Mount Buffalo from Mount Hotham, Victoria

40 Great Walks
in Australia

Tyrone Thomas
Andrew Close

Contents

Introduction

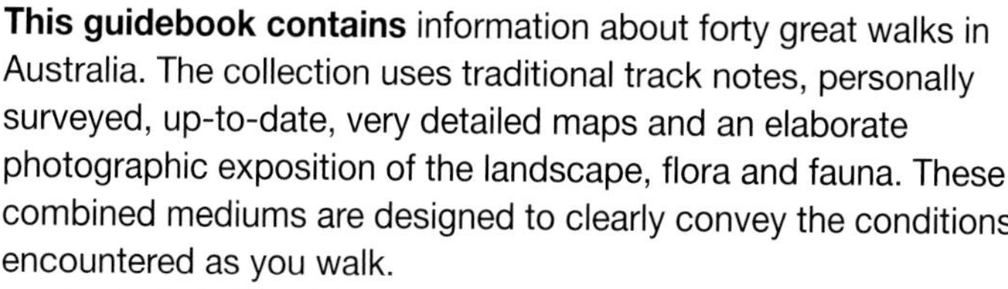

This guidebook contains information about forty great walks in Australia. The collection uses traditional track notes, personally surveyed, up-to-date, very detailed maps and an elaborate photographic exposition of the landscape, flora and fauna. These combined mediums are designed to clearly convey the conditions encountered as you walk.

Australia is the oldest, driest, flattest and smallest continent. It therefore follows that by world standards, the terrain is very ancient, fantastically eroded and geologically interesting. Many primitive plant and animal species are evidence of the uniqueness of the country, evolving in isolation from other land masses. Even the most famous of Australian animals, the kangaroo, is in effect a living fossil. Classification as a continent gives some impression of the vastness of the landscape to be explored, yet conveniently, the huge area is just one country, with no problems of political boundaries to be crossed.

For safety reasons, some spectacular places have been omitted. The incredible Bungle Bungles of north-west Western Australia, for instance, are very remote with access requiring a four-wheel-drive vehicle. The most challenging mountain ascent of Federation Peak, in Tasmania, is probably best left to skilled rock climbers, it being so rugged as to be beyond the capability of most bushwalkers. The forty selected walks are a representation of rainforest, desert, coast, volcanic features, inland gorges and mountain scenery. Many of the selected walks are in the southern two-thirds of Australia, as far northern Australia is often too hot for comfortable walking. Additionally, in the south there is a longer seasonal window for walking.

Walks are graded as easy, medium, or hard. Time taken to complete walks will vary greatly, depending upon the experience of individuals. Track notes are therefore provided with references that give both exact distances and variable times, excluding lunch or other significant breaks. Weather conditions will influence times greatly. The direction of each walk is described, either clockwise or anticlockwise, and is intended for ease of navigation or effort.

A word of warning to all: do not underestimate the distances involved in travelling overland and the subsequent time, fuel and water necessary for the journey. Australia is huge and naturally lends itself to air travel over the longer hauls. Hitch hiking is to be discouraged. Towns are sometimes hundreds of kilometres apart and, especially inland, day time temperatures soar. When driving, avoid fatigue by taking frequent breaks (every two hours) and try not to drive between dusk and dawn as native animals are more active at night.

Our intention is to introduce you to a wide variety of environments in which you can interact fully with respect to the landscape, flora and fauna around you. Special sections deal with safety, mapping and navigation to assist you.

We have walked all routes in the book as near to publication date as possible. All track notes and the complete map coverage were simultaneously compiled. Our maps generally show all walking and four-wheel-drive tracks on the entire map coverage so that you have an option to create your own walk routes or short cuts or vary the described walks. Our first walk map is at 1:12 500 scale and all others are at 1:25 000 scale. Unfortunately many official maps fail to show vast numbers of tracks and other information relevant to bushwalkers. Our aim is to provide accurate recent maps with information that is generally not available for walkers elsewhere, for your convenience and safety.

Andrew Close

Tyrone Thomas

It is our policy to walk all routes fully to ensure correctness. However, it must be expected that changes will occur in some places with the passing of time. Likewise, it is impossible to know in advance of particular and unusual problems, such as bushfires, bridge washouts, landslides and other occurrences. Every care has been taken in compiling notes and maps, but no responsibility will be accepted for any inaccuracies or for any mishap that might arise out of the use of this book. Take account of your medical condition, bushcraft skills, ability to navigate, your equipment and your safety. Please read pages 218–229 for more information. The walks in this book are unsuitable for children unless they are accompanied by an adult. The authors and publisher welcome advice of any errors or desirable amendments to bring future editions of the book up to date.

Tyrone Thomas
Andrew Close

Walks location map

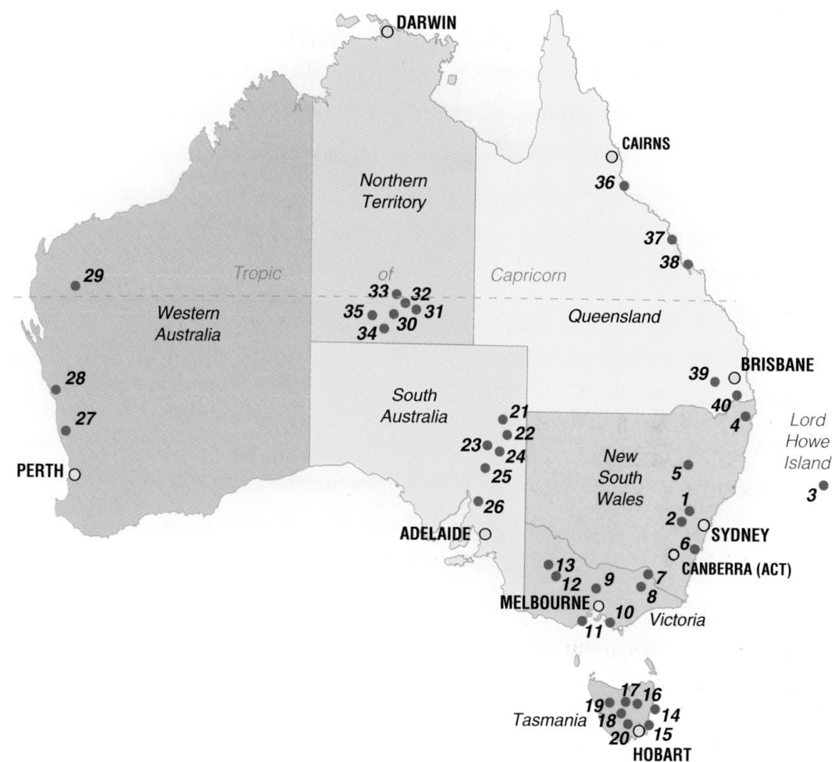

1 Valley of the Waters, Blue Mountains, NSW
2 Grand Canyon, Blue Mountains, NSW
3 Mount Gower, Lord Howe Island, NSW
4 Mount Warning, Northern Rivers, NSW
5 The Breadknife, Warrumbungle Ranges, NSW
6 Pigeon House Mountain, South Coast, NSW
7 Little Pine Mountain, North-East, VIC
8 Mount Feathertop, Alps, VIC
9 Camels Hump–Mount Towrong, Mount Macedon, VIC
10 Cape Woolamai, Phillip Island, VIC
11 Point Addis, Surf Coast, VIC
12 Briggs Bluff, Grampians, VIC
13 Mount Stapylton, Grampians, VIC
14 Wineglass Bay–Hazards Beach, East Coast, TAS
15 Raoul View–Tunnel Bay, Tasman Peninsula, TAS
16 Quamby Bluff, Great Western Tiers, TAS
17 Walls of Jerusalem, Central Plateau, TAS
18 Cradle Mountain Circuit, Cradle Mountain, TAS
19 Tullah–Lake Herbert, Tullah, TAS
20 Tarn Shelf–Lake Webster, Mount Field, TAS
21 Arkaroola Creek, Flinders Ranges, SA
22 Chambers Gorge, Flinders Ranges, SA
23 Bunyeroo Gorge, Flinders Ranges, SA
24 ABC Range, Flinders Ranges, SA
25 Mount Ohlssen Bagge, Flinders Ranges, SA
26 Hidden Gorge, Mount Remarkable, SA
27 Pinnacles Desert, Cervantes, WA
28 Murchison Gorge, Kalbarri, WA
29 Mount Bruce, Pilbara, WA
30 Kings Canyon, George Gill Range, NT
31 Kalarranga–Mpaara, Palm Valley NT
32 Mpulungkinya, Palm Valley, NT
33 Ormiston Gorge, Macdonnell Ranges, NT
34 Uluru Circuit, Red Centre, NT
35 Kata Tjuta, Red Centre, NT
36 Macushla–Cape Richards, Hinchinbrook Island, QLD
37 South Molle Island, Whitsunday Islands, QLD
38 Cape Hillsborough, Mackay, QLD
39 Mount Cordeaux, Main Range, QLD
40 Green Mountains, South-East Rim, QLD

Index to walk/hike suggestions

Walk no.	Walk area	Walk km	Walk hours	Walk grade	Page
21	Arkaroola Creek, SA	8	3	medium	122
22	Chambers Gorge, SA	9	4	medium	126
23	Bunyeroo Gorge, SA	8	2.5	easy	130
24	ABC Range, SA	9.6	4	medium	134
25	Mount Ohlssen Bagge, SA	7.5	4	hard	138
26	Hidden Gorge, SA	16.6	two days	medium	142
27	Pinnacles Desert, WA	5	2	easy	150
28	Murchison Gorge, WA	8	3.5	medium	154
29	Mount Bruce, WA	9.6	5	medium	159
30	Kings Canyon, NT	10.5	4.5	medium	166
31	Kalarranga–Mpaara, NT	8	3	medium	171
32	Mpulungkinya, NT	13	5.5	medium	175
33	Ormiston Gorge, NT	8.5	4	medium	179
34	Uluṟu Circuit, NT	10.7	3.5	medium	183
35	Kata Tjuṯa, NT	7.4	3	medium	188
36	Macushla–Cape Richards, QLD	7	3.5	easy	194
37	South Molle Island, QLD	12.6	5	medium	198
38	Cape Hillsborough, QLD	9	4	easy	203
39	Mount Cordeaux, QLD	12.6	5	medium	208
40	Green Mountains, QLD	18.8	8	hard	213

Overview of Australia

Mount Connor and parakeelya, Northern Territory

Australia, often referred to as 'The island continent' or 'Great Southern Land', is 4000 km from east to west and 3200 km from north to south. Extending across 30 degrees of latitude, one third of the land mass is within the tropics, however, most of the country is of a desert or arid nature. Australia has the distinction of having the longest, uninterrupted coastline in the world. The Great Barrier Reef in Queensland and Ningaloo Reef in Western Australia are major coastal features.

The majority of more temperate, habitable regions occupy a relatively narrow band on the eastern and south-eastern slopes of the Great Dividing Range (or the Divide as it is commonly known), with an even narrower band on the extreme west and south-west of the country. The Divide is so named as it effectively separates the rivers that run east and south to the sea from rivers that flow west mainly to the interior. It also markedly affects the climate on either side.

Walkers can expect to find lush vegetation on the coastal side of the Divide in all four eastern states and great coastal walks. Along the Divide, northern regions have an abundance of tropical and sub-tropical rainforest while southern regions have temperate and sub-alpine forests. The predominant alpine areas are the Snowy Mountains in southern New South Wales, the Victorian Alps in north-east

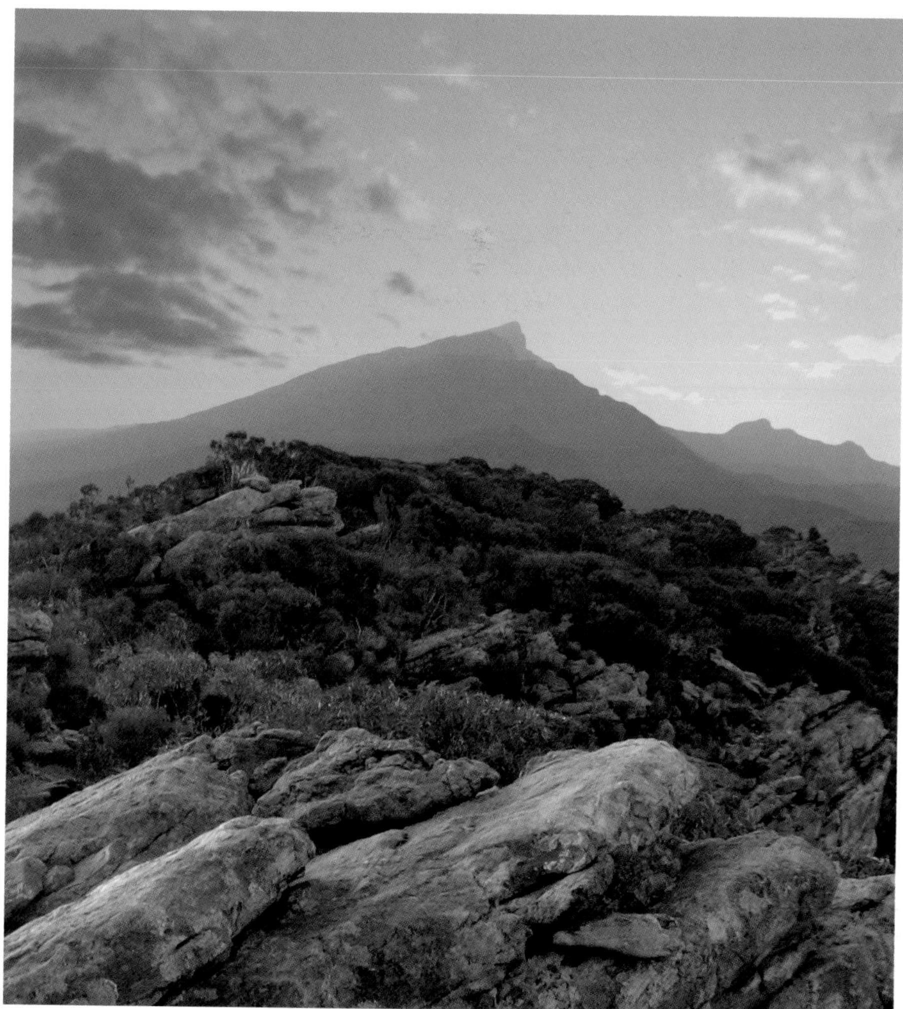
View to St Mary Peak, South Australia

Victoria, and the Central Highlands of Tasmania. The Murray, with its largest tributary the Darling, is the longest river system. The Murray descends from the Snowy Mountains and flows to its mouth in South Australia.

On the drier inland side of the Divide, open woodlands and grasslands give way to vast arid areas and desert. The walks focus upon unique geological features of gorges, rocky plateaus and escarpments including places such as Uluru and Kata Tjuta.

The vast Nullarbor Plain, straddling South Australia and Western Australia, is an ancient sea floor of limestone, which has been uplifted by tectonic activity. This plateau is sparsely vegetated with plants such as low growing saltbush. Below the surface are caves such as Koonalda. The Nullarbor Plain is bounded by desert and the Southern Ocean.

The landscape

The Australian land mass was once part of the 'super-continent' known as Pangaea (all-land) surrounded by Thalassa (all-sea). Laurasia (Europe, Asia and North America) was later separated from Pangaea leaving a southern land mass known as Gondwana, which became Australia, New Zealand, South America, Antarctica, Africa and India. This has been deduced from the matching shapes of the coastlines and types of rock of once neighbouring land masses. Many fossilised remains contained within sedimentary rocks were exposed when the continents drifted apart and show similarities. Also present-day plant species of the same type can be found on neighbouring land masses now widely separated by oceans.

The movement of the tectonic plates caused much volcanism, resulting in the formation of metamorphic rock, granite or basalt. Volcanic eruptions in Australia occurred as recently as 4800 years ago. Activity has been concentrated mostly on the eastern side of the country. Folding, buckling and faulting caused a major mountain building event leading to the creation of the Great Dividing Range. This occurred when the Pacific Plate collided with and was drawn (subducted) below the Indo-Australasian Plate. The subduction zone mostly resulted in violent volcanic activity where melting of the crust of the Earth occurred deep below the surface. However, in the case of the Blue Mountains, the Sydney Sandstone block was uplifted from the sea floor to create the wonderful escarpment walking areas we see today at Valley of the Waters and Grand Canyon.

Granite occurs at many places along the range. Granite is formed when molten rock wells up below thick overlying rock, but does not break the surface. Slow cooling leads to the formation of this hard,

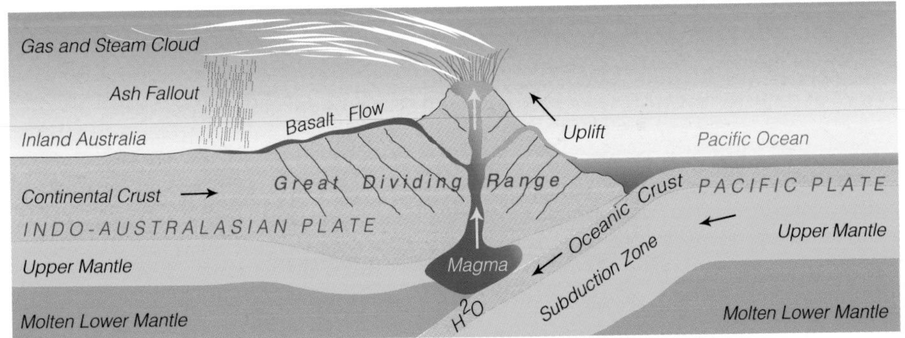

Volcanic formation of the Great Dividing Range

dense rock. Examples exposed by erosion can be viewed at Wilsons Promontory in Victoria, Freycinet Peninsula in Tasmania, the New England region of New South Wales and south-west Western Australia. Quartzite eroded from granite creates spectacular white sand beaches and azure water as sunlight is reflected from the sand under the water.

Basalt results from molten rock that is either ejected into the atmosphere or oozed through cracks in the crust of the Earth. Notable examples of basaltic volcanic activity featured as walks in this book are the Breadknife, Lord Howe Island and Mount Warning in New South Wales. Much arable farming land is located in the vicinity of extinct basaltic volcanoes, where the mineral enriched soils are for the most part deep and fertile.

The topography of Tasmania is dominated by a central plateau that has largely been eroded by glacial action, leaving a number of peaks and ridges capped with dolerite rock. In the south-west, older quartzite is exposed and eroded. In the south-east and south-west, considerable sinking of the land has occurred and seas have risen following past ice ages, submerging former valleys, creating a labyrinth of bays. Towards the north, the plateau has resisted erosion more than other places and the dramatic Great Western Tiers have resulted along a broad fault line. The retreating ice sheet has relieved the underlying land of its enormous downwards pressure allowing it to tilt and rise. Wonderful walks exist in the alpine areas amid glacier-carved features, such as Tarn Shelf and Cradle Mountain, which have many lakes and tarns.

On the mainland, water will always be in short supply. However, the Great Artesian Basin makes it possible for life to exist in the Australian interior as it contains vast reserves of water. It was formed as the land on the western side of the Divide subsided, with its lowest point at Lake Eyre in north-eastern South Australia. Some rainfall from northern Australia travels from the Queensland section of the Divide by river. For the most part it seeps underground extremely slowly, through porous sedimentary rock aquifers into the final collection point at the Lake Eyre basin. Further south on the Divide, more water flows by the river system but still moves through aquifers of sandstone, mudstone and limestone. The location of limestone caves suggests a former alignment of reefs and ancient coastline from earlier times when much of the Australian interior was an inland sea. As a result many Australian soils contain high levels of salt left behind from retreating oceans or later washed from higher to lower lands.

Multiple layers of sediment, compressed under primeval seabed, began

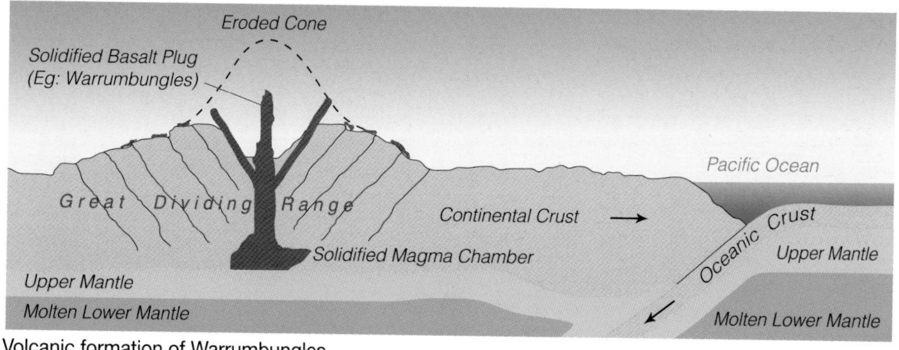

Volcanic formation of Warrumbungles

Kalarranga Amphitheatre, Northern Territory

the formation of the monolith Uluṟu. Gradual upheaval of the crust of the Earth has tilted the original rock some 90 degrees. These sedimentary layers of arkose, rich in feldspar with iron ore, give the rock its characteristic red hue. The crust of the Earth buckled to create such places as the Macdonnell Ranges near Alice Springs and both the Musgrave Ranges and Flinders Ranges in South Australia. Elsewhere much of the interior has been heavily eroded to form vast plains.

A huge percentage of land on the western side of the continent contains some of the oldest rock in the world. As a result there are fantastic geological formations from the buckling and eroding. The Kimberley and Pilbara regions are notable for their fair share of features such as the Bungle Bungles and Murchison Gorge. The walk at Mount Bruce in the Pilbara is amid some of the largest deposits of iron ore in the world, a legacy of the high iron composition of early Earth.

Hamersley Gorge, Western Australia

The climate

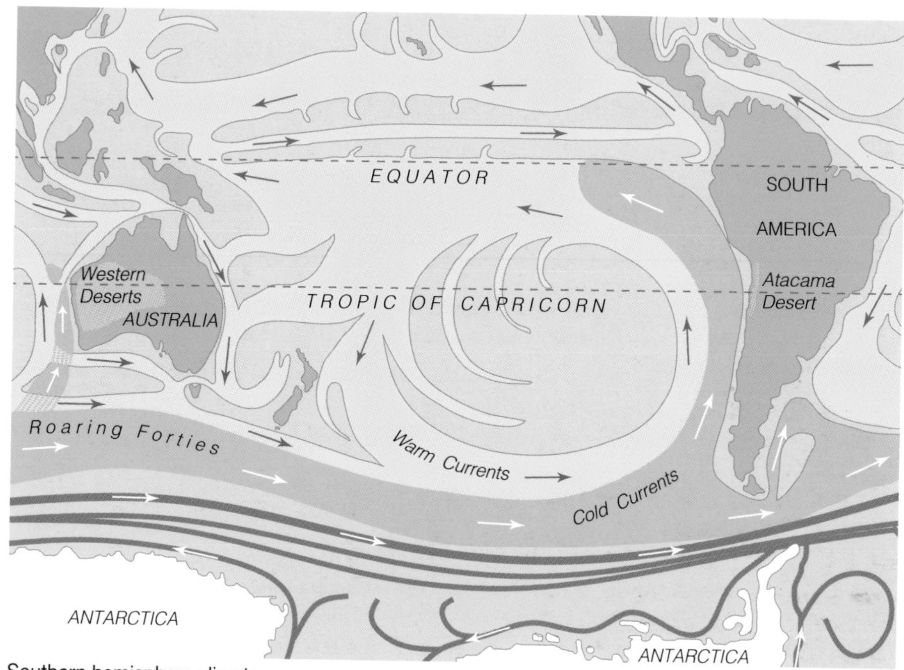

Southern hemisphere climate

Temperature and humidity can vary widely, from below zero to the high forties. The presence of deep winter snow can come as a surprise to some overseas visitors but many agree Australia is a sunburnt country. Cyclonic weather every summer across the whole of the northern part of the country releases huge quantities of water on to the landscape. The two dominant seasons are known as 'the wet' and 'the dry'.

South of the Tropic of Capricorn, a more temperate, four-seasonal climate exists. The prevailing weather comes from the west. However, much of the east coast is mostly influenced by dominant south-east trade winds. The majority of rain delivered by this weather system falls on the eastern slopes of the Divide where a maritime climate exists. This leaves the inland side of the range much drier. Monsoons in the north can affect southern areas, but the south can suffer prolonged periods of drought, especially during times of 'el Niño'. This occurs when large masses of cold water combined with cold air currents impinge on the eastern shoreline, reducing rainfall drastically.

The large land mass of Australia accentuates wind flows around high and low pressure cells. As the sun warms air at the equator, it rises into the troposphere, loses its rainfall and cools. The air then sinks back to Earth as dry air at about 30 degrees south latitude and north latitude creating deserts on the western sides of continents. At the southern hemisphere solstice, the dry air band lies right across middle Australia. It is for this reason that deserts exist as far south as the Mallee district in Victoria.

Southern Australia is greatly influenced in winter by the appearance of westerly winds known as the roaring forties. Tasmania bears the brunt of these wind patterns as they encircle the globe. There is no land mass apart from Cape Horn at the tip of South America to slow the winds that hit the west coast of Tasmania causing unpredictable climatic conditions. For this reason it is essential that walkers in the Tasmanian wilderness prepare for this unpredictable influence.

The flora

One hundred million years ago the Australian land mass was located much further south. Most of its eastern half was covered with cool temperate rainforest of Gondwana origin, such as the myrtle beech, cycads, ferns, Wollemi pines and other coniferous plants. The last links with Gondwana were severed when Australia moved northward from Antarctica and became an island continent. As it drifted in isolation north-east towards the equator, the climate shifted from cool/wet to warm/dry. Differing microclimates then appeared with a diverse range of temperature and rainfall zones suitable for colonisation by a wider variety of plants. As sea levels lowered, a land bridge provided connection between Australia at Cape York and spread the equatorial rainforests of Asia into Australia. Rising sea levels later submerged the land bridge forming the Torres Strait between Cape York and Papua New Guinea. This composite of Asian and Gondwana flora is evident in the rainforests in Papua New Guinea, Queensland and New South Wales. Vegetation includes trees with buttressed trunks, lianas (vines), epiphytes and conifers, such as araucaria. The demarcation between Southern Asian and Australian plants and animals is today known as Wallaces Line. In 1876, Alfred Russell Wallace divided the world into zoological and geographical regions. Even though the land to either side of the line is only 24 km apart, a clear distinction can be observed between Lombok and Bali.

The Tasmanian part of the then unified Australian land mass remained joined to Antarctica longer than Africa or South America, so it has the largest concentration of Gondwana flora, which in some places has remained mostly unchanged, especially in the alpine highlands at Tarn Shelf, Cradle Mountain, and the Walls of Jerusalem.

Climatic changes forced plants from Gondwana origin to adapt, or face extinction. Species that were able to evolve led to the creation of new forms. The Myrtaceae family produced genus such as *eucalyptus* and *kunzea*, capable of adapting to the increasing dry climate and nutrient deficient soils. It also produced further genera, such as *syzygium* (lilly pilly) and *melaleuca* (paperbark), to colonise damp and swampy areas. The Mimosaceae family produced genus, such as *acacia*

Opposite page (clockwise from top left):
Banksia (*Banksia attenuata*)
Sturt desert pea (*Swainsona formosa*)
Everlasting (*Helichrysum acuminatum*)
Cycad (*Macrozamia communis*)
Grass tree (*Xanthorrhoea australis*)
Golden wattle (*Acacia pycnantha*)
Flowering gum (*Eucalyptus ficifolia*)
Kangaroo paw (*Anigozanthos manglesii*)

(wattles), which rose to prominence with the changing climate. Known as phyllodinae, leaves were reduced to phyllodes, or spines, to limit evaporation and conserve moisture. These highly evolved sclerophylls effectively deal with nutrient-deprived soils by creating their own nitrogen through nodules on their roots. This has enabled acacias to colonise many arid inland areas where eucalyptus are less prevalent. Sclerophyll adaptation secured a niche for both Myrtaceae and Mimosaceae families in the modern Australian flora. The most instantly recognisable 'Australian' forms of vegetation are eucalyptus and acacia. Australia has a diverse range of eucalyptus forest and acacia scrublands, which extend to Papua New Guinea and New Caledonia. Epicormic shoots and lignotubers enable eucalyptus to regenerate quickly after fire. It is for this reason they have become dominant trees. Banksias, grevilleas and numerous, often prickly, woody species require heat (usually fire) to scarify their seeds before they can germinate. These adaptations are not found in the ancient Gondwana plants notably nothofagus, which are restricted to small, damp, unburned pockets of forest in the wetter regions of eastern Australia.

In the main, Australia has two types of desert flora:

1. perennials, which can survive over long periods of drought (e.g. mulga, saltbush, desert oak, spinifex)
2. short-lived ephemeral annuals, which erupt out of the ground after periods of rain where they grow rapidly, flower and set seeds. The seeds lie dormant until favourable conditions return (e.g. Sturt desert pea and parakeelya).

The interior deserts effectively isolate non-desert flora from each other. This case in point is notable in the far south-west of Western Australia. Plants there have both barriers of desert and ocean effectively isolating plant species from each other. They have evolved in a relatively constant habitat over aeons, resulting in more specialised forms. The Kangaroo paw is a fine example. Although Gondwana in origin, at one time they were surrounded on all sides by ocean when much of the interior was an inland sea. An ancient sea floor of limestone is visible today as the Nullarbor Plain.

The Nullarbor Plain contains huge deposits of calcium carbonate in the form of decaying marine organisms that have a high pH (alkaline) composition. As the majority of Australian natives prefer acid soils, the Nullarbor acts as a plant distribution barrier between eastern and western Australia. The flora of south-west Western Australia is more like that of South Africa than eastern Australia. The Proteaceae family is well represented in both countries with a wide diversity of forms and foliage. In Australia, these include banksias, grevilleas and hakeas. Western Australia is renowned for its proliferation of wildflowers. A number of eucalyptus trees including the karri and jarrah forests of the south-west do not appear naturally elsewhere in the country. Australia has been the ongoing recipient of foreign plant species from migratory birds, seed borne on wind, by ocean currents, and those brought in by mankind.

Opposite page (clockwise from top left):
Scoparia (*Richea scoparia*)
Tasmanian waratah (*Telopea truncata*)
Nothofagus (*Nothofagus gunnii*)
Soft tree fern (*Dicksonia antarctica*)
Spear lilly (*Doryanthes palmerii*)
Christmas bell (*Blandfordia punicea*)
Bangalow/piccabean palm (*Archontophoenix cunninghamiana*)
Fuchsia heath (*Epacris longifolia*)

The fauna

Prior to the inundation of the land bridges by rising ocean levels, animals were able to migrate between the land masses that comprised Gondwana. Since these were cut off, animals have been effectively isolated on their respective continents. Between Asia and Australia, Wallaces Line marks a boundary of different animal species, just as it does with plant species. The end result is similar animals evolving along different lines.

For example, the Australian platypus and the echidna are known as monotremes. These two unusual animals have a reptilian ancestry, in that they both lay eggs, and yet are warm-blooded, aligning them more closely with other mammals. The platypus has an electrically sensitive, duck-like bill for seeking out aquatic prey in its stream-side habitat. It has webbed feet, nests in burrows and is essentially an aquatic animal. The echidna closely resembles a porcupine, with many thick, fierce spines along its upper body. A diet of ants has resulted in the development of a long snout and strong front legs with claws, to facilitate digging out the ants and termites nests. It has fairly poor eyesight, relying on a sense of smell to find food. Found in mountain and forest country, echidnas can travel quite considerable distances and are surprisingly good climbers. They lay a single egg which develops in a pouch.

Marsupials nurture their young in a pouch on the lower abdomen (e.g. kangaroos, possums, wombats, koalas, numbats and bandicoots). They are widespread throughout the country and vary in size from mice-like antechinus to the giant red kangaroo. An unusual feature of marsupials is they give birth to highly under-developed young that then climb through the fur to reach the pouch, which contains the teats for suckling. Kangaroos have the unusual feature of being able to suckle a 'joey' out of the pouch, while a developing embryo is suckling in the pouch and a fertilised embryo is waiting in the uterus. The tree kangaroo from Papua New Guinea is well adapted to arboreal life in the Queensland Wet Tropics. Throughout the country, the border between pastoral lands and desert landscapes are the best locations to view kangaroos, emus and members of the parrot family. The Tasmanian devil is the largest carnivore still in existence; it rears up to four young in its pouch.

Two species of crocodile inhabit northern waters and both are protected. The fresh water crocodile is quite docile; however, the saltwater crocodile is dangerous. Approximately 130 species of frog occur in Australia. Two of the more unusual types are the 'gastric-brooding frog', which is unique in that it temporarily transforms its stomach into a uterus to hatch the young, and the 'water-holding frog', a desert dweller, which conserves moisture during times of drought by forming an underground cocoon and immersing itself until the drought is over. Among the lizards, perhaps the best known is the frill-necked lizard. When under attack it extends the coloured frill around its neck and makes

Opposite page (clockwise from top left):
Kookaburra (*Dacelo novaeguineae*)
Koala (*Phascolarctos cinereus*)
Wombat (*Lasiorhinus latifrons*)
Tasmanian devil (*Sarcophilus harrisii*)
Rainbow lorikeet (*Trichoglossus haematodus*)
Rock wallaby (*Petrogale penicillata*)
Echidna (*Tachyglossus aculeatus*)
Red kangaroo (*Macropus rufus*)

a hissing sound. It makes its escape by running at high speed on its back legs.

Approximately 100 of the 140 species of snake are venomous. The largest non-venomous snake is the scrub python or amethystine, which can reach 7 m in length. The most venomous land snake is the tiger snake, which reaches up to 2 m in length, followed by the Queensland Taipan, almost 3.5 m long. Gippsland in Victoria is home to the largest earthworm in the world, growing to over 3.5 m and almost 2 cm in diameter. Related to the earthworm are leeches. They are not considered dangerous; however, the anti-coagulant they inject upon attachment can cause extended bleeding when removed. They are found mostly in damp woodland, especially near water courses. The funnel-web spider is the most poisonous arachnid in Australia. The male is unusual in being several times more toxic than the female. It is restricted to coastal areas of New South Wales. The famous red-back spider is the opposite, with the female capable of inflicting a painful and highly venomous bite.

Over 700 bird species exist in Australia, at least two of which have an interesting call or song. The bellbirds, as their name suggests, emit a loud call closely resembling a shrill bell. They are most likely to be found in damp bushland. Lyrebirds have the ability of mimicking other bird calls and even extend their range to cover chainsaws and mobile phones! The brush turkey and smaller scrub fowl are commonly found scratching around in the leaf litter.

The largest Australian bird is the flightless emu at 1.5 m tall. The male incubates the eggs, which can weigh almost a kilogram. A similar bird, the cassowary, an immigrant from Papua New Guinea, is superbly adapted for the rainforest with its helmeted head which allows it to ram through the jungle at high speed. Related to the European kingfisher, kookaburras are renowned for their laugh. There are two types: the laughing jackass of eastern Australia and the blue-winged variety found in the north to north-west. Galahs and sulphur-crested cockatoos are among more than 50 species of parrot, the smallest of which, the budgerigar, is found in large flocks in more arid regions. The 2.5 m wingspan of the wedge-tail eagle makes it the largest bird of prey. It occurs throughout the country but is more prevalent in arid regions.

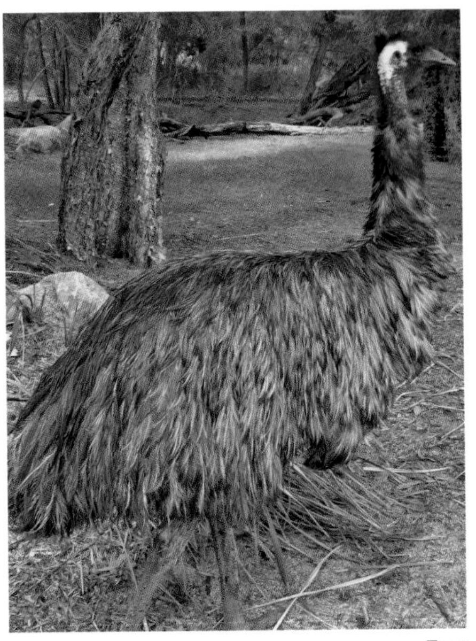

Emu

Galahs

Map legend

	Information
	Ranger
P	Carpark
	Toilet
	Lookout
	Picnic Area
	Picnic Area with Shelter
HUT	Hut / Enclosed Shelter
	Car Camping
	Bush Camping
	Retail Building
	Point of Interest
][	Bridge
31	Highway Sealed
	Main Road Sealed
	Road Unsealed
	Four-wheel-drive
	Gate or Barrier
	Railway

START	Walk Start / Walk Route and Direction
	Walk Route on Sealed Road
	Walk Route on Unsealed Road
	Walk Route on Four-wheel-drive
	Other Walking Tracks
Falls	Stream with Falls and Flow Direction
	Lake / Reservoir / Sea
	Swamp / Intermittent Lake
	Cliffline / Rock Scree
Mount Amos △ 445m	Major Peak and Height
Hansons + Peak	Mountain Apex / Named Peak
250	Contour with Elevation
	National Park
	Park Other
	Private Land
	Residential Area
	Sand / Beach
N 0 500m Scale 1:25,000	Scale Bar / Distances Metric Geographic True North

NEW SOUTH WALES

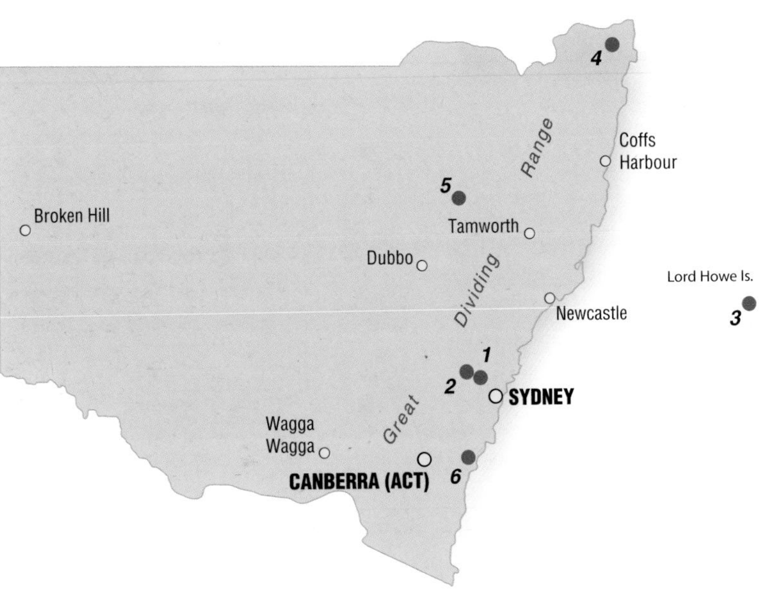

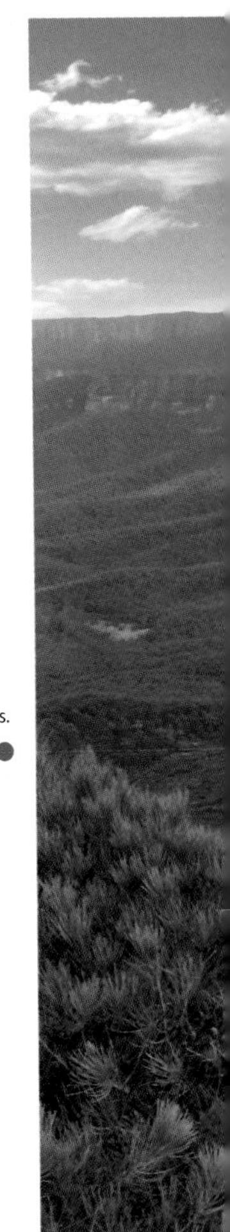

1	Valley of the Waters	Blue Mountains National Park
2	Grand Canyon	Blue Mountains National Park
3	Mount Gower	Lord Howe Island National Park
4	Mount Warning	Mount Warning National Park
5	The Breadknife	Warrumbungle National Park
6	Pigeon House Mountain	Morton National Park

Byangee Walls from Pigeon House Mountain

New South Wales is the oldest state. Sydney, the capital city with its harbour setting, has many walks within easy reach. A feature is the fantastically eroded sandstone cliffs and canyons of the Blue Mountains. Off the east coast, sub-tropical Lord Howe Island is a green, volcanic jewel in the Tasman Sea. Northern New South Wales has a sub-tropical climate limited to the eastern slopes of the Great Dividing Range. The ascent to Mount Warning is through lush rainforest. Inland, the spectacular volcanic features of the Breadknife and the Grand High Tops, in the Warrumbungle Range, are of much geological interest. In the southern Great Dividing Range is craggy Pigeon House Mountain. Further south in the Snowy Mountains is the highest peak in the country: Mount Kosciuszko.

Australian Capital Territory

Canberra, the capital of the nation, is ideal for many walks through its parks and at Lake Burley Griffin.

VALLEY OF THE WATERS

Blue Mountains, New South Wales

Walk:	6.5 km circuit
Time required:	Including minimal breaks, 3 hours
Grade:	One day, medium with many steps to negotiate
Environment:	Sandstone cliffs, forest and waterfalls
Last review date:	November 2008
Map reference:	New South Wales Lands, 1:25 000 Katoomba and Map 1 (note scale 1:12 500)
Best time to visit:	Suited to any season but may be cold and slippery in winter from June to August

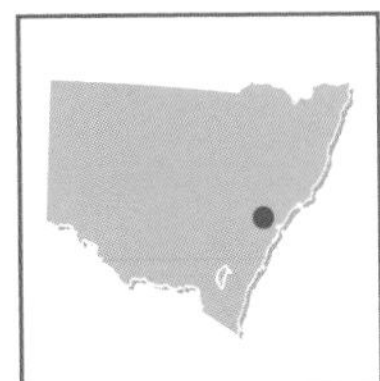

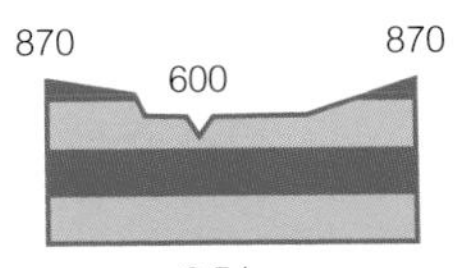

The small township of Wentworth Falls may be overlooked by most visitors to the Blue Mountains region as they make their way to better-known Katoomba.

Wentworth Falls, Blue Mountains

1 VALLEY OF THE WATERS

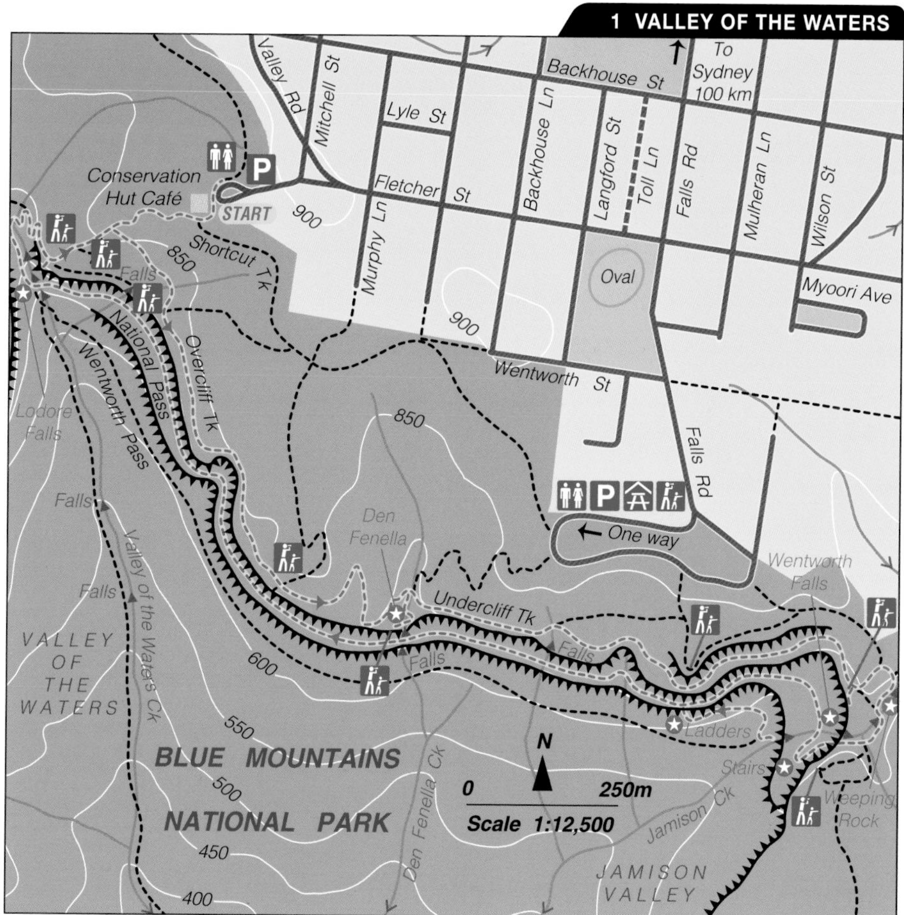

Mt Victoria	J	F	M	A	M	J	J	A	S	O	N	D	Year
Rain av. mm	110	97	80	76	45	58	42	50	47	63	70	72	810
Temp av. max. °C	22	22	20	17	12	10	9	10	13	16	19	21	15
Temp av. min. °C	12	12	11	8	5	3	2	3	4	7	9	11	7

However, here you will discover magnificent areas of natural beauty with superb walk opportunities. This is essentially a cliff-side walk, which takes in many fine waterfalls and cascades, dramatic changes of vegetation and many great viewpoints.

Access is along the Great Western Highway to Wentworth Falls village, which is about 100 km from Sydney. Rail travel is available from Sydney to Wentworth Falls station, some 2 km from the walk start. Coaches operate along the highway too. There are plenty of accommodation options in the Blue Mountains especially around Katoomba.

Turn off the Great Western Highway on to Falls Road at Wentworth Falls, take the third turn on the right into Fletcher Street, then after 500 m veer left to Conservation Hut café carpark. The walk, leading clockwise, starts here where there is tourist information, toilets and perhaps the opportunity for a café snack after the walk.

Head off from the café west, past Shortcut Track, down many steps for 200 m to turn left and descend a further 200 m to Lyrebird Lookout at the rim of massive sandstone cliffs. This provides a great view of the Valley of the Waters and the walking track far below. Later in the day you will be ascending through this lush rainforest below, within shade and seeing several large waterfalls to their best advantage. Overcliff Track runs along the cliff-rim south-south-east and you follow it for more views. A few slightly boggy spots are encountered where water seeps down ferny slopes. After 500 m, you meet a track junction and Breakfast Point Lookout, which is a few metres to your right.

Continue on Overcliff Track as it swings east and descends via a switchback and past closed Lady Sees Lookout to Den Fenella Creek and a track intersection within another 500 m. This intersection marks the end of Overcliff Track and the start of Undercliff Track. However, you should take an especially good 200 m return side trip downstream among beautiful ferns to a small waterfall then on out to the Den Fenella Lookout before continuing.

Follow Undercliff Track and soon it starts to live up to its name, providing most attractive walking along sandstone bedding way above the Jamison Creek valley and massive Wentworth Falls. After 600 m, you reach another track intersection and you turn right to go a few metres to Fletchers Lookout with its wonderful view of the two major drops of Wentworth Falls.

Back at the intersection, it is best to avoid the direct track down to the lip of the falls and instead go north-east to first

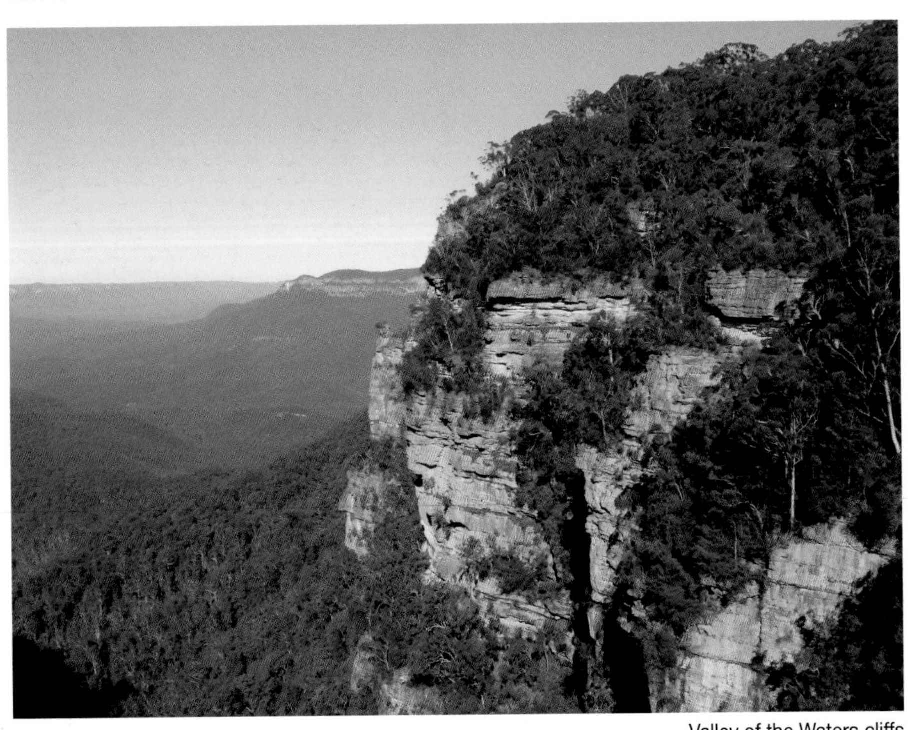

Valley of the Waters cliffs

see lovely Weeping Rock, which is just upstream. On the way you bypass a track from the Falls Road carpark area and link to Darwins Track at the creek. Weeping Rock is then south, just downstream a few metres short of the top of Wentworth Falls. This location is most attractive and ideal for a break. Charles Darwin, while on his way to Bathurst, visited Wentworth Falls and noted that in his opinion the region was 'desolate and untidy'.

Flagstones allow you to cross Jamison Creek at the lip of Wentworth Falls then you cross a small side creek and start the big descent. Keep right and head down some well defined and precipitous steps from the cliff-rim. These steps have been hewn from the cliff-face in the 1890s and must have involved an unimaginable amount of time and quite dangerous work. The view from them is quite stunning. The falls plunge in two stages. National Pass opened in

Wentworth Falls

Wentworth Falls base

1908 and it crosses the stream amid spray between the two drops. If there has been recent heavy rain, a raincoat would be advisable. Cut stone blocks provide access across the creek. Quite often the wind, being channelled up the valley, will blow the water upwards as it spills over the top.

National Pass, the track you should follow, then rises a little via steps and you get glimpses back to the falls. This track continues for some 1.8 km on what surely is the most spectacular cliff-walk in Australia and about the best overall walk in the Blue Mountains. The sandstone cliffs are in horizontal beds and this remarkable track follows around the contour of the bedding on a tiny ledge. The cliffs have been carved out in places to permit a through route and for much of the way you are under cliff overhangs. You even pass behind waterfalls. The views of the Jamison Valley are often uninterrupted as there is little foreground vegetation to block the view. Fine stonework of steps and carved sandstone blocks will draw your attention.

Some 300 m from the falls along National Pass, you reach the top of Slack Stairs, which is a long series of ladders and stairs down the cliffs to give access to a lovely pool and beach at the base of the lower drop of the falls. We highly recommend the side trip which is 600 m return, provided due account is taken of the effort needed to climb for the return. We designate a medium rather than easy grade to this walk because of this side trip which uses steep ladders and many steps. The beach is a splendid place for a rest and the rainforest is also most attractive.

Retrace back up the ladders avoiding Wentworth Pass, continue on National Pass then towards its end you descend a little into rainforest at the base of cliffs and reach the Valley of the Waters Creek. Wentworth Pass links in from the left and you turn upstream. A number of smaller and two major waterfalls plunging from the soaring cliffs can then be seen to best advantage as you climb historic steps. There are wonderful fern glade settings of ground ferns and mosses especially and rock overhangs in what must surely be the most perfectly formed and picturesque spot in the Blue Mountains.

Next, you climb via zigzags, bypass a left-side track, climb further to Empress Lookout and Queen Victoria Lookout and get great views of the rainforest, cliffs and valley below. The latter lookout is a few metres to the right of the main track and Overcliff Track lies ahead. You should turn left up a spur track eastwards via more steps and within 400 m complete the walk back at Conservation Hut café.

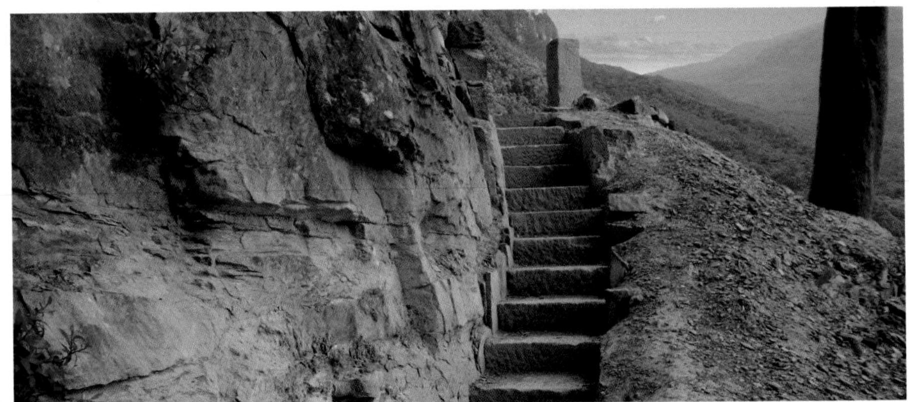

Sandstone steps on National Pass

2 GRAND CANYON
Blue Mountains, New South Wales

Walk:	13.5 km circuit
Time required:	Including minimal breaks, 5 hours
Grade:	One day, medium with many steps to negotiate
Environment:	Sandstone cliffs, forest and waterfalls
Last review date:	November 2008
Map reference:	New South Wales Lands, 1:25 000 Katoomba and Map 2
Best time to visit:	Suited to any season but may be cold and slippery in winter from June to August

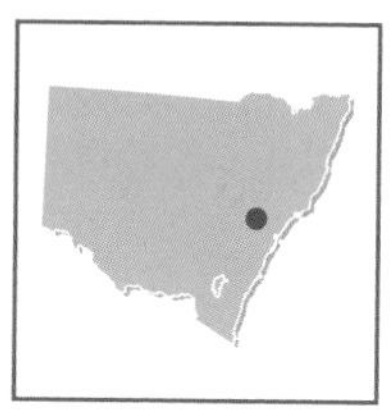

Govetts Leap, Evans Lookout and Grand Canyon are undoubtedly major attractions of the Blackheath district in the Blue Mountains. Each result from tremendous erosion of sandstone. The floor of the Grose River valley north-east of the three points is up to 600 m below. Grand Canyon is really a contorted hanging valley which is rapidly being eroded by Greaves Creek as it plunges into the main valley at Beauchamp Falls. Deep chasms and plunging waterfalls are sure to leave no one disappointed. While the walk is suited to any season, it is perhaps best enjoyed after rainy periods when the waterfalls are at their most spectacular phase.

Access is along the Great Western Highway to Blackheath, which is about 116 km from Sydney. Trains are available for access to Blackheath. There are plenty of accommodation options in the Blue Mountains at Blackheath and especially around nearby Katoomba. For this walk, travel to the Blue Mountains National Park visitor centre just east of Blackheath. You might like to spend time in the centre before setting off on the walk. You start on the adjacent Fairfax Heritage Walk pathway to nearby cliff-tops. This path leads down through excellent bushland with many wildflowers. It includes the George Phillips Lookout at the cliff-rim. You see Horseshoe Falls from this vantage point and a great panorama of the Grose Valley plus its major surrounding cliffs. When 1.8 km from the visitor centre you reach Govetts Leap Lookout where there is a good picnic

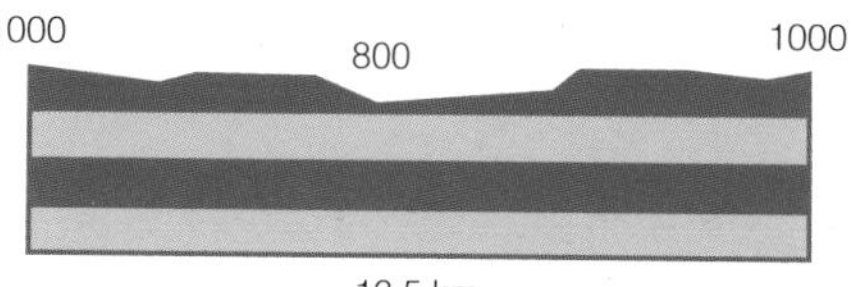

Mt Victoria	J	F	M	A	M	J	J	A	S	O	N	D	Year
Rain av. mm	110	97	80	76	45	58	42	50	47	63	70	72	810
Temp av. max. °C	22	22	20	17	12	10	9	10	13	16	19	21	15
Temp av. min. °C	12	12	11	8	5	3	2	3	4	7	9	11	7

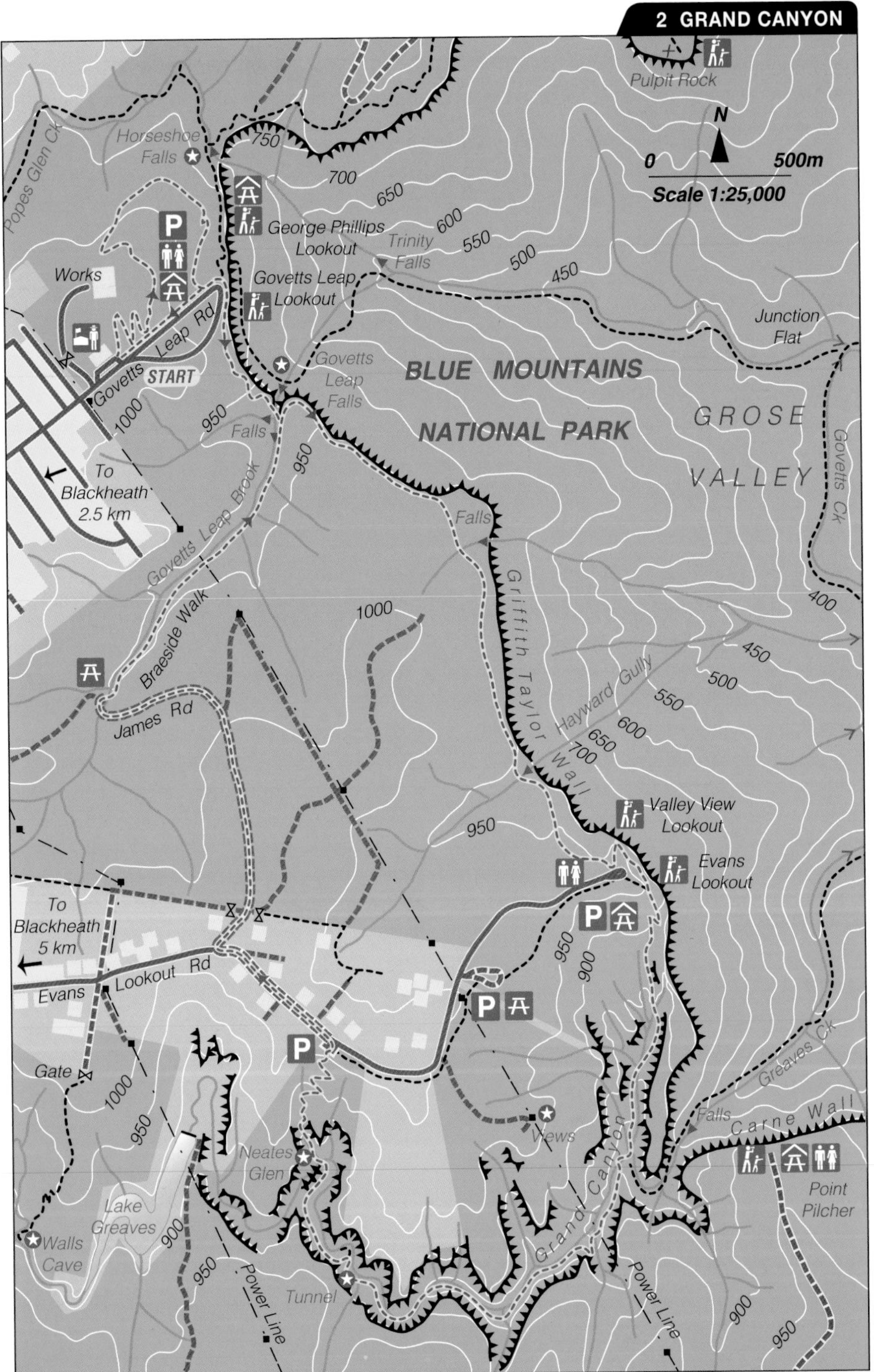

Pulpit Rock
N
0
500m
Scale 1:25,000
Horseshoe Falls
750
700
650
600
550
500
450
Popes Glen Ck
George Phillips Lookout
Trinity Falls
Govetts Leap Lookout
Works
Govetts Leap Rd
START
Junction Flat
Govetts Leap Falls
BLUE MOUNTAINS
NATIONAL PARK
GROSE
VALLEY
Govetts Ck
1000
950
Falls
To Blackheath 2.5 km
Govetts Leap Brook
Griffith Taylor Wall
Braeside Walk
James Rd
400
Hayward Gully
Valley View Lookout
Evans Lookout
To Blackheath 5 km
Evans Lookout Rd
900
Gate
Greaves Ck
Carne Wall
Views
Neates Glen
Grand Canyon
Point Pilcher
Lake Greaves
Walls Cave
Power Line
Tunnel

Morning light over Grose Valley

area. The scenery here is breathtaking and popular with tourists. The Blue Mountains are so named because of an unusually blue haze compared to other mountain areas. Evidently minute eucalyptus oil droplets in the atmosphere diffuse light to cause the illusion.

Follow a foot track south along the cliff-rim. Within 750 m you should reach the head of Govetts Leap Falls (these days also known as Bridal Veil Falls) after a short sharp descent. Cross Govetts Leap Brook and bypass Braeside Walk which is your later return streamside route, so as to climb south-east along the cliff-rim. Another excellent lookout is reached as you start to climb. The track continues near the cliff-rim for 2.5 km to Evans Lookout carpark and its picnic area. On the way you will probably see many lizards and some termite mounds plus a wide variety of plants. These include waratah (*Telopea speciossima*), honeyflower (*Lambertia formosa*) and several species of banksia, callistemon and hakea.

Both Valley View Lookout and Evans Lookout give more spectacular views to the Grose Valley from near the carpark and you should visit both lookouts via a triangular track route. After a break, locate the access track to Grand Canyon heading south. This soon descends steeply into a very pleasant gully and gorge with abundant ferns. At 1.2 km from Evans lookout, this gorge meets Greaves Creek. Here you should turn right and head upstream from this confluence and follow the floor of the canyon. During the walk through the canyon, the sandstone walls become deeper and closer together, with numerous crossings of the creek required as you progress. Cliffs soar above you and in some places descend into darkness below. After some 500 m, it will be necessary to climb away from the creek up a number of well-formed steps to a walkway skirting the cliff-face. Here the sedimentary layering of sandstone is clearly evident with variations of colour due to impurities. The track gradually turns east

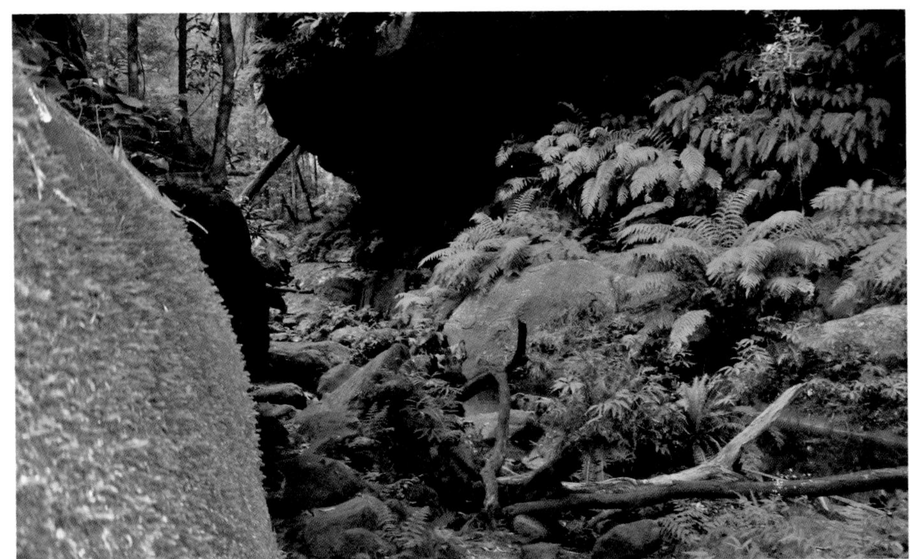

Grand Canyon floor

with many rock overhangs and the creek is now far below you in the narrowest part of the canyon. You may wish to stop for lunch here in a cool part of the canyon. After another 1.5 km and once through a 10 metre-long tunnel at an ancient rock fall, the canyon floor becomes flatter

Carne Wall

with the stream temporarily disappearing underground.

Approximately 30 m from this tunnel, a number of steps constructed on the rock face must be climbed. The track then continues for 700 m to a sharp bend in the stream. Here you cross the creek and leave the main gorge to climb a ferny side gorge via switchbacks for 800 m to a carpark at Evans Lookout Road.

Turn left along the road and within 500 m the road bends west and meets James Road. Turn sharp right to follow this gravel road for 1.5 km to Govetts Leap Brook and Braeside Walk. The way is relatively flat with sparse bushland. Turn right and head down the foot track beside Govetts Leap Brook for 1.3 km returning to the head of Govetts Leap Falls. The route is mainly through open heathland along the east bank. Once back at the falls turn left and retrace the 750 m up the hill and along the cliff-rim to Govetts Leap Lookout. Finally follow a foot track up the north side of Govetts Leap Road for 400 m to return to the visitor centre.

3 MOUNT GOWER

Lord Howe Island, New South Wales

Walk:	8.5 km retrace
Time required:	Including minimal breaks, 8 hours
Grade:	One day, hard with island registered guide required
Environment:	Coastal cliffs and steep mountain ascent
Last review date:	Walked September 2001. Updated through Lord Howe Island Board January 2009
Map reference:	New South Wales Lands, 1:15 000 Lord Howe Island and Map 3
Best time to visit:	September to May, winter can be windy and misty

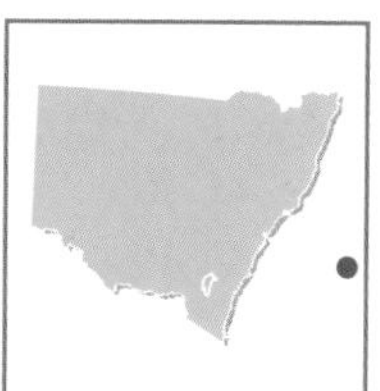

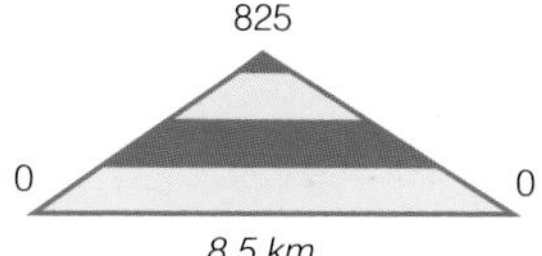

Tahiti, Moorea, Bora Bora and Lord Howe Island are all South Pacific sub-tropical islands of incredible beauty. Their magnificence has resulted from the combination of high island volcanic plug topography with surrounding tropical seas and coral reefs. Lord Howe Island is equal in scenic and natural attractions to any of the better known tourist venues of Polynesia. Furthermore, Lord Howe Island is part of New South Wales and unlike the other destinations is relatively close to the Australian east coast. It is also, perhaps, one of the best kept tourist secrets in the world. It does not have the trappings of mass tourism and therefore represents a truly natural paradise. In fact, a special Act of Parliament (*The Lord Howe Island Act 1953*) protects the people and the environment from commercial exploitation and large scale development. Clearly the aim is to limit the tourist industry to minimise the human impact on the island biodiversity. One gathers that the islanders are intent on keeping their island low key. Lord Howe Island, named after an eighteenth-century admiral in the British navy, was discovered on 17th February 1788, less than a month after settlement at Sydney Cove.

There are at least 239 native plant species on Lord Howe Island, and some 113 of these occur nowhere else in the world. There are some 500 fish species and 60 coral species living in the lagoon, reef and surrounding sea. There are 18 species

Lord Howe Is	J	F	M	A	M	J	J	A	S	O	N	D	Year
Rain av. mm	121	117	138	114	153	176	143	105	106	114	111	104	1505
Temp av. max. °C	25	25	24	23	21	19	18	18	19	20	22	23	22
Temp av. min. °C	20	20	19	17	16	14	14	13	14	15	17	19	17

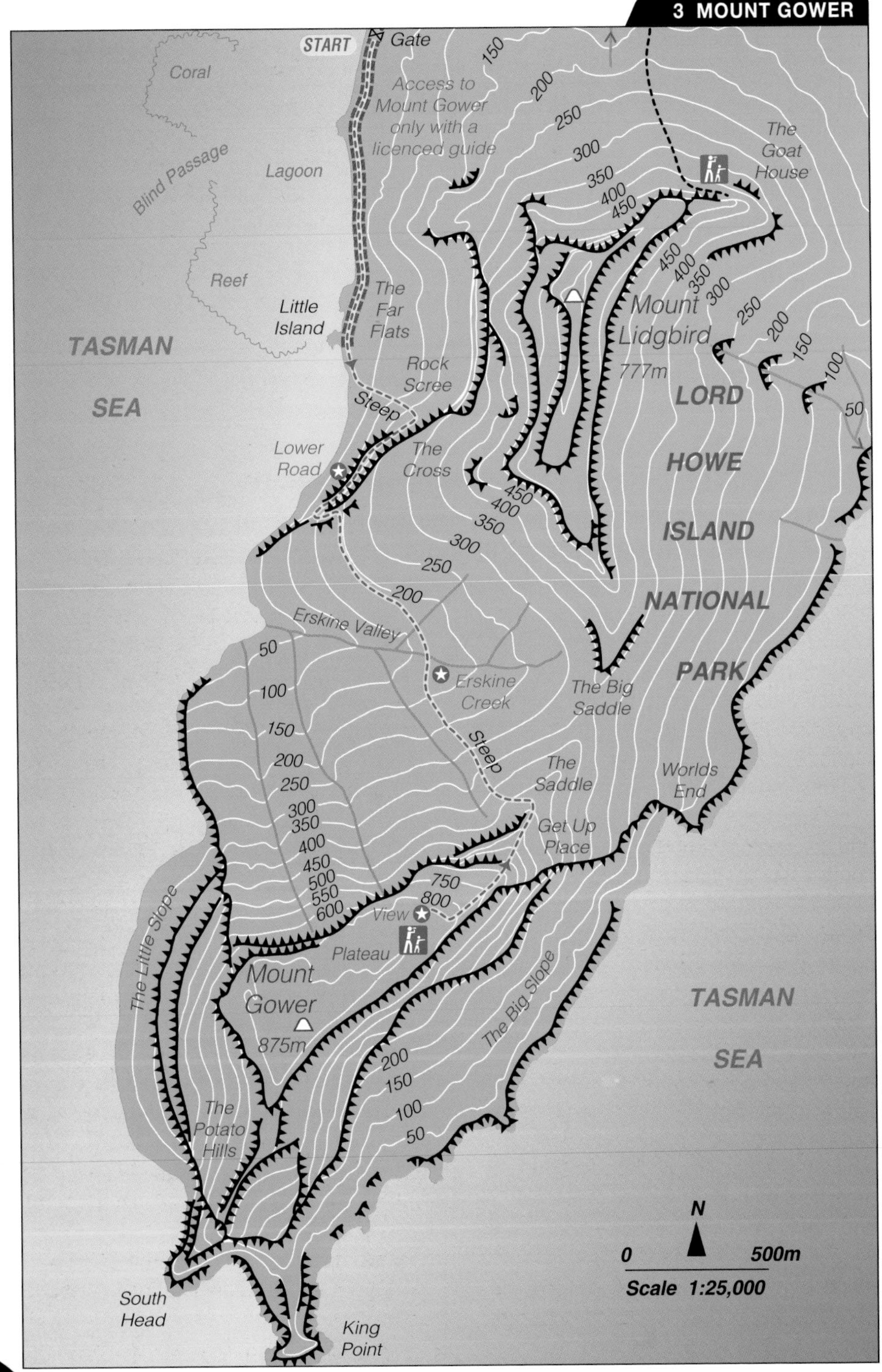
START
Gate
Coral
Access to Mount Gower only with a licenced guide
Blind Passage
Lagoon
The Goat House
Reef
Little Island
The Far Flats
Mount Lidgbird
777m
TASMAN
SEA
Rock Scree
Steep
LORD
HOWE
ISLAND
NATIONAL
PARK
Lower Road
The Cross
Erskine Valley
Erskine Creek
The Big Saddle
Steep
The Saddle
Worlds End
Get Up Place
View
Plateau
Mount Gower
875m
The Little Slope
The Big Slope
TASMAN
SEA
The Potato Hills
South Head
King Point
N
0
500m
Scale 1:25,000

Mount Lidgbird, Mount Gower and reef

of land birds, including the rare Lord Howe Island woodhen, and many species of sea birds ranging from large gannets to terns. Boobies, mutton birds and wideawakes (sooty terns) nest in large numbers on isolated parts of the coast. There is total protection of all plant life, bird life and marine life and the island has United Nations World Heritage classification.

Lord Howe Island is approximately 800 km north-east of Sydney and 800 km south-east of Brisbane; it is roughly east of Port Macquarie. It is the centrepiece of 28 smaller islets and rock stacks set on a submarine ridge between Australia and New Zealand. The main Australian east coast current keeps the ocean warm and thereby enables the most southerly living coral in the world to flourish. However, nearby cold currents add to marine diversity. The island is about 11 km long, crescent shaped and aligned north-south. Its narrowest point, between Old Gulch and North Bay beach, is only about 250 m wide. Its widest point is 2.8 km. Some 75 per cent of the island is declared a permanent park preserve to protect flora and fauna. The eastern coastline consists mostly of rugged ocean cliffs with small surf beaches and the west coast is mainly lagoon and coral reef. The coastline is readily accessible for only about 8 km. The lagoon is 6 km long and generally just 1–2 m deep.

The volcanic activity that created the island occurred earlier in the north than in the south where there are massive vertical-sided peaks known as Mount Gower (875 m) and Mount Lidgbird (777 m). These two peaks, especially, create the appearance of a typical South Pacific 'Bali Hai'. The island was once much larger but over time has been eroded by the elements.

Lord Howe Island walks, unlike most in this publication, entail a good deal of expense for transport and accommodation. For the enthusiastic walker, the outlay is certainly warranted. Air fares are expensive by Australian standards. It should be appreciated that the short island runway prevents larger planes operating; therefore each flight can only transport up to about 36 people. There are regular flights throughout the week from Sydney, Brisbane and Port Macquarie.

Accommodation cost is high due

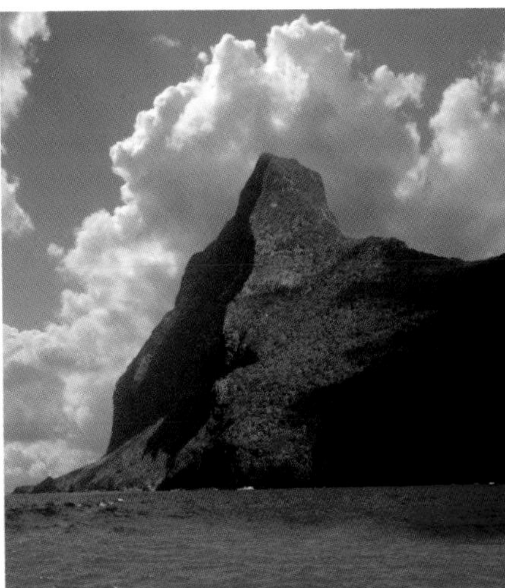

Mount Gower 'Get Up Place'

to isolation and high transportation cost of supplies. Full-board guest house accommodation and self-contained or motel style apartments have to be used. In effect, camping is not permitted. It is limited to islanders and only at North Bay.

There are general stores on the island, but merchandise, again, is costly. Several restaurants are available. The usual mode of transport is by hired bicycle with just a few vehicles being available for hire. Some accommodation operators run mini buses for their guests. Walkers can, in fact, reach most parts of the island and return in a day. There is an extensive walking track network. The island has a small hospital and limited search and rescue services so you should be vigilant about your safety.

Lord Howe Island has a maritime climate and frosts do not occur. The seas are mostly warm and there is a moderately good rainfall spread throughout the year, but heavier in winter. Winter rain and winds cause a definite tourist off season so some accommodation closes during June, July and August. February is the driest month and has a minimum monthly average temperature of 20 degrees Celsius.

Special points to remember include:

- take a torch for evening strolls
- dress at restaurants is smart casual
- airline luggage limits are 14 kg
- an environmental levy is included in the airfare
- coral is sharp; do not go barefoot
- glass bottom boat trips are available to see the reef
- snorkelling gear can be hired
- the island has an interesting museum
- there are no snakes or poisonous spiders.

As mentioned, the twin peaks that form the southern end of Lord Howe Island are Mount Lidgbird and Mount Gower and the latter is our suggested walk. Mount Lidgbird summit at 777 m is rarely climbed, is unsafe and should not be attempted. The grey-black volcanic rock of both peaks conveys an awesome, eerie impression, especially near the cliff-bases.

The ascent of Mount Gower is only allowed with a licensed guide by whom a fee is charged. Island regulations and policy under the Permanent Park Preserve plan of management make it illegal to climb without a guide. At the time of last review there were two guides registered with the Lord Howe Island Board with climbs operated two to three times each week during the peak season (December to May) and lesser ascents at other times. You need to be prepared for a difficult, hard climb. Contact with guides is preferable through your accommodation venue but advice could be given through the Lord Howe Island Board.

The requirement for a guide is said to be because of an awkward section known as the Lower Road, which involves negotiating a 500 metre-long ledge with about a 150 m sheer drop to the sea. Approaching the summit there is an awkward climb at the Get Up Place. Clearly there is an advantage in using a guide on any walk in an unfamiliar location, if for no other reason than to ensure the most interesting spots are visited and to have flora and fauna described. As well, the rare Lord Howe Island woodhen has the Mount Gower summit as one of its main habitats. Providence petrels nest there also. Numerous plant species occur, many of which grow nowhere else in the world. There is a definite need to prevent undue intrusion especially on the summit plateau.

The plateau is covered with luxuriant, dripping, mossy cloud forest. The tops are often shrouded in mist and on rainy days the whole area appears most forbidding, with waterfalls plunging over huge cliffs into the sea.

There are excellent views to be had from the peak, especially from the knife-edge northern approach spur. The island appears dwarfed in a vast expanse of ocean. The colours of the lagoon waters and the coral reef, together with the line of breakers along the outer reef edge, are simply magnificent. The huge bulk of Mount Lidgbird dominates the foreground.

Closer at hand is an impressive display of unusual plants and there is a big range of birds, most of them sea birds. They are a special feature of Lord Howe Island. They visit each summer in hundreds of thousands, for breeding.

The rare woodhen is a flightless bird and displays no fear of man. By 1978, there were said to be just 30 birds in existence, so in 1980 three pairs were taken into captivity and used for raising chicks. By 1984, 92 birds were released and now over 200 birds live on the island.

To start the walk to Mount Gower it is best to use bicycle or other transport to reach the south end of sealed Lagoon Road. Rather than walking the road, the time and energy would be better spent on the mountain.

The distance from the end of Lagoon Road to Little Island, then up to the peak, is only 4.25 km (8.5 km return), but progress will be slow and island guides allow 8 hours.

From the south end of Lagoon Road and a gate, a four-wheel-drive track needs to be walked for 1.2 km to Little Island. The track remains close by the sea. The guides need to be booked well in advance and poor weather can see your guide advising against tackling the ascent as rocks can be slippery.

After the initial 1.2 km coast walk to Little Island, rock hop the boulder-strewn beach southwards for about 130 m to locate the indistinct start of the ascent track. The pad leads off immediately adjacent to the southern edge of rock scree. This scree is now partly covered by vines. Palms on the slopes stretch right to the rocky beach immediately north of the scree, causing the scree to be more obvious through lack of trees. Once located, the pad is easy to discern. The track rises very quickly and about 50 m from the beach there are ropes to aid you on the steep climb. About 150 m elevation is gained in about 300 m distance from the beach to the base of the cliffs and an overhang. These cliffs are part of the western buttress of Mount Lidgbird.

Mount Gower summit view

It is then necessary to begin a contouring walk south at the cliff-base. Shortly afterwards ropes are again provided as the pad leads on to a distinct narrow ledge. This ledge (Lower Road) gets quite breathtaking with a 150 m sheer drop to the sea below. Some inexperienced people could become nervous at this point. Ropes stretch along the side of the track for about 400 m of the 500 metre-long Lower Road. The pad then turns east around the end of the cliff-face and there is a climb up a rocky crest for about 150 m. The way is then via a basically contouring track east into the Erskine Valley for about 600 m to where the creek is forded on flat rocks. The volume of water in the creek varies greatly, depending upon the weather. There is always adequate water for a good drink and at times there can be a real torrent. The whole area is deep within damp forest and is a great place for a rest. The stream is home to a number of rare species and includes shrimps. How they got there is quite a mystery.

Next, the track swings south-east and climbs steadily for 700 m, gaining 350 m elevation up the crest of a spur to a high ridge linking Mount Lidgbird and Mount Gower. Dense forest, including the usual palms, extends right up to the ridge. The ridge is attained well above and south of the main 400 m Lidgbird Gower saddle (The Big Saddle). Once on the ridge, there is a very steep ascent of a knife-edge spur. Ropes are again provided in a particularly steep section known as 'Get Up Place'. In this area there is a rise in elevation of about 350 m in about 600 m, so exposure becomes acute as the summit plateau is neared. Sea birds are often seen soaring in the updraughts. Views become spectacular. The vegetation is heavily wind pruned and stunted and the prevailing misty conditions usually mean that great care is needed on slippery rocks. Also you need to be careful not to step on or interfere with the bird nesting burrows.

Mount Eliza and palms

At the top the main attraction is the view just past a knob. The large collection of endemic plants is a real feature. Orchids are abundant. You need a long break in this wonderful spot and should not venture on to the environmentally sensitive plateau. The remainder of the walk involves a retrace with much care being exercised in slippery places.

After the walk seems an ideal opportunity to take the tourist boat trip which circumnavigates the island. The boat passes right alongside both the east and west cliff-faces of Mount Gower and really highlights how very steep and huge the cliffs are. The eastern face gives an impression of having been subjected to an enormous prehistoric landslide into the sea which must have caused a tsunami in New Zealand. Also, as you round the southern tip of the island, the famous rock spire, Balls Pyramid, can be seen about 23 km to the south. It rises sheer from the sea in a 550 m high spire.

4 MOUNT WARNING

Northern Rivers, New South Wales

Walk:	8.8 km retrace
Time required:	Including minimal breaks, 4 hours 30 minutes
Grade:	One day, medium
Environment:	Mountain ascent in rainforest
Last review date:	August 2007
Map reference:	New South Wales Lands, 1:25 000 Burringbar and Map 4
Best time to visit:	April to November. December to March can be hot and humid. Avoid the summit during storms

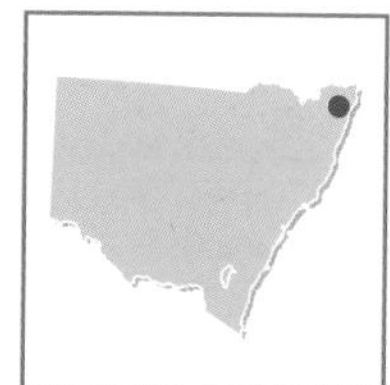

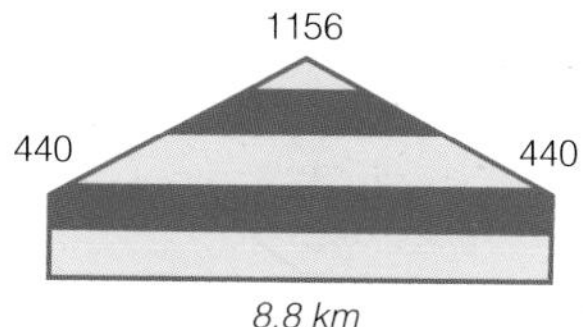

The Gold Coast in Queensland has developed as the premier tourist beachside centre with the best that Australia offers in facilities, including extensive air services to and from the rest of Australia and from New Zealand. The attractions are not only associated with the beaches along the coast but also inland, where the Border Ranges contain superb rainforests, waterfalls and national parks. Surfers Paradise has the most tourist development, but the tourist area extends from Southport in Queensland to Tweed Heads in New South Wales and beyond.

A glance at the 1:250 000 scale government Tweed Heads map sheet, reveals the immensity of a vast ancient (early tertiary) volcano, which we are told last erupted about 23 million years ago. It is adjacent to the Gold Coast, on the border of northern New South Wales and southern Queensland. The Tweed River and other streams have eroded and enlarged the central explosion crater, but left an 'island' of harder, more acid lava rock dome, called Mount Warning. It was named by Captain Cook as he discovered the east coast of Australia. Geologists believe the mountain once attained about 2000 m, nearly double the present 1157 m height. The flanks of the former, huge basaltic dome of the mountain remain along the state border in the form of the McPherson and Tweed Ranges, but erosion has created great low angle spurs (or planeze) with deep gorges between them. Such dramatic features as the Pinnacle, mark the rim of the eroded crater where the harder surface rocks have given way. The erosion caldera is about 30 km in diameter.

A most informative and enjoyable ascent of Mount Warning can be taken from the Breakfast Creek carpark serving the national park, which encompasses the peak. Access is via Murwillumbah in New South Wales and the south arm of the Tweed River valley, then up the valley of Karrumbyn Creek. Many Gold Coast visitors find the walk to be an excellent outing during their holiday.

Byron Bay	J	F	M	A	M	J	J	A	S	O	N	D	Year
Rain av. mm	164	184	208	183	179	164	107	92	66	102	120	143	1720
Temp av. max. °C	27	27	26	24	22	19	19	20	22	23	24	26	23
Temp av. min. °C	20	20	19	17	15	12	11	12	14	16	17	19	16

Murwillumbah has a good range of accommodation options and there are also places to stay close to Mount Warning but not in the national park. Be aware that the mountain (Wollumbin) is considered sacred to Aboriginal people and they prefer its summit not be climbed. Despite this fact, thousands of people ascend the peak each year. You should remain on the provided walking track if you choose to climb. There is no public transport towards the mountain beyond Murwillumbah. You should not leave valuables in vehicles in the carpark at the trackhead as thieves evidently operate in the area. Carry drinking water and do not start the walk late in the day. Keep off the summit during thunderstorms as lightning frequently strikes the top. There is a pleasant picnic area on more level ground down the road from the carpark if needed. There is also a table, seats and toilet at the carpark.

A 4.4 kilometre-long foot track leads from the carpark to the summit. It starts off well graded with many steps and zigzags, but for the last short steep ascent above about 1000 m elevation it has a long chain hand-hold to assist with scaling sloping rocks. Seats along the way, plant labels on some trees and distance markers also help make the walk more enjoyable. The rocks near the summit can be slippery when wet.

Bangalow palms

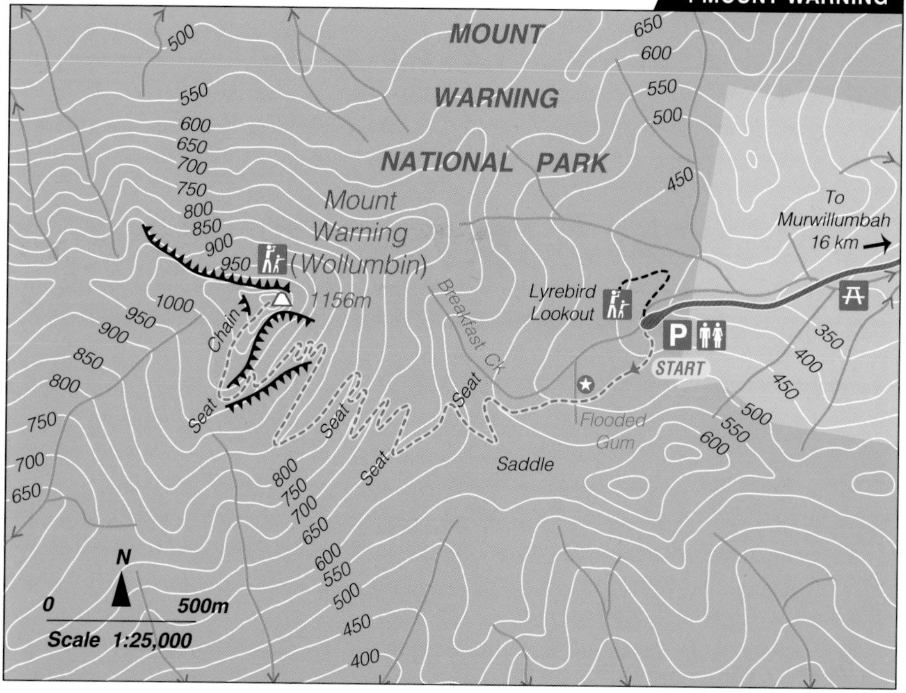

MOUNT
WARNING
NATIONAL PARK
Mount
Warning
(Wollumbin)
1156m
Chain
Seat
Seat
Seat
Seat
Breakfast Ck
Lyrebird
Lookout
START
Flooded
Gum
Saddle
To
Murwillumbah
16 km
N
0
500m
Scale 1:25,000

Flooded gum

Mount Warning

The rainforests in the area are part of the much larger, World Heritage-classified Gondwana Rainforests of Australia. Rainforest is therefore abundant and is most dense on the igneous rock areas of the main peak and associated peaks where soil depth and moisture is deeper. White booyong and palms are especially prevalent on the sheltered, lower reaches. These are called bangalow palms by Aborigines in New South Wales and piccabeen palms by the Aborigines of Queensland. Brush box trees (*Lophostemon confertus*) are common and some 400 m from the walk outset you pass an enormous flooded gum (*Eucalyptus grandis*). Buttressed trees, such as the huge strangler figs, are common. Daughwood, tamarind and glossy laurel are also seen. The mid-level forest includes numerous tree species, such as lilly pilly, rosewood, corkwood, cedar, coachwood and beech. There are also many epiphytes, such as orchids, elkhorn, staghorn, climbing ferns and birds nest ferns plus many vines. Lawyer vines (*Calamus muelleri*) with their nasty tendril barbs should be avoided. Vines are characteristic of rainforest environments. High cliff-faces have many giant spear or gymea lilies (*Doryanthes palmeri*) which are noted for their giant red flower heads late each spring and early summer. The exposed, summit rock faces feature shrubby montane heath and grassy plants such as tussock, grass tree, blunt-leaf mountain wattle, yellow tea tree, bottlebrush and broad-leaved cassinia.

You are sure to see and hear lyrebirds, scrub turkeys, green catbirds, whipbirds and quails but most wildlife tends to be nocturnal. Numerous species of bats, spiders, possums, pademelons, lizards and frogs are common. Leeches can be a problem in wet weather.

Four viewing decks on the summit provide the best possible panoramas, and plaques illustrate and name the features to be seen. Views occur only on the upper reaches and at the summit where there are spectacular outlooks to the erosion crater walls which, on average, are 15 km distant. On the top, the north coast of New South Wales and the high-rise buildings of the Gold Coast are within view as is the Tweed River, distant Cape Byron and the nearby towns of Murwillumbah, Tyalgum and Uki. The top of Mount Warning, by reason of elevation and easterly aspect, is the first part of the Australian mainland to receive sun rays at dawn. There are no branch tracks along the route of the climb, so you need simply ascend and descend via the same route. Lunch is suggested on the top before you retrace the way down the mountain.

5 THE BREADKNIFE
Warrumbungles, New South Wales

Walk:	13.7 km circuit
Time required:	Including minimal breaks, 6 hours
Grade:	One day, medium
Environment:	Volcanic lava plugs, forest and mountain ascent
Last review date:	August 2007
Map reference:	New South Wales Lands, 1:30 000 Warrumbungle National Park and Map 5
Best time to visit:	Suited to any season but avoid hot days

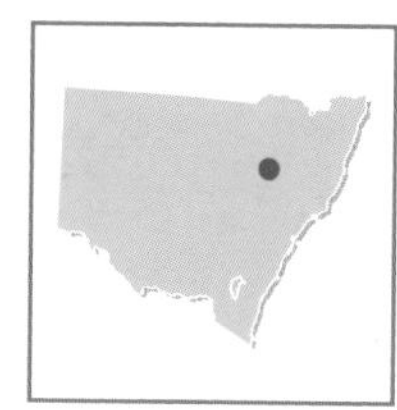

Some 400 km inland and west of Coonabarabran is Warrumbungle National Park. This area contains many significant igneous rock columns, plugs, domes and mesas, which are the remains of composite volcanic activity occurring some 13 million years ago. Much erosion of softer ash and other ejected material has since occurred with a radiating stream flow pattern emerging. These streams link to be part of the present Castlereagh River system. In stark contrast to the now exposed plugs and domes, formations such as the Breadknife occur when cracks in the side of the volcano allowed magma to well up from below. Rapid cooling formed stronger rock. The lava was a viscous, trachyte type, rich in silica. In many cases this process blocked the throat of volcanic vents and this often led to explosive discharges, which can blow large quantities of rock great distances. Such features as Belougery Spire and Crater Bluff are excellent examples of plugs.

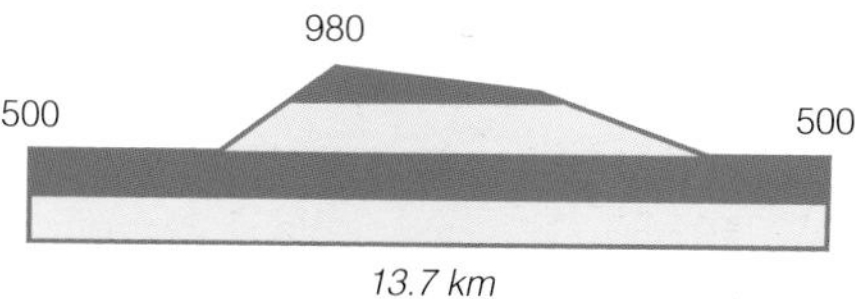

The park is noted for a wide variety of flora and fauna. White cypress pines (*Callitris glaucophylla*), and black cypress pines (*Callitris endlicheri*), rough barked apple, grass trees and 17 different species of eucalyptus occur. Up to 35 varieties of orchid proliferate. Of note is the shiny leaved hopbush (*Dodonaea viscosa*). You will most likely encounter grey kangaroos, echidnas, wedge-tailed eagles, emus and galahs.

Generally speaking, the park is quite dry and lack of water is often a problem. Hot summer days are best avoided and it is essential to carry plenty of drinking water during walks. You are advised to bring in water from a treated source.

Climbing the rock faces of the

Coonabarabran	J	F	M	A	M	J	J	A	S	O	N	D	Year
Rain av. mm	90	80	62	53	54	57	55	53	49	59	63	66	745
Temp av. max. °C	31	30	28	23	19	15	14	16	20	24	27	30	23
Temp av. min. °C	15	14	11	7	3	1	0	1	3	7	10	13	7

5-1 THE BREADKNIFE

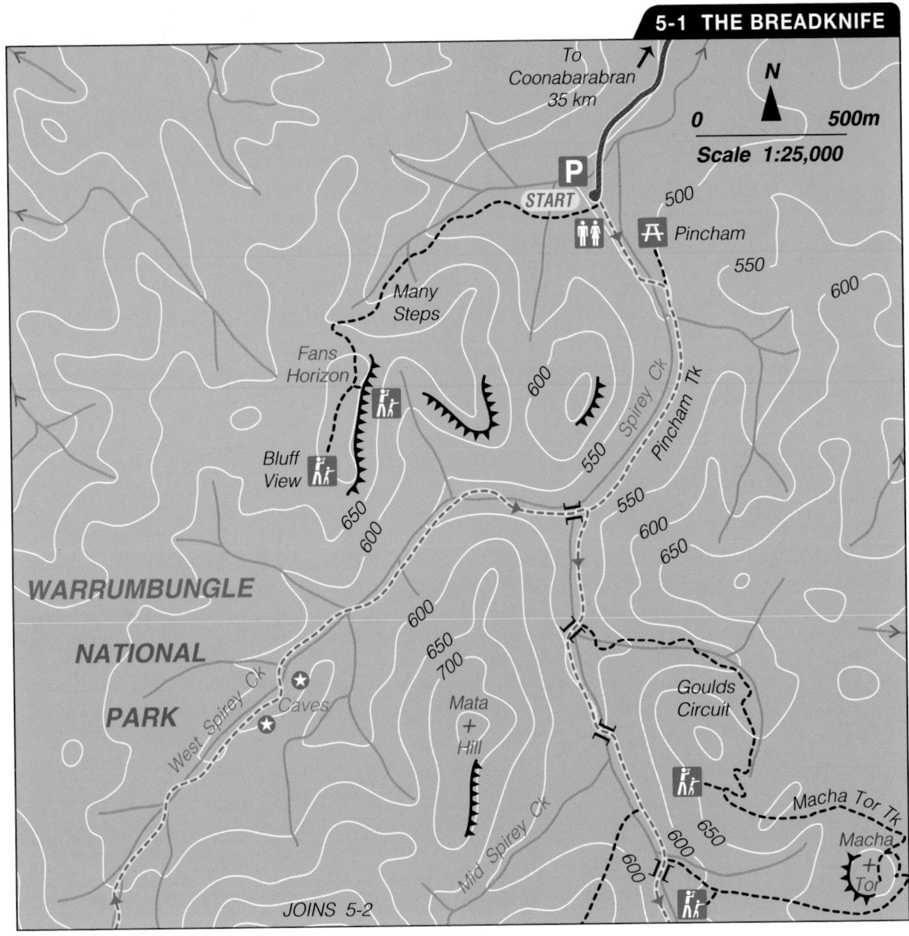

Breadknife is not allowed by park authorities, but rock climbing is popular at designated sites within the park: a permit for which is required. The park has an extensive system of walking tracks and the climb to the Breadknife and the Grand High Tops is among the most popular.

This walk goes to the Breadknife and beyond to Spirey View beginning at Camp Pincham. The land in this area was donated by a grazier Alfred Pincham. Camp Pincham carpark is at the end of a side road, 800 m south from the main park road. The spot also services a side trip to Fans Horizon just 1.6 km each way.

The remoteness of the park means private transport is needed for access. The town of Coonabarabran has good facilities and accommodation. Coach services operate along the highway through the town. There is excellent camping with full facilities within the park. Local wildlife has become tame to the presence of humans and may prove troublesome near food.

From the carpark at Camp Pincham head off south, past a bush camp area, via Pincham Track in the valley of Spirey Creek for 1.2 km. Bypass this right-fork West Spirey Creek Track, as this is your return route, from across the creek at this point. Some 500 m later, avoid the left-fork Macha Tor Track, so as to continue in the wooded

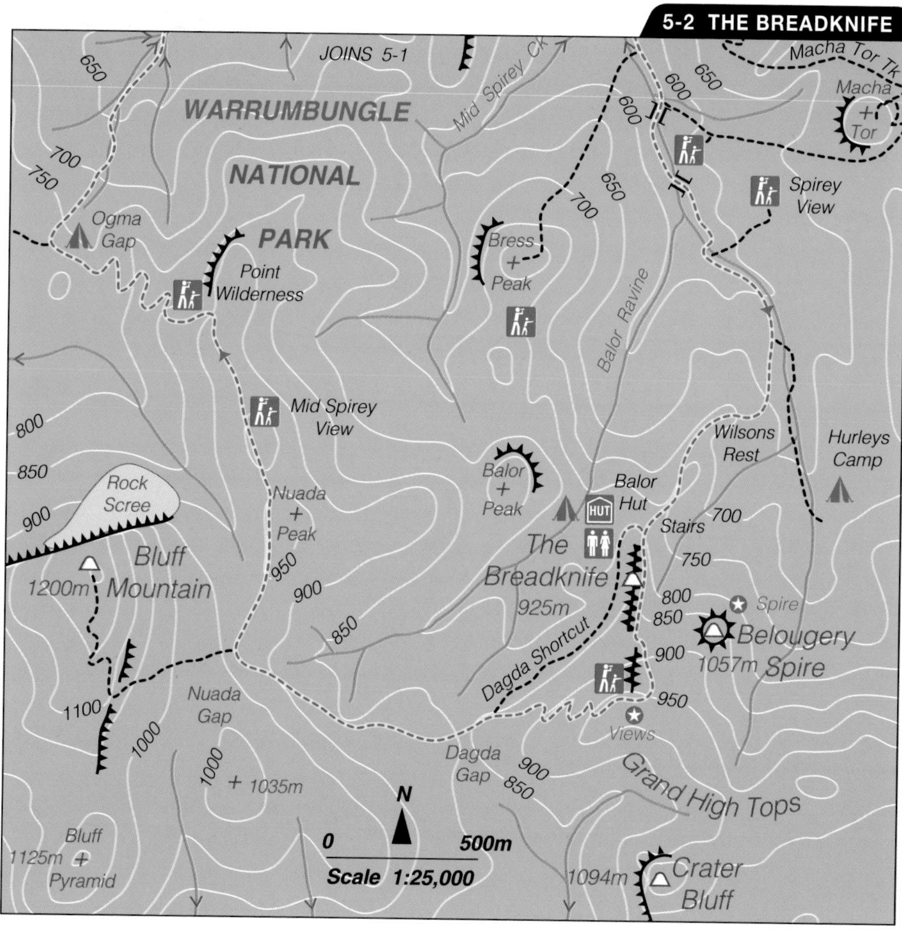

valley on the main track. Three other lesser side pads are also passed.

When 3.7 km from the walk start, you begin to leave the valley at the Hurleys Camp turnoff. Start a steady climb up past a seat at Wilsons Rest. Excellent views of Belougery Spire and western cliffs help to make this climb more pleasant. It is a 1 km climb mostly by paved path and stairway to a track junction. Here you are at the lower end of the Breadknife. Cypress pines provide some shade on hot days. The right fork leads within 70 m to locked Balor Hut (bookings required for use), toilet and viewpoint, where a welcome rest is afforded. You may well consider lunch here, as it is less exposed than 700 m further ahead, atop the summit.

Next, retrace your steps and take the ongoing track uphill, climbing alongside the eastern base of the blade formation. After 400 m you will reach the upper end of the Breadknife. However, you need to climb a little further for spectacular views. Follow the track east around the base of another rock blade; Lughs Wall is parallel to, and south-east of, the Breadknife. As you reach its top end, walk 10 m west on to the blade for the view over the Breadknife and beyond.

Next, continue up the rocky slopes, following orange reflective track markers.

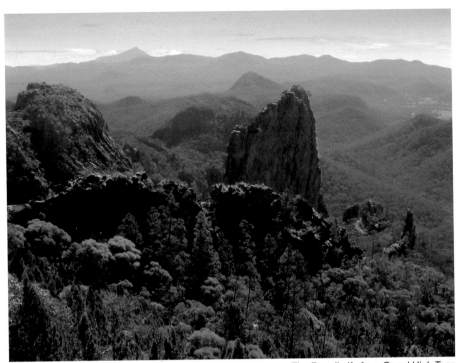

The Breadknife from Grand High Tops

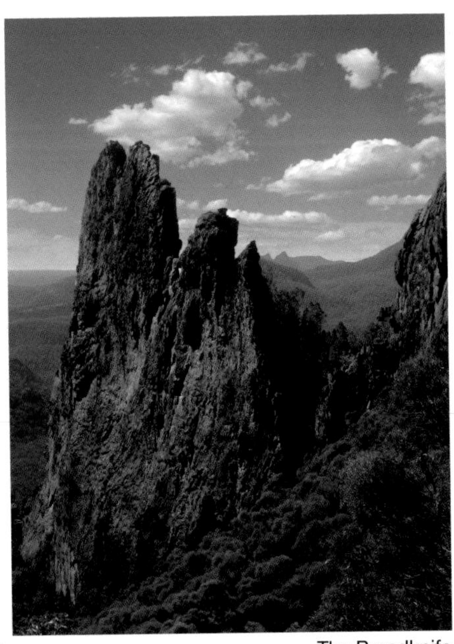

The Breadknife

Within 300 m you will reach the Grand High Tops, offering commanding views of Belougery Spire, Crater Bluff and surrounds. It is probably the best panorama in the park and is especially good towards the now familiar landmark of the Breadknife.

From the tops, head 600 m west, at first keeping high, then steeply descending to Dagda Gap. Keep heading west from the track junction at the gap. You pass through sparse forest amid some cypress pines to reach Nuada Gap after another 1.2 km. Here you avoid the left fork to Bluff Mountain and continue along the tops, past Nuada Peak to Mid Spirey View. Take time here to appreciate the view of Bluff Mountain and its cliffs which dominate the scene to your west. Evident are the basalt columns that form the core of the bluff with expansive scree slopes near the base. When 1.7 km from Nuada Gap you reach

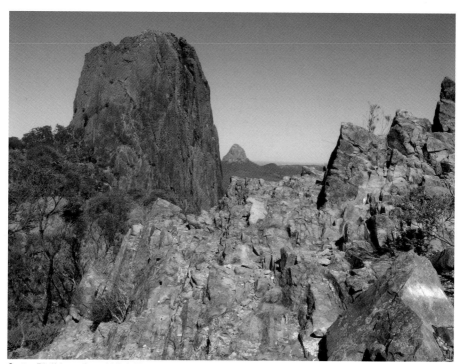

Crater Bluff from Grand High Tops

Point Wilderness and another outlook. Continue down zigzags for 600 m past Ogma Rocks to Ogma Gap and Ogma bush camp site. A small clearing here is most suitable for a rest.

Next, turn down the right-fork track, north-east towards Camp Pincham. The track is steep and somewhat rough at first. It then flattens out to follow the West Spirey Creek valley through relatively cooler woodlands with abundant plant species. The sheltered gully forms a microclimate for a wide variety of ferns and orchids. At two points there are small caves to the right of the track. The bushland here is tranquil compared to the exposed high places visited earlier. After 3 km, cross the creek, rejoin your outward route and retrace the 1.2 km along the Spirey Creek Track back to Camp Pincham carpark.

Belougery Spire

PIGEON HOUSE MOUNTAIN

South Coast, New South Wales

Walk:	4.8 km retrace
Time required:	Including minimal breaks, 2 hours 30 minutes
Grade:	One day, medium
Environment:	Forested mountain ascent
Last review date:	November 2008
Map reference:	New South Wales Lands, 1:25 000 Milton and Map 5
Best time to visit:	Suited to any season.

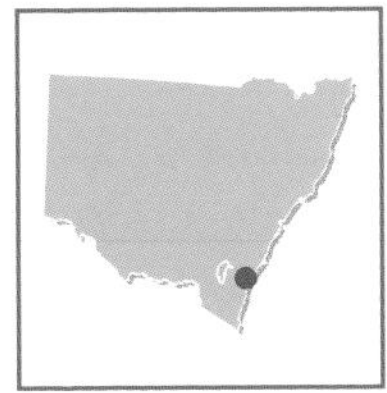

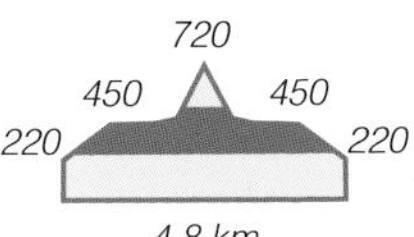

Captain James Cook named Pigeon House Mountain in 1770, when he saw the abrupt knob of the sandstone summit from off the east coast. It is said he thought it resembled a dovecote. The peak is 720 m above sea level and commands spectacular views of the coast and westwards to the ranges of the Budawang Wilderness. The whole region westwards is characterised by a very heavily dissected and eroded sandstone plateau with massive cliffs, canyons and domes. A good return walk can be taken to the peak from a minor picnic ground at a road end on a southern spur of the mountain. The reward for effort is the panorama from the summit.

Pigeon House Mountain cliffs

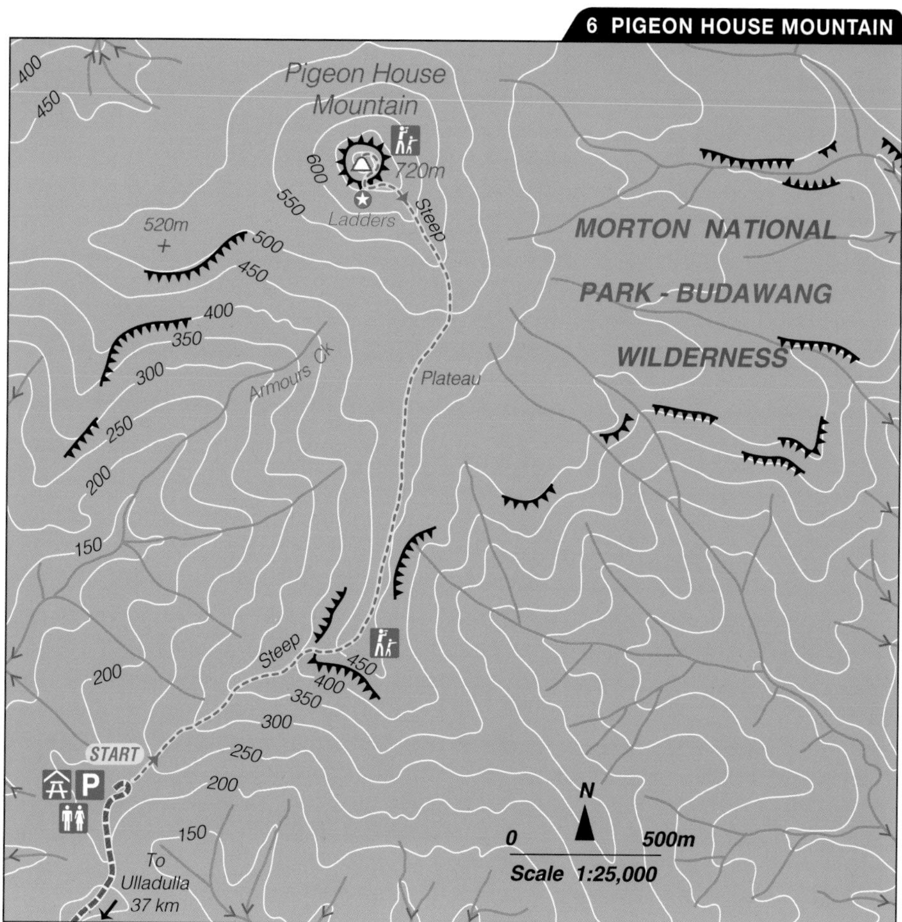

Access to the start is from Milton to Brooman and Nelligen Road, up Clyde Ridge Road 7.8 km, then 1.2 km north (right fork) to the picnic area. A 500 m ascent is needed to reach the summit from the picnic area, so, the walk is a bit taxing. The final ascent up through 50 m high cliffs is by way of a series of long ladders with some exposure.

From the picnic area, a track leads steeply north-east up to a rocky outcrop some 700 m away and 230 m higher. The pad scales the spur and then swings north and leads across a plateau for about 1 km. The plateau section makes for very pleasant walking and allows for a break after the steep climb. There is a good view of Pigeon House Mountain summit ahead. Vegetation is typical of the Sydney sandstone country with hardy shrubs and fairly stunted trees

Nowra	J	F	M	A	M	J	J	A	S	O	N	D	Year
Rain av. mm	103	82	99	89	85	104	98	55	59	60	59	77	970
Temp av. max. °C	27	27	26	23	19	17	17	18	21	23	25	26	22
Temp av. min. °C	16	16	15	12	10	8	7	8	9	11	13	15	12

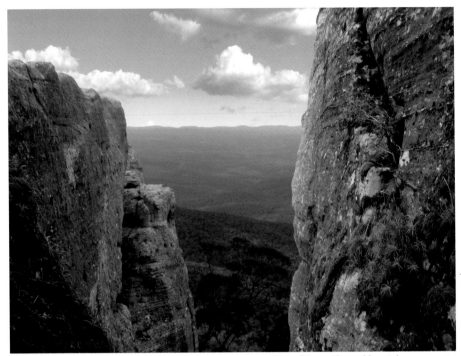

Pigeon House Mountain access gap

because of shallow soils. Soon, however, the track enters taller eucalyptus forest and rises again steeply up to the base of cliffs at the south-east side of Pigeon House Mountain. The forest is taller and denser because of the pyramid shaped outwash of the mineralised soils from the summit of the peak. This outwash, which is like rock scree, is more fertile and creates the iconic shape of the mountain.

Just to the left of the cliffs' approach point, ladders give direct access to the summit via a gap in the cliffs. There is some exposure because of the great length of the ladders. You see orchids growing on the rock faces as you climb these ladders. At the top it is necessary to wander about to get the best vantage point for each direction. Not only do you get the tremendous views deep into the Budawang Wilderness, but also to the coast around

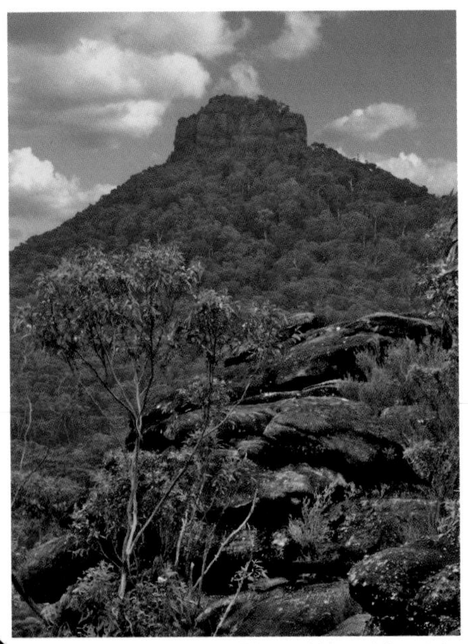

Pigeon House Mountain

Byangee Walls from Pigeon House Mountain

Ulladulla. The wilderness view includes the Clyde River valley as it cuts its way through from the Southern Tablelands. You can see deep into the Budawang Wilderness to such specatular features as the Castle, Byangee Walls and Monolith Valley. Each of these places is largely inaccessible to all but those prepared to walk for days.

A hard grade walk into remote Monolith Valley is particularly rewarding. Labyrinths of sandstone chasms, beehive-shaped domes, huge rock overhangs and massive cliffs abound.

The summit of Pigeon House Mountain is one of the best places from which to view this remarkable wilderness.

Lunch could be enjoyed atop the summit before retracing the route using the same walking track. Be most careful when descending the ladders.

Budawang Wilderness

VICTORIA

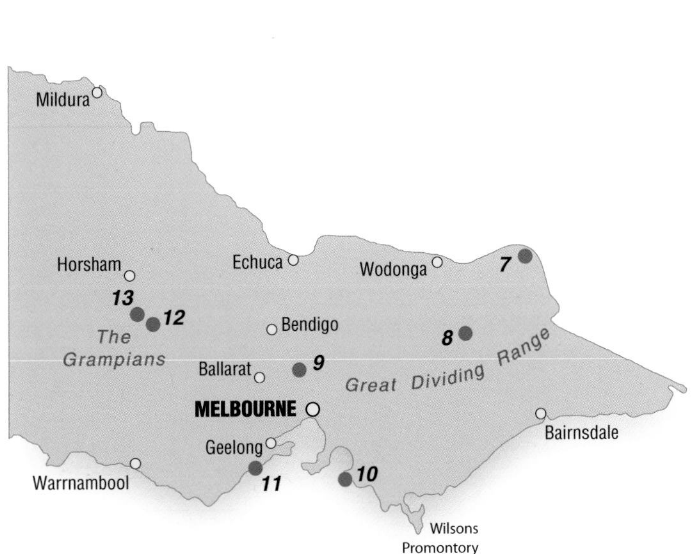

7	**Little Pine Mountain**	Burrowa-Pine Mountain National Park
8	**Mount Feathertop**	Alpine National Park
9	**Camels Hump–Mount Towrong**	Macedon Regional Park
10	**Cape Woolamai**	Phillip Island Nature Park
11	**Point Addis**	Point Addis Marine National Park
12	**Briggs Bluff**	Grampians National Park
13	**Mount Stapylton**	Grampians National Park

Cape Woolamai, Phillip Island

Victoria has a wide variety of regions. Melbourne, the capital city, has many fine tracks along the Yarra River, the coast and nearby hills. To the east the Great Dividing Range dominates, with opportunities for high-country walking. A walk above the tree-line along the Razorback to Mount Feathertop in summer is an exceptional alpine experience. The lower levels of the Great Dividing Range provide year-round walking at places such as Pine Mountain and Mount Macedon. At famous Phillip Island, Cape Woolamai has high granite cliffs and beautiful white sand beaches. The south-west coast includes the rock formations known as the Twelve Apostles and the Great Ocean Road. At Point Addis there is coastal cliff scenery and one of the best beaches in Victoria. In the west, the sandstone escarpments and generally rugged terrain of the Grampians provide excellent walking opportunities, notably in the northern Grampians at Briggs Bluff and Mount Stapylton.

7 LITTLE PINE MOUNTAIN
North-East, Victoria

Walk:	8 km retrace
Time required:	Including minimal breaks, 4 hours
Grade:	One day, medium
Environment:	Granitic mountain ascent
Last review date:	November 2008
Map reference:	Vicmap, 1:50 000 Corryong (limited use) and Map 7
Best time to visit:	Suited to any season

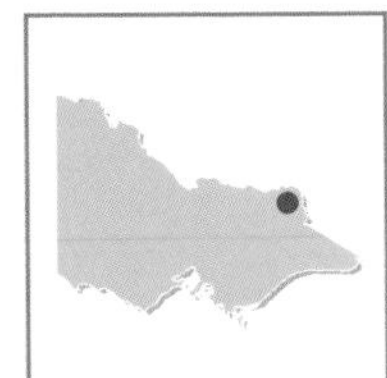

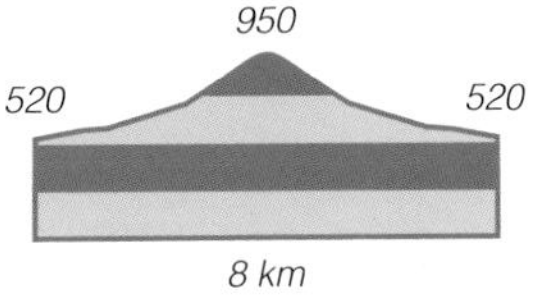

The upper Murray River valley near Corryong is a most scenic part of Victoria and includes the fairly large and mountainous Burrowa-Pine Mountain National Park. The Pine Mountain section of the park is a complex granite monolith said to be about 30 km wide at its base. Like all granite, it was formed underground aeons ago and later exposed by massive erosion. The summit attains 1062 m and the complexity of the mountain means walking to the summit is strenuous with many sharp ups and downs and numerous bare rock surfaces. These can become slippery when mossy and wet. Some 4 km up the mountain there is an extremely beautiful 950 m un-named peak which we have called Little Pine Mountain. It has huge expanses of bare rock and splendid outlooks so we suggest this is an ideal goal for a walk. To go further renders the grade quite hard and requires a very full day.

The mountain supports vast numbers of black cypress pines (*Callitris endlicheri*). The peak is of botanical significance because of several rare species including Pine Mountain grevillea (*Grevillea jephcottii*), fan grevillea (*Grevillea ramosissima*), broad-leafed hopbush (*Dodonaea rhombifolia*) and phantom wattle (*Acacia phasmoides*). Some of the more common plants include patersonia, correa, dianella, stylidium and xanthorrhoea.

Best access is from the small riverside community of Walwa at the state border and Murray River. However, if you need accommodation then you need to use

Granite boulders and hills

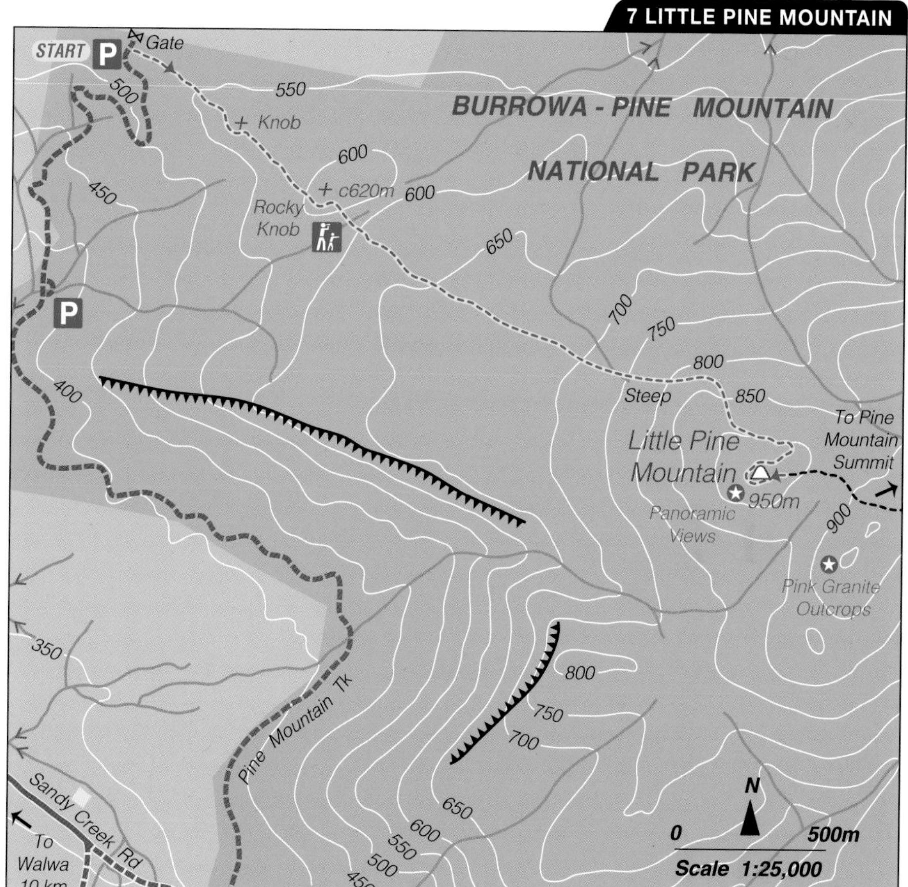

places such as Wodonga or Corryong. From Walwa, you go south on Shelley Road 2.2 km and south-east along Sandy Creek Road 9 km. You then turn left to travel 4.6 km on Pine Mountain Track which is a dry weather only road. It is in reasonable condition, although the last 1.7 km is a little steep and rocky. The walk begins on a saddle at 530 m above sea level. However, with adverse conditions, some drivers may wish to walk the last 1.7 km from a convenient small parking bay which is just before the rise to the saddle.

The first half of the ascent leads basically south-east up a quite broad spur to about 680 m elevation. Orange and red triangular track markers indicate the route. On the way two rocky knobs are skirted on their southern side. The second of these is Rocky Knob. It has a reasonable outlook.

Corryong	J	F	M	A	M	J	J	A	S	O	N	D	Year
Rain av. mm	51	45	53	51	63	77	80	82	71	80	63	60	776
Temp av. max. °C	31	31	27	22	16	12	11	14	17	21	25	28	21
Temp av. min. °C	14	14	11	7	4	2	2	3	5	7	9	12	7.5

Pine Mountain wildflowers

Rocky Knob

Beyond this point the ascent gets much steeper and includes some rock scrambling especially above the 900 m level. You round a switchback and emerge on bare rock expanses that cover much of the higher knob of Little Pine Mountain. The track markers lead you in a semicircle around and over the summit for best vantage points. The track continues downhill east but we suggest you take a break, enjoy the surrounds and then retrace the way, even though the ongoing track appears enticing. The Little Pine Mountain summit area features pink granite and many wildflowers when in season.

Pink granite outcrops

8 MOUNT FEATHERTOP

Alps, Victoria

Walk:	24.7 km retrace (Day one 11 km; Day Two 13.7 km)
Time required:	Including minimal breaks, two days (Day one 4 hours 30 minutes; Day Two 6 hours)
Grade:	Two days, medium, backpack required
Environment:	Alpine meadow and mountain ascent
Last review date:	February 2009
Map reference:	Vicmap, 1:25 000 Harrietville and Feathertop and Map 8
Best time to visit:	November to April. Totally snowbound in winter from June to September

At 1922 m, Mount Feathertop is the second highest mountain in Victoria and is perhaps the only one that looks like a true, craggy alpine peak. A wintertime snow cornice has resulted in its name. From most directions, any climb is difficult. The Razorback, a defined ridge approach, however, offers high level walking at about 1700 m elevation with views nearly all the way to Mount Feathertop. The route starts from Diamantina Hut on the Great Alpine Road about 3 km west of Mount Hotham ski resort. The ridge provides a relatively easy walk and is the most popular of access routes. In summer the walk to the peak provides some of the best of alpine walking.

Ancient sedimentary rock, heavily folded and later metamorphosed, then deeply eroded, has resulted in the striking landform seen today.

It is noted that the Razorback access attracts inexperienced walkers, some of whom set out far too late. All walkers would benefit by starting to walk before 10 am. Also, be forewarned that the sudden physical exertion at the higher altitude can cause light-headedness and even altitude sickness for some people. The district is heavily covered with snow in winter and usually in spring. It is unwise for most people to walk to the peak in such deep snow conditions. The summit area is very dangerous as unstable cornices result in avalanches and lives have been lost in the past. Tom Kneen Track, near the summit, commemorates one of those who have died when a cornice collapsed. Great care must be exercised during any walk in foggy conditions. Remember that in this area sudden unpredictable weather changes are frequent. Some of the track sidles the eastern, slopes of the Razorback offering limited protection from the worst

Bright	J	F	M	A	M	J	J	A	S	O	N	D	Year
Rain av. mm	71	53	57	72	105	116	136	138	124	104	83	75	1136
Temp av. max. °C	29	29	26	21	16	12	12	13	16	20	23	26	20
Temp av. min. °C	10	11	8	5	3	1	1	2	3	5	7	9	6

8-1 MOUNT FEATHERTOP

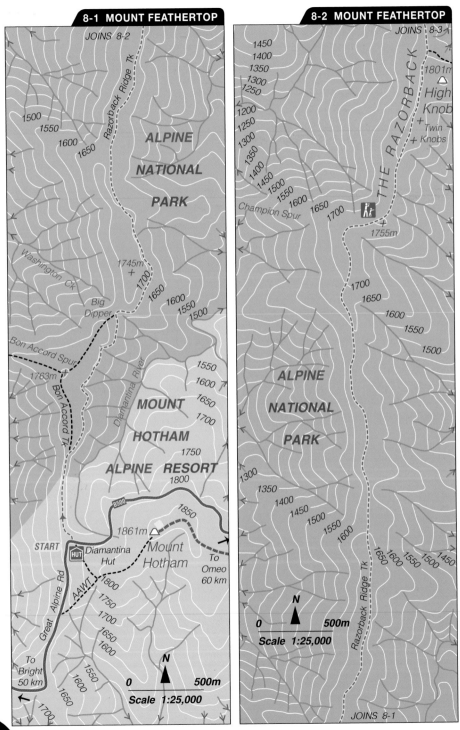

JOINS 8-2
Razorback Ridge Tk
ALPINE NATIONAL PARK
1500
1550
1600
1650
Washington Ck
1745m
1700
1650
1600
1550
1500
Big Dipper
Bon Accord Spur
1763m
Bon Accord Tk
Diamantina River
1550
1600
1650
1700
MOUNT HOTHAM ALPINE RESORT
1750
1800
B500
1850
1861m
Mount Hotham
START
HUT
Diamantina Hut
To Omeo 60 km
AAWT
1800
1750
1700
1650
1600
Great Alpine Rd
To Bright 50 km
1550
1600
1650
1700
N
0 500m
Scale 1:25,000

8-2 MOUNT FEATHERTOP

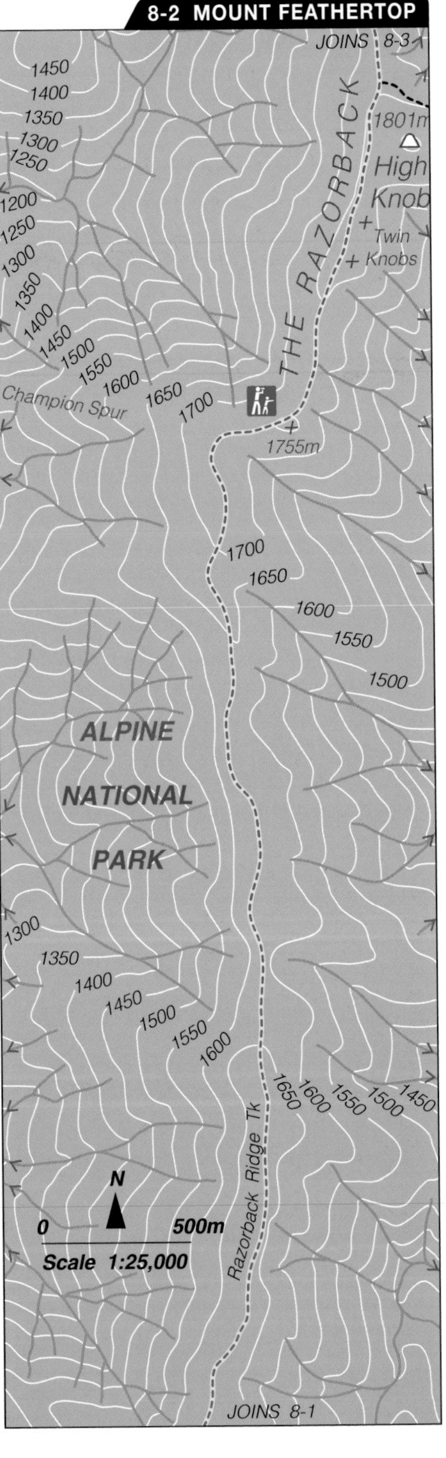

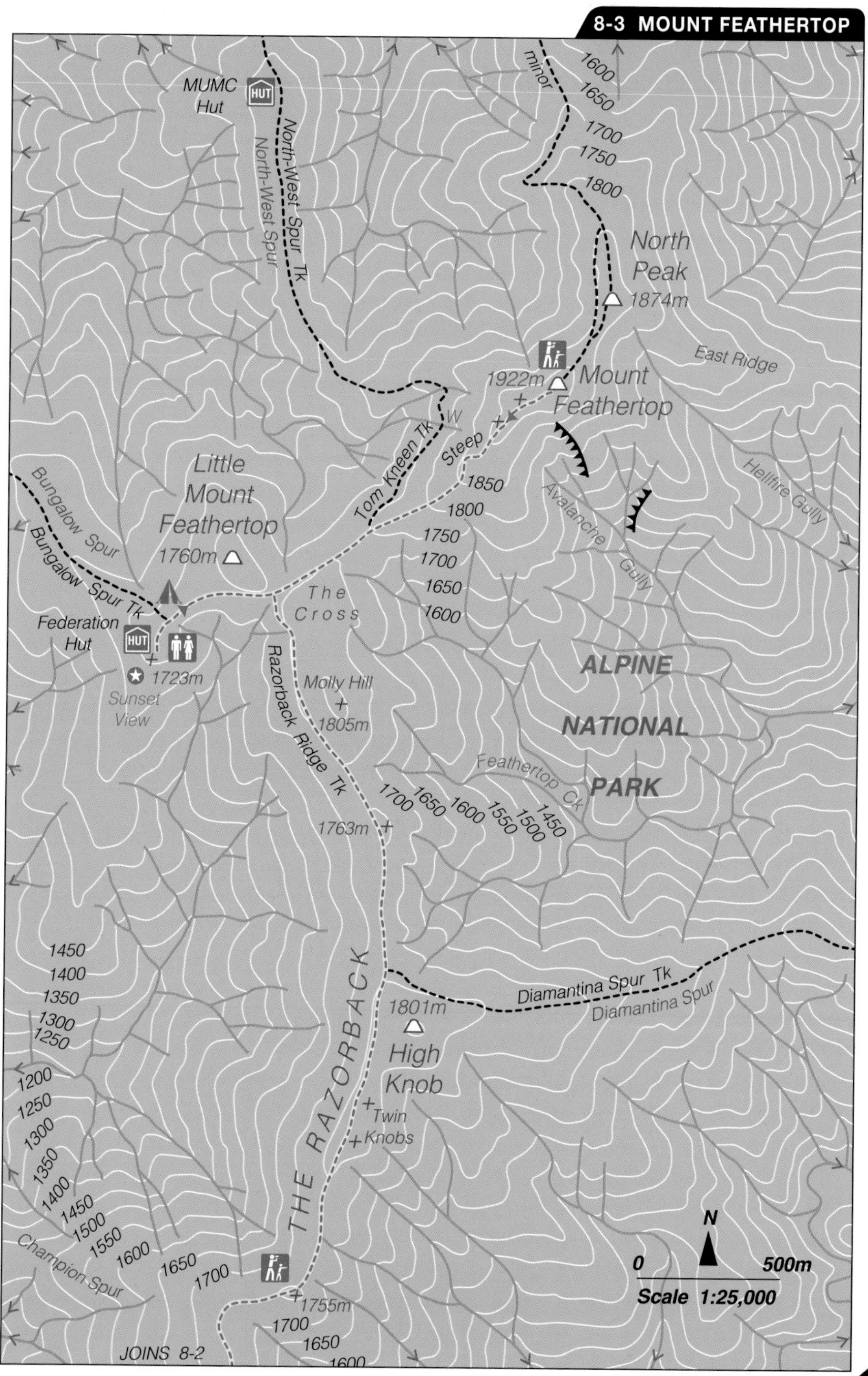
MUMC Hut
North-West Spur Tk
North-West Spur
minor
1600
1650
1700
1750
1800
North Peak
1874m
East Ridge
1922m
Mount Feathertop
W
Steep
Tom Kneen Tk
1850
1800
1750
1700
1650
1600
Avalanche Gully
Hellfire Gully
Little Mount Feathertop
1760m
Bungalow Spur
Bungalow Spur Tk
Federation Hut
1723m
Sunset View
The Cross
Molly Hill
1805m
Razorback Ridge Tk
ALPINE NATIONAL PARK
Feathertop Ck
1700
1650
1600
1550
1500
1450
1763m
1450
1400
1350
1300
1250
Diamantina Spur Tk
Diamantina Spur
1801m
High Knob
THE RAZORBACK
Twin Knobs
1200
1250
1300
1350
1400
1450
1500
1550
1600
1650
1700
Champion Spur
1755m
1700
1650
1600
JOINS 8-2
N
0
500m
Scale 1:25,000

The Razorback and Mount Feathertop

of the prevailing westerly weather. Carry a stove if you wish to cook. Open fires are not permitted on Mount Feathertop or its approaches.

Grassy spots outside Federation Hut, near Mount Feathertop, are suggested for camping and the hut is designated for an emergency refuge only, so you need to carry a tent. The former burnt hut has been rebuilt since 2003. You should not rely on tank water at the hut. The nearest good spring water is about 1 km away from the hut on the western slopes of the Mount Feathertop summit via Tom Kneen Track, so you should be self-sufficient with drinking water.

In 2003, wildfire raged throughout the Alps so millions of snow gums along the slopes of the Razorback and elsewhere in the sub-alpine zones died. Regeneration mainly from lignotubers of the rootstock is slow because of harsh climate but this classic Victorian walk holds great interest. The stark, silvery, dead snow gum trunks contrast well against the deeper greens of the taller timber in the lower montane zones. The stratification of vegetation is most pronounced. Regeneration of the alpine herblands and heathfields above the treeline is progressing well and the myriad everlasting and other daisy flowers are a sight to behold. The regrowth of mint bush, alpine celery and trigger plants is remarkable given the harsh exposure to the elements of wind, snow and erosion of soil.

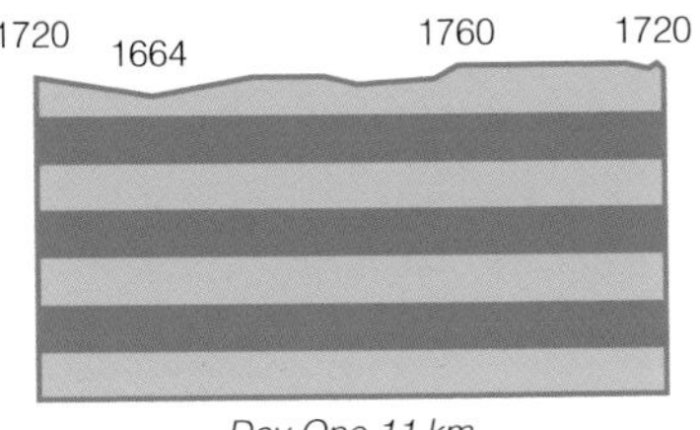

Day One 11 km

DAY ONE

From Diamantina Hut, just west of the top of Mount Hotham, head off north on the ridge crest track over exposed grassy tops, above the treeline and with broad views. There are regenerating snow gums

Mount Feathertop in winter

(*Eucalyptus pauciflora*) on the lower slopes to either side. Snow poles mark the route. Within about 600 m of the start of the walk, the foot track divides. You should veer right here rather than continue to follow the widely spaced snow pole line over a hill to Bon Accord Spur. Instead, you should sidle down eastern slopes into the Big Dipper, a deep saddle 2 km from the walk start. The track then sidles further on eastern slopes to regain the tops gradually. Nearby Mount Loch is to your right and ahead to the right you see Mount Fainter. Between them is the deep valley of the Diamantina River flowing into the Kiewa River West Branch. Once on the crest, expansive views westwards include Mount Buffalo and the Ovens River valley. The track stays near the crest and when 6 km from the walk start it begins to rise to the top of the Champion Spur.

At 7 km, the top of Champion Spur is rounded with a short eastwards section of walking to a rocky top. From this point onwards, the scenery becomes quite magnificent. Soon, you pass Twin Knobs where rocky bluffs and summertime wildflowers entice some walkers to camp on tiny grassy clearings within a sheltered depression. This idyllic spot could make a very pleasant place for your lunch break.

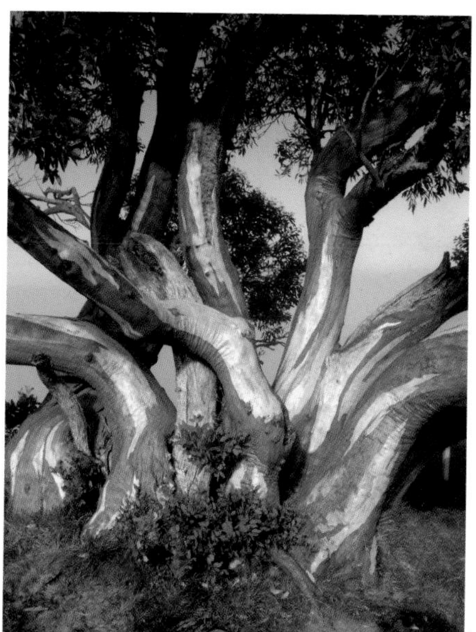
Snow gum at the Cross

High Knob, the top of the Diamantina Spur, lies just north and the track to follow veers left along its western side. At the north end of the High Knob bypass (1.8 km from the top of the Champion Spur), Diamantina Spur Track joins from the Kiewa River West Branch.

Continue northwards on the crest for 700 m, then sidle left another 800 m on the western slopes of Molly Hill down to a saddle known as the Cross. This saddle is 10.3 km from Diamantina Hut and has a magnificent old snow gum at a track junction. Turn left and descend 400 m distance to Federation Hut and camp site on a lovely grassy section of ridge just at the tree line. Snow gums provide shelter and a few escaped the fire. The hut is beside the Bungalow Spur Track from Harrietville. Once settled into camp, ensure that at sunset you walk the 150 m on to the tiny hill behind the hut and toilet to see the sun sink low over Mount Buffalo.

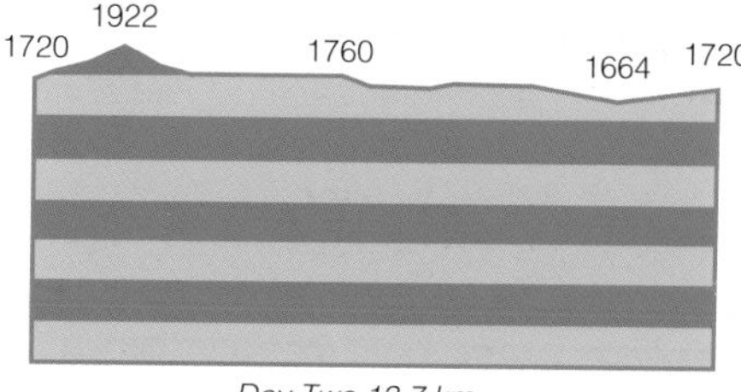

Day Two 13.7 km

DAY TWO

Ideally you should rise and walk early so that morning sunlight is seen to best advantage on the summit of Mount Feathertop. Having slept the night at the higher altitude your body should be better acclimatised, making climbing easier. You could carry your pack for the 400 m up to the Cross and drop it while you make the

Sunset from Federation Hut

Mount Buffalo from Mount Hotham

3 km return side trip. The summit is some 200 m higher than the hut. The ascent should only be made in fair or good weather. Take warm clothing to the exposed summit.

From the Cross, head north-east 400 m sidling the slopes of Molly Hill to another saddle. Here, the Tom Kneen Track veers off left. Continue another 1.1 km up the main spur crest track to the top and enjoy the great panorama. There are three high points and the most distant one is the highest.

The rest of the activities for the day involve retracing to the Cross then along the Razorback route back to Diamantina Hut. No doubt you will note lizards, snakes, grasshoppers, beetles and birds including birds of prey. A good place for lunch might again be at the Twin Knobs.

Mount Feathertop summit view

CAMELS HUMP–MOUNT TOWRONG

Mount Macedon, Victoria

Walk:	17 km
Time required:	Including minimal breaks, 6.5 hours
Grade:	One day, medium
Environment:	Cool temperate forest and views
Last review date:	February 2009
Map reference:	Vicmap, 1:25 000 Macedon and Map 9
Best time to visit:	Suited to any season, but can be cold and misty in winter

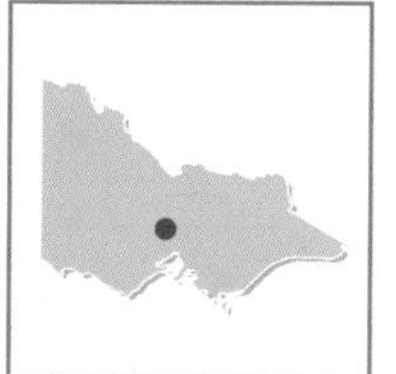

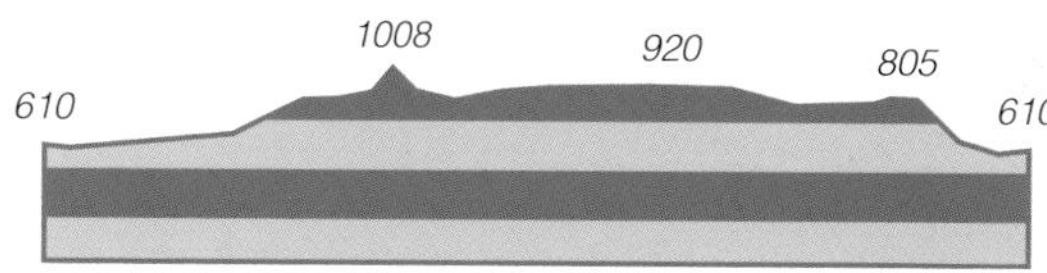

Central Victoria has a most interesting geological attraction at Mount Macedon on the Great Dividing Range. The mount is a large, extinct volcano and significant landmark 65 km north-west of Melbourne. The last eruption point centred upon Camels Hump, some 8.3 million years ago. The lava from that eruption flowed south to form the ridge up which the main Mount Macedon Road now runs. Turritable Creek and Willimigongon Creek have eroded the southern slopes heavily to either side of the main road.

Camels Hump represents a lava plug at 1008 m and is the highest point, with Mount Macedon at 1001 m and Mount Towrong at 805 m. These three high points are along a summit ridge in a large horseshoe-shaped arc. Many geologists claim this to be the old crater rim. However, some experts believe this arc is not the volcanic crater rim but rather the very eroded remains of a once much higher mountain.

Rich volcanic soils remain to nourish sturdy, tall forests of messmate (*Eucalyptus obliqua*), manna gum (*Eucalyptus viminalis*) and alpine ash (*Eucalyptus delegatensis*). Tree ferns are common on the southern and eastern flanks. With so much of the cool temperate forests of Victoria burned in recent years, this heavily forested country now is somewhat unique as it has fully recovered from fire in 1983. During any bushwalk you will encounter wildlife, such as rosellas, small birds and wallabies and perhaps koalas, echidnas, yellow-tailed

Macedon	J	F	M	A	M	J	J	A	S	O	N	D	Year
Rain av. mm	48	51	54	65	77	85	82	86	88	83	66	56	840
Temp av. max. °C	23	23	20	15	11	9	8	9	12	16	19	22	16
Temp av. min. °C	11	12	10	8	6	4	2	3	4	6	8	10	7

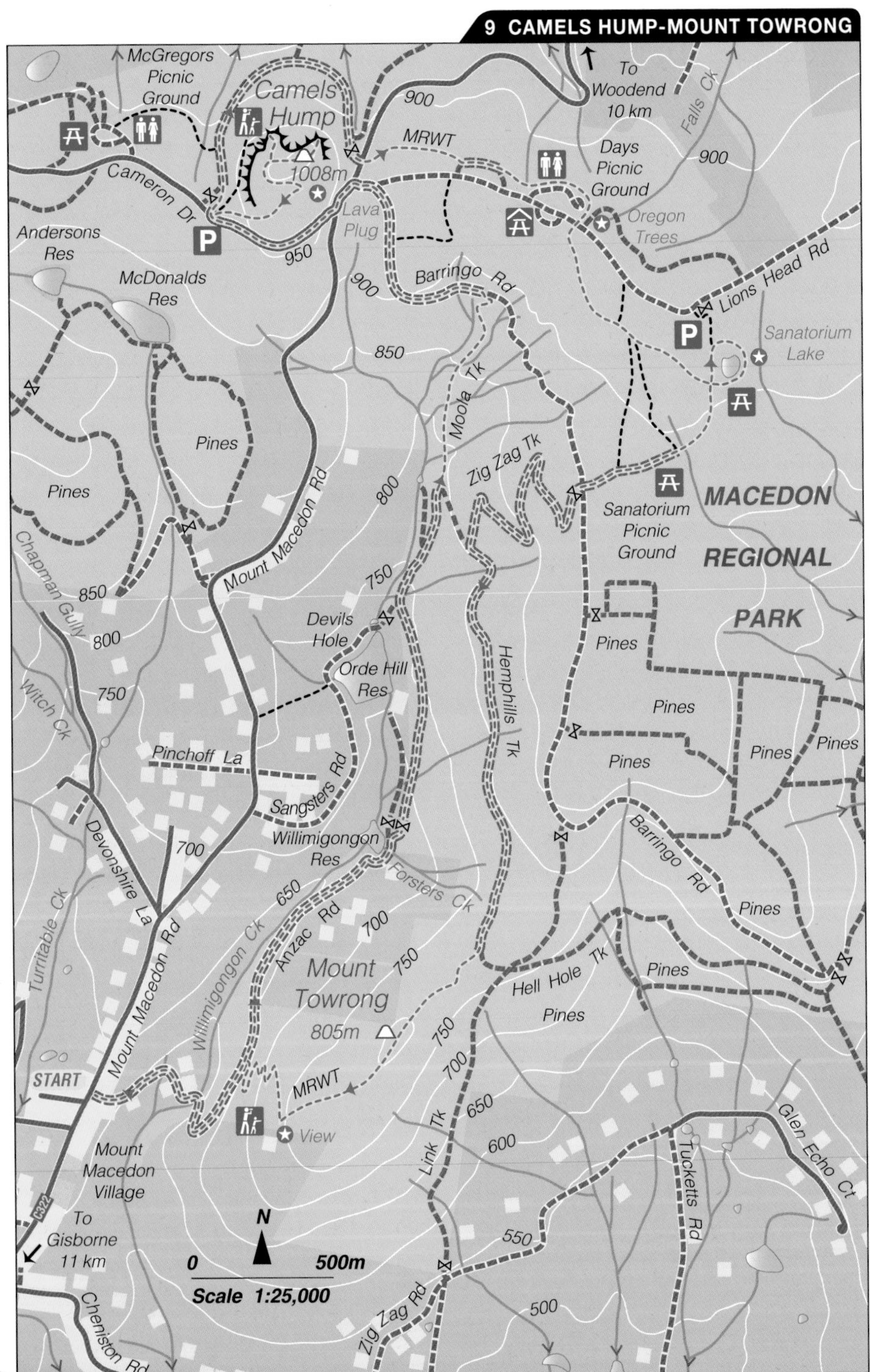

McGregors Picnic Ground
Camels Hump
1008m
Cameron Dr
Lava Plug
To Woodend 10 km
Falls Ck
900
MRWT
Days Picnic Ground
Oregon Trees
Andersons Res
McDonalds Res
950
900
Barringo Rd
Lions Head Rd
Sanatorium Lake
850
Moola Tk
Zig Zag Tk
Pines
Pines
800
Mount Macedon Rd
Sanatorium Picnic Ground
MACEDON REGIONAL PARK
Chapman Gully
850
750
Devils Hole
800
Orde Hill Res
Hemphills Tk
Pines
Witch Ck
750
Pines
Pinchoff La
Sangsters Rd
Pines
Pines
Pines
Willimigongon Res
Devonshire La
700
Forsters Ck
Barringo Rd
650
Anzac Rd
700
Pines
Turritable Ck
Mount Towrong
750
Hell Hole Tk
Pines
Willimigongon Ck
Mount Macedon Rd
805m
Pines
750
700
START
MRWT
650
View
600
Link Tk
Tucketts Rd
Glen Echo Ct
Mount Macedon Village
C322
To Gisborne 11 km
N
0
500m
Scale 1:25,000
550
Zig Zag Rd
500
Cheniston Rd

black cockatoos and sulphur-crested cockatoos.

There are numerous walking tracks that can be followed. The main Macedon Ranges Walking Track periodically marked with signs (MRWT) leads in an arc and passes each of the three high points of the mountain. This suggestion, starting at Anzac Road near the Mount Macedon village, includes the eastern parts of this track system so as to visit Camels Hump, picnic areas, picturesque Sanatorium Lake and Mount Towrong. You pass through both wet and dry sclerophyll forests. The altitude on the mountain tops at around 1000 m can give rise to cold conditions with some snowfalls in winter, so you should be prepared with warm clothing. Snow gums grow on some of the high points. Resist walking this route in reverse to the suggested notes as the north end of Moola Track is too hard to locate.

Parts of the mountain are also renowned for the presence of some of the best private ornamental gardens in

Crimson rosella

Australia. Rhododendrons, azaleas, maples and many other exotic plants thrive on the acidic soil. In the late 1800s, the wealthy of Melbourne established large Indian Hill Station type properties on the mount and competed with each other for the finest garden. Many of these properties remain. Autumn and spring are very special times of the year at Mount Macedon when it has colourful foliage.

Start the walk at Anzac Road corner 300 m up the main road from the general store area of the village and go east into gravelled Anzac Road. It winds down around ferny bends to cross Willimigongon Creek, negotiates a hairpin bend, then can be followed north up the creek valley in forest to Willimigongon Reservoir, 1.7 km from the main road. Anzac Road is a pleasant, quiet bushland road. As you walk it you pass some steps at the Mount Towrong Track 900 m from the walk start. This track is your return route. Along the road, you pass some private gardens. At the reservoir end of Anzac Road, skirt the east side of the reservoir and you reach a division of tracks. The left-fork, water board route is gated and you need to pass a barrier taking the right fork. This begins with a steep pinch, but the climb is fairly short. For 900 m you walk in tall wet sclerophyll forest, up, then down the slopes to another track junction, just north of Orde Hill Reservoir. Once a sanatorium was located here at the junction of Sanatorium Creek. It was part of the early resort facilities of the mountain.

Turn up the valley on Moola four-wheel-drive track and soon bypass a left side track so that within 500 m you come to a hairpin bend. Right at the switchback you need to stoop to pass under a large fallen tree trunk and continue straight ahead (north). The historic Moola foot track is your ongoing route. It leads uphill in wilderness for 700 m to emerge at Barringo Road. It

Snow gums on Camels Hump

gets quite ferny in dense wet sclerophyll forest. Ground and tree ferns proliferate as do emerald green moss-covered logs. The last few metres are steeply up a ramp at the road embankment. Turn left and follow the quiet, gravel road through more fine forest for 900 m and you arrive on the crest of the Great Dividing Range at sealed Mount Macedon Road and Lions Head Road junction.

Next, head towards the summit of Camels Hump, which is immediately to the west of the junction. Go just 100 m to your left and turn right up sealed Cameron Drive. Be careful here as cars and tourist buses use this road and there is no footpath. Within just 500 m you reach a carpark servicing Camels Hump. A well-formed easy grade track can then be climbed for 600 m to the lava plug summit, via a hairpin bend. Near the top the track splits to link to each of the two 'humps' of the camel. The right fork is the highest point and has a formal lookout at 1008 m but you should visit both summits. Composed of svolvsbergite, Camels Hump is one of only four known places in the world where this type of rock occurs. Named for the Svolvaer Goat lava plug near the town of Svolvaer in far northern Norway, it is also found at nearby Hanging Rock (Mount Diogenes) and Brocks monument at Hesket. Lunch is suggested on the summit with famous Hanging Rock in view in the foreground and the Cobaw Ranges beyond. The lunch spot is 6.6 km from the walk start. You need to explore the two summits for best views but be careful of the cliffs. Rock climbers frequent the area. East of the formal lookout there is a most interesting rocky viewpoint to the country northwards including to Hanging Rock. The exposed areas are a habitat for snow gums.

After a break, retrace the path to Cameron Drive. At the carpark there is a rock climbing access track off right. Avoid it and go down an adjacent track to the left within a gully on to the MRWT and you follow it for the rest of the walk. This can then be descended around the west side and northern rocky ramparts of Camels Hump. Near a low point on the track, avoid a left side turnoff and begin to climb south-east and south. When 1.35 km from the Camels Hump carpark, you return to the main Mount Macedon Road.

The ongoing MRWT is across the road and you follow it mostly on foot track as it leads east 800 m in bush to large Days picnic ground. A break in this pleasant area might be appropriate before you continue. If you walk the northern edges of the clearing you see splendid examples of manna gums and you may find wallabies grazing in the quieter parts. Bird life is prolific. At the eastern end of the clearing, mature Oregon trees are a feature. From these trees cross Lions Head Road to the south side in the picnic ground to follow the foot track towards Sanatorium Lake. After another 900 m of forest walking and temporarily using part of a bridle track, the walking track divides.

Veer left to go 300 m to Sanatorium Lake, where there are intersecting foot tracks, an information board, picnic tables and an eastbound track leading around the edge of the water. The tiny and picturesque lake was once a reservoir, but it is unclear whether the supply was for a nearby nursery or a sanatorium in the valley below, or both. Walk the lake shore pad anticlockwise to complete a 350 m loop back to the intersection. You may notice many birds and probably some frogs. Koalas also live here. Next, turn south, to walk down through more damp forest 400 m to most pleasant Sanatorium picnic ground, set among fine exotic, deciduous trees including many poplars. In autumn there is a carpet of golden leaves beneath your feet. The nursery once existed here.

Follow the picnic area access road west 400 m and cross Barringo Road on to Zig Zag four-wheel-drive track. Head down it in forest for 1.4 km to the fifth hairpin bend then turn left on to Hemphills four-wheel-drive track. This leads south 1.6 km within more forest to the crest of the Mount Towrong ridge just 100 m west of a saddle. Here you turn right (south). Climb a little for 600 m, still in forest, with glimpses of Melbourne off left and reach a rock cairn marking the summit of Mount Towrong at 805 m. There are filtered views in dry sclerophyll forest. Continue from the cairn and you start the 1.4 km descent to Anzac Road. The pad gets progressively steeper and the rocky open slopes provide spectacular views of Mount Macedon village, the famous Mount Macedon Memorial Cross and to the south-west and south of the Great Dividing Range especially.

At Anzac Road, turn left, walk down around the hairpin bend, to and across Willimigongon Creek and up around the ferny road bends 900 m to the main road and walk end. If time permits it is well worthwhile driving to the Mount Macedon Memorial Cross for a splendid evening view of the surrounding districts.

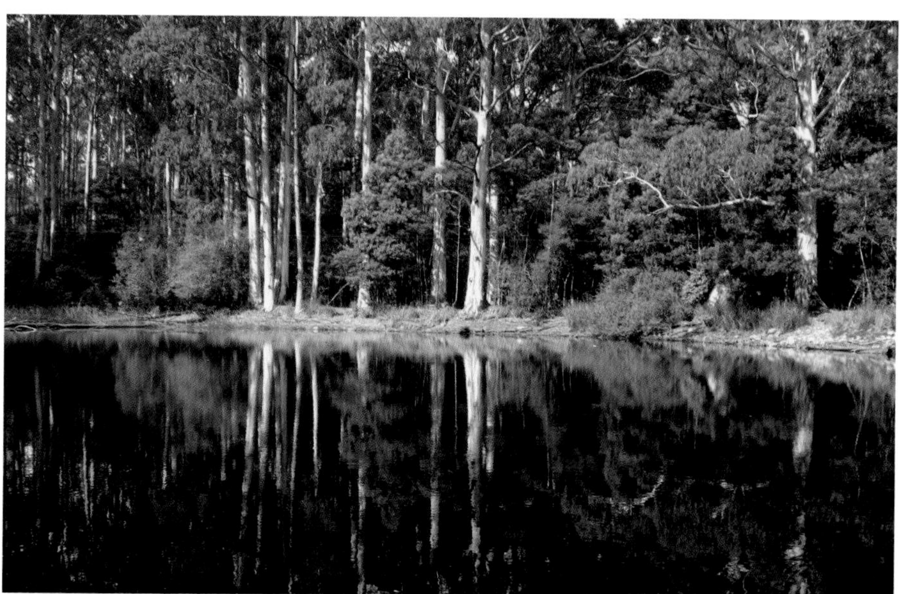

Manna gums, Sanatorium Lake

10 CAPE WOOLAMAI

Phillip Island, Victoria

Walk:	11 km
Time required:	Including minimal breaks, 4 hours
Best time to visit:	Suited to any season
Grade:	One day, easy
Environment:	Coastal beaches, dunes and cliffs
Map reference:	Vicmap, 1:25 000 Phillip Island and Map 10
Last review date:	February 2009

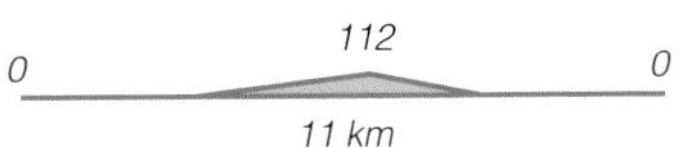

At the eastern end of Phillip Island is a rugged, 112 m high headland of pink granite known as Cape Woolamai. The Bunurong Aboriginal word 'Woolamai' has been chosen as a name for the cape as it resembles the shape of the fish snapper. The cape features high cliffs and granite rock which includes pinnacles, caves and a blowhole. There are sweeping views from the tops. A mixture of granite, sandstone and other rock types result in a remarkable sight along the shore with great inter-tidal rock shelves and reef platforms plus most colourful boulders sculptured by the waves. Adjoining the headland is a dune area with famous Woolamai surf beach to the south and sheltered Cleeland Bight beach to the north.

The whole eastern extremity of the island is protected as a fauna reserve within the Phillip Island Nature Park system. Rare hooded plovers and fairy penguins frequent the area and large rookeries of up to a million short-tailed shearwaters (mutton birds) congregate for their breeding season. These migratory birds each year fly an impressively long circuit of the Pacific, first to New Zealand, then around the western Pacific all the way to the Aleutian Islands off Alaska, along the west coast of North America, then across the Pacific and down the east coast of Australia. They arrive at Cape Woolamai around 24th September each year. A single egg is laid in a burrow in October and the parents take turns at sitting on the egg until it hatches in January. They leave in late April or early May for their long migratory flight. A large number of birds including pacific gulls, terns, sandpipers and ibis also frequent the reserve.

We strongly advise that you time your visit around low tide as much walking at sea level is suggested. This ensures you maximise your enjoyment and exploration of the inter-tidal zone and its wonders with relative safety. A circuit on track via surf beach and rocky coast, amongst the

Wonthaggi	J	F	M	A	M	J	J	A	S	O	N	D	Year
Rain av. mm	49	46	61	78	97	96	99	102	89	87	69	61	934
Temp av. max. °C	24	25	23	20	17	14	14	14	16	18	20	22	19
Temp av. min. °C	13	13	12	10	9	7	6	7	8	9	10	12	10

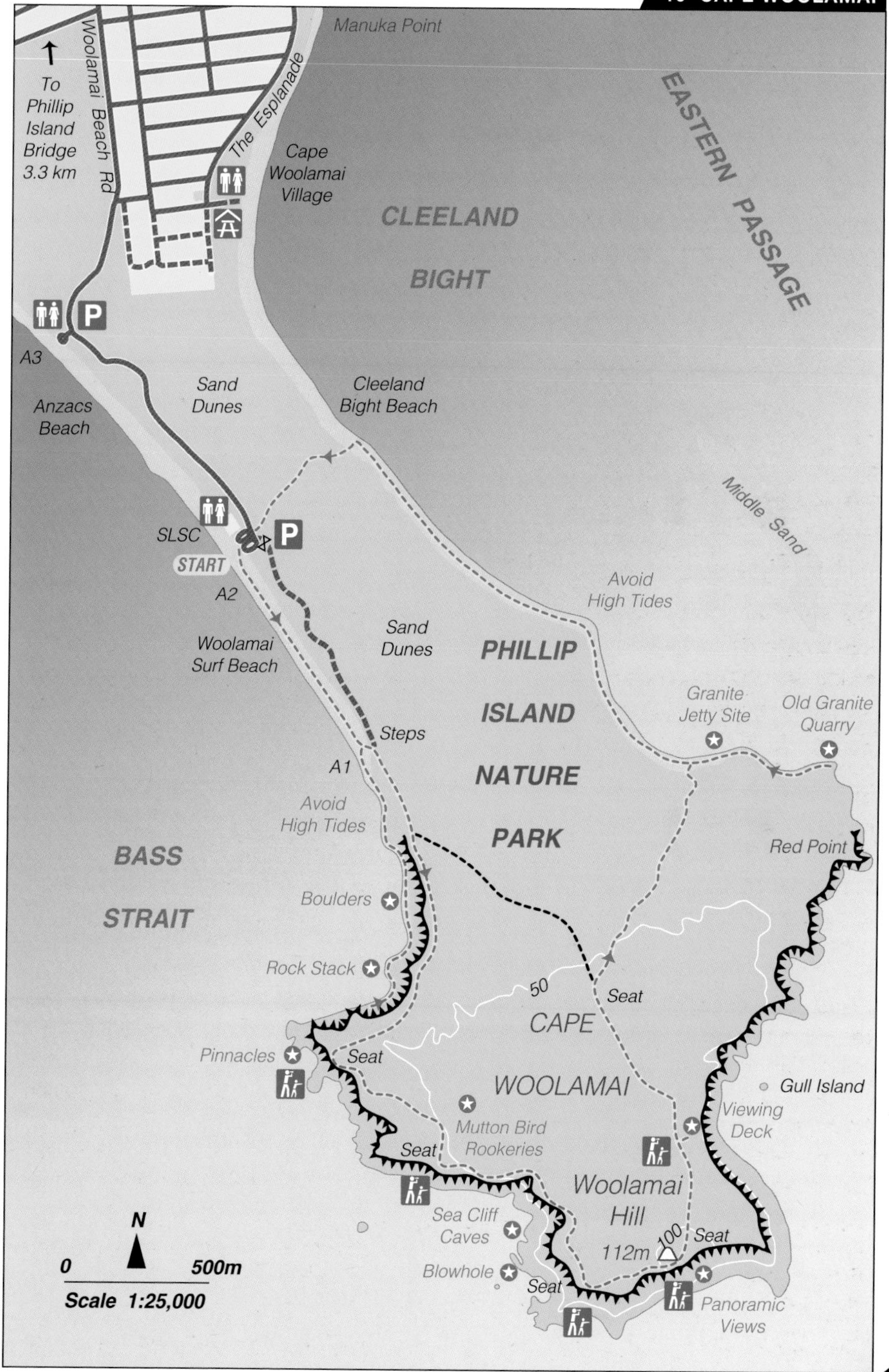

Manuka Point

To Phillip Island Bridge 3.3 km

Woolamai Beach Rd

The Esplanade

Cape Woolamai Village

CLEELAND BIGHT

EASTERN PASSAGE

A3

Anzacs Beach

Sand Dunes

Cleeland Bight Beach

Middle Sand

SLSC

START

A2

Woolamai Surf Beach

Sand Dunes

PHILLIP ISLAND NATURE PARK

Avoid High Tides

Granite Jetty Site

Old Granite Quarry

Steps

A1

Avoid High Tides

BASS STRAIT

Red Point

Boulders

Rock Stack

50

Seat

CAPE WOOLAMAI

Pinnacles

Seat

Gull Island

Viewing Deck

Mutton Bird Rookeries

Seat

Woolamai Hill

Sea Cliff Caves

100

Seat

112m

Blowhole

Seat

Panoramic Views

N

0 500m

Scale 1:25,000

Cape Woolamai and sea birds

rookeries and over the headland is most interesting especially about January and February. The cape and dunes have a good foot track network which should not be left for any reason: burrows of the mutton birds abound and if walked upon, they easily collapse killing the fluffy chicks and adults. Be mindful not to frighten the birds. Swimming is another attraction during warmer weather.

From the western end of the Phillip Island bridge, travel 2.5 km west to Woolamai Beach Road. Turn south, then go 2.8 km to Woolamai Surf Life Saving Club carpark and start the walk. In late summer it is advisable to carry repellent to combat insects such as march flies. It is best to avoid the Christmas to New Year period, as large crowds head for the beach at the surf club.

Descend from the carpark on to the beach and set off south-east. Some 900 m from the surf club, steps lead up cliffs to a foot track near their rim and this is your later walk route. An emergency triangular marker A1 is at this location.

A coastal side trip 1 km each way is a highlight of the walk. Fine white sand beach, granite cliffs and shoreline rock hopping plus dense, bright green foliage on some cliff-faces draw your attention. There is a variety of rock types, textures, shapes and colours. The marine life in many tidal rock pools create a lot of interest. Lichen on rocks, algae (including Neptunes Necklace algae), and seabirds, such as pacific gulls and oyster catchers, frequent the area. After passing between cliffs and a prominent rock stack and when 1 km from the steps you reach a rocky bluff where the sea usually prevents further progress and granite boulder hopping becomes awkward and slippery. For safety and conservation reasons it is unwise to venture further. You need to retrace back to the sandy beach and steps.

Colour coding for several foot tracks exists from these steps and you should follow the blue route. This doubles with the black coded route for much of the suggested walk. Go south-east on the track

Rock stack on Woolamai Beach

above the cliffs for 300 m until it divides, then veer right and take the cliff-rim track another 900 m from where you can look down on inspiring sea-cliff formations known as the Pinnacles. There is a seat at the best viewing spot.

The track can then be followed further in barren country around cliff-tops, gently climbing higher and higher past several outlooks and two more seats; and at one place there are views to large caves at the base of cliffs. The mutton birds seem to be especially prevalent in this general locality. The track then reaches a shipping beacon, 2 km from the Pinnacles. Panoramic views of Mount Dandenong, the Strzelecki Ranges and Wilsons Promontory can usually be seen from this, the highest point of the walk at 112 m.

The track should then be descended north-west to a cliff-rim viewing deck and broad vista along the Bass Coast and beyond. Next, head downhill for 800 m to a seat some 200 m short of a track intersection. This seat is located in a sheltered bushland setting; an ideal spot for a lunch break roughly midway through the walk. Capeweed, a South African plant, has overrun the summit, but banksias, sheoaks, wattles, tea tree and paper bark can all be seen as you descend northwards and pause at the seat. Revegetation of these once barren tops has been most successful in this locality.

After lunch and once at the track junction, veer right (north-east) and go down through denser bushland to Cleeland Bight beach fronting Eastern Passage 1 km distant. There is a short steep descent among trees and scrub on to the beach. Granite blocks at the ruins of a former jetty can be seen at the beach just to the east. Granite was once quarried in the area. This is a good spot for a swim if desired. The

The Pinnacles

Cape Woolamai cliff-caves

water is usually calm and quite sheltered and there are good views up the channel of Eastern Passage to Phillip Island bridge.

After a break, a side trip 400 m each way to the former granite quarry is most rewarding. It is at a headland and the abundant granite has orange lichen growing on it at the high tide mark. More cut granite blocks are seen at this once busy quarry, which is now an idyllic secluded place to relax and unwind.

After the side trip, the final stage of the walk is to follow the beach north-west for 1.7 km to a partly obscured signpost on a dune. There are large dunes to the left all the way to this point. This sign marks your route on foot track for 500 m through dunes, across an isthmus, back to the Woolamai Beach surf club and end of the walk.

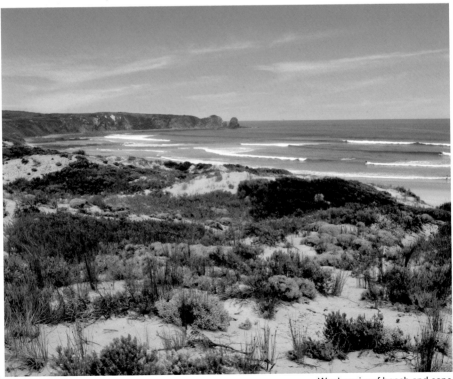

Woolamai surf beach and cape

11 POINT ADDIS
Surf Coast, Victoria

Walk:	11.5 km circuit
Time required:	Including minimal breaks, 4 hours
Grade:	One day, medium
Environment:	Coastal scrub, cliffs and surf beach
Last review date:	December 2008
Map reference:	Vicmap, 1:25 000 Torquay and Anglesea and Map 11
Best time to visit:	Suited to any season but best during beach weather

Point Addis (Kitjarra Ngitj) and Bells Beach are situated at perhaps the most attractive part of the Surf Coast and could be considered as having some of the best ocean beach scenery anywhere near Melbourne. Bells Beach is world-renowned in surfing circles. Behind the dramatic, high sea cliffs at Point Addis is Ironbark Basin, home to thousands of red ironbark trees (*Eucalyptus tricarpa*). The long-distance Surf Coast Walking Track passes through the Basin and several other walking tracks exist. A number of viewpoints from cliff-tops are a highlight too. The Great Otway National Park now protects the coastal land frontage and the Point Addis Marine National Park protects the fringing sea. The area is near Torquay, a town with full facilities.

A great circuit walk can thus be enjoyed. You do need to first check for the time of high tide as the Pixie Cave area and a short rocky headland beach at Jarosite Headland near Bells Beach Southside can be flooded at high tide. Also, no drinking

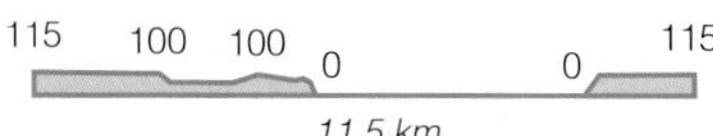

water is available at any point. These notes describe the circuit as an anticlockwise route for easiest progress within Ironbark Basin. The description starts at a gate beside Jarosite Road.

Jarosite Road connects the Great Ocean Road with Bells Beach and leads off the Great Ocean Road just north of Point Addis Road. The walk starts at a park gateway along the south side of Jarosite Road about 700 m east of Addiscott Road and Peregrine Close intersection. Just inside the gate, two tracks veer off into the bushland and you should take the right fork southwards.

The forest here is of the somewhat stunted ironbarks with many grass trees in the understorey. The track swings west and after 500 m you pass Jarosite Track, off left. That track leads to a former Jarosite mine that existed near the top of the sea cliffs. Jarosite is a sulphate of potassium and

Geelong	J	F	M	A	M	J	J	A	S	O	N	D	Year
Rain av. mm	36	31	30	48	49	45	50	49	50	57	49	38	533
Temp av. max. °C	24	24	22	20	16	14	13	15	16	18	20	22	19
Temp av. min. °C	12	13	12	9	7	6	5	5	6	7	9	10	9

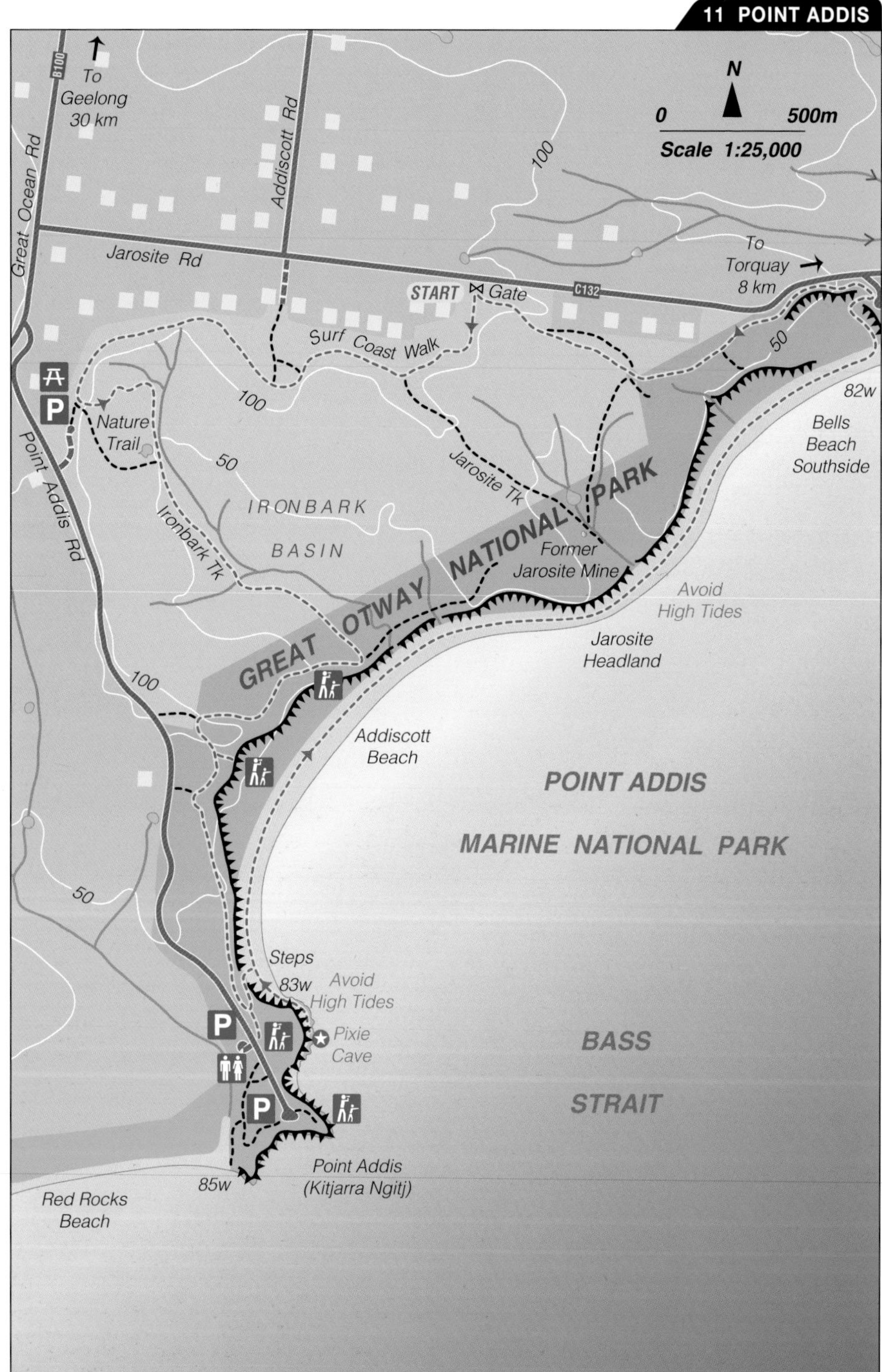

To Geelong 30 km
B100
N
0 500m
Scale 1:25,000
Addiscott Rd
Great Ocean Rd
100
Jarosite Rd
To Torquay 8 km
START
Gate
C132
Surf Coast Walk
50
100
82w
Nature Trail
Bells Beach Southside
Point Addis Rd
50
Jarosite Tk
IRONBARK
BASIN
Ironbark Tk
PARK
NATIONAL
Former Jarosite Mine
OTWAY
Avoid High Tides
GREAT
Jarosite Headland
100
Addiscott Beach
POINT ADDIS
MARINE NATIONAL PARK
50
Steps
83w
Avoid High Tides
Pixie Cave
BASS
STRAIT
Point Addis (Kitjarra Ngitj)
85w
Red Rocks Beach

Red ironbark

iron. Red ochre from the mine was used in paint for former Victorian trains such as the old 'Red Rattlers'. The track to follow continues west near the southern edge of private properties then turns south-west. It remains at about 100 m above sea level within the ironbark forest. When 2.1 km from the walk start you reach a nature trail circuit off left and this spot is just north of a carpark serviced from Point Addis Road. The two ends of the nature trail are about 20 m apart and the loop descends into Ironbark Basin where the forest becomes denser and includes messmate trees and many acacia species.

Take the left arm of the nature trail for the more interesting descent. You lose over 50 m within 400 m to a small dam and a track fork is just past the dam. Instead of following the nature trail up to the right, go south-east down Ironbark Track towards

Pixie Cave at Point Addis

the coastal cliff-tops. The track flattens out within the Basin and leads into coastal heathland. After 1.3 km you reach the cliff-rim. Broad views of the coast and cliffs are afforded.

The track turns right and climbs sharply to a lookout platform then leads south-west above the cliff-rim. After 900 m you end the climb and pass a former four-wheel-drive track off right, to soon arrive at another viewing deck. The next section of track features display boards relating Aboriginal history and information. As you go southwards you bypass another pad off right and within 800 m descend to meet the main beach access track for the Point Addis east-side beach (emergency beach access 83W). We suggest you climb 100 m further to the roadway via the beach access track so as to view the tremendous panorama from Addiscott Lookout deck at the roadside. Toilets are just downhill across the road too.

Retrace the 100 m then continue on down many steps on to the beach then

Addiscott Beach cliffs

Jarosite Headland

consider lunch on the sand, perhaps in the usually sheltered corner of the beach just to your right. This spot is often more suited for swimming than in any nearby big surf. If the tide safely permits you should take a side trip around the cliff-base for about 200 m to see Pixie Caves where the sea has eroded these arches.

After the lunch break, a 4 km beach walk north-eastwards to Bells Beach Southside begins. Except at very high tide times, most of the distance is broad sandy beach backed by high cliffs. About 1 km along the beach you enter an official clothing optional beach area and here some tea tree and low dunes below the cliffs, which once provided some shade in hot weather, are now fenced off for revegetation. Further along the beach you reach some rocks at Jarosite Headland and the beach becomes narrower. It is here that you need to take care and avoid high tides. There can be some shade at times at the cliff-base but the cliffs are unstable and you could conceivably be subject to danger from falling rock. The cliffs are of stratified beds of various coloured ochres, mudstone and clays. After beachcombing for 4 km, you reach a concrete path which leads off the beach as another headland begins. At the 82W sign you ascend to the carpark at Bells Beach Southside. Extensive coastal views can be enjoyed from the carpark area.

Where you reach the carpark, the Surf Coast Walking Track leads off westwards above the cliffs. At first it is near the south side of Jarosite Road and soon temporarily uses the actual road verge. After 1 km among coastal heathland, and with some gradual climbing needed, you reach a fork of three tracks. The left fork leads to the former Jarosite mine site and the other two tracks parallel each other then rejoin after 400 m. The left of these two routes is the narrower, but more pleasant option, as the right fork is adjacent to private properties. Once the tracks rejoin, you walk 300 m further west and thereby complete the walk at the Jarosite Road gate. If time permits, a short drive to the carpark at the south end of Point Addis Road is most worthwhile, especially near sunset.

Point Addis cliffs

Walking on Addiscott Beach

12 BRIGGS BLUFF
Grampians, Victoria

Walk:	12 km retrace
Time required:	Including minimal breaks, 5 hours
Grade:	One day, medium
Environment:	Sandstone formations and cliffs with sparse vegetation
Last review date:	January 2009
Map reference:	Vicmap, 1:25 000 Mount Stapylton and Map 12
Best time to visit:	Suited to any season but avoid hot days

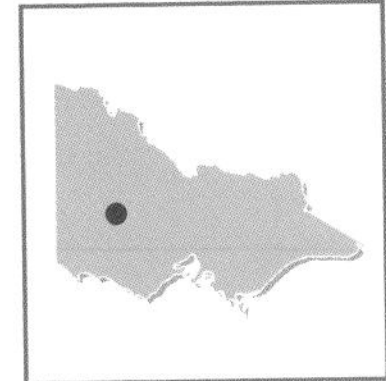

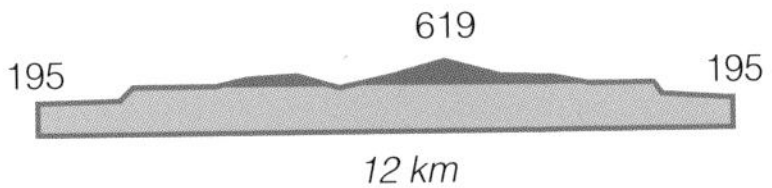

The Grampians ranges have long been one of the foremost tourist attractions in Victoria. These rugged sandstone mountains are situated between Melbourne and Adelaide and not far from the highway linking the two cities. They therefore attract tourism from both states. Wildflowers in spring feature throughout the four main ranges: Victoria, Serra, Mount William and Mount Difficult. Each range has been subjected to tilting and buckling resulting in escarpments. Additionally they have been fantastically sculptured by the erosive forces of wind and water.

This walk is in the northern section of the Grampians National Park where you climb to Briggs Bluff to take in expansive views across the Wimmera plains, see most interesting geological features and enjoy an overall feeling of wilderness. It is through the more rugged of Grampians terrain and amid some of the best walking country in Victoria. Private transport is needed for access. Nearby Horsham and Stawell both have a full range of accommodation options, public transport access and hire car availability. To reach the walk start at Roses Gap, you need to travel mostly sealed Roses Gap Road from the Western Highway between the two towns.

The foot track is rough in places and sturdy footwear is essential. The track to Briggs Bluff commences at the small Beehive Falls carpark, 600 m west of the intersection of the Halls Gap–Mount Zero Road and Roses Gap Road.

At first, a broad, fairly level track leads for 1.4 km south and south-east up the west bank of Mud Hut Creek to a bridge amid ferns and 100 m short of lovely, 25 metre-high Beehive Falls. The cliffs in this area get very colourful at times when the sun is low. After you cross the bridge below the falls, the track gets much

Horsham		J	F	M	A	M	J	J	A	S	O	N	D	Year
Rain	av. mm	23	25	23	32	46	50	47	49	46	44	33	27	445
Temp	av. max. °C	30	30	26	21	17	14	13	15	17	21	24	27	20
Temp	av. min. °C	13	13	11	8	6	4	3	4	5	7	9	11	7

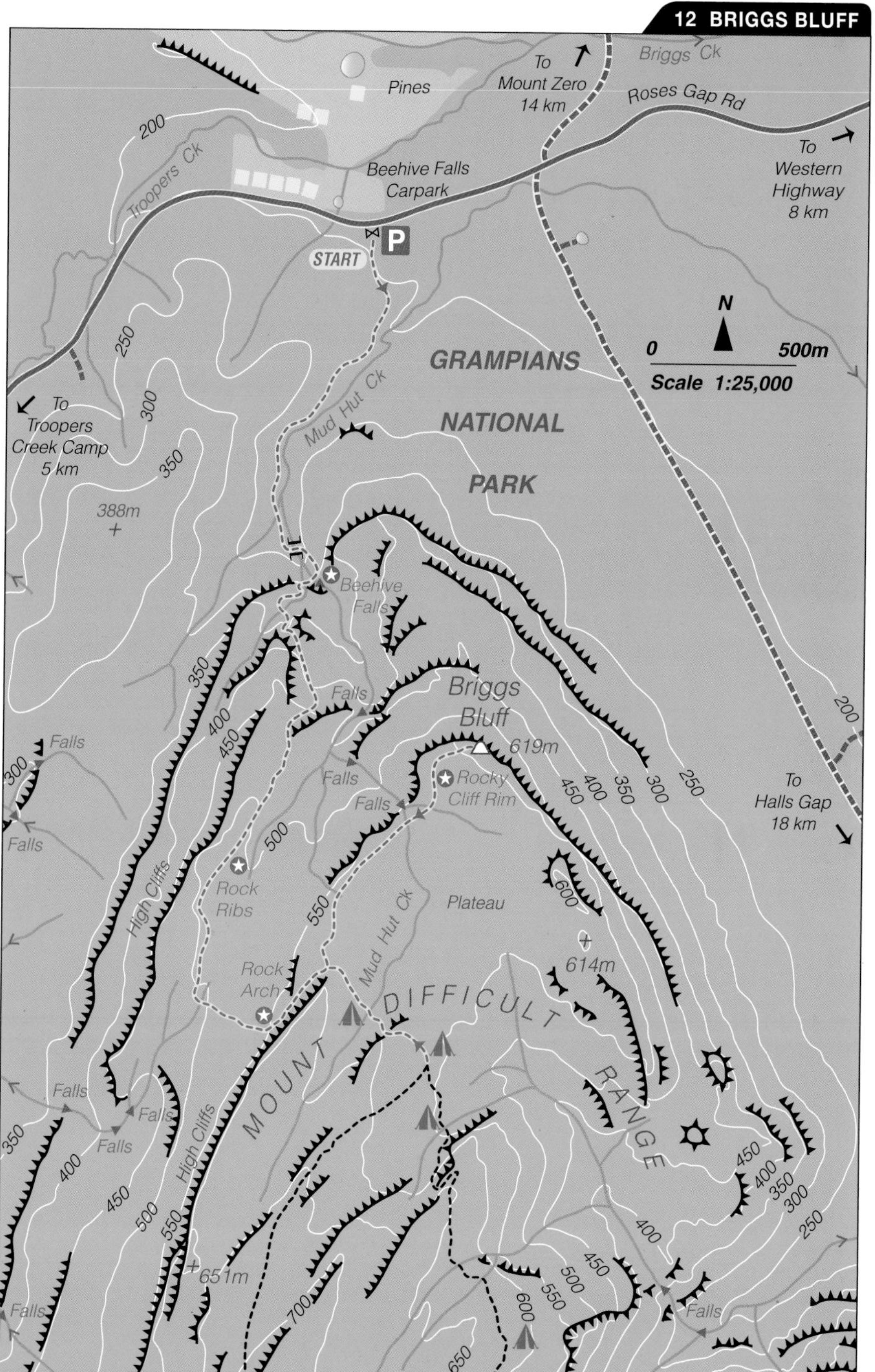
Briggs Ck
Pines
To Mount Zero 14 km
Roses Gap Rd
To Western Highway 8 km
Troopers Ck
Beehive Falls Carpark
START
P
GRAMPIANS NATIONAL PARK
N
0 500m
Scale 1:25,000
Mud Hut Ck
To Troopers Creek Camp 5 km
388m
Beehive Falls
Briggs Bluff
619m
Rocky Cliff Rim
Falls
To Halls Gap 18 km
High Cliffs
Rock Ribs
Plateau
614m
Rock Arch
MOUNT DIFFICULT RANGE
651m
200
250
300
350
400
450
500
550
600
650
700

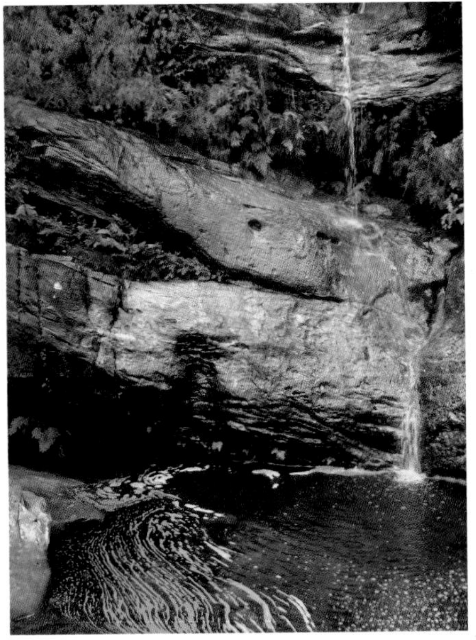

Beehive Falls

rougher underfoot and you need to climb significantly.

Take a short break and enjoy the cascading water, swallows and butterflies. Also take care not to slip as you use stream bed rocks to cross below the falls and then scramble up a steep, somewhat awkward, rocky track until the nearby top of the cliff is reached. A second, usually dry, small waterfall should be passed during this rough ascent.

The pad then swings south-west then south-east to cross a gully and ascends into wild, rocky, sandstone terrain with the impressive cliffs of Briggs Bluff as a backdrop. Continue up past many rocky turrets, pancake-shaped formations, ravines, and escarpments, then swing south-west on to a ridge. Cliff-lines abound in this locality. After the gradient eases, there is a very pretty rocky stream gully to

Briggs Bluff summit and cliffs

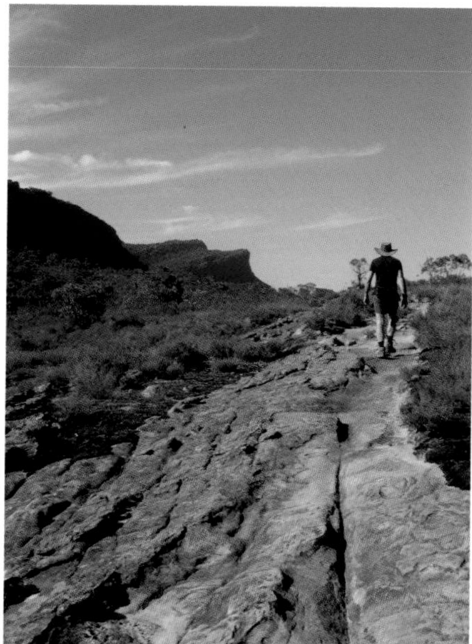

Rock ribs and Mount Difficult

the east of the pad. In this area the track follows rock ribs which are aligned so that Mount Difficult is highlighted straight ahead. Triangular painted track markers on

Rocky cliff-rim, Briggs Bluff

the rock ribs need to be followed carefully. About 2 km from Beehive Falls, the track crosses near a broad saddle after swinging east and rises up towards most impressive cliffs containing many high, wind-scoured caverns. Boulders converge to form a cavern-like arch across the track as you reach the base of cliffs. The track then swings north-east up a broad rock ramp formation to reach the cliff-tops and a track junction 2.6 km from Beehive Falls and 4.2 km from the walk start.

For now take the right fork for just 600 m for a lunch break in most delightful surroundings. The way is down a little to cross usually dry Mud Hut Creek and its adjacent bush camp within 300 m. You then head over a rocky spine and down to a second bush camp within another 300 m at a junction of foot tracks. The view here to vast plains and craggy heights and the shade of trees make this an ideal lunch spot.

After the break, retrace the 600 m and turn down the right-fork pad. It soon swings north to lead along bare rock near a rocky cliff-rim, then across a couple of minor streams that form the headwaters of Mud Hut Creek and up the rocky slopes of Briggs Bluff. It is 1.2 km from the track junction to the bluff crest.

In the interests of your safety, and especially if you dislike heights, keep well away from the northern face of the bluff especially when it is windy as there is a 200 m sheer drop over the rim. Views here are spectacular and include much of the northern Grampians. Mount Stapylton is in view to the north-west. After you have taken in the vista of the vast Wimmera plains, make your way back to the walk start but omitting the side trip taken for lunch. Take particular care descending back to the base of Beehive Falls. A short pause by the water before retracing to the carpark will make a fitting end to the walk.

MOUNT STAPYLTON

Grampians, Victoria

Walk:	8 km total, 5.2 km retrace plus 2.8 km retrace
Time required:	Including minimal breaks, 4 hours
Grade:	One day, medium with considerable height exposure
Environment:	Sandstone formations and cliffs with sparse vegetation
Last review date:	January 2009
Map reference:	Vicmap, 1:25 000 Mount Stapylton and Map 13
Best time to visit:	Suited to any season but avoid hot days or high winds

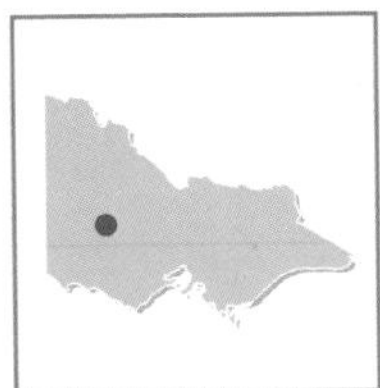

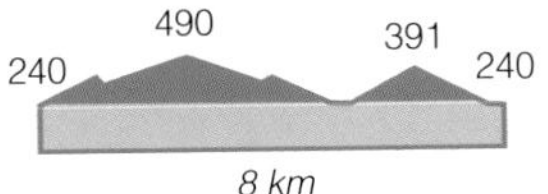

At the extreme north end of the Grampians is the Mount Zero picnic ground adjacent to the lower edge of Flat Rock. This locality, including nearby Mount Stapylton, is among the most rugged of places in the Grampians and has extremely good walking. However, reaching the very top of Mount Stapylton is quite awkward. At busy times, such as Easter and Christmas, hundreds of people attempt to climb Mount Stapylton every day. Many do not reach the summit. In the interests of your safety you should omit the last section because of the exposure on bare rock even though painted triangles on the bare rock define a route to the top. We suggest you climb to an outstanding view point, which is within 200 m of the summit, avoid the awkward section and instead also go up nearby Mount Zero for a fantastic overview of the whole district.

The walk area is situated near Horsham and Stawell and both towns have a full range of accommodation options, public transport access and hire car availability. To reach the walk start at Mount Zero picnic ground you need private transport to travel unsealed roads from the Western Highway between the two towns. The average annual rainfall is about 450 mm compared with 900 mm at places as close as Halls Gap. Trees mostly on sandy country are fairly sparse and the general impression is of outback Australia. Sandstone, folded, twisted, eroded and uplifted is the feature of the area. Red oxide, ochres and white or yellow sand with high silica content create a colourful contrast among the rocks.

From Mount Zero picnic ground, walk south-east up impressive Flat Rock, a broad sandstone slope with about a 20–25 degree angle. It is somewhat like the Elephants Hide rock formation near

Horsham	J	F	M	A	M	J	J	A	S	O	N	D	Year
Rain av. mm	23	25	23	32	46	50	47	49	46	44	33	27	445
Temp av. max. °C	30	30	26	21	17	14	13	15	17	21	24	27	20
Temp av. min. °C	13	13	11	8	6	4	3	4	5	7	9	11	7

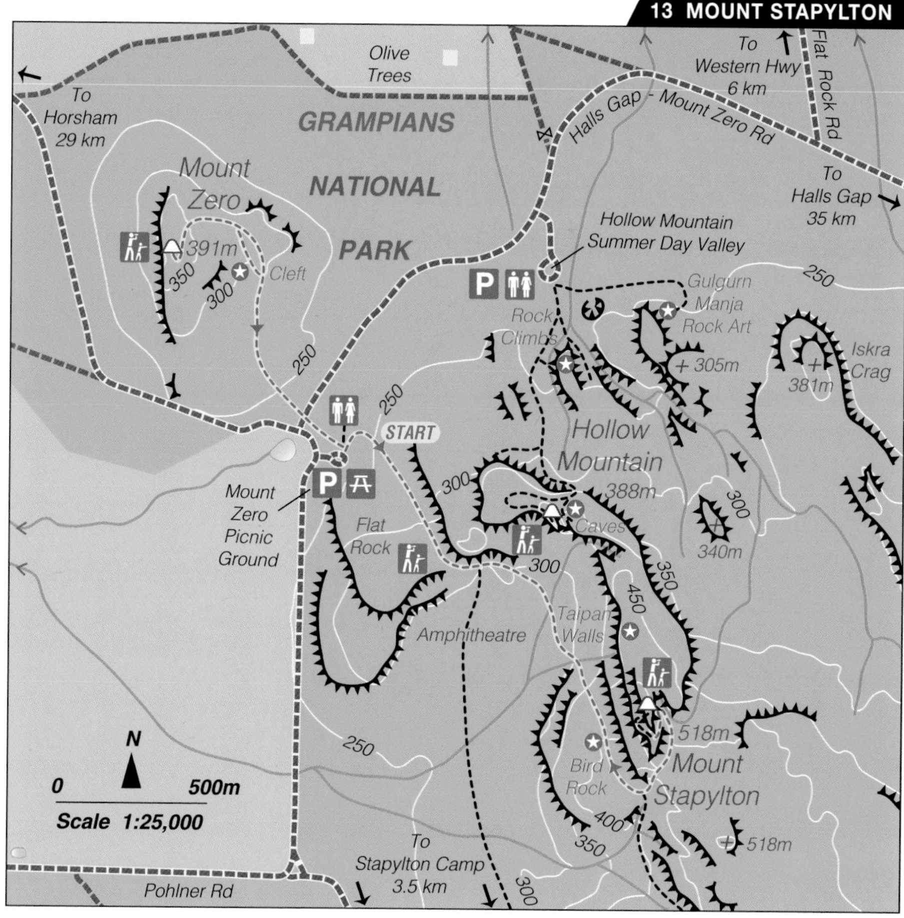

Halls Gap. Painted triangles on the rock reveal the route to follow to the higher south-eastern edge. It tends a little to the left as it rises. At the top of Flat Rock, the pad is just south of a cliff-line. There are great views towards the mountain peaks of the Asses Ears and the western part of the Grampians. The track then descends slightly and crosses the floor of a huge amphitheatre on the southern side of Mount Stapylton. Vegetation is far denser on the sandy floor with much banksia, callitris, acacia and eucalyptus in a dry sclerophyll environment. Massive colourful cliffs ring much of the amphitheatre and are a rock climbing venue. If you glance up to your left you may see climbers scaling the enormous, sheer rock faces such as the upper and lower Taipan Walls. The amphitheatre is known as the Horseshoe to rock climbers.

Within the amphitheatre, avoid a right-fork pad 800 m from the walk start (Pohlner Road and Stapylton Camp access) and continue on the left-fork track uphill, south-east via a broad rock ramp formation created by geological fault lines. Watch the painted track markers carefully and they lead right past a large bird-shaped rock (Bird Rock) which is best viewed from below when silhouetted against the sky. The track alignment mainly uses bare rock surfaces from which you obtain broad views. Almost level ground is attained just south of Mount Stapylton summit and you reach another track junction 2 km from the walk start.

Avoid the track off south (Pohlner Road and Stapylton Camp access) and continue on the left fork. The way is then more rocky and leads over a small saddle with the ramparts of Mount Stapylton just up to your left. You go down and across a small hollow and swing west up a gully into a ravine area just east of the Mount Stapylton summit. As the ravine narrows, the pad divides at abutting rock. Here arrow markers on rocks indicate the left fork to take.

Bird Rock

This left fork rises up bare sloping rock immediately. It passes a big and lovely wind-scoured cave in the cliffs, right alongside the climbing route. Some 100 m up the slope there is a rocky viewpoint where the way seems to end. Many people make this their turn-around point in rugged wild terrain with great views. We suggest you also turn back here. (Red painted triangles do indicate an ongoing route down a few metres to a lower broad rock ledge and then off right along ledges to the awkward summit ascent.) The panorama is of much of the northern Grampians and of truly rugged terrain.

After a break, simply retrace the route back to the walk start but do not be lazy and miss out on a really great

Mount Stapylton and Taipan Walls

short extension to nearby Mount Zero. It is an almost conical-shaped rocky little sandstone peak, which marks the extreme northern end of the Grampians. It stands apart within a sandy heath woodland area adjacent to the vast farming plains of the Wimmera. A foot track only 1.4 km long links the Mount Zero picnic ground with the summit where there is a cairn and excellent views. These views are especially good later in the day when sunlight highlights the massive cliffs of the Taipan Walls and of Mount Stapylton generally. You will no doubt be amazed at the wild and lofty places you just visited on Mount Stapylton. Beside the track in spring you will find several varieties of greenhood orchids, spider orchids and bearded orchids. Near the summit there is a lot of round-leaf mint bush. Grampians thryptomene (*Thryptomene calycina*), an endemic, grows exceedingly well around the peak.

From the north side of the picnic ground the track leads off north-west and within 250 m intersects the Halls Gap–Mount Zero Road. The sandy pad then soon starts to rise, gradually veering to the right and reaching rocky outcrops and small cliffs. Painted triangles on the rocks then define the way. Soon the track divides temporarily and you should climb the right fork. The rejoined pad then leads near the crest of a spur, swings left and westwards towards some fairly easily negotiated rocks and handrails, which assist access to a fenced summit and 360 degree outlook.

If possible spend some time here as the sun sinks and the red and yellow sandstone faces are seen to best advantage. However, you need to descend the peak before darkness because of the rough terrain. Near sunset you are rewarded by commanding views along the western margins of the Grampians while in the foreground you see thousands of olive trees on nearby private lands. To finish the day, retrace the track back down to the picnic ground. However, as you progress, take the right fork where the track divides to get a final great surprise for the day at a quite narrow rock cleft through which you need to squeeze.

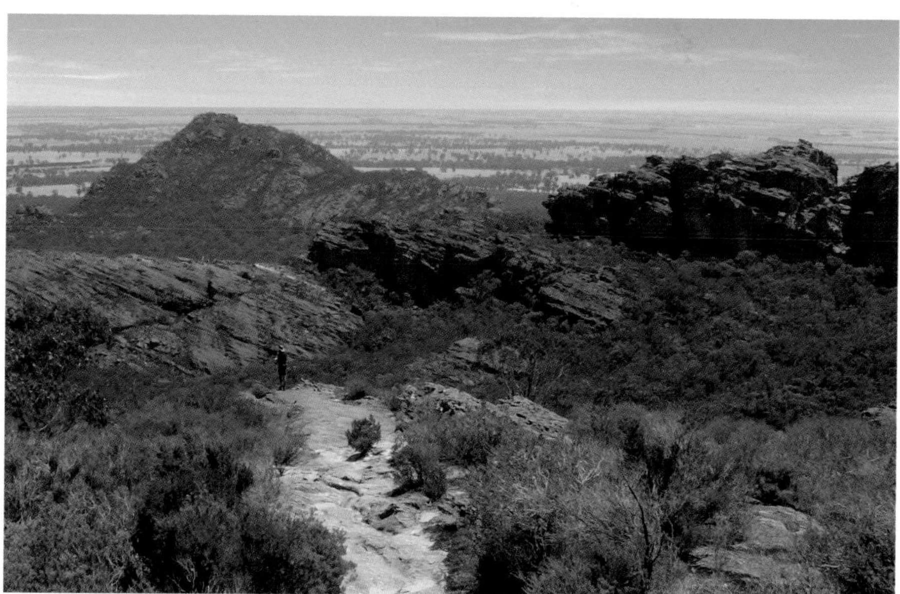

Mount Zero and Hollow Mountain

TASMANIA

TAS

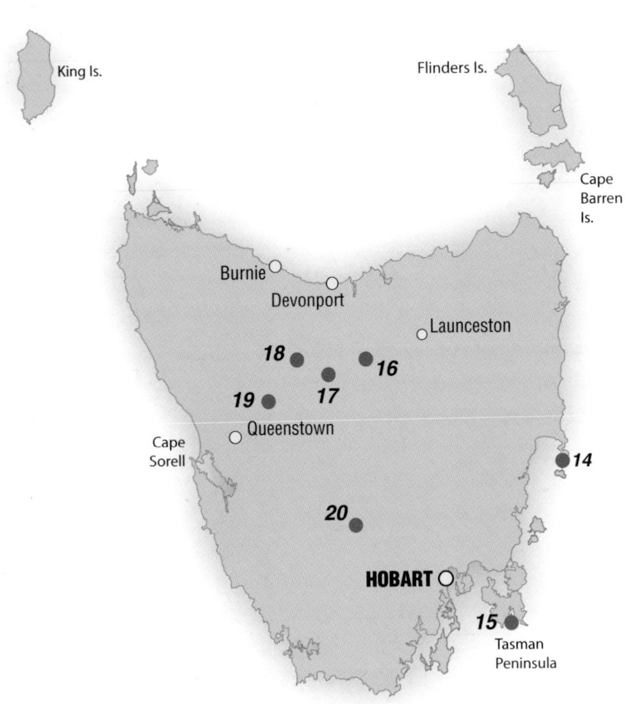

14	Wineglass Bay–Hazards Beach	Freycinet National Park
15	Raoul View–Tunnel Bay	Tasman National Park
16	Quamby Bluff	Great Western Tiers
17	Walls of Jerusalem	Walls of Jerusalem National Park
18	Cradle Mountain Circuit	Cradle Mountain–Lake St Clair National Park
19	Tullah–Lake Herbert	Mount Farrell Regional Reserve
20	Tarn Shelf–Lake Webster	Mount Field National Park

Dove Lake, Cradle Mountain

TAS

Tasmania provides walkers some of the most remote, rugged and challenging terrain in Australia. Mount Wellington, with its massive dolerite cliffs, dominates the capital city of Hobart. Nearby are many wonderful walks. The east coast, especially at Freycinet Peninsula, has superb white sand beaches backed by rugged granite mountains. The Tasman Peninsula with its high dolerite rock sea cliffs, feature in the walk to Tunnel Bay. Northwards, on the Great Western Tiers is the ascent to lofty Quamby Bluff. The glaciated central highlands offer great alpine walks at Walls of Jerusalem and Cradle Mountain. Immense peaks, carved by former glaciers, tower over crystal-clear lakes and a sense of being in ancient Gondwanaland surrounds you. Out westward, the alpine walk to Lake Herbert has magnificent scenery. Nearer to Hobart, at Mount Field, is Tarn Shelf. This exposed alpine walk amid many tarns and unique alpine plants offers superb wilderness walking.

14 WINEGLASS BAY–HAZARDS BEACH

East Coast, Tasmania

Walk:	13 km circuit
Time required:	Including minimal breaks, 4 hours 30 minutes
Grade:	One day, medium
Environment:	Beaches, granite outcrops and coastal heathland
Last review date:	May 2007
Map reference:	Tasmap, 1:25 000 Coles Bay and Graham sheets and Map 14
Best time to visit:	Suited to any season but winter, June to August can be cool

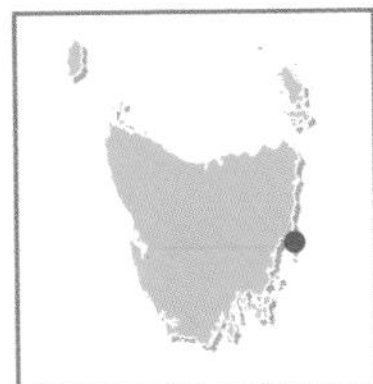

Freycinet Peninsula on the east coast of Tasmania is renowned for its very beautiful beaches backed by massive granite peaks known as the Hazards. The same type of granitic scenery also exists in Tasmania at Bicheno, Mount William and Flinders Island. About 370 million years ago, the volcanic granite welled up amongst rock folds and later was exposed by erosion during bouts of sinking and uplifting.

This circuit walk at Freycinet Peninsula, within national park, provides the opportunity for a break at both Wineglass Bay and Hazards Beach with swimming or lazing at either or both beaches. Wineglass Bay is undoubtedly the most beautiful spot, so it is suggested that the longer break and perhaps lunch could be taken there. These breaks will naturally extend the estimated 4 hours 30 minutes walk time. Usually the only drinking water is at the south-east end of Wineglass Bay, which also happens to be a bush camp site. This water supply can get brackish at times; therefore carry some water and also sunscreen.

Access to the peninsula and its national park is via the Tasman Highway from the small towns of Swansea or Bicheno. Coaches operate along the Tasman Highway. Separate coaches link Bicheno to Coles Bay. However, overall, private transport is best used. Coles Bay is a small settlement with a general store, fuel, café and boat ramp.

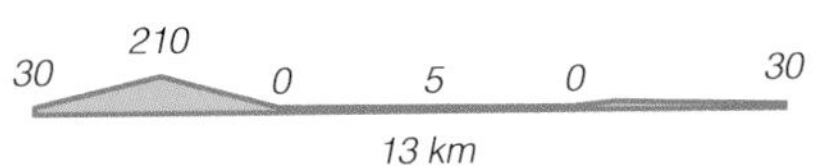

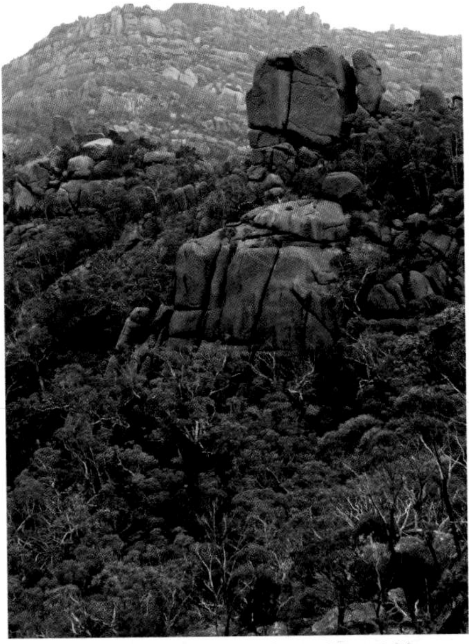

Pink granite on Mount Mayson

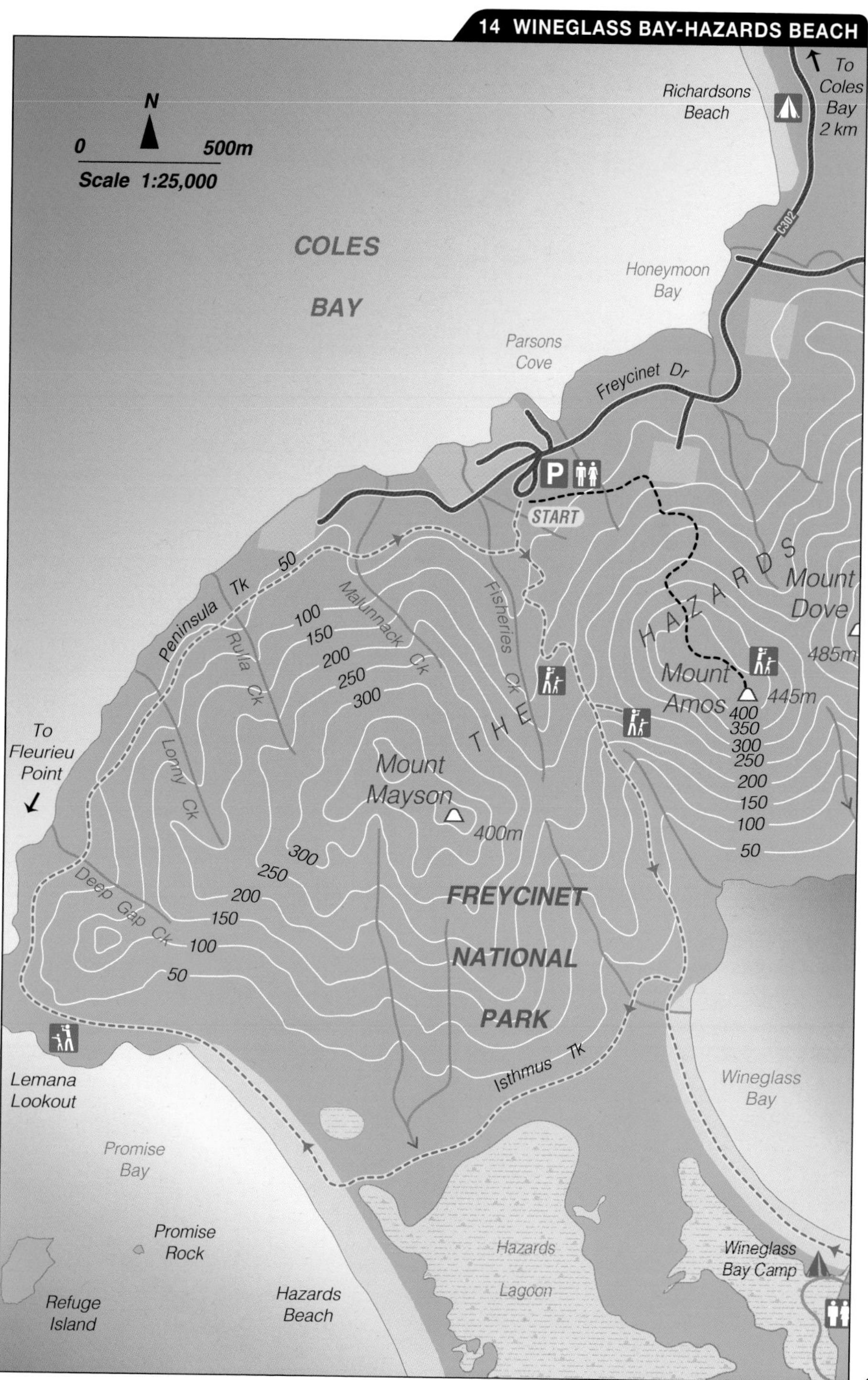
N
0
500m
Scale 1:25,000
COLES
BAY
Richardsons
Beach
To
Coles
Bay
2 km
C302
Honeymoon
Bay
Parsons
Cove
Freycinet Dr
START
Peninsula Tk
Rulla Ck
Malunnack Ck
Fisheries Ck
Lonny Ck
Deep Gap Ck
THE HAZARDS
Mount
Dove
485m
Mount
Amos
445m
Mount
Mayson
400m
To
Fleurieu
Point
FREYCINET
NATIONAL
PARK
Isthmus Tk
Lemana
Lookout
Promise
Bay
Promise
Rock
Refuge
Island
Hazards
Beach
Hazards
Lagoon
Wineglass
Bay
Wineglass
Bay Camp

Bicheno		J	F	M	A	M	J	J	A	S	O	N	D	Year
Rain	av. mm	53	56	56	60	56	60	52	49	43	56	57	69	672
Temp	av. max. °C	21	21	20	18	16	14	14	14	16	17	18	19	17
Temp	av. min. °C	12	13	11	10	8	6	6	6	7	8	10	11	9

Camping is available within the park. Around Coles Bay are bed and breakfasts, cabins and resort accommodation. Other accommodation options are available at the more distant towns of Swansea and Bicheno.

South of Coles Bay village, you pass the park ranger station and 3.8 km further on is the walk start at the Peninsula Walking Track carpark. From the southern end of the carpark, bypass the Mount Amos Track and head south-south-east across a gully on a good foot track. Here you turn left. You then climb steps on an excellent graded track. This is in an area of well-drained granitic soils with a westerly aspect, so vegetation is fairly sparse. You may see wallabies in the area. Granite has been used extensively for construction of the many steps and associated track drainage. When 1.5 km from the carpark you reach a saddle between Mount Amos and Mount Mayson, both rugged pink granite peaks. The saddle is 210 m above sea level and granite boulders surround the locality. The pink tint of the Hazards is caused by iron oxide in feldspar. The granite rock of the peaks consists of the feldspar (pink or cream), micas (black) and quartz (white and glassy).

At the saddle, take a side trip (200 m return) to the left on to a viewing deck to get your first view of lovely Wineglass Bay ahead. This lookout is the goal of most walkers at Freycinet Peninsula and once

Wineglass Bay from Mount Amos

past it, you tend to have a bit of paradise mostly to yourself.

Leave the saddle and descend the ongoing track for 1.5 km, to the north-west end of the Wineglass Bay beach. The damp forest as you descend contrasts with the dry slopes west of the saddle. Some 30 m before the track links to the beach, Isthmus Track from Hazards Beach is on your right. This track is your later route. Some of the granite rocks at the beach have colourful orange and silver lichens growing on them.

Walk the full 1.5 km long white, quartz-derived sand Wineglass Bay beach to reach the sheltered far end in about 25 to 30 minutes. There is a bush camp area and a creek mouth at the spot and the usually calm sea here is great for swimming.

Enjoy lunch and preferably take a long break before retracing the beach to turn left on to Isthmus Track. Follow it for a virtually flat 2 km walk to Hazards Beach. The track passes banksia stands with much bird life. In spots near Hazards Lagoon and swamp, there is some board walk. The track then crosses dunes to the west side of the peninsula.

Turn north-west (right) at Hazards Beach and go the 1 km to the end of the beach. Another break in this sheltered corner might appeal. There are good views south to the backbone range of the peninsula and across Great Oyster Bay. Refuge Island is seen in the foreground.

Next, follow the Peninsula Walking Track from the beach end. The track climbs up away from the shore, passes a small, sheltered cove and soon reaches rocks at Lemana Lookout. Next, it rounds Fleurieu Point, stays roughly parallel to the coast but rises up slopes and crosses a number of creeks. It is 4 km from the north end of Hazards Beach back to the carpark. The latter part crosses slopes, to avoid private property near the shore. Because of the westerly aspect, this final leg of the walk can seem hot and tiring on some summer afternoons.

Wineglass Bay Beach

RAOUL VIEW–TUNNEL BAY

Tasman Peninsula, Tasmania

Walk:	12.6 km retrace
Time required:	Including minimal breaks, 5 hours
Grade:	One day, medium
Environment:	Coastal cliffs, forest and heathland
Last review date:	January 2008
Map reference:	Tasmap, 1:25 000 Raoul and Map 15
Best time to visit:	Suited to any season but winter can be cold

Tunnel Bay on the Tasman Peninsula has long been a favourite in walking circles. The remote bay is located near rugged Cape Raoul with road access from the small tourist settlement of Port Arthur via Nubeena Road for 8.9 km, then on Stormlea Road south for 9.2 km, avoiding Robinsons Road and Thorntons Road, both off left.

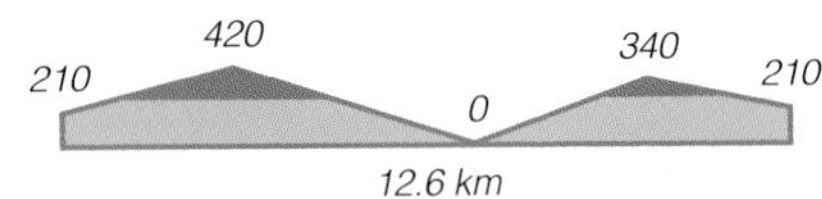

The road continues further to a farm gate, but there are no parking spots so leave transport and walk the final 300 m to the gate. An old walking track direct to Tunnel

Cape Raoul

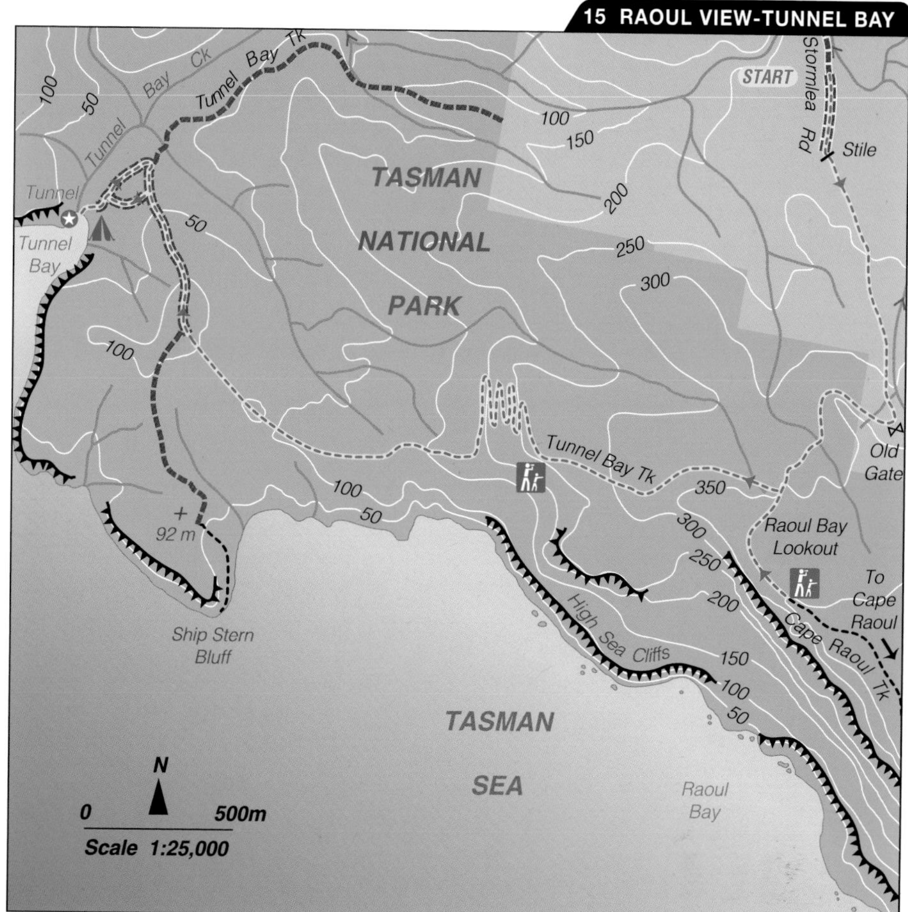

Bay (still shown on some maps) has been closed to avoid private property. Tunnel Bay is now approached via the start of the Cape Raoul Track. It passes the Ship Stern Bluff area. Exposed cliff-rim outlooks are included in this walk so you should exercise great care at these spots especially if it is windy or wet.

Go as far as the gate, but do not enter. Instead, cross a stile and veer left along the fence line, following track markers along the lower edge of a paddock. The foot pad leads uphill so that forest is entered. You meet an old gate 900 m from the road. Turn right here on to a roughly contouring pad westwards in forest; enter the Tasman National Park, cross a gully in which cutting grass thrives, then climb south. After going 550 m, a track junction is reached.

A side trip of 1.2 km return is highly recommended here. You should climb the Cape Raoul Track to a spectacular outlook

Port Arthur		J	F	M	A	M	J	J	A	S	O	N	D	Year
Rain	av. mm	90	63	89	95	84	107	107	119	103	103	81	97	1154
Temp	av. max. °C	19	19	18	16	14	11	11	12	13	14	16	17	15
Temp	av. min. °C	11	11	11	9	8	6	6	6	6	7	8	10	8

on a cliff-rim some 400 m above sea level and have a good rest. You get a great panorama to Cape Raoul and the Raoul Bay cliffs in the foreground. Further, just a few metres on a side pad off right along the cliff-rim, your view is to the west to Tunnel Bay and Ship Stern Bluff (the rest of your walk). There is also a wide view to Bruny Island, Fluted Cape on the island, the south coast, Mount Wellington and many other distant peaks. The high cliffs here catch the full force of prevailing westerly weather so mists swirl in and keep vegetation damp and thriving. There are taller eucalyptus trees and great groves of banksia as an understorey.

Once back at the main Tunnel Bay Track junction, head westwards for 1 km to emerge from forest at a remarkable rocky outlook point. You are nearly 250 m above the sea and only about 500 m from the shoreline. This is another good place for a rest. The view is quite splendid but not as broad and high as that from the Cape Raoul Track outlook. A switchback route then facilitates descent, in eucalyptus forest at first, then in dense tea tree to the Ship Stern Bluff locality. Here you are on a plateau at some 100 m above sea level.

Some 2 km from the outlook, and 150 m lower, you should join the old Ship Stern Bluff to Tunnel Bay four-wheel-drive track on a small hilltop amid much tea tree. Walk north from this crest for 600 m steeply down into Tunnel Bay Creek valley. Views of Tunnel Bay are good during the descent. Near the bottom of the hill, the track forms a triangle and you should turn left at the first junction to make the short cut via another four-wheel-drive track for just 350 m to the rocky beach front of Tunnel Bay. You can then enjoy lunch, fossick about the rocks, which are mainly large rounded boulders, and see the tunnel. It is a sea cave in the form of an arch and a long corridor through rock enables you to look out to sea as if

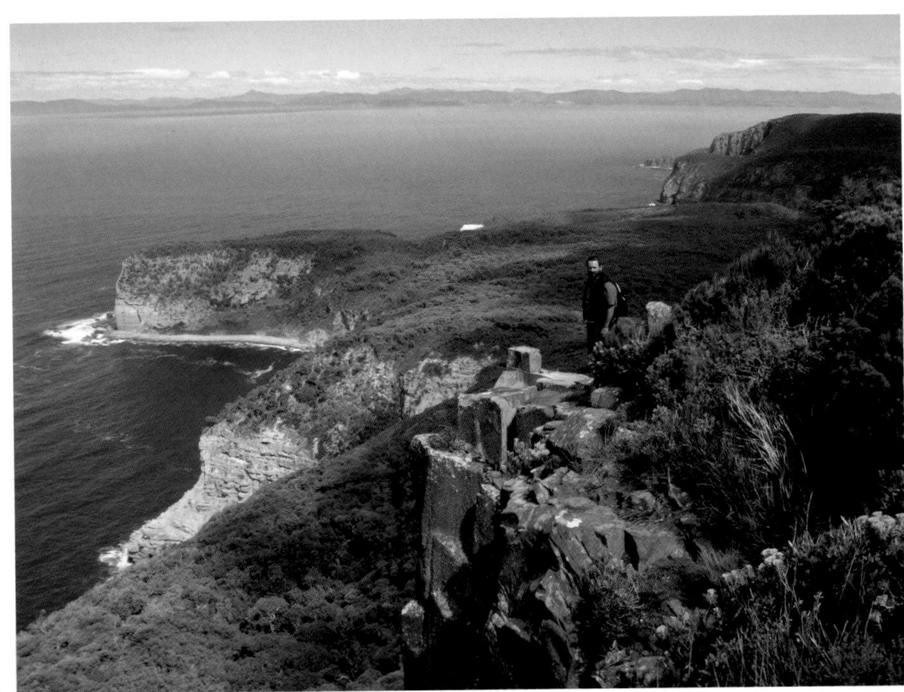

Ship Stern Bluff and Tunnel Bay

Tunnel Bay and cliffs

peering through a key hole. There is an exposed camp place near the rocky shore. The rocks have a lot of the succulent pig face (*Carpobrotus rossii*) growing on and around them as if trying to get heat from the rocks. The plant has become dominant as the front line vegetation at the cove except in sheltered places. It is easily damaged so you do well to walk elsewhere, away from these plants and indeed other plants which struggle to survive. The bay is quite wild and unsafe for swimming or for entering the water. Even sea weed is pulverised by the action of waves on rocks. Windswept cliffs around the cove are densely covered with casuarina.

When returning to Stormlea Road, do not go far on the old four-wheel-drive track northwards (Tunnel Bay Track) as it is closed off at private property. Walk it just 200 m then turn right for the climb. Thereafter you reach and pass the short cut used earlier, then you retrace the track routing already described omitting the side trip to the Raoul Bay Lookout.

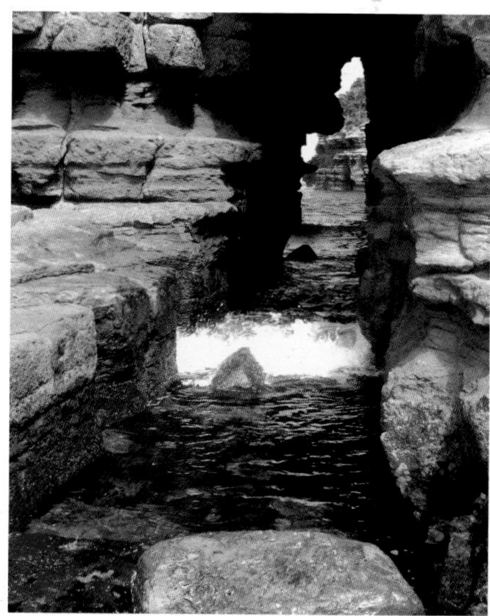

The Tunnel

QUAMBY BLUFF
Great Western Tiers, Tasmania

Walk:	6 km retrace
Time required:	Including minimal breaks, 4 hours
Grade:	One day, medium with rough, steep pinch
Environment:	Forest, rock scree, cliffs and exposed alpine tops
Last review date:	November 2007
Map reference:	Tasmap, 1:25 000 Quamby Bluff and Map 16
Best time to visit:	Suited to warmer months, snow likely in winter

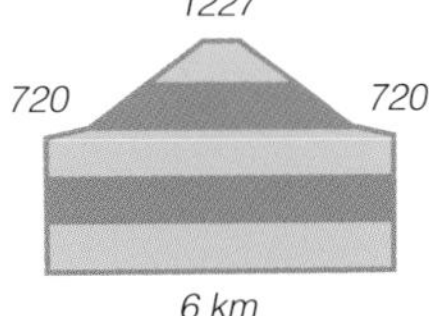

South from the town of Deloraine some 20 km via the Lake Highway, the dolerite rock ramparts of Quamby Bluff dominate the scene to the west of the highway. The bluff is geologically similar to the nearby Great Western Tiers and adjoining plateau

Ascending rock river

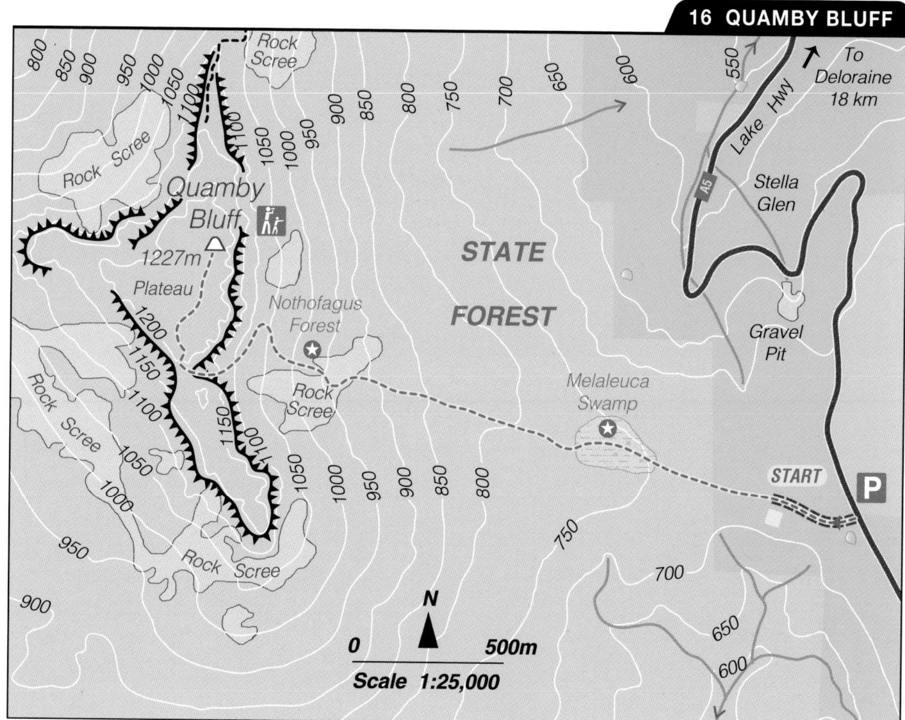

above the tiers. However, millennia of erosion and ice scouring by glacial action has caused it to be a somewhat isolated peak that reaches 1227 m high and also has a summit plateau.

There are tracks to the summit from both the north and the east, but these track notes describe the slightly easier and more popular eastern approach. It is a wonderful experience, steep and rough, but most rewarding. Take warm clothing and carry water. There is a 500 m rise in elevation. Abandon plans for the trip if the weather looks poor. Be aware that you have to scramble on boulder and scree fields. Rocks can move underfoot despite appearing stable and it is therefore best to keep both hands ready to grab on to rock when ascending or descending these awkward sections.

Access to the walk start is from the Lake Highway, which climbs via some hairpin bends through Stella Glen in forest. When 1.2 km south of the last hairpin, the highway has a level grade in farming country. A 300 metre-long farm access road leads off west here, directly towards the mountain. Parking is available beside the highway but in dry weather you can park near a farm house via the side road. Letter box No. 4 beside the highway indicates where you need to turn if you wish to go the extra distance.

From the farm house road end the walking track to follow enters pleasant

Launceston	J	F	M	A	M	J	J	A	S	O	N	D	Year
Rain av. mm	50	29	33	51	65	66	76	84	66	54	49	46	668
Temp av. max. °C	24	25	22	19	16	13	13	14	16	18	20	22	18
Temp av. min. °C	12	12	10	7	5	3	2	4	5	7	9	11	7

bushland and surprisingly rises very gently for the first 1 km. It even crosses through a small melaleuca swamp and you pass a partly open clearing. Suddenly the mountain slopes confront you and it is all stops out for a 420 m rise in elevation. The forest which includes a lot of myrtle (*Nothofagus cunninghamii*) gets denser and the ground surface gets quite rocky and moss covered. Dianella grows well in this area. When 1.5 km from the walk start, you meet the lower edge of a massive dolerite boulder and scree field scoured from the cliffs above, during past ice ages. These boulders are known as peri-glacial rock. They move extremely slowly as a rock river, accentuated by ice fracturing during expansion and contraction. Watch the track markers of small rock cairns carefully to climb across a narrow section of the field to again enter myrtle forest. This forest forms

Descending rock river

Nothofagus forest, Quamby Bluff

Quamby Bluff outlook

a tongue of vegetation with the boulder field, devoid of vegetation, to either side. Great views are here. The track steepens on a sharp spur crest then you ascend via a hairpin bend to an even steeper section. This brings you into a very rocky and usually windy saddle with a view westwards to the Great Western Tiers.

Follow more markers over boulders to climb north from the saddle and get above cliffs which surround the summit plateau. Within just 200 m you are on the plateau, then it is a flat 400 m walk north to the summit trig. However, the plateau is extremely exposed; it can be boggy underfoot with a lot of prickly scoparia (*Richea scoparia*), so progress is slow. You need to take extra care, especially if fog closes in. Low alpine shrubs cover the tops but fortunately do not obscure tremendous views. On a clear day, you can see much of northern Tasmania.

After a break, retrace the same route but be most careful in picking your way if fog is about. Also take great care descending the tangled roots of the myrtle forest and the rock scree.

Quamby Bluff

WALLS OF JERUSALEM

Central Plateau, Tasmania

Walk:	21.5 km (Day one 6.5 km; Day two 15 km) retrace
Time required:	Including minimal breaks, two days (Day one 4 hours; Day two 9 hours)
Grade:	Two days, medium, backpack required
Environment:	Forest and exposed alpine tops
Last review date:	January 2008
Map reference:	Tasmap, 1:25 000 Walls of Jerusalem National Park and Map 17
Best time to visit:	Suited only to summer, snowbound in winter

The glaciated tops of the world-renowned Norwegian mountains have a counterpart on the Central Highlands of Tasmania, which is almost as magnificent but hardly known. A glance at the Mersey sheet 1:100 000 scale government map readily illustrates the similarity to Norwegian topography. A band of country about 12 km wide and 40 km long has some 4000 alpine lakes and tarns within it. Although the sea does not verge on it as it does with Norwegian fiords, Lake St Clair and, to a lesser extent, lakes Myrtle, Meston, Louisa and Adelaide bear a distinct resemblance. Interestingly, the map shows some Norwegian names such as Lake Solveig and Lake Sonja.

In the midst of this lovely place, an unusual complex of five main peaks surround a central basin. Names with a biblical theme have been given by Reg Hall, a Launceston resident, and are attached to these features. The complex is called the Walls of Jerusalem. To reach the central basin, walkers normally pass through Herods Gate or sometimes one of four other passes or gates called Jaffa, Ephraims, Damascus and Gate of the Chain. Lakes include Salome, Sidon and Tyre and there is both a Pool of Siloam and a Pool of Bethesda. There is a Wailing Wall, Zion Hill and the Temple. Walls of Jerusalem National Park, declared in 1981, incorporates this section of the Central Highlands.

One drawback to the area is the isolation and extreme vulnerability to exposure. It is basically a plateau averaging about 1200 m above sea level, with peaks reaching nearly 1500 m. A number of people have died of exposure here, so it is absolutely essential that walkers are well experienced in how to deal with any problems that may arise and are adequately equipped with all seasons gear. Carry drinking water and a small stove if wishing to cook as this is a fuel-stove only area.

Devonport	J	F	M	A	M	J	J	A	S	O	N	D	Year
Rain av. mm	44	36	46	61	76	80	97	90	75	66	57	53	777
Temp av. max. °C	21	21	20	18	15	13	13	13	14	16	17	19	17
Temp av. min. °C	12	13	11	8	7	5	5	5	6	7	9	10	8

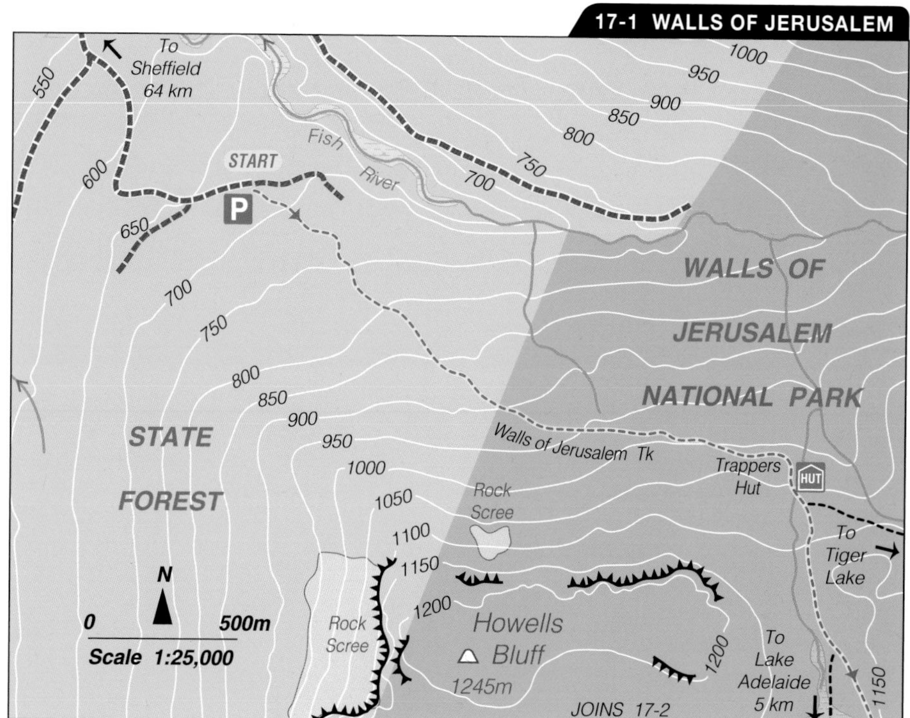

You should abandon your walk plans if the weather is deteriorating. Even in summer, blizzard conditions can occur. Wind chill can be extreme due to the presence of numerous alpine lakes and tarns.

Despite the rugged, barren appearance, the locality is very fragile with slow-growing plants, ancient pencil pines and easily erodible soils. Park authorities urge you to stay on the tracks designated for walking, so you should comply in order to protect the area, thereby preserving it for future generations to enjoy. Camp areas get degraded easily and therefore no camping beyond Herods Gate is permitted for this walk. In order to address this issue, wooden platforms have been constructed upon which tents can be pitched near Herods Gate. Guy ropes can be anchored to the platforms. Tap water and toilets are also provided here. Platforms are limited in number but some are sufficiently large for several tents.

Access can be from the small town of Sheffield, or from Mole Creek or Moina, then south up the Mersey River valley past Lake Parangana and Lake Rowallan dam wall. Some 4.7 km south of the dam wall, Mersey Forest Road crosses the Fish River and just beyond it, a lesser, left-side road leads off uphill south-east 1.1 km to a carpark on the slopes of Howells Bluff. This carpark is on the south side of the road at about 670 m elevation.

Cradle Mtn	J	F	M	A	M	J	J	A	S	O	N	D	Year
Rain av. mm	80	75	82	128	162	160	212	201	148	130	113	103	1594
Temp av. max. °C	18	18	16	13	10	8	7	8	10	12	14	16	13
Temp av. min. °C	7	8	7	5	4	2	1	1	2	3	5	6	4

JOINS 17-1
Lake Loane
WALLS OF JERUSALEM NATIONAL PARK
Walls of Jerusalem Tk
Solomons Jewels
Junction Lake Tk
Wild Dog Ck
Stretcher Lake
N
0 500m
Scale 1:25,000
JOINS 17-3
1150
1200
1100
1250

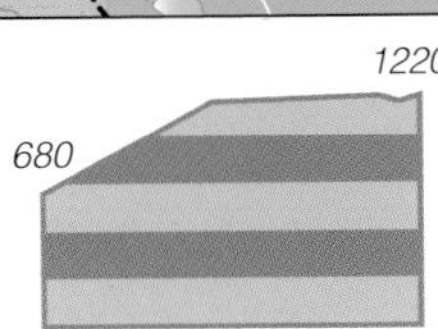

Day One 6.5 km

DAY ONE

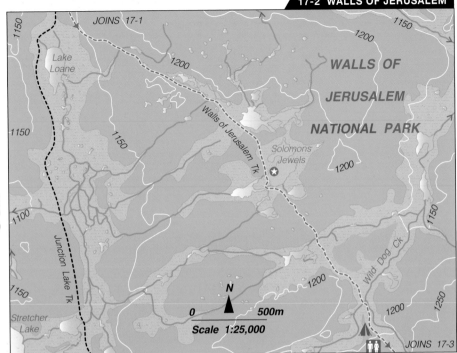

From the carpark a foot track rises gradually up the mountainside. The walk plan allows for the significant climb with a heavy pack on the first day leaving time to enjoy many lovely spots. A registration booth for walkers is just up the track from the carpark. Be aware that your entry in the record is only checked by authorities if you are reported missing.

Climb the well-defined and marked track south-east. It is aligned on north-facing slopes with scrub and mixed forest including a lot of lomatia and tea tree. To prevent tiredness because of the altitude rise, you are advised to stop frequently.

After 2.5 km and a steep pinch, you reach Trappers Hut near an often dry creek. The hut is a bit dilapidated but is an invaluable refuge in bad weather. It is a good place for another rest after much climbing. Avoid a lesser track to Tiger Lake off to your left at the hut.

Next, climb south-south-east 500 m to a fairly indistinct saddle where there is a track fork, just short of Lake Loane. The vegetation here changes markedly to alpine types. You see a lot of spaghnum mosses, bog plants, scoparia, alpine fern and snow gums. Avoid the right-fork, Junction Lake Track, as it leads to Lake Adelaide and beyond. Veer left, south-east towards the Walls of Jerusalem. The track is fairly pronounced with good markers.

You climb further, then the route levels out a bit and a rest is recommended. Here, views improve. Many of the peaks of the southern part of the Cradle Mountain–Lake

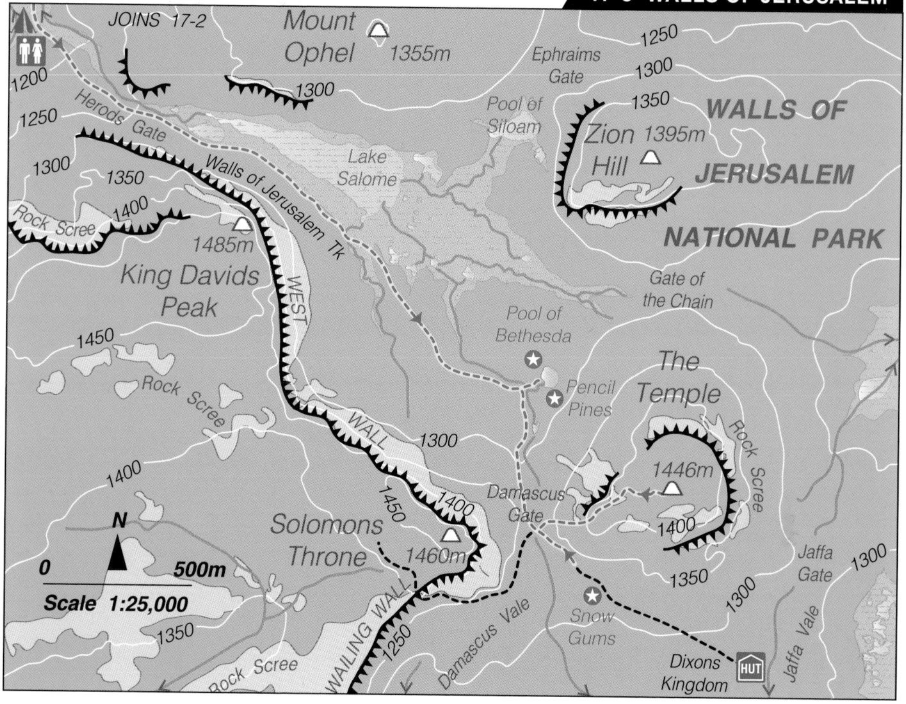

St Clair National Park come into view. These include notable peaks such as the Acropolis, Mount Ossa and the Du Cane Range. The next phase of the walk includes a number of delightful alpine tarns named Solomons Jewels. These tiny lakes are surrounded by mossy vegetation, pencil pine and snow gum trees. They tend to grow in less exposed spots. There are higher areas ahead and so a rest here is recommended. There is plenty of evidence of ice scouring on the surrounding rocks. Jurassic period dolomite rock abounds.

As Wild Dog Creek is neared, planks forming extensive boardwalk protect the alpine vegetation on the creek flats and indeed for much of the walk ahead. As you start to climb beyond the creek you reach three side tracks, each off to your right, to separate areas of camp platforms and your destination for the day. The toilet is at the uppermost site.

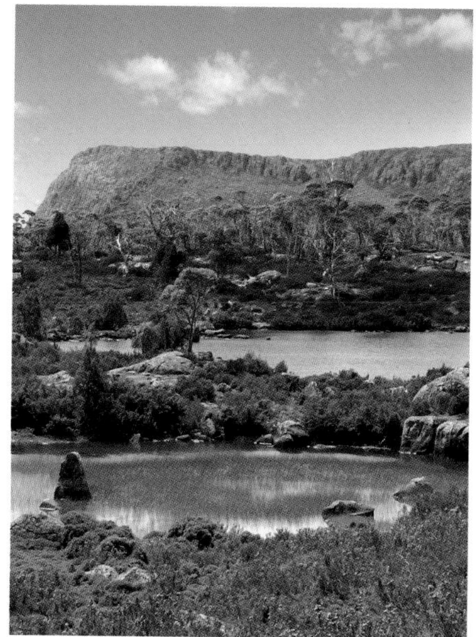

Solomons Jewels

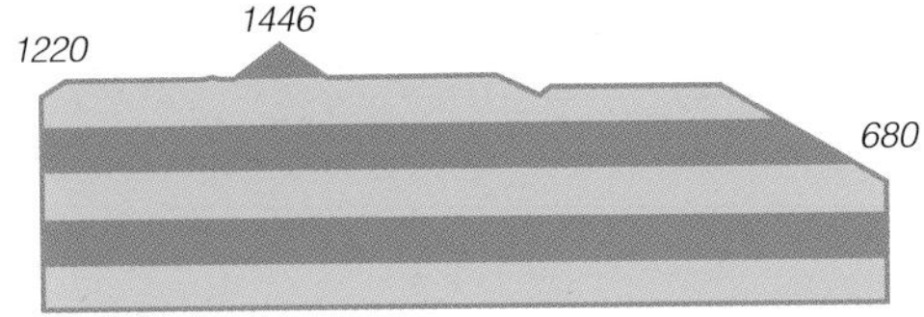

Day Two 15 km

DAY TWO

The plan is to go to the summit of the Temple, return for lunch at camp site and then collect your gear for the retrace to the carpark. The side trip is 8.5 km and you rise from about 1200 m to 1446 m.

From camp there is a climb through alpine vegetation for 600 m to Herods Gate. A small stream cascades down from the natural gate and drains a central basin within the walled area. At the gate, Lake Salome appears ahead; it partially fills the basin and is surrounded by steep slopes and major cliffs. Behind you are Barn Bluff and Cradle Mountain many kilometres away. The basin vista of wild terrain, glaciated rock walls, primitive conifers and other plants is indicative of vegetation in prehistoric times.

Keep to the boardwalk and head into the basin for 2 km, so as to be well to the east end of Lake Salome. The full circle of walls can be now viewed. The central basin can be a bleak place but awe inspiring. Just to stop on the planks and look up to the towering cliffs and ponder the beauty of the place with its changing moods, light and shadows is most atmospheric. One of the main types of vegetation beside the track is scoparia (*Richea scoparia*), a very prickly plant with leaves like a pineapple head. When in flower in mid summer, it is most beautiful, ranging from white to deep red. As much of the valley blooms it is a sight to behold and it is a significant drawcard for a later visit. The Pool of Bethesda lies south-east of Lake Salome and at the

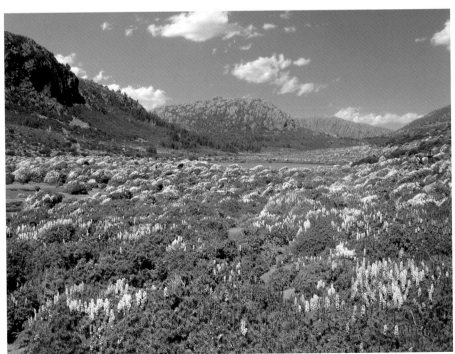

Lake Salome and scoparia

2 km stage a 200 m side track off left leads to this tarn amid some very ancient pencil pines (*Athrotaxis cupressoides*). Some of these conifers are said to be up to 1000 years old. A pause by the water in this idyllic spot would be most rewarding before climbing the Temple. The Pool of Bethesda was once designated for camping and is now a day use area. To reduce your ecological footprint you should stay on the main formed track and resist following former minor tracks created by past campers.

Retrace the 200 m and turn left to continue up the main central basin track on more boardwalk for 600 m and you reach Damascus Gate some 70 m higher. On the crest there is an intersection with the track straight ahead descending towards Dixons Kingdom hut. We suggest you go down it about 150 m for a great panorama. The view is down Damascus Vale and Jaffa Vale

Pool of Bethesda

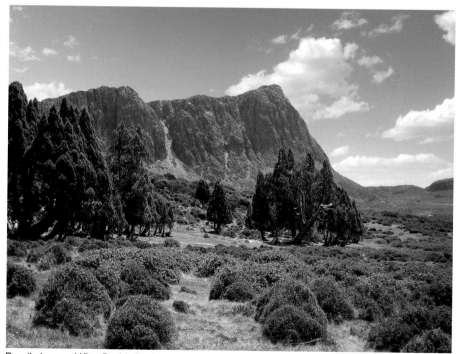

Pencil pines and King Davids Peak

En route to the Temple

to distant peaks and Lake Ball. Snow gums growing in the area are some of the oldest in Tasmania. The trees are fire sensitive but the damp, waterlogged soils and alpine conditions have meant fire has not occurred for a very long time. These trees are growing in more sheltered areas shielded by the nearby cliffs close to Damascus Gate. This side trip is especially good for anyone not wishing to scramble up the dolerite rock scree to the Temple. It is also a less exposed option. The rock scree movement around the Temple is said to be some of the most active in Tasmania.

Retrace to the crest, ignore the steep track on your left up to Solomons Throne and climb in the opposite direction steeply east-north-east. You ascend through patches of dolerite rock scree and within 600 m reach the summit of the Temple. The last section includes a short dip. At the top you will see an unsurpassed vista of the Central Plateau and virtually all of the mountains of the Cradle Mountain–Lake St Clair National Park. After a break on the top, return to camp, enjoy lunch and a rest before packing up your gear and retracing down to the walk end.

The Temple summit view

CRADLE MOUNTAIN CIRCUIT

Cradle Mountain, Tasmania

Walk:	15.2 km (Day one 5.7 km; Day two 9.5 km) circuit
Time required:	Including minimal breaks, two days (Day one 3 hours; Day two 5 hours)
Grade:	Two days, hard, backpack required
Environment:	Alpine moorland, glacially formed lakes and views
Last review date:	January 2008
Map reference:	Tasmap, 1:25 000 Cradle and Map 18
Best time to visit:	Suited only to summer and snowbound in winter

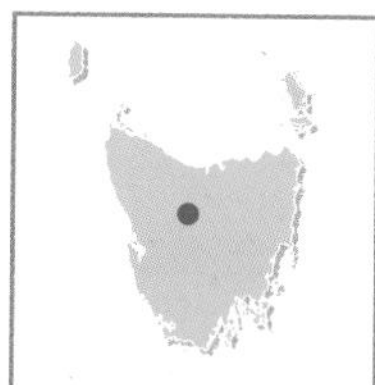

Cradle Mountain, at 1545 m, is renowned as one of the most photographed, visited and internationally known mountains in Australia. For a sunburnt country, it is a remarkable alpine-looking peak. It is mostly snow covered in winter. The famous long-distance Overland Track to distant Lake St Clair leads right past the peak, which features jagged dolerite rock, like many high Tasmanian peaks.

Access to Cradle Mountain is usually from Devonport. The tourist office in Devonport can arrange for coaches or private transport operators to take you from Devonport if needed. Accommodation at Cradle Mountain is located just outside the national park. It varies from camping and self-catering cabins to somewhat more luxurious lodge-type hotels at Pencil Pine. Devonport is a small city with ferry and air services to the mainland.

The most scenic parts of the northern end of the Cradle Mountain–Lake St Clair National Park are included in this longer walk aimed at visitors who wish to have an overnight experience without having to use the busy Overland Track huts at Waterfall Valley. Scott–Kilvert hut at Lake Rodway is the alternative.

In summer, transport needs to be left at the Transit Terminal just outside the national park entrance. The shuttle bus service should be used to reach Dove Lake carpark as it is not advisable to leave cars there overnight unless there is no alternative.

The carpark is at the northern extremity of Dove Lake where foot tracks lead off in each direction to circuit the lake. Cradle Mountain and Weindorfers Tower dominate the skyline at the south end of the glacier-formed lake. Carry appropriate clothing and footwear for all seasons, especially warm clothing, as you are headed into remote, elevated highland and exposed country. Set out before 10 am on the walk to take

Cradle Mtn		J	F	M	A	M	J	J	A	S	O	N	D	Year
Rain	av. mm	80	75	82	128	162	160	212	201	148	130	113	103	1594
Temp	av. max. °C	18	18	16	13	10	8	7	8	10	12	14	16	13
Temp	av. min. °C	7	8	7	5	4	2	1	1	2	3	5	6	4

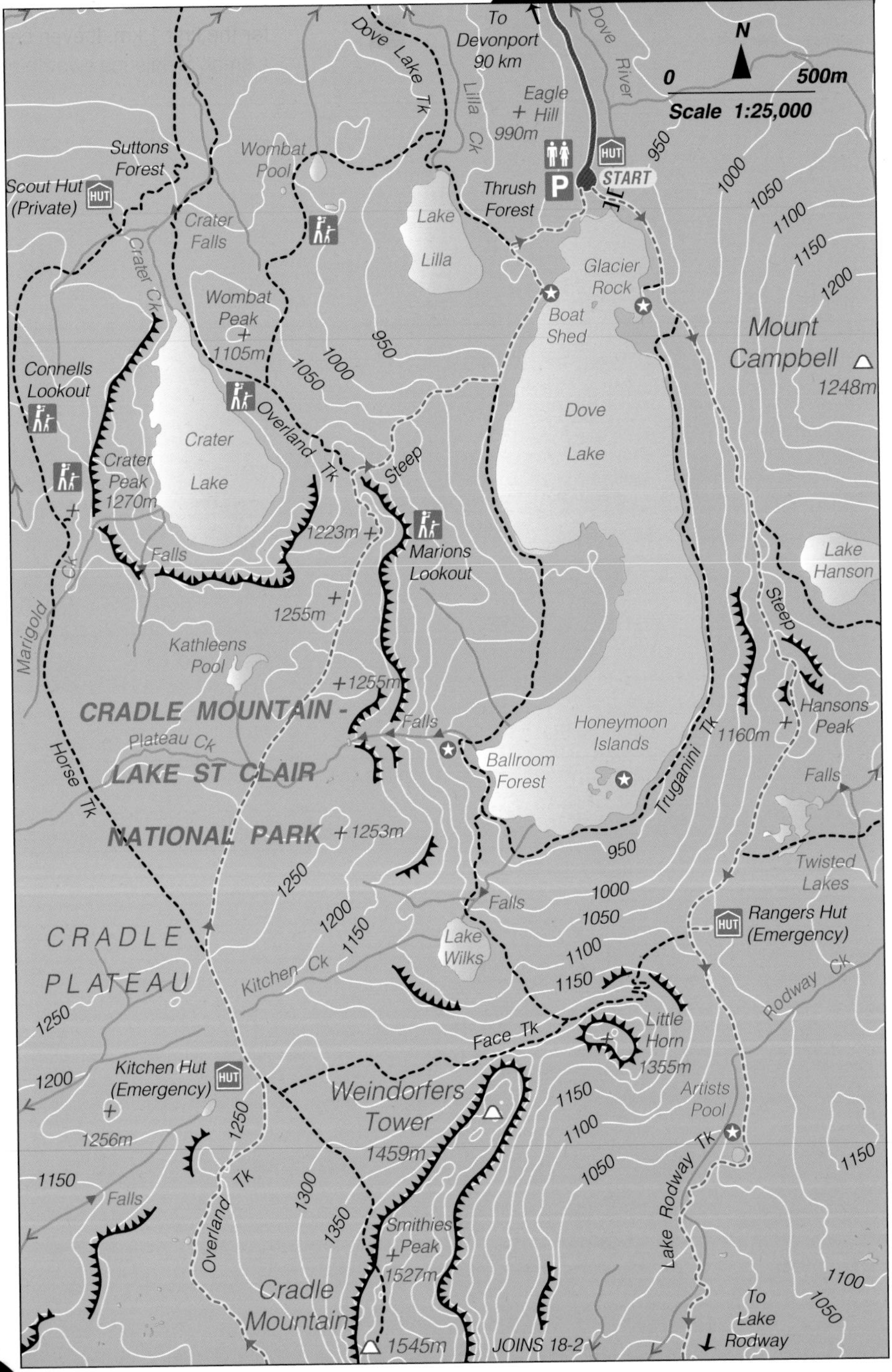

To Devonport 90 km
Dove Lake Tk
Dove River
Lilla Ck
Eagle Hill 990m
N
0 500m
Scale 1:25,000
Suttons Forest
Wombat Pool
Scout Hut (Private)
HUT
START
Thrush Forest
Crater Falls
Lake Lilla
Crater Ck
Glacier Rock
Wombat Peak 1105m
Boat Shed
Mount Campbell 1248m
Connells Lookout
Overland Tk
Dove Lake
Crater Lake
Crater Peak 1270m
Steep
1223m
Marions Lookout
Falls
Lake Hanson
Marigold Ck
1255m
Steep
Kathleens Pool
1255m
Hansons Peak
CRADLE MOUNTAIN - LAKE ST CLAIR NATIONAL PARK
Plateau Ck
Falls
Honeymoon Islands
Truganini Tk
1160m
Horse Tk
Ballroom Forest
Falls
1253m
Twisted Lakes
Falls
Rangers Hut (Emergency)
CRADLE PLATEAU
Lake Wilks
Kitchen Ck
Rodway Ck
Little Horn 1355m
Face Tk
Kitchen Hut (Emergency)
Weindorfers Tower 1459m
Artists Pool
1256m
Lake Rodway Tk
Falls
Overland Tk
Smithies Peak 1527m
Cradle Mountain 1545m
JOINS 18-2
To Lake Rodway

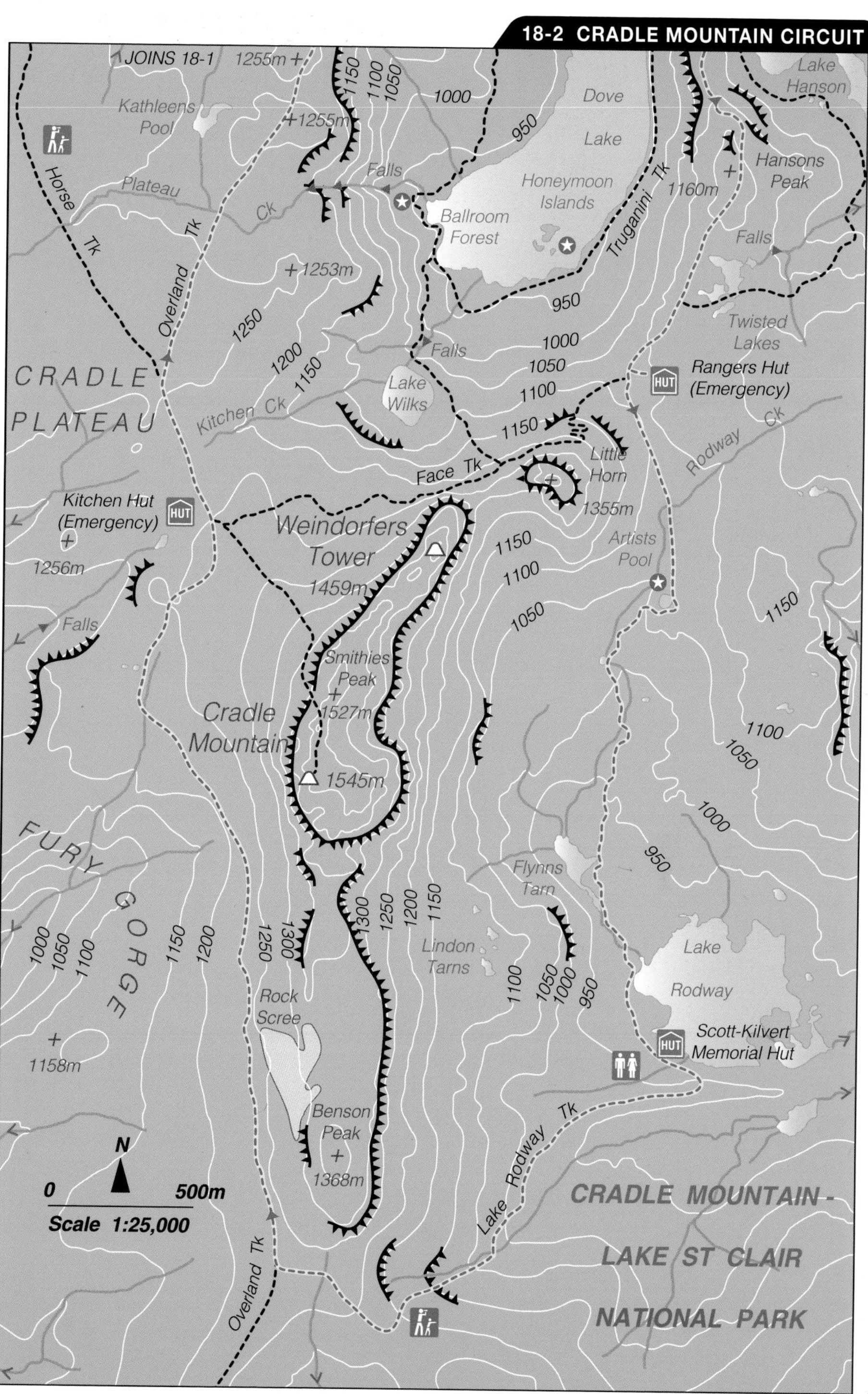

JOINS 18-1
1255m
Kathleens Pool
Horse Tk
Plateau Ck
Overland Tk
+1255m
Falls
Dove Lake
Honeymoon Islands
Ballroom Forest
Truganini Tk
1160m
Lake Hanson
Hansons Peak
Falls
1253m
Twisted Lakes
Falls
Lake Wilks
Rangers Hut (Emergency)
CRADLE PLATEAU
Kitchen Ck
Face Tk
Little Horn
1355m
Rodway Ck
Kitchen Hut (Emergency)
1256m
Weindorfers Tower
1459m
Artists Pool
Falls
Smithies Peak
1527m
Cradle Mountain
1545m
FURY GORGE
Flynns Tarn
Lindon Tarns
Lake Rodway
Rock Scree
Scott-Kilvert Memorial Hut
1158m
Benson Peak
1368m
Lake Rodway Tk
N
0 500m
Scale 1:25,000
CRADLE MOUNTAIN - LAKE ST CLAIR NATIONAL PARK

advantage of cooler morning temperatures as a steep climb with your heavy pack is involved from the outset. You also gain an advantage of securing a place in the hut at busy times. Avoid deteriorating weather and proceed only if it is fine. Park authorities ask that you register your intentions.

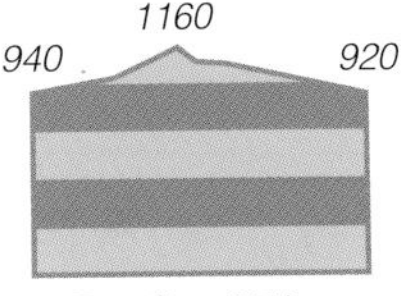

Day One 5.7 km

DAY ONE

From the carpark at Dove Lake, walk south-east over a foot bridge spanning the Dove River to cross button grass flats. After just 500 m, bypass the popular lower level lake circuit route. Head south-east steeply uphill to your left for 700 m to reach a saddle and junction of foot tracks. On the way you pass through lovely thickets of tanglefoot (*Nothofagus gunnii*) and in summer you may be fortunate to see some stunning blooms of Tasmanian Christmas bell (*Blandfordia punicea*). The track is rather rocky underfoot. At the saddle Lake Hanson is seen to the south-east and Dove Lake continues to be in view to the west. Several small beaches and the Honeymoon Islands look inviting from above.

Take the right-fork, southerly track, to steeply ascend very exposed Hansons Peak which is 500 m away. At one part a chain is provided to assist the scramble up bare sections of rock. Keep well apart from the rest of your party to avoid sending rocks on to those below. From the top of Hansons Peak, 230 m higher than Dove Lake, the view to Little Horn, Weindorfers Tower and more distant Cradle Mountain is especially good and a reward for the effort of the

Artists Pool and pencil pines

steep climb. Dove Lake, Lake Hanson and the Twisted Lakes are all in view.

A more gradual descent of the southern slopes follows for another 500 m to reach a track junction near the Twisted Lakes, which are a most fascinating example of glacier-formed tarns on the alpine tops. Pencil pines grow by the tarns and the adjacent rocks have both colourful lichen and glacial striations on them. Little Horn and Weindorfers Tower are then just ahead. An option here is to take a 200 m side trip along the Twisted Lakes Track to better appreciate this magnificent place. Next, continue 350 m south then reach Face Track off right at cross tracks. Face Track, as the name suggests, traverses cliff-lines near the towering mountain peaks of Little Horn and Weindorfers Tower. Rangers emergency hut is located 75 m to your left and is a good place for lunch in the shelter given the likelihood of cold winds produced by the high peaks and Dove Lake.

A most beautiful and relatively sheltered route lies ahead for the next 2.6 km, although the pad can get wet and muddy underfoot. As this day walk is quite short, take your time to appreciate this serene, tranquil setting. The route is much lower than the western side of Cradle Mountain and the sheltered conditions permit the growth of a wide variety of very beautiful plants including conifers and tanglefoot. You see pencil pines, rock outcrops, colourful lichens, tarns and the alpine plants with a backdrop of massive, towering cliffs on the east side of the mountain. Picturesque Artists Pool is right beside the track and is surrounded by gnarled pencil pines. Further on you see a series of cascades and more alpine tarns including larger Flynns Tarn. After fairly easy downhill walking, you reach the A-frame Scott–Kilvert Hut near Lake Rodway. The hut is a memorial to a tragedy when a teacher named Scott and a student named Kilvert perished in a blizzard in 1965. The large hut was later erected to prevent a re-occurrence of the same fate. Water and toilets are provided near the hut.

Benson Peak

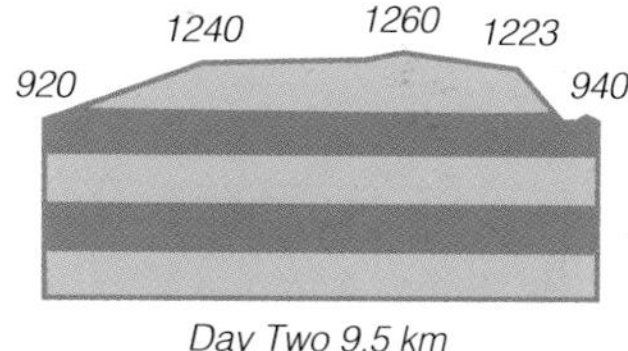

Day Two 9.5 km

DAY TWO

Start early in the day as the distance is much longer. The first 2.5 km involves a somewhat gentle, then steeper ascent around the southern end of the Cradle Mountain complex near Benson Peak so as to join the main Overland Track on exposed tops. As you depart the hut you are within forest and you climb on to a lateral moraine left by a former glacier. Swing west then south-west and eventually leave the shelter

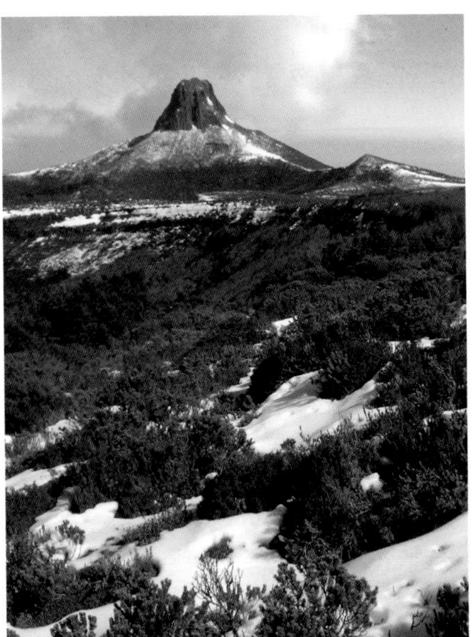
Barn Bluff

of the forest. The track steepens and reaches steps to pass up through a cliff-line at a tiny cascade. The cliffs are comprised of conglomerate rock. Above these small cliffs, take the time to rest and enjoy the view back towards Hidden Lake below, Lake Rodway off left and distant Devils Gullet on the Great Western Tiers. Scoparia, bauera, waratah, hakea, ferns and mosses are beside the track. Climb further into more exposed country and perhaps rug up to keep warm as a ridge crest is reached.

At this southern extreme of the mountain you see the many rugged peaks to the centre and southern end of the national park. Barn Bluff takes centre stage straight ahead. Gradual climbing follows over open alpine country of stunted vegetation and rock for the last 500 m to the Overland Track. The strong winds of

Hansons Peak and Dove Lake from Marions Lookout

Dove Lake and boatshed

the prevailing westerly weather here create difficult growing conditions for many plants, unlike the sheltered lower country behind you. Evidence of past glacial action is demonstrated in the cliffs and basin shape of nearby Cradle Cirque.

Turn right (north) and use the Overland Track for much of the rest of the walk. The way ahead is clearly defined but leads over rocky ground. You are likely to meet far more people on the track from here. For 2.7 km you contour roughly parallel with the cliffs of the very rocky western side of the Cradle Mountain complex. You then pass the beginning of the Fury River and Fury Gorge. The stream at this spot is but a trickle. You then climb a little to a saddle north-west of the Cradle Mountain summit. The whole stretch is exposed and provides broad views. Dolerite rock columns dominate the skyline of the peaks like shards piercing the sky. The Fury River gorge contains extremely dense rainforest fed from the western slopes of Cradle Mountain.

Some 200 m beyond the right-fork track to Cradle Mountain summit is the Kitchen Hut (emergency use only). The area is good for a rest and perhaps to watch distant walkers climbing and descending the summit.

Next, climb slightly north-west on bleak open slopes and veer right when 400 m from the hut. Continue north-north-east across the Cradle Plateau and Plateau Creek. Within 1.5 km you reach the rim of the plateau at Marions Lookout. Broad views including to distant Mount Roland, the Great Western Tiers and the Walls of Jerusalem can be enjoyed here. You also see Crater Lake 100 m lower to the left and Dove Lake 300 m lower to the right. Much of your outward journey of the previous day and walk end is also in view. There are great photographic opportunities.

Descend the rocky Overland Track for another 200 m then turn right on to a direct descent towards the northern end of Dove Lake. Chain handhold assists you for most of the steepest section ahead. Surprisingly you lose height very rapidly and re-enter vegetation on the sheltered eastern slopes below Marions Lookout. After 900 m of steady descent you link to the main Dove Lake lower circuit walking track used by countless numbers of visitors. Turn left and follow the path for just 400 m and you come to a historic boat shed on the shore at a tiny beach. This most celebrated photo location gives you a vista of both the lake and the now familiar mountain.

To finish the walk, climb just 200 m up the ongoing track, turn right and descend to the carpark 300 m away.

19 TULLAH–LAKE HERBERT

Tullah, Tasmania

Walk:	8.5 km retrace
Time required:	Including minimal breaks, 5 hours
Grade:	One day, medium
Environment:	Eucalyptus forest, button grass and exposed alpine tops
Last review date:	January 2008
Map reference:	Tasmap, 1:25 000 Tullah and Map 19
Best time to visit:	Suited to summer months only

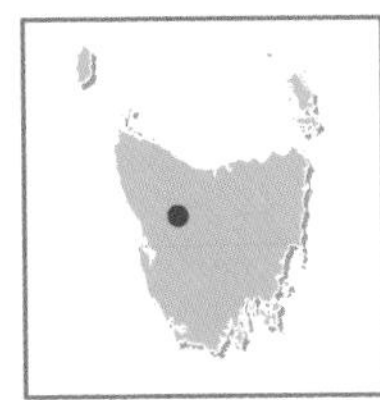

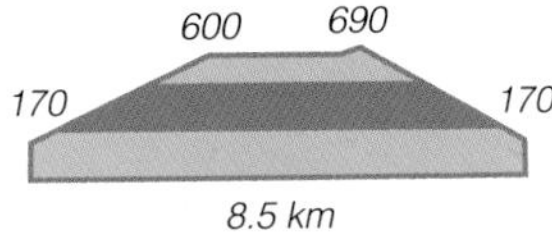

This walk starts from an elevation of just 170 m at Tullah township on the Murchison Highway and leads up to near the summit of 711 m high Mount Farrell. The peak overshadows the former hydro-electric construction township. The mountain is largely surrounded to the west by Lake Rosebery and to the north and east by Lake Mackintosh plus the Murchison River and its gorge to the south. The mountain has a history of mining since the late 1800s. Alpine Lake Herbert, near the summit and southern end of the mountain, has supplied water for mining in the past. The old pipeline route and accompanying track linking the lake and town have been used as access for picnics by the lake for about one hundred years.

Lakes Mackintosh and Rosebery have been constructed much later for power generation. This altered the densely forested valleys into vast and somewhat beautiful lakes. The lower flanks of the mountain are forested. Above the treeline is extensive button grass. Higher still are exposed cliffs dominated by white and pink quartzite embedded in conglomerate rock. Accommodation is available at Tullah but Burnie to the north is the nearest large place with full facilities.

It is our opinion that this outstanding climb equals some of the best of walking in Tasmania. There is a strong component of true wilderness without the disadvantage of being too remote or too physically demanding. In fact, if the weather does change it is possible to descend the mountain rapidly. There is mostly a fairly gentle grade to the track although a few steeper sections occur especially at the outset. The lack of people, regulations, helicopters overhead and entry fees are a refreshing change. Further, there are stupendous panoramas in all directions from the tops including eastwards to Cradle Mountain, Barn Bluff and Mount Ossa. Fine views of nearby Mount Murchison are

Rosebery		J	F	M	A	M	J	J	A	S	O	N	D	Year
Rain	av. mm	130	82	103	151	173	200	209	211	233	195	147	134	1952
Temp	av. max. °C	21	22	20	17	14	11	11	12	13	16	19	21	16
Temp	av. min. °C	10	10	9	8	6	4	4	4	5	6	8	10	7

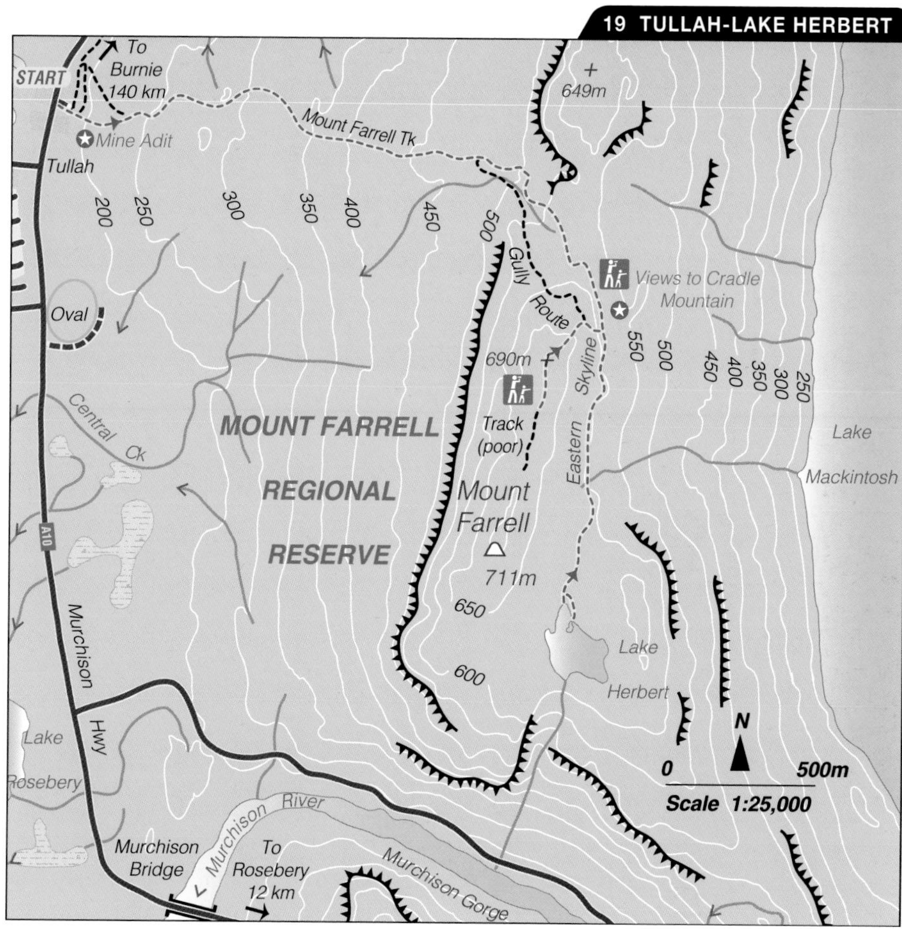

to the south. Here you can really get back to nature and enjoy solitude. Even though it is situated in the west of the state and therefore subject to bad weather, the walk route for the most part is fairly sheltered. On the higher skyline area the track roughly contours eastern flanks shielded from prevailing westerly weather by the mountain crest. However, it is wise to carry adequate warm clothing and water on the trip.

Leave transport beside the highway rather than attempt to use a rough short section of side road to a small turning point 100 m up the road. The spot is opposite tearooms. Nearby is an interesting museum with local exhibits on mining, early settlers and hydro-electric power development.

Head up the rough road 100 m to a former mine ruin and adit and avoid two tracks off left along the contour. Red arrows then mark the easterly walk route ahead. You enter eucalyptus and tea tree forest immediately so the canopy provides shelter and shade as you climb steeply at first. The track soon levels out and climbs step-like for some 1.5 km before rising above the tree line and emerging on button grass. At this point the views begin and gnarled, rocky outcrops erupt out of the landscape ahead. About 300 m onwards the track divides and you should follow the middle option. The left track rejoins the middle track shortly but the right fork leads to Mount Farrell summit via an awkward gully route and a possibility of encountering snakes. We suggest another, higher option towards the summit later. A further 300 m onwards you reach the ridge crest 2 km from the walk start and turn south where you get tremendous views to Lake Mackintosh and many mountains to the east. This is a great place to pause.

Ahead is what we have named the Eastern Skyline. You contour and climb slightly over button grass and low herbage where you see alpine flora and especially blandfordia plants. You are protected from the westerly weather by the summit ridge for all of the 1.4 km to Lake Herbert and have Lake Mackintosh way below you. At the 500 m stage you pass the Mount Farrell crest track which we suggest you follow on your way back. Lake Herbert, Mount

Lake Herbert

Lake Herbert and Mount Murchison

Murchison and the trig point on Mount Farrell summit then come into view. You could pause to climb on to some rocks beside the track for fine views to distant Mount Murchison looming beyond the lake.

At the lake, Mount Murchison is obscured by the southern end of Mount Farrell. The track leads directly to the north end of the 600 m high lake where you should head a few metres to the left and go out on to a small rocky peninsula for superb views of the lake environment. Tadpoles, frogs and yabbies are plentiful. Take a lunch break by the water.

Next, retrace 1 km and veer left on a track up a crest at a short man-made cutting. Almost immediately, double back left (south) and ascend the defined crest rather than going down hill. (This down hill gully route is the upper end of the awkward gully summit option.) Keep to the very crest and climb steeply so that within 500 m you reach the top of a high, rocky summit at 690 m elevation. Here you see great views of Tullah township for the first time. Lake Rosebery is in view as is Mount Farrell summit and imposing Mount Murchison. Take a break and congratulate yourself for reaching this high point. The track does continue along the crest southwards but significantly deteriorates and is difficult to follow. We suggest you go just 300 m to where you obtain a view down on to Lake Herbert from near a large rock outcrop. Beyond here the track turns downhill to your right and becomes very minor. It then stops without reaching the actual summit. Be content to turn back here and retrace the route to Tullah avoiding the gully route. At the start of the retrace on a clear day you will see eastwards from left to right, distant Cradle Mountain, Barn Bluff and Mount Ossa to best advantage.

Eastern Skyline and Lake Mackintosh

TARN SHELF–LAKE WEBSTER

Mount Field, Tasmania

Walk:	13 km circuit
Time required:	Including minimal breaks, 6 hours
Grade	One day, medium but can be very wet underfoot
Environment:	Alpine meadow and glacially formed tarns
Last review date:	May 2007
Map reference:	Tasmap, 1:25 000 Dobson and Map 20
Best time to visit:	Suited only to summer and snowbound in winter

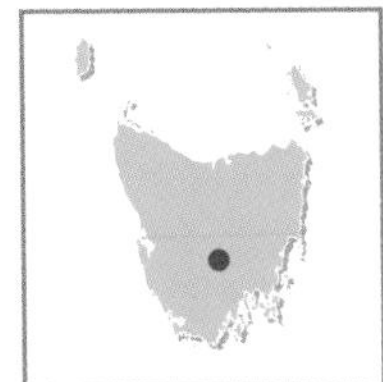

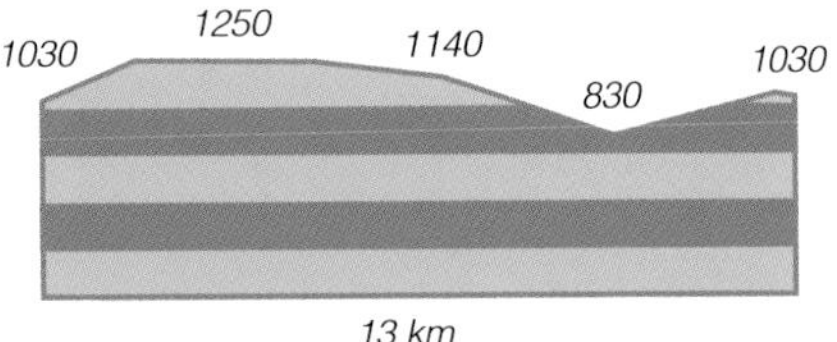

Ice has shaped many of the mountains of Tasmania in the past and Mount Field is a typical example of the tremendous changes that have occurred. Mount Field West and Mount Field East form the extremities of what once was a plateau. With the passing of time ice has scoured out much of the plateau, leaving a series of ridges. Much of the area is of dolerite rock. If you study a map, K Col is clearly a central point in ridges from Mount Field West, along the Rodway Range to Mount Mawson and between Florentine Peak and the Newdegate Pass area. Glacial action has gouged huge valleys and left typical flat valley floors, steep walls, truncated spurs and an abnormal set of watercourses all radiating out from K Col.

Retreating glaciers left behind an accumulation of debris rock known as moraines. These have caused natural dams behind which lakes, such as Hayes, Belcher, Belton, Seal and Webster, have remained in the valleys. On or near the tops, ice has scoured out innumerable hollows that are now filled with water, an example being the remarkable Tarn Shelf.

A very educational circuit walk can be taken to see the effects of glacial action. As with most similar areas, the scenery is excellent. The suggested starting point is at the Lake Dobson carpark 15 km up the narrow winding road from the Mount Field National Park entrance. This carpark services some ski lodges.

Be sure to pick a fine day, so that the glacial valleys can be seen from the tops. Forget the walk if the weather is poor. A shelter hut is at the walk start and three other shelter huts exist along the walk route. This is perhaps indicative of the

New Norfolk	J	F	M	A	M	J	J	A	S	O	N	D	Year
Rain av. mm	39	34	38	47	44	49	48	46	49	55	47	49	550
Temp av. max. °C	23	24	21	17	14	10	10	12	14	17	19	21	17
Temp av. min. °C	10	11	9	7	4	2	1	2	4	6	8	9	6

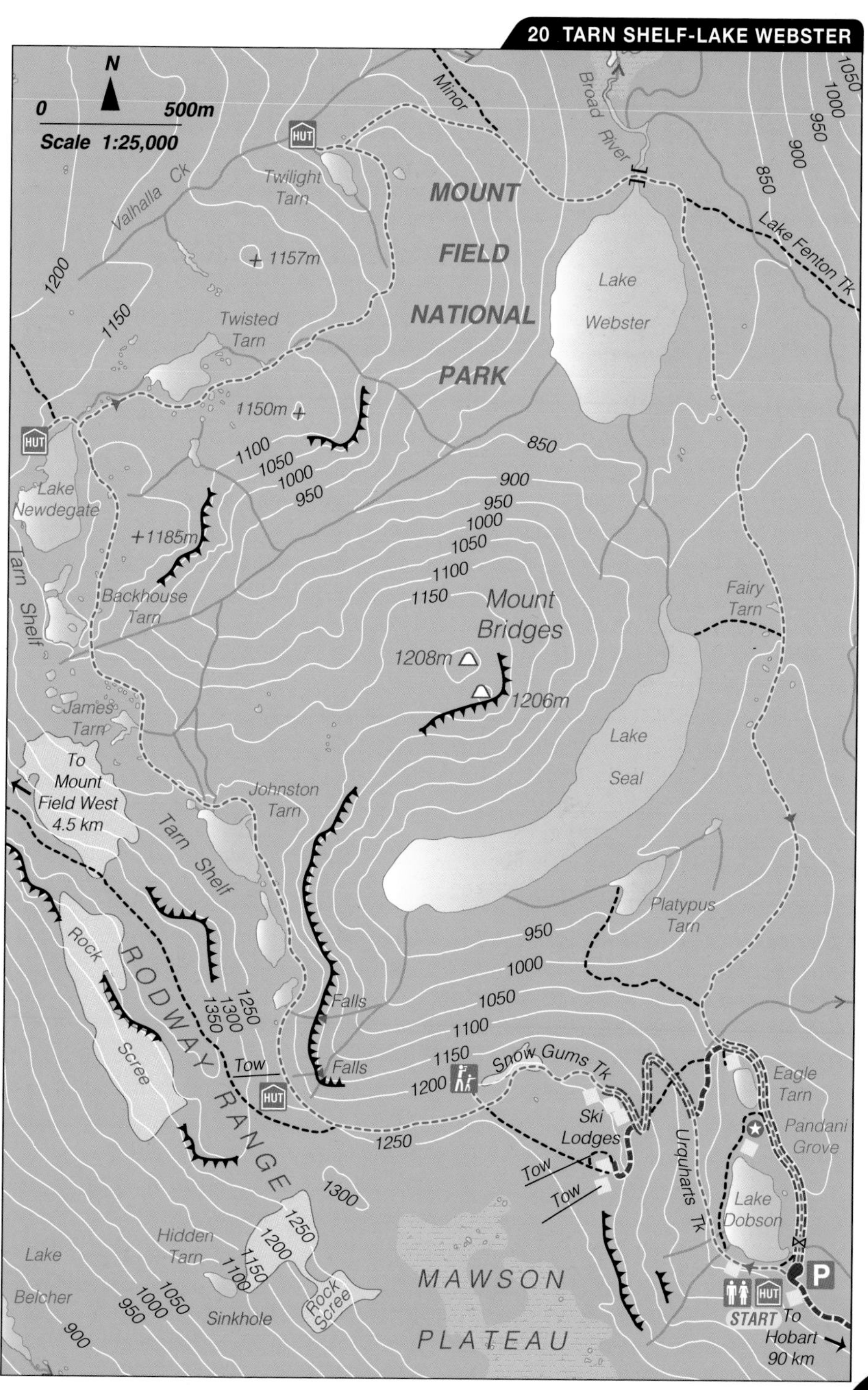
N
0 500m
Scale 1:25,000
HUT
Twilight Tarn
MOUNT FIELD NATIONAL PARK
Minor
Broad River
Lake Webster
Lake Fenton Tk
Valhalla Ck
1157m
Twisted Tarn
1150m
Lake Newdegate
1185m
Backhouse Tarn
Tarn Shelf
Mount Bridges
1208m
1206m
Fairy Tarn
James Tarn
To Mount Field West 4.5 km
Johnston Tarn
Lake Seal
Platypus Tarn
Rock Scree
RODWAY RANGE
Falls
Tow
Snow Gums Tk
Ski Lodges
Urquharts Tk
Eagle Tarn
Pandani Grove
Lake Dobson
Hidden Tarn
Lake Belcher
Sinkhole
Rock Scree
MAWSON PLATEAU
START
To Hobart 90 km
P

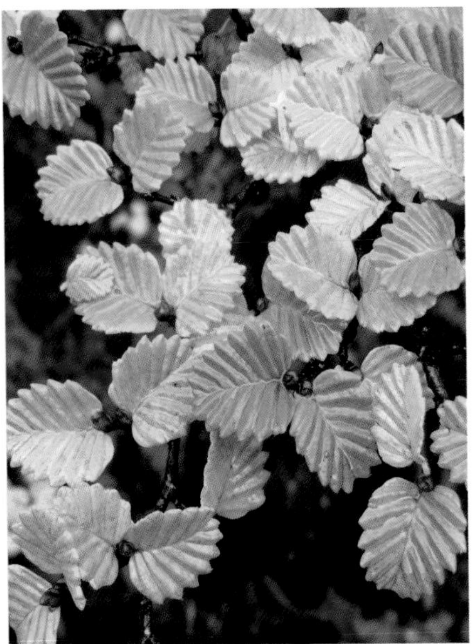

Deciduous fagus

need to be careful in such exposed alpine country where snow can occur at any time of the year. Late April and early May is a great time to see the resplendent autumn tints on the Tarn Shelf.

Deciduous fagus also known as tanglefoot (*Nothofagus gunnii*), a small endemic tree grows in the area and is stunningly beautiful as it sheds its leaves. An annual pilgrimage walk to Tarn Shelf on Anzac Day (25th April) to see the fagus at its best has become a tradition. The yellow-orange hues of the trees reflect in the many alpine tarns.

Access to the park is from Hobart and private transport is needed. Accommodation is limited to camping at the park entrance, some cabins and a small hotel at the tiny settlement of National Park. It is better to use the town of New Norfolk where many options exist.

Take the western shore walking track

Pandani palms at Lake Dobson

Lake Seal

around Lake Dobson shore for 250 m, passing the Wellington Ski Club building and innumerable alpine plant species along the way. The upper plant storey is of pandani palm (*Richea pandanifolia*), banksia, snow gum, pencil pine, waratah and tea tree. The lower plant storey includes prickly scoparia, bauera and a host of mosses, notably sphagnum and cushion plants. Lichens of varying colour cover rocks creating interesting patterns. Boardwalk covers wet patches of the track. Veer left next, to climb Urquharts Track for 500 m through forest to a roadway at a hairpin bend. Turn up the road past an outlook point towards ski slopes and lodges. After 500 m take the right fork of the road. Pass three ski lodges and at the nearby road end, head on to Snow Gums walking track. Small animals such as Tasmanian devils and tiger quolls may be seen in this area.

Climb the track west-north-west 500 m via herb- and rock-covered scree slopes, to a track intersection, on some open tops. Here, go a few metres north to Lake Seal Lookout. The lake is almost vertically 300 m below the lookout, and you can see clearly how ice has carved the landscape to form the lake and cliffs. Boardwalk is provided on the tracks in this area.

Next, go west from the intersecting tracks for 600 m, then fork right towards Tarn Shelf and Lake Newdegate. Rodway ski tow and a shelter hut are just ahead. It is then 3 km to Lake Newdegate. Much of the way is along the Tarn Shelf. Descend from the shelter hut then continue on to the broad ice-scoured ledge of Tarn Shelf which is on the slopes of the Rodway Range. Panoramic views are a feature of the whole area. Ice scour marks can clearly be seen on the rocks and scoured hollows contain many delightful tarns. This alpine environment is a paradise for plant enthusiasts and walkers.

Pineapple grass

The track is very rocky with many small rises and falls, so progress will be slow. At the northern end of the shelf formation is the larger tarn: Lake Newdegate. The track leads to the north end of the lake where there is a nine-bunk hut and minor track junction. Lunch could be considered at the hut.

Turn right (east) to cross 1 km of alpine plateau with more track boardwalk and tarns including lovely Twisted Tarn. The way is then down through stunted eucalyptus north for 800 m to Twilight Tarn where there is another small hut near its north end. This hut is rather rustic and just 200 m west, off the main track. You could have a rest here.

Descend again east for 1.4 km through more dense eucalyptus forest to the outlet of Lake Webster. The overgrown Mount Lord Track links in on your left during this

Lake Newdegate

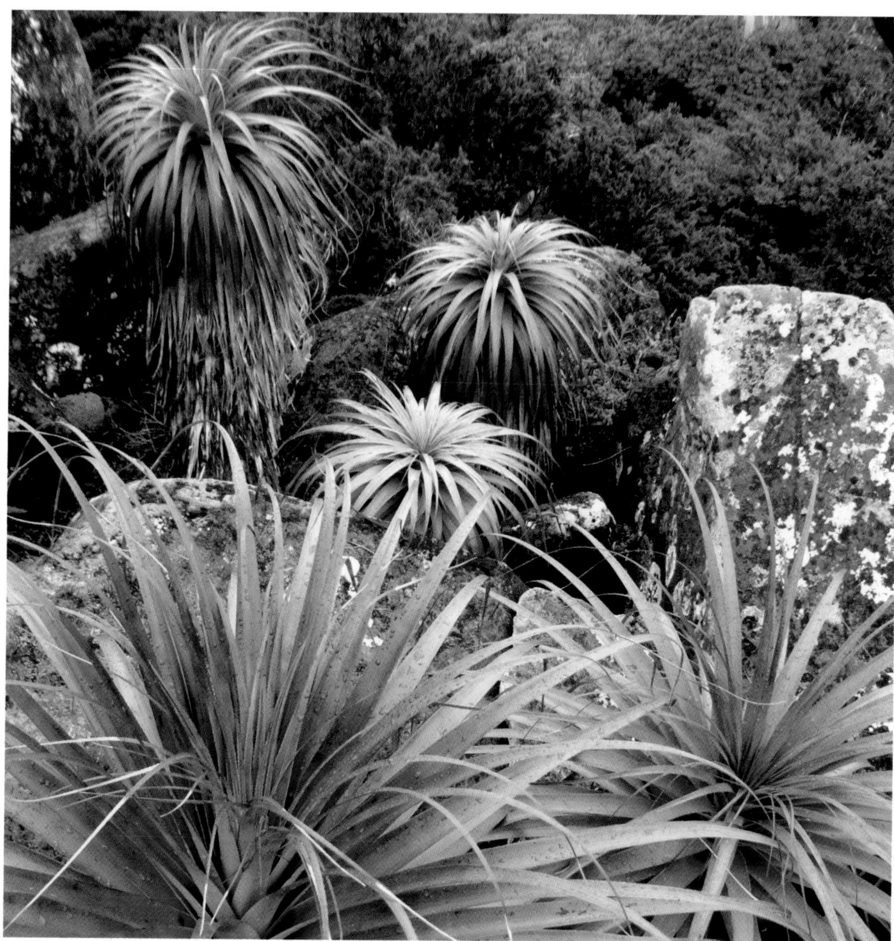
Pandani palms

descent. At the lake outlet, there is a foot bridge, across the Broad River.

To the east of the lake there is a small button grass plain, typical of many glaciated valley floors. The soil is too sour to grow trees except on ridges of moraine. The ongoing track forks right, away from Lake Fenton Track. Go south across the button grass plain, then rise on to a rather large moraine ridge. The track then gradually ascends for 3.2 km back to the ski village access road. Banksias, waratahs and eucalyptus form much of the vegetation at first, then the plant life becomes far more varied.

About midway up the rise, in the area of Fairy Tarn and other tiny ridge-top tarns, bypass a track off west to the outlet to Lake Seal. This finger lake is a typical glacier-formed lake and can be seen from the main track as you climb. When within 200 m of the road and the end of the climb, bypass a track off right down to Platypus Tarn.

The road is reached at a bend. Go down the road for 800 m past the east side of each of Eagle Tarn and Lake Dobson to return to the Lake Dobson carpark. The roadside is prolific with pandani as well as a very diverse range of other plants.

SOUTH AUSTRALIA

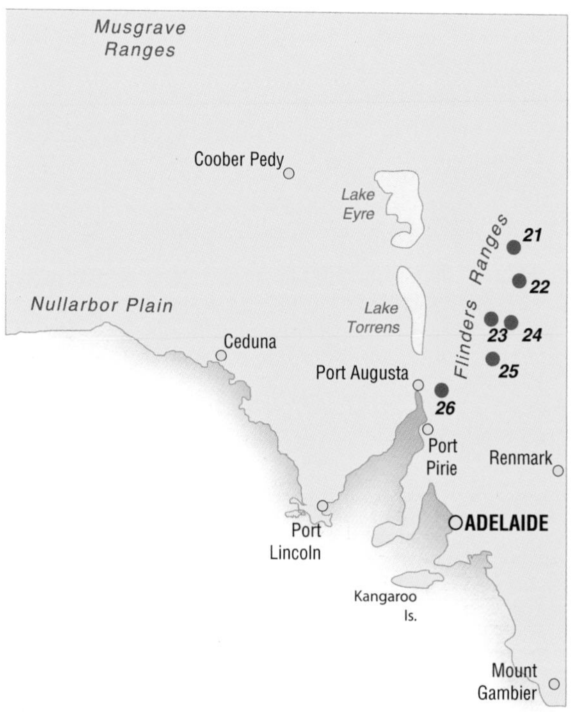

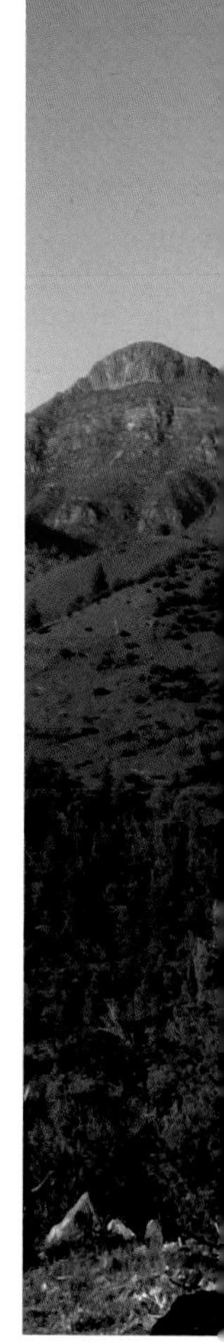

SA

21	**Arkaroola Creek**	Arkaroola Wilderness Sanctuary
22	**Chambers Gorge**	Northern Flinders Ranges
23	**Bunyeroo Gorge**	Flinders Ranges National Park
24	**ABC Range**	Flinders Ranges National Park
25	**Mount Ohlssen Bagge**	Flinders Ranges National Park
26	**Hidden Gorge**	Mount Remarkable National Park

Heysen Range, Flinders Ranges

The South Australian capital, Adelaide, is set by the Torrens River. It is backed by the Adelaide Hills which are part of the Flinders Ranges. They reach far inland and contain some of the oldest rocks in Australia. Spring wildflowers are a feature, as is the abundant wildlife. In the far north, some of the best shorter walks are at Arkaroola Wilderness Sanctuary and Mount Chambers Gorge. Further south, closer to famous Wilpena Pound, is the ABC Range with its panoramic vistas. Nearby, Bunyeroo Gorge cuts through the range. The ascent to Mount Ohlssen Bagge offers a fine view into the Wilpena Pound, an example of a 'geo-syncline' (a bowl-like formation caused by uplift of the crust of the Earth). Rugged, arid country gorges, such as Hidden Gorge, occur further south at Mount Remarkable. The famous long-distance Heysen Trail for walkers traverses the length of the Flinders Ranges, including through the Mount Remarkable and Flinders Ranges National Parks.

21 ARKAROOLA CREEK

Flinders Ranges, South Australia

Walk:	8 km circuit
Time required:	Including minimal breaks, 3 hours
Grade:	One day, medium
Environment:	Arid, deeply dissected, ranges
Last review date:	September 2008
Map reference:	Lands Department 1:50 000 Wooltana and Map 21
Best time to visit:	April to November. Summer is extremely hot

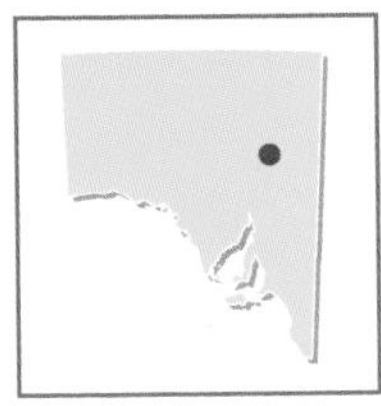

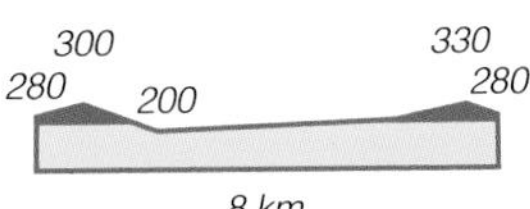

In the remote, far northern Flinders Ranges lies a very ancient landscape with twisted, buckled and heavily eroded features. It is perhaps the farthest north that you are able to go in a conventional vehicle. Since 1967 an enterprising family has created Arkaroola Resort near a former homestead. The resort is now the hub of its own wilderness sanctuary through which the usually dry Arkaroola Creek runs. A range of affordable accommodation is available. A 150 km network of four-wheel-drive tracks and walk routes have been created by the resort and several great walks result. One of the best takes you along Arkaroola Creek and into Bararranna Gorge. You need to carry water and protect yourself from the strong sunlight in this very arid and often hot environment. It is best to start the walk before 9 am to avoid the heat of the day.

Of interest to the scientifically minded person, Arkaroola Resort boasts astronomical observatories, a seismograph (for measuring earth tremors) and an onsite geologist and astronomer. There is a large exhibition room housing mineral and fossil relics found in the vicinity as well as interesting information on former mining activities.

Some 5.6 km east of Arkaroola Resort via the access road, travel north on Paralana Hot Springs Road 4 km to a small carpark near the former Welcome Mine. The access road is good two-wheel-drive unmade road. This mine yielded ore of 40 per cent copper, which was shipped to Wales for processing. As is often the case with such pure deposits, other economically important minerals, such as copper, gold and uranium, were found nearby. Interestingly uranium and copper deposits are detectable in plant material, and some animal and ant droppings.

Walk up the road north-east for 400 m to a saddle where you can view the

Arkaroola		J	F	M	A	M	J	J	A	S	O	N	D	Year
Rain	av. mm	34	35	29	14	18	14	15	15	16	19	16	24	249
Temp	av. max. °C	34	33	30	25	20	17	16	19	23	26	30	33	26
Temp	av. min. °C	20	19	16	11	7	4	3	5	8	12	15	18	12

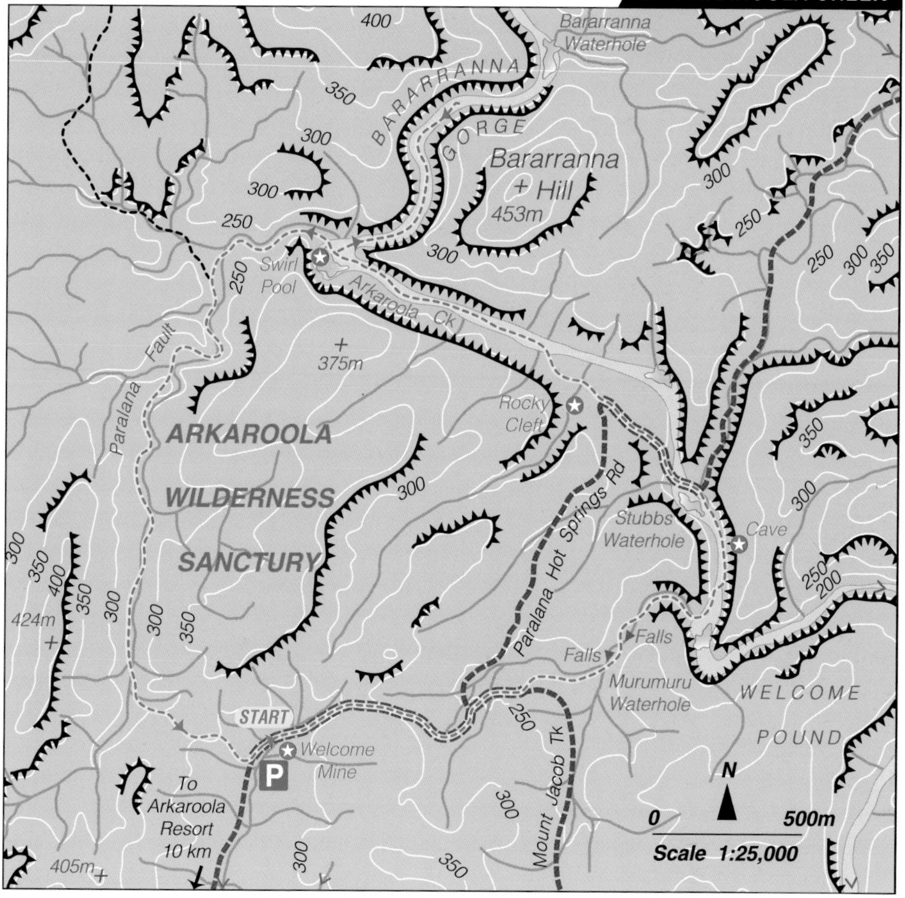

Welcome Pound formation. From here descend 500 m to a track junction where you turn east on to Mount Jacob four-wheel-drive track. After 200 m veer left and descend a rocky gully on foot track to the head of a usually dry waterfall. There are several of these as you continue. Negotiate the dry creek bed, which consists of 700 million year old glacial tillite, to reach the confluence with Arkaroola Creek, some 900 m from where you left the four-wheel-drive track. Red gums are dotted throughout the creek vicinity. Turn north and walk along the stream bed, with large boulders and waterholes and with caves in the cliffs. After 500 m you reach the Paralana Hot Springs Road located near Stubbs Waterhole. From here you turn north-west up the road for 500 m to a hairpin bend. Stop here briefly to view the jagged cliffs that line the route that you have just walked. A foot track leaves the hairpin bend and leads north-west whereupon you rejoin Arkaroola Creek bed.

Continue between high cliffs exhibiting dramatic rock strata. This includes an interesting rocky cleft. At a sharp bend after 1 km you meet a confluence with a western gully at a swirl pool. There are large amounts of flood debris trapped in tree bases, a startling indication of the depth of the water when the creek is flooded.

Arkaroola Creek

Rocky cleft

After stopping for a break here, take a side trip 1.2 km return north-east through Bararranna Gorge. Large boulders, the remnants of ancient glaciers, are littered along the gorge floor and there is a great variety of rock colour. Potholes (gnamma), produced by the action of pebbles swirling in turbulent water, erode the rock surface. You may be fortunate to see a yellow-footed rock wallaby. These mammals display great agility as they dart up the precipitous cliffs. When almost 600 m into the gorge, try to keep to the left bank in order to view a large vertical rock slab in midstream. It exhibits several different ripple markings on its western face. The ripples are remnants from an ancient seabed floor. You need to retrace the gorge from about this point even though the gorge continues for some distance.

Once back at the swirl pool, turn right (west) up the main side gully on marked foot track. After 500 m, turn south at

Ripple stones, Bararranna Gorge

SA

another gully confluence. From here the creek bed that you basically walk, sits upon the Paralana Fault (still seismically active). Follow the track up over a small saddle and walk the gully upstream (south) partly on a former four-wheel-drive track. Gradually climb south for 1.8 km. Finally, leave the gully climbing steeply to your left via the track and over a saddle, down to the walk end within 500 m.

Walking Arkaroola Creek

CHAMBERS GORGE

Flinders Ranges, South Australia

Walk:	9 km circuit
Time required:	Including minimal breaks, 4 hours
Grade:	One day, medium
Environment:	Remote, rugged, semi-desert gorge
Last review date:	September 2008
Map reference:	Lands Department 1:50 000 Wertaloona and Map 22
Best time to visit:	April to September. November to March is extremely hot

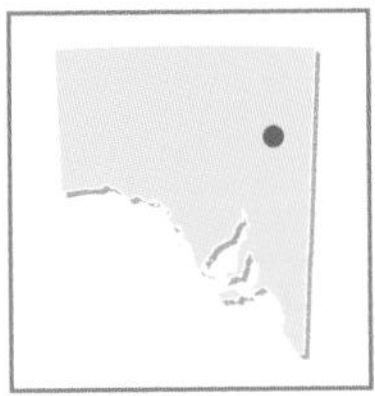

This walk is quite remote, some 550 km north of Adelaide. It is in the northern Flinders Ranges not far from Lake Frome. Mount Chambers Creek passes through Chambers Gorge into Lake Frome. Best access is from Blinman where limited accommodation and stores are available.

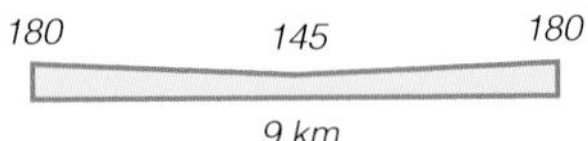

You need to carry plenty of water for the walk and wear a hat and sunscreen. For best comfort, start this walk before 9 am. Following heavy rains, expect access roads

Mount Chambers

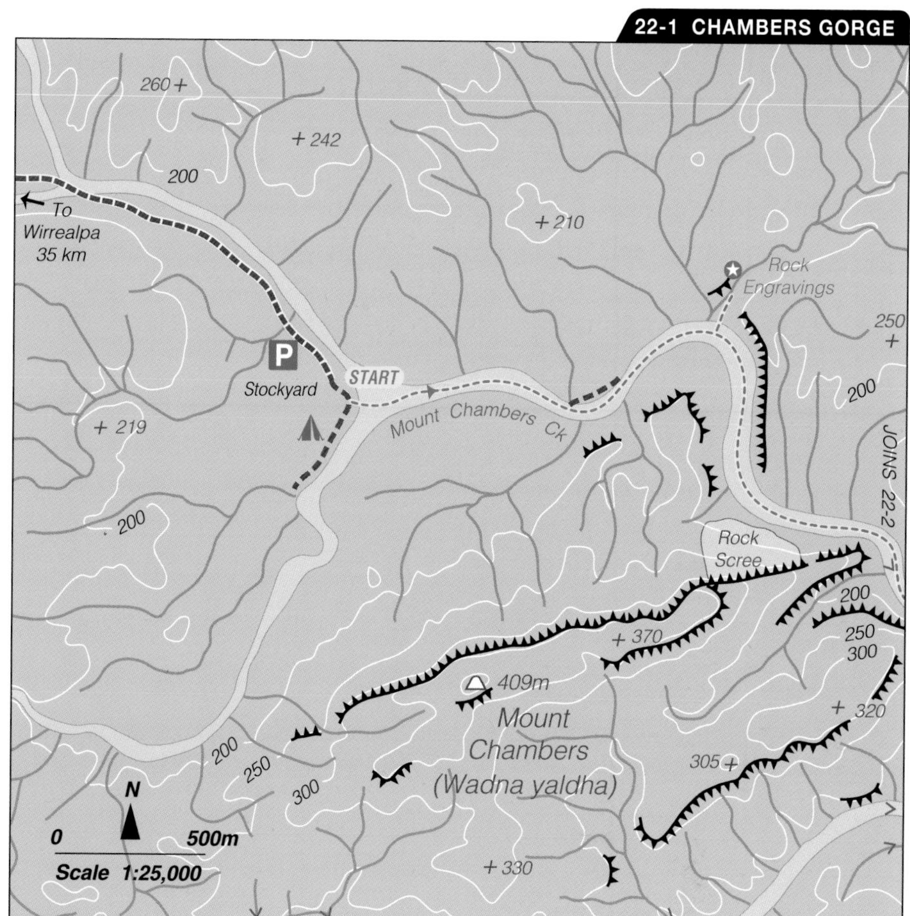

and the gorge to be impassable. From Blinman, you travel east to Wirrealpa then north-east along the Arkaroola Road 70 km into semi-desert. The long journey is well rewarded as the gorge is particularly scenic and of much geological interest. The cliffs are a deep reddish-brown colour. While there is often water in waterholes, you should not drink it, as it is intensively used by wildlife and possibly contaminated by upstream mining activities. The presence of the water in the semi-desert attracts vast numbers of birds and other animals.

After 4 km drive from the main Arkaroola Road, park at a campground (no facilities) and near an old stockyard. From here start to walk east, which is upon the usually dry bed of Mount Chambers Creek. This first section gives splendid views of Mount Chambers (known by the Aboriginals

Arkaroola		J	F	M	A	M	J	J	A	S	O	N	D	Year
Rain	av. mm	34	35	29	14	18	14	15	15	16	19	16	24	249
Temp	av. max. °C	34	33	30	25	20	17	16	19	23	26	30	33	26
Temp	av. min. °C	20	19	16	11	7	4	3	5	8	12	15	18	12

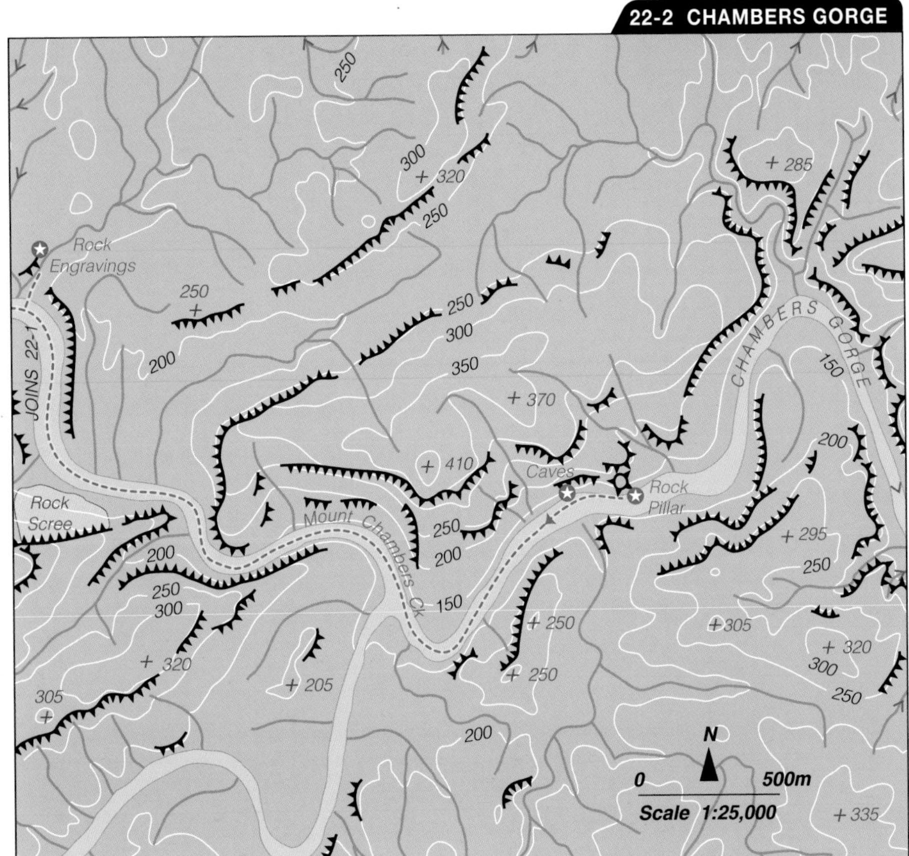

of the Flinders Ranges as Wadna yaldha).

After 1.5 km locate a site of Aboriginal petroglyphs (engravings) on the north bank at a pronounced bend, 50 m from the main watercourse. The site is located on low cliff overhangs. Faint impressions in the rock are more easily viewed with the sun at a low angle.

Return to the main creek bed and continue downstream (south) into the deepening gorge. The creek bed is littered with rock fragments of varying colours and shale-like composition, originating from distant hills. From here, sheer cliffs dominate and have a definite loose, layered structure. They date back some 600 million years. You will soon come to a distinctive grey-green band of rock crossing the creek bed. Ahead are extensive scree slopes tumbling down from Mount Chambers. The creek turns east and widens considerably. Red gums line the riverbed and tea tree helps to anchor the sandbars found midstream. You may come across seedlings of paper daisy, wild hops, salvation jane and the occasional Sturt desert peas.

From here on, the high cliffs cast large shadows on to the creek bed. When 3.5 km from the walk start, a significant confluence is encountered from the south-west. Shortly after, Mount Chambers Creek takes a sharp bend to the north-east and 1 km from the confluence you reach a prominent rock pillar on the north bank. This is the

Mount Chambers from gorge floor

Chambers Creek

suggested walk turn-around spot and a good place to have lunch even though the gorge continues further with similar scenery.

As you retrace following lunch, look for two caves at the base of the north bank cliffs. These are obviously used by animals for shelter from the elements. There is a large melaleuca thicket adjacent suggesting the presence of underground water. Along the route, note the upper level of flooding as indicated by the debris trapped high up in nearby trees and water marks on the cliffs. On your retrace upstream ensure you keep to the main watercourse and not veer into any side valley, especially those leading south. Your return is basically in a westerly direction.

BUNYEROO GORGE
Flinders Ranges, South Australia

Walk:	8 km retrace
Time required:	Including minimal breaks, 2 hours 30 minutes
Grade:	One day, easy
Environment:	Remote mountain desert, rugged gorge and creek
Last review date:	September 2008
Map reference:	South Australian Lands Department 1:50 000 Oraparinna and Map 23
Best time to visit:	May to October. Avoid hot days November to April

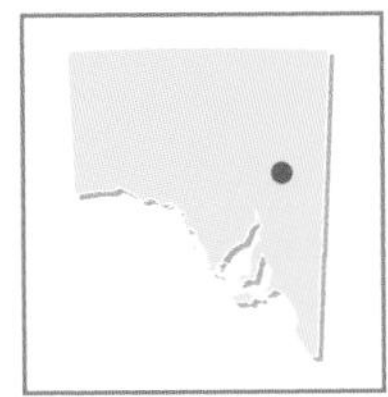

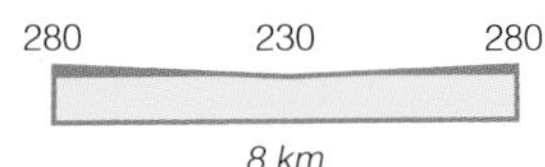

Bunyeroo Creek is a most beautiful spot for an easy walk. The creek banks are often green and therefore perhaps more inviting than other gorges and watercourses in this part of South Australia, especially on warmer days. The often-dry watercourse, remarkably, passes right through the rugged Heysen Range forming Bunyeroo Gorge.

SA

Bunyeroo Gorge gums

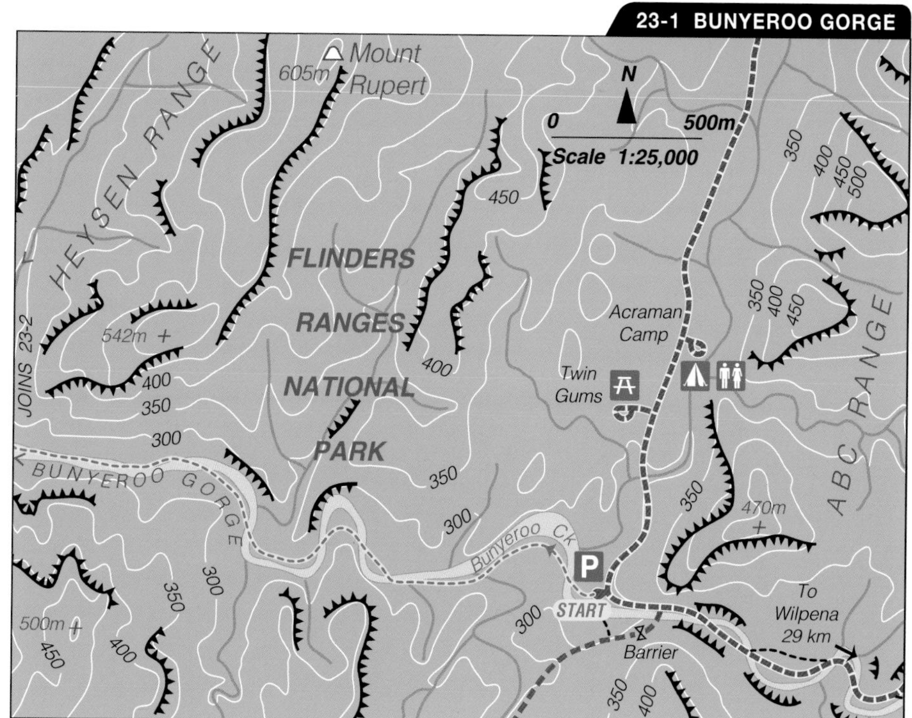

Access is via scenic Bunyeroo Road. It starts 4.8 km north of the Wilpena turnoff along the Wilpena–Blinman Road. You need to go 20 km along Bunyeroo Road to a carpark at the head of the gorge. This carpark also services a circuit walk through the ABC Range. You should avoid periods of heavy rain as some roads north of Wilpena may be closed to prevent damage to the road and for your safety. The general scenery and views from parking bays along the Bunyeroo Road are outstanding. The closest accommodation options are at Wilpena and Rawnsley Park.

From the carpark it is only 4 km walk westwards, through the gorge and as far as a nearby windpump. There is a rough track to follow but it is not fully continuous. Some pegs help you follow the track sections. Walking is normally easy amid sparse vegetation or on sandy creek bed. There are plenty of stepping stones to cross the creek. You occasionally cross attractive, gently sloping mounds. Some rocks contain colourful minerals. Following torrential rains, a large volume of water is trapped within the narrow gorge. This can move huge boulders some distance downstream. River red gums and massive, ancient cliffs make it a very memorable place. A common tree in the ranges, also seen here, is the native pine (*Callitris glaucophylla*). Various wattles, hop bush, daisy bush and salvation jane are often seen. The presence of any water,

Wilpena		J	F	M	A	M	J	J	A	S	O	N	D	Year
Rain	av. mm	20	15	8	7	57	51	62	43	20	17	7	17	324
Temp	av. max. °C	31	31	29	23	16	14	12	14	18	24	26	28	22
Temp	av. min. °C	16	16	13	8	5	4	2	2	5	9	12	14	9

FLINDERS RANGES NATIONAL PARK

HEYSEN RANGE

Bunyeroo Ck

Wind Pump

BUNYEROO GORGE

542m +

500m +

JOINS 23-1

300
250
300
350
400
350
300
350
350
400
450
450
400
350
300

N

0 500m

Scale 1:25,000

Bunyeroo Creek rock

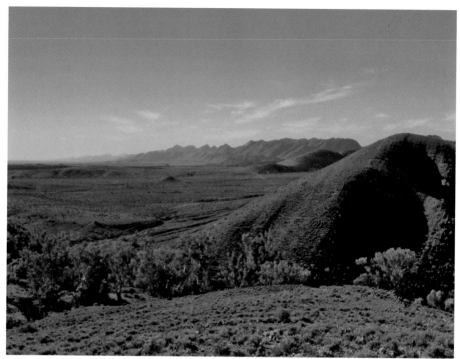

Bunyeroo Gorge outlet

attracts surrounding wildlife. Members of the parrot family and emus are usually prevalent. However, drought conditions will adversely affect numbers. The farthest point of the walk is where the gorge opens out to the vast, alluvial plains with Lake Torrens in the distance. Near this spot and on private land is a windpump and tank supplying livestock. This is the western extent of the park in this gorge and is where you should turn around.

Take a moment to relax and unwind and enjoy the wilderness. If you are lucky you may spot a rock wallaby.

On your retrace upstream, watch the marker pegs. Ensure you keep to the main watercourse and not veer into any side valley, especially those leading south. Your return is in an easterly direction.

Rock wallaby

ABC RANGE

Flinders Ranges, South Australia

Walk:	9.6 km circuit
Time required:	Including minimal breaks, 4 hours
Grade:	One day, medium
Environment:	Scenic arid hill country
Last review date:	September 2008
Map reference:	Lands Department 1:50 000 Oraparinna and Map 24
Best time to visit:	May to October. Avoid hot days November to April

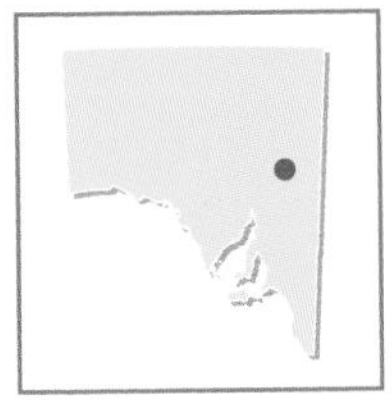

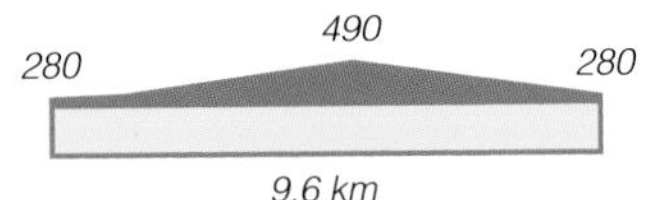

This walk follows Wilcolo Creek at the outset and then takes you to a high vantage point from which you can view the Heysen Range and the north-east escarpment of Wilpena Pound. To the north, the upper reaches of Bunyeroo Creek can be seen. Early morning walkers will be rewarded with excellent photographic opportunities. The route is anticlockwise and begins at Bunyeroo Gorge carpark in a particularly attractive part of the Flinders Ranges.

Leave the Wilpena to Blinman Road some 10 km from Wilpena to travel along scenic Bunyeroo Road for 20 km.

View from ABC Range

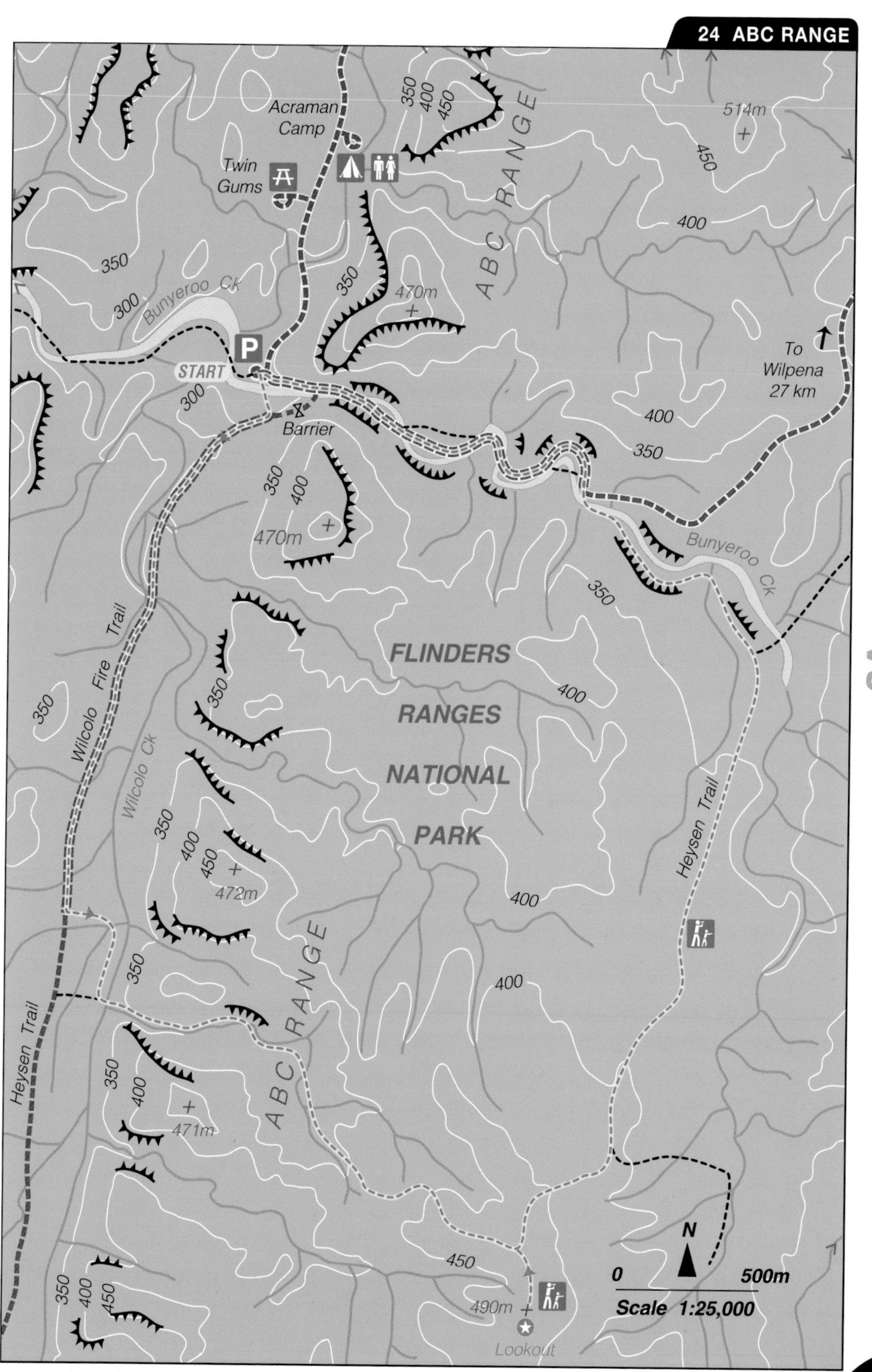
Acraman Camp
Twin Gums
ABC RANGE
514m
450
400
350
300
Bunyeroo Ck
470m
P
START
Barrier
To Wilpena 27 km
FLINDERS RANGES NATIONAL PARK
Wilcolo Fire Trail
Wilcolo Ck
472m
Heysen Trail
471m
490m
Lookout
N
0 500m
Scale 1:25,000

Wilpena		J	F	M	A	M	J	J	A	S	O	N	D	Year
Rain	av. mm	20	15	8	7	57	51	62	43	20	17	7	17	324
Temp	av. max. °C	31	31	29	23	16	14	12	14	18	24	26	28	22
Temp	av. min. °C	16	16	13	8	5	4	2	2	5	9	12	14	9

Note that heavy rain may make roads impassable. Park at Bunyeroo carpark, which has no facilities. Some 800 m north is small Acraman campground with a toilet and limited tank water. It is set amid the most attractive scenery of the ABC Range. Also nearby is the delightful Twin Gums picnic area. Wilpena and Rawnsley Park are not too far away, with accommodation and basic supplies.

Start the walk south across Bunyeroo Creek via a short foot track on to Wilcolo Fire Trail, which doubles as the long-distance Mawson cycle trail. Continue for 2.1 km on the wide track, through a syncline valley, which is a division between the ABC and Heysen ranges. As you walk, the unfolding view is of St Mary Peak through fairly dense callitris woodland. The understorey subsists on purple coloured, pulverised shale, forming a thin, poor soil. After walking 2.1 km, turn left (east) on to a foot track and descend a steep bank 200 m to Wilcolo Creek. Turn south up the creek and within 200 m meet the junction with the Heysen Trail.

Cross the creek eastwards following the Heysen Trail markers, which takes you up a narrow, rocky side gully with some pronounced cliffs. Steadily climb east on good foot track. After 500 m you have passed through a narrow section of the

Bunyeroo Valley

Heysen Range from ABC Range

ABC Range. Most of the remaining 1.4 km climb ahead is on the southern slopes to another track junction. Consider a break, within reasonable shade on these slopes, with occasional good views south. Upon reaching the track junction at a crest, take a south side track to an outlook 200 m away. Here you are at 490 m elevation with a 360 degree panorama. A plaque indicates the closest major mountains. The dominant vegetation is silver wattle (*Acacia rivalis*) with large patches of salvation jane. The view takes in the Heysen Range to the west.

Retrace the 200 m and turn right to begin a descent to a wide track within 400 m. The next 2 km spur crest walk has excellent views, as you make your way north, down the wide track to the creek. Here the Heysen Trail separates to cross the creek. Keep on the left bank, heading downstream, above cliffs before again descending to the creek bed. Shale-like rock fragments litter the bed and red gums provide shade and sanctuary for wildlife including possums and birds. The trees grow on the bed as well as the banks indicating the presence of underground water. The direction you walk in is north-west. The existence of emus is indicated by their cow pat-like droppings. The cliffs that bound the creek are the nesting sites of circling swallows. Their mud nests can be seen clinging to the rocks. Fairly reliable water in the creek allows the swallows to construct these engineering marvels, cemented by their own saliva. After 900 m join the road through upper Bunyeroo Gorge, travelling west. Follow the road for 1.5 km, among large red gums with numerous creek crossings below high cliffs to the walk end.

MOUNT OHLSSEN BAGGE
Flinders Ranges, South Australia

Walk:	7.5 km retrace
Time required:	Including minimal breaks, 4 hours
Grade:	One day, hard
Environment:	Arid, mountain ascent
Last review date:	September 2008
Map reference:	Lands Department 1:50 000 Wilpena and Map 25
Best time to visit:	May to October. Avoid hot days November to April

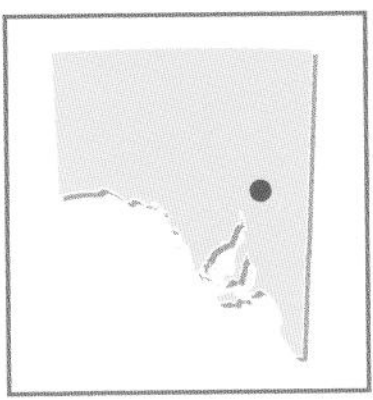

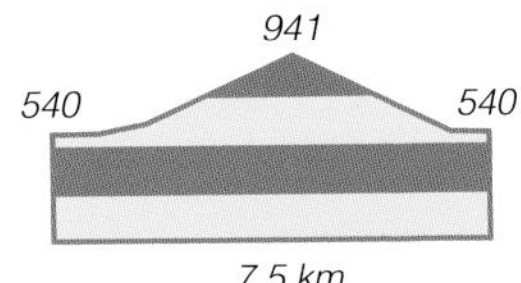

The Flinders Ranges around Wilpena occupy part of one of the oldest landscapes in the world. Geologists claim they are between 600 million and a billion years old. Spectacular, steep, saw-toothed ridges, uplifted, folded, buckled and fractured, are their prominent feature, with many rugged gorges cut through the ridges by streams that rarely flow.

Mount Ohlssen Bagge

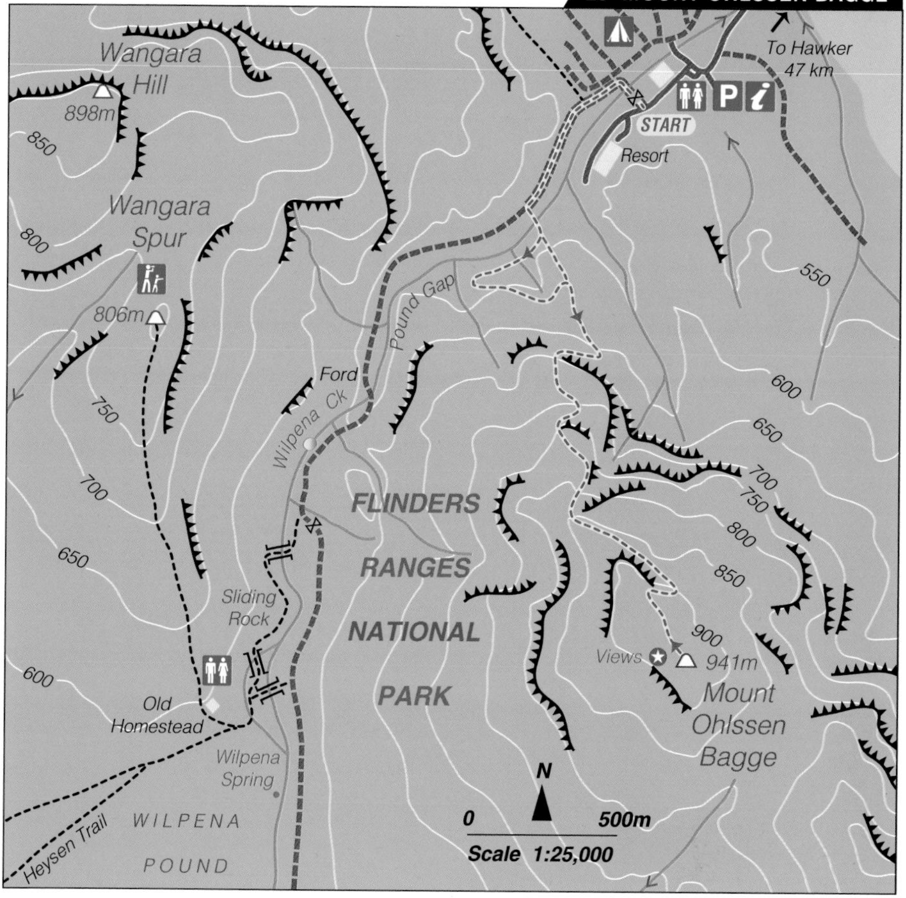

Explorer and navigator Matthew Flinders named the extensive ranges, parts of which now are protected as national parks. The ridges around Wilpena mostly consist of quartzite, which is very resistant to weathering, and the rock colours vary from brilliant reds through to dark chocolate-brown. Softer, eroded rock below the quartzite is mostly of sandstone, mudstone and shale often as alluviums. The twisting ranges mostly form typical dip slopes and escarpments.

The main tourist focus of the Flinders Ranges is Wilpena Pound, some 450 km north of Adelaide. Wilpena is an Aboriginal name meaning 'bent fingers' and when viewed from the air, Wilpena Pound is a remarkable, 16 km by 6 km, geological feature. Its huge saucer-shaped synclinal form is easily appreciated from a higher

Wilpena	J	F	M	A	M	J	J	A	S	O	N	D	Year
Rain av. mm	20	15	8	7	57	51	62	43	20	17	7	17	324
Temp av. max. °C	31	31	29	23	16	14	12	14	18	24	26	28	22
Temp av. min. °C	16	16	13	8	5	4	2	2	5	9	12	14	9

vantage point. Such pounds occur in other parts of the Flinders Ranges but Wilpena is the most noteworthy. Its shape, like two cupped hands, is formed with dramatic cliffs around the exterior of the basin.

The unique vegetation is also of great interest. Many of the usually dry watercourses are lined with beautiful river red gums and each spring, by October, most of the surrounding ranges are covered in red hop flowers, mauve salvation jane and other wildflowers. Native pines are common and mallee, grass trees and wattle are prolific on the higher slopes. Overall though, vegetation is sparse and permits good views. Euros, wallabies, kangaroos, including the big red kangaroo, emus, eagles, hawks and birds of the parrot family are present although following years of drought, their numbers have declined. Also seen are galahs, finches, budgerigars, and corellas.

Wilpena resort and campground is located at a breach in the wall of the pound where Wilpena Creek drains the internal basin. The creek here has a more reliable water flow than most other parts of the ranges so many fine river gums are seen. A store adjacent to a visitor centre has a fair range of supplies. Some 15 km south is an alternative at Rawnsley Park. It has a full range of accommodation and a store.

With an average annual rainfall of just 324 mm, hot north winds and summer temperatures frequently reaching well over 40 degrees from November to March, tourists tend to avoid Wilpena in summer. However from May to October conditions are very pleasant normally. Winter temperatures can drop to freezing overnight due to clear skies, but each day is usually comfortably warm.

To view the pound formation you need to climb high and many walkers head for St

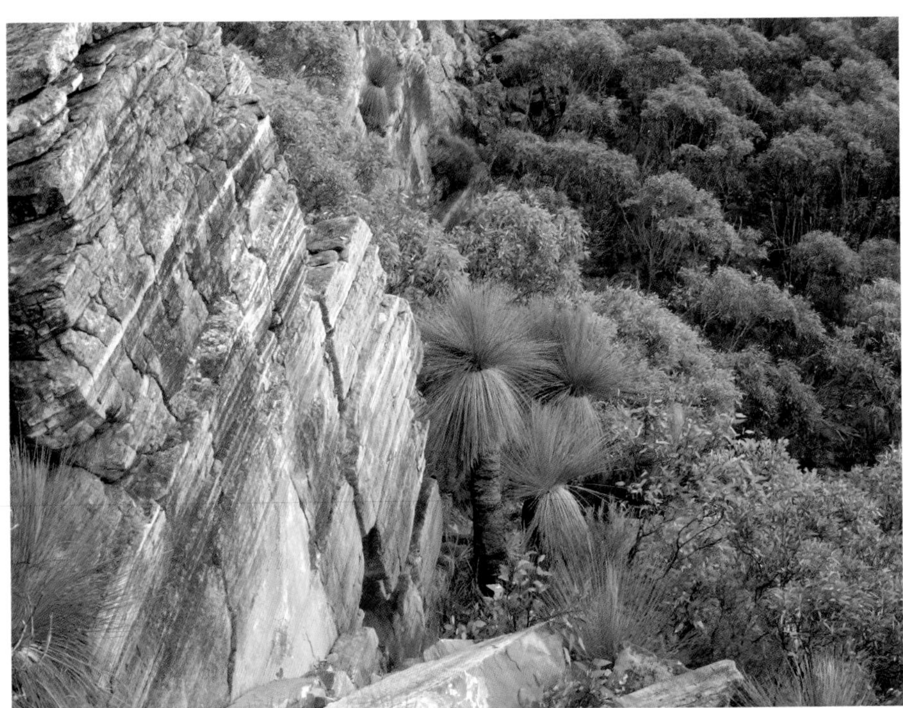

Sandstone and grass trees

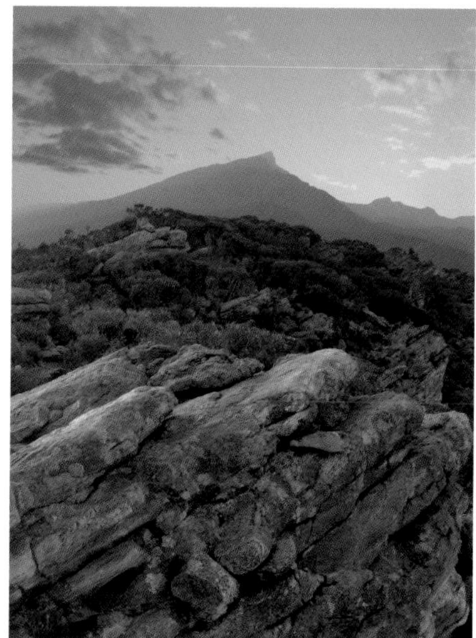

View to St Mary Peak

Mary Peak. The local Aboriginals ask that this sacred summit not be climbed so we suggest you climb Mount Ohlssen Bagge for an even better walk. The climb is very steep in places, quite rugged and rocky underfoot with poor track marking but the distance is not great and certainly much less than to St Mary Peak. For most of the way you have good views but for the best panorama of Wilpena Pound you need to go right to the top.

From the visitor centre you need to take the main four-wheel-drive track west past the camp area, along the north bank of Wilpena Creek as if going into the floor of the pound. Shade from large trees and attractive cliffs ensure enjoyment for this 800 m stretch. You then turn left on to walking track so as to re-cross Wilpena Creek. Once on the south bank you should turn right and take a nature trail for 1 km. Seats are placed along this track with its attractive creek flats and gradual climb on to a spur where you rejoin the direct ascent track to Mount Ohlssen Bagge and turn right. It is then 'all stops out' for 2.3 km of steep, rugged climbing amid interesting sandstone and other rock strata.

The poor, rocky soils support sparse, woody plants, such as banksias, grevilleas and sheoaks, with many grass trees on the higher reaches. There are a number of zigzags as you ascend. Along the summit ridge and at the actual top there are stunning views in all directions to places over 100 km away. Besides the interesting geological shape of the pound you see the northern part of Spencer Gulf and much of the Flinders Ranges.

No doubt a long rest will be appreciated before you retrace the route. On the return you should bypass the nature trail loop in favour of the short direct option.

Wilpena Pound rim at sunset

HIDDEN GORGE

Mount Remarkable, South Australia

Walk:	16.6 km (Day one 7 km; Day two 9.6 km) circuit
Time required:	Including minimal breaks, two days (Day one 3 hours 30 minutes; Day two 4 hours 30 minutes)
Grade:	Two days, medium, backpack required
Environment:	Steep hill climb and gorge
Last review date:	September 2008
Map reference:	Lands Department 1:50 000 Melrose and Map 26
Best time to visit:	April to October. Avoid hot days November to March

SA

Mount Remarkable National Park provides some relatively strenuous walking opportunities. Invariably the reward for effort is a broad panorama or the serenity of such places as Hidden Gorge. The park boasts 14 walks including part of the long-distance Heysen Trail. For this walk you rise nearly 350 m and you cover a fair distance. However, the last 5 km is downhill. All water should be carried and hot days avoided. The park is closed on proclaimed total fire ban days. Although the walk can be completed in a day during cooler weather, we recommend an overnight wilderness stop on the banks of Alligator Creek at Hidden Camp. The campsite has no facilities, however, the remoteness has an attraction all of its own.

Over the two days you walk the valleys of Mambray and Alligator creeks and then climb through Hidden Gorge to the Battery Ridge, before returning south down the pronounced spur of the ridge, bypassing the Bluff. The reddish-brown quartzite rock formations surrounding you are best viewed late or early in the day. This walk suggestion therefore has the first day of walking later in the day and an early rise on the second day.

Access to the park is from Highway No. 1 between Port Pirie and Port Augusta into the Mambray Creek park entrance. You should leave transport at the easternmost carpark and picnic ground. Port Pirie has the nearest full accommodation and supply options.

The vegetation seen during this walk includes some fine river gums along Mambray Creek. Their white trunks contrast well with the reddish-brown rocks nearby and thousands of native white pines (*Callitris glaucophylla*). Sheoaks cling precariously to the cliffs and grow on very thin poor soils. There are many species of eucalyptus, acacia, callistemon and

Port Pirie	J	F	M	A	M	J	J	A	S	O	N	D	Year
Rain av. mm	19	18	18	28	38	41	34	35	36	33	24	22	344
Temp av. max. °C	32	32	30	25	20	17	16	18	21	25	28	30	24
Temp av. min. °C	18	19	16	13	11	8	8	8	10	12	14	16	13

JOINS 26-2
N
0 500m
Scale 1:25,000
THE BATTERY
The Battery Tk
MOUNT REMARKABLE NATIONAL PARK
The Bluff
Mambray Ck
Mambray Creek Tk
START
To Port Pirie 45 km
Mount Cavern Tk

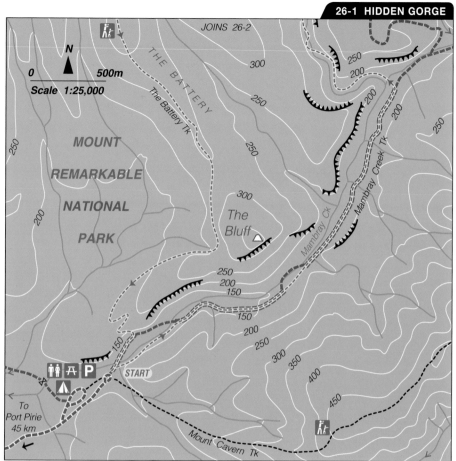

xanthorrhoea. Yellow-footed rock wallabies, euros and other members of the kangaroo family may be seen.

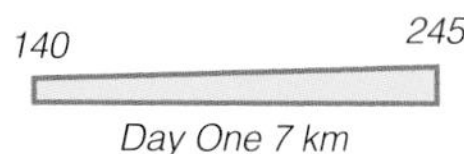

Day One 7 km

DAY ONE

The first day is of easy grade and short so you do not need to start until the afternoon. Lunch at the Mambray Creek picnic ground, perhaps after the long drive from Adelaide, may be an option. You head off for 3 km eastwards up the Mambray Creek valley, mainly on a fire access four-wheel-drive track. Short foot track sections skirt past creek fords so wet feet can be avoided. There are a number of pleasant pools along the way. The river gums in the locality usually harbour galahs and other parrots. Mambray Creek then meets Alligator Creek, which at this spot breaches the southern wall of a huge geological pound formation. Viewed from nearby Mount Cavern, you see a distinct geological resemblance to more-famous Wilpena Pound. The breach is quite narrow, given the huge water catchment of the pound. The foot track passes through the breach.

The ranges of the Mount Remarkable National Park feature extremely old rock

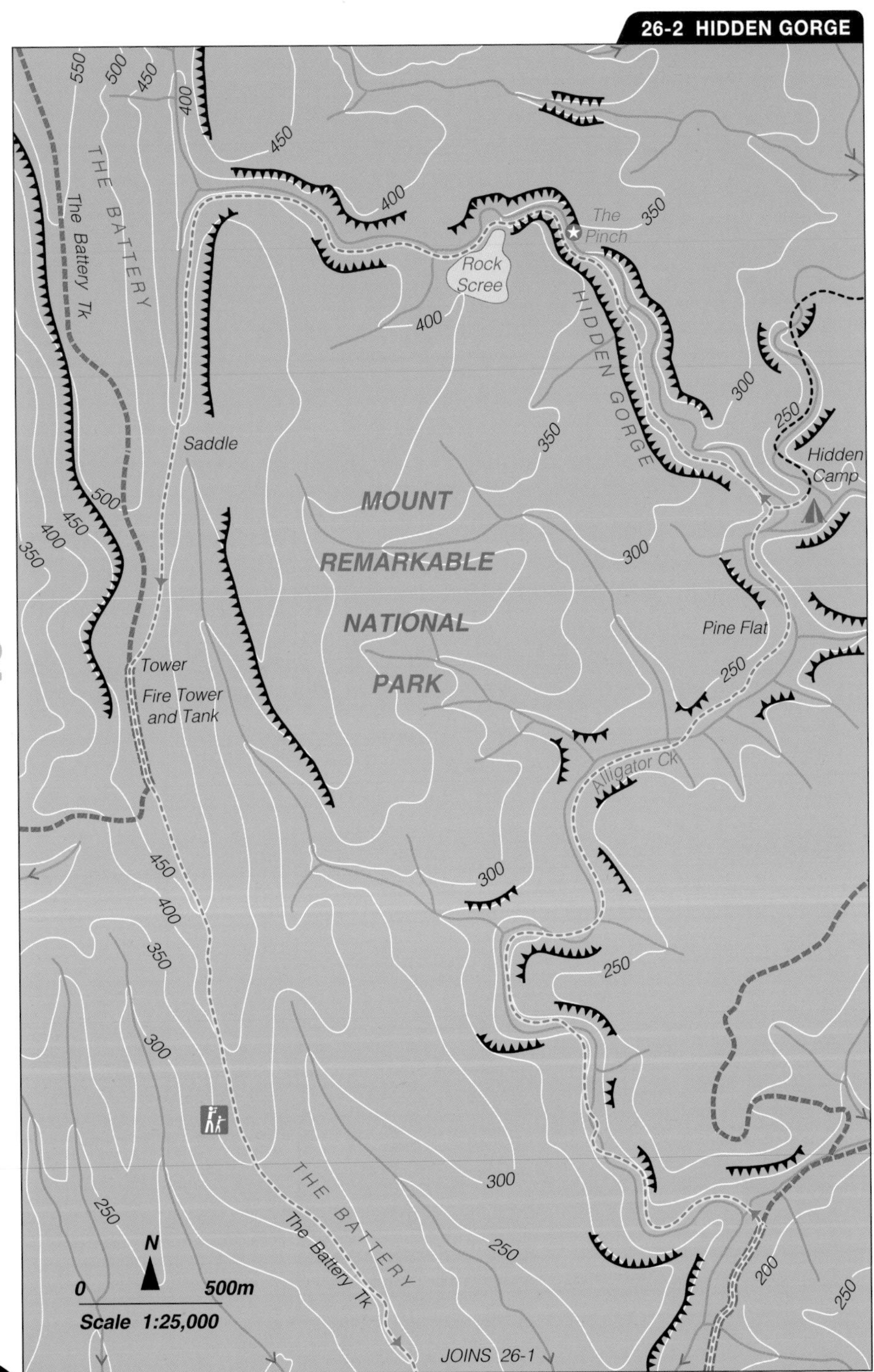
THE BATTERY
The Battery Tk
The Pinch
Rock Scree
HIDDEN GORGE
Saddle
MOUNT
REMARKABLE
NATIONAL
PARK
Hidden Camp
Pine Flat
Tower
Fire Tower and Tank
Alligator Ck
THE BATTERY
The Battery Tk
JOINS 26-1
N
0
500m
Scale 1:25,000

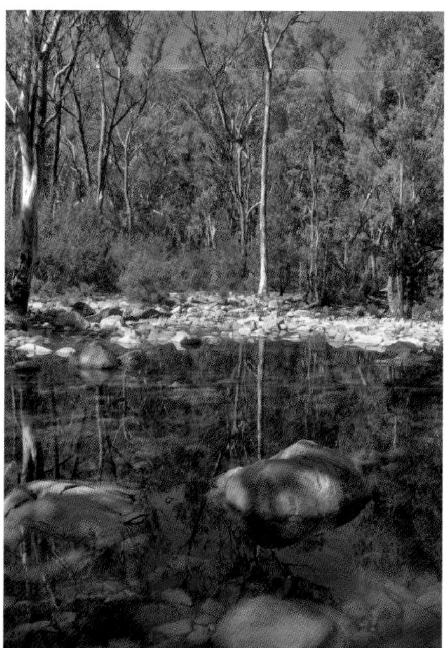

Mambray Creek

formations created by many different factors. Rhynie sandstone (800 million years old), pink and greyish-white ABC Range quartzite (600 million years old) and glacial Apilla tillite occur. The harder quartzite is on the higher country and the softer sandstone, tillite and some mudstone are in the lower regions where their erosion has created gorges.

Once past the breach in the pound formation, you follow a foot track along Alligator Creek for 4 km within the pound. The creek twists its way in a gorge and the foot track is good and well marked as the terrain gets more rugged. Just north of Pine Flat there is a track turnoff into Hidden Gorge. This is your route for the following day. Your bush camp for the night is 100 m from the junction along the track to your right. The rest of the day can be spent relaxing by the stream in this wilderness spot.

Hidden Gorge rock strata

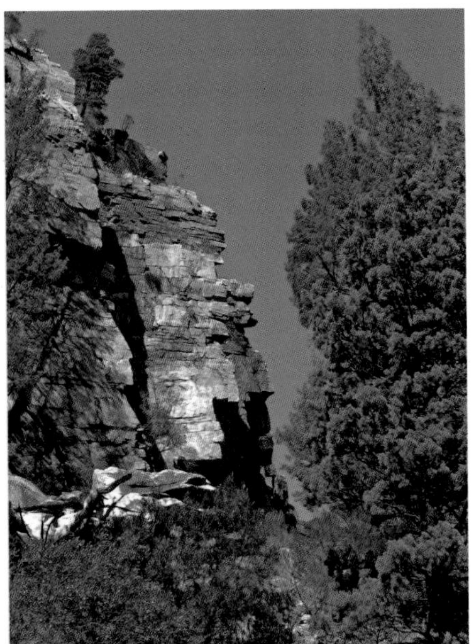

Cypress pines and cliffs

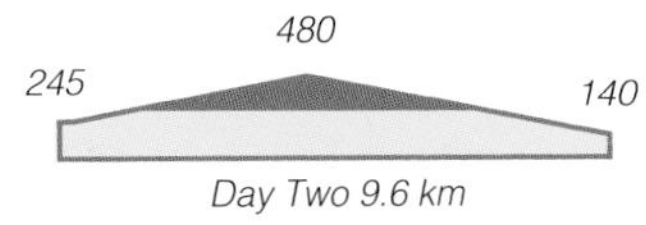

DAY TWO

Progress in Hidden Gorge will be much slower due to rocky terrain. At first retrace the 100 m to the track junction and turn right. After just 500 m you find the sheer height of the gorge walls increases and you are often required to follow the creek bed. Relatively high cliffs and a very narrow section, which we call 'the Pinch', will entice you to linger and view the beauty. The overhanging walls are barely 15 m apart. After the Pinch, both sides of the gorge have collapsed, almost plugging the way and you need to climb to the left to negotiate the obstruction. Some 3 km from the Hidden Camp turnoff, the track leaves the gorge throat and turns south to

Hidden Gorge cliffs

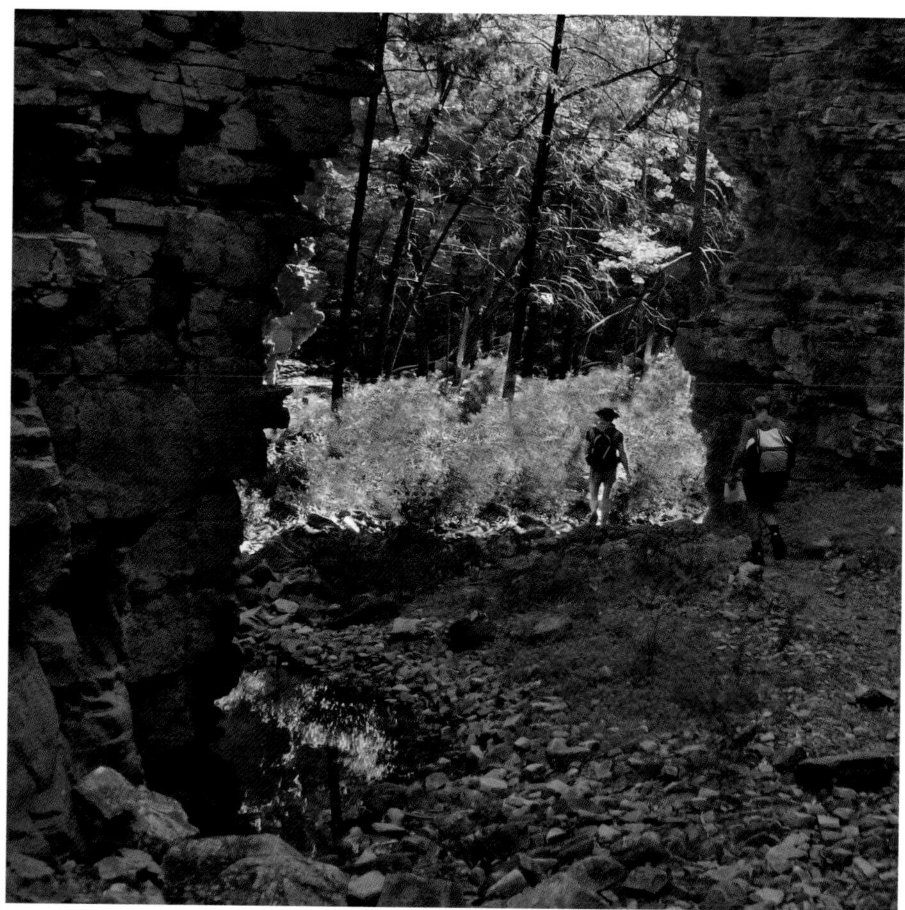
The Pinch, Hidden Gorge

ascend for 900 m close to a cliff-line so as to reach a saddle. Continue uphill beyond the saddle for another 950 m and you join a fire access trail on the crest of the Battery ridge to a small communications tower. You may experience a marked change in temperature on the ridge compared to the sheltered gorge below. Go south on the fire access trail for 150 m then near the base of a fire watchtower there is a small water tank fed by a roof top and shelter, but you should not rely upon this water.

Continue south on this four-wheel-drive track for some 300 m then where it turns west, veer left on to foot track down a spur crest. Ahead, the panorama encompasses the whole of the head of Spencer Gulf. The sun-baked crest has sparse, dry sclerophyll scrub with many grass trees and yellow-footed rock wallabies.

Continue south on the ridge-top track and down across the western slopes of the Bluff for 4 km to eventually arrive back at Mambray Creek. A couple of track zigzags are negotiated as you near the creek. From here a four-wheel-drive track leads south-west 300 m downstream, to the end of the walk at the picnic area.

WESTERN AUSTRALIA

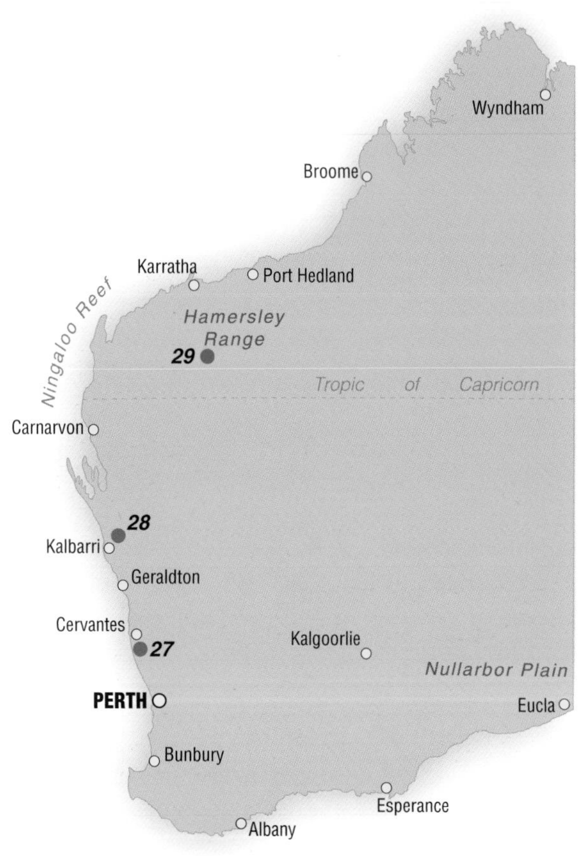

27	Pinnacles Desert	Nambung National Park
28	Murchison Gorge	Kalbarri National Park
29	Mount Bruce	Karijini National Park

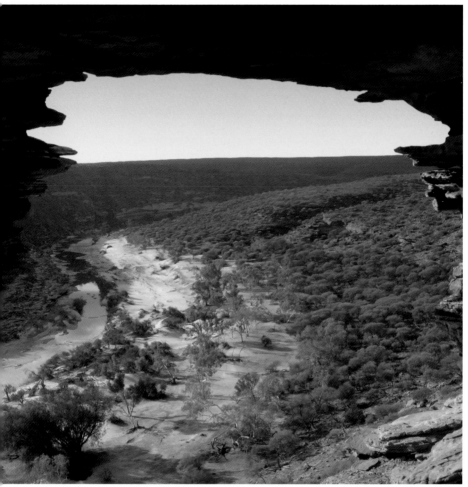

Rock window, Murchison Gorge

Western Australia is the largest of all the states. Perth, the capital, is one of the most remote cities in the world. Western Australia is famous for its spring wild flowers. Southwards the 350 km Bibbulmun Walking Track from Perth to Albany traverses mixed forest with tall kauri and jarrah trees and coastal heathland. North of Perth, the Pinnacles Desert near Cervantes offers a unique walking experience. Near Kalbarri, the Murchison River cuts its way to the Indian Ocean through the red rock walls of stunning Murchison Gorge. Further afield the Pilbara Ranges of the north-west boast an incredible wealth of iron ore and other minerals. The summit walk to Mount Bruce is near the mines. Likewise in the very remote north, the Kimberley plateau also features very ancient rock cliffs, waterfalls and gorges. In the East Kimberly are the amazing beehive-shaped rock formations known as the Bungle Bungles.

PINNACLES DESERT
Cervantes, Western Australia

Walk:	5 km circuit
Time required:	Including minimal breaks, 2 hours
Grade:	One day, easy
Environment:	Desert sands with limestone pinnacles
Last review date:	August 2007
Map reference:	Map 27
Best time to visit:	May to October. Avoid hot days November to April

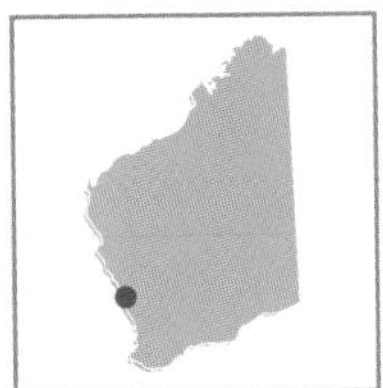

20 20
5 km

The Pinnacles in Nambung National Park are a well-known feature in coastal sandy desert country. They are located 17 km by sealed road south-east of the small town of Cervantes, which is 245 km north of Perth. The town has limited accommodation except for a well-appointed backpacker hostel and a motel. The park has no accommodation. The main attraction of the park is the thousands of limestone pinnacles, which protrude by as much as 3.5 m from the orange-yellow desert sands. The majority of the formations are needle-like, some having sharp edges, occasionally perforated by holes. They stand like silent sentinels, reminiscent of Stonehenge or the monuments of Easter Island. However, the Pinnacles are definitely not man-made. There is also fine coastal scenery elsewhere in the park. Most visitors to the Pinnacles drive a sandy 3.5 km circuit from the park entrance gate where a fee is charged. Adjacent is a carpark and interpretive centre. Those driving the circuit stop frequently to admire the formations and take photographs. There is a viewing deck and a number of high points from which panoramic views are afforded out to the coast. Seeing the Pinnacles from these vantage points allows you to better appreciate them. The whole of the area lies at close to sea level.

The geology of the Pinnacles is rather interesting. They consist of sand and limestone. The whole district including offshore islands and bluffs has limestone underneath it and forms a major aquifer from which the town of Cervantes draws all its water. Over time sands made up of sea shell fragments from the nearby coast have washed ashore and blown inland forming dune systems some of which are the oldest in Western Australia. During winters, sinking rainwater, which is slightly acidic, dissolves the calcium carbonate (lime) contained in the alkaline shells that form the dunes. During summers the

Cervantes	J	F	M	A	M	J	J	A	S	O	N	D	Year
Rain av. mm	9	12	30	40	80	120	110	90	55	35	12	7	600
Temp av. max. °C	37	38	37	32	29	26	25	26	27	29	31	35	31
Temp av. min. °C	23	24	23	19	17	15	14	14	14	16	18	21	18

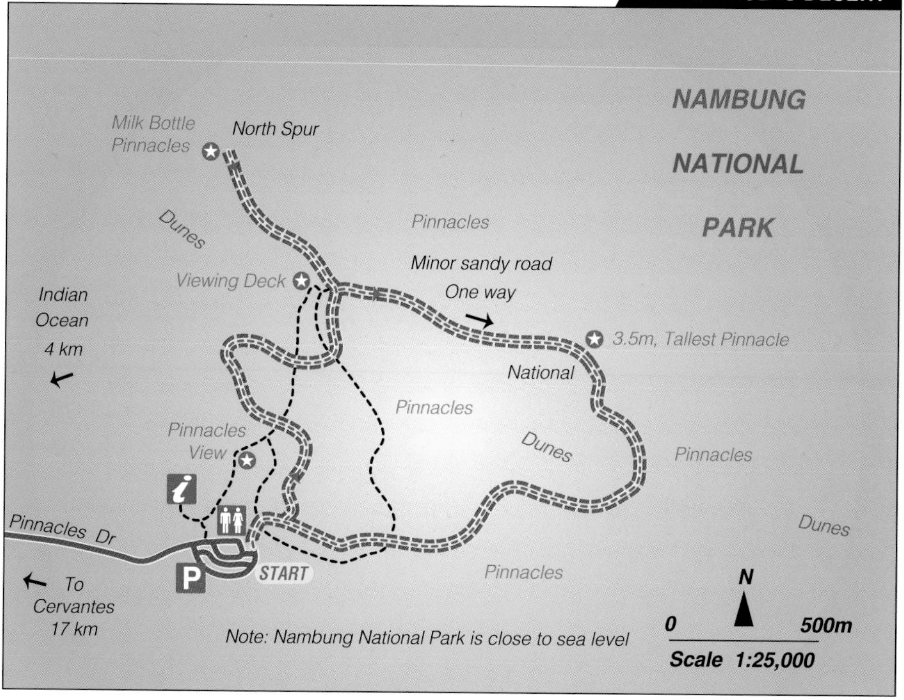

NAMBUNG
NATIONAL
PARK
Milk Bottle Pinnacles
North Spur
Dunes
Pinnacles
Viewing Deck
Minor sandy road
One way
Indian Ocean
4 km
3.5m, Tallest Pinnacle
National
Pinnacles
Pinnacles View
Dunes
Pinnacles
Pinnacles Dr
START
Dunes
To Cervantes
17 km
Pinnacles
N
0
500m
Note: Nambung National Park is close to sea level
Scale 1:25,000

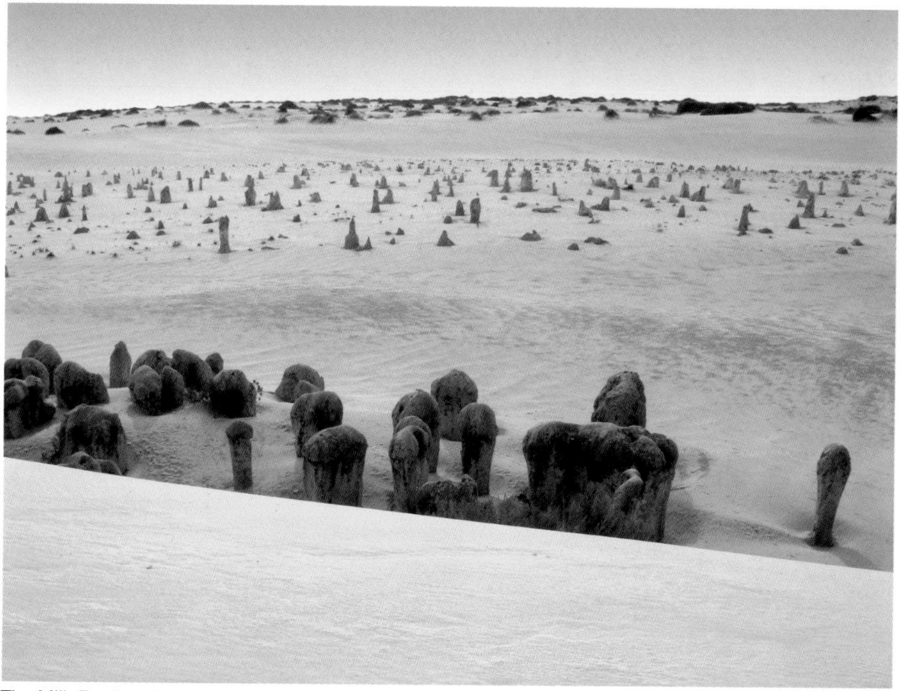

The Milk Bottles, North Spur

Tallest pinnacle

drying of the material forms calcrete. This hard surface capping has been aided by the presence of plants that accentuate the leaching process. Roots sent down by plants have caused cracking and erosion of the underlying soft quartz sand and limestone. Subsequent wind erosion over time has created the columns we see today. The alternate exposure and submerging of pinnacle formation by dune movement is continual.

Despite shifting sands, numerous plants have adapted to these arid conditions. Acacias prefer the leeward side of dunes while succulents and the more salt-resistant or frontline species grow on the windward side of dunes. The further inland, the larger the plant species. Banksias, dryandras and casuarinas are common while some small wildflowers can be viewed in season. Animal life includes emus, kangaroos, skinks, pythons, Goulds monitors, and many birds especially birds of prey and parrots.

There is a rather short walking track circuit from which you see some of the pinnacles. However, we suggest that to fully appreciate the experience, ignore the walk loop, leave your car at the carpark, walk into the desert and complete an alternative 5 km clockwise circuit by foot. Make sure you are totally self-sufficient with water, as none is available in the park. Avoid hot days and preferably walk in early morning or late afternoon for best comfort and photographic conditions. The 5 km suggested walk route includes a side trip to the North Spur. This takes you along much of the sandy road route, so you should take into account the presence of vehicular traffic, which travels a one-way route in a clockwise direction and is usually light so it does not mar the experience.

From the carpark and interpretive centre area, you walk the ongoing road east to a nearby road fork then turn left for great views of pinnacles. Thereafter, a

Galahs on pinnacle

Lizard

major feature of the walk is a viewing deck 1.3 km from the walk start. You get a vista over the Pinnacles and toward the coast. Some 100 m later there is a side track off left to take. Follow North Spur 700 m to the road end where you will find a collection of notable pinnacles called the Milk Bottles, nestled at the foot of an imposing dune system. Here you have a chance to truly appreciate this unique desert environment. The hardened calcrete capping on the milk bottle formations is most noteworthy.

After you complete the side trip you continue along the sandy road for 700 m to be right alongside the highest recorded pinnacle at 3.5 m. Thereafter, the remaining 1.15 km of sandy road needs to be walked back to the carpark amid more pinnacles and interesting desert dune vegetation. Congratulate yourself for completing this very unusual desert walk, which is one of very few desert areas that one can safely traverse on foot.

Wind-scoured pinnacles

MURCHISON GORGE
Kalbarri, Western Australia

Walk:	8 km circuit
Time required:	Including minimal breaks, 3.5 hours
Grade:	One day, medium some rock scrambling involved
Environment:	Cliff-rim and river gorge walk
Last review date:	August 2007
Map reference:	1:100 000 Kalbarri and Map 28
Best time to visit:	May to October. Avoid hot days and the wet season November to April

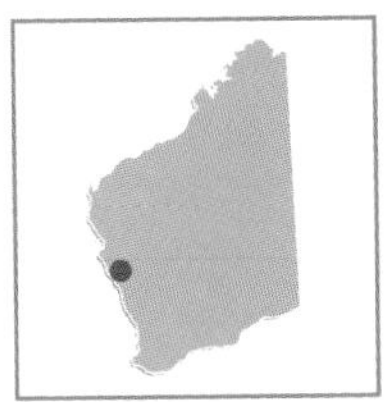

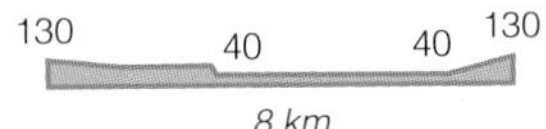

Upstream of the coastal tourist town of Kalbarri, some 600 km north of Perth, the Murchison River flows through stunningly beautiful scenery of reddish-brown rock, glistening white-sand beaches and large rock pools. At Murchison Gorge the river takes an almost complete 7 km loop in one of the most scenic parts of the district. Kalbarri has a large range

Natures Window

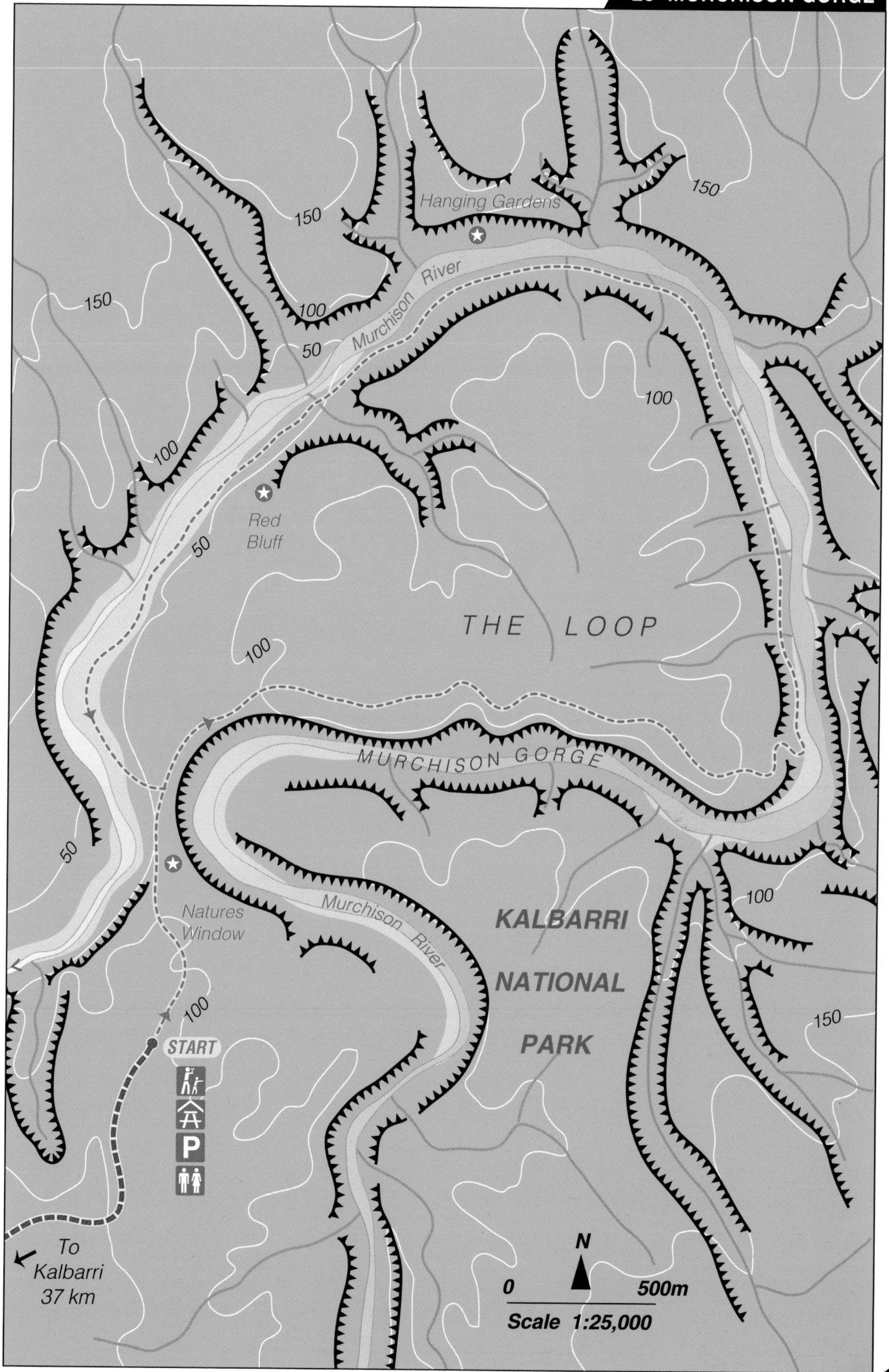
Hanging Gardens
150
150
150
100
50
Murchison River
100
100
Red Bluff
50
THE LOOP
100
MURCHISON GORGE
50
Natures Window
Murchison River
KALBARRI NATIONAL PARK
100
150
100
START
To Kalbarri 37 km
N
0
500m
Scale 1:25,000

Kalbarri	J	F	M	A	M	J	J	A	S	O	N	D	Year
Rain av. mm	6	6	21	24	53	90	73	51	26	23	6	1	379
Temp av. max. °C	33	34	33	28	25	22	21	22	23	25	27	31	27
Temp av. min. °C	19	20	19	15	13	11	10	10	10	12	14	17	14

of accommodation options and tourist information office, so is ideal as a base for this walk.

Approximately 400 millions years ago, a process of sedimentation began to take place. This left a relatively flat plateau which as recently as one million years ago was eroded by the early Murchison River to form the gorge. From its beginnings the river now flows 700 km west to its mouth at Kalbarri.

This part of Australia could be described as geologically stable from its earliest beginnings to the present day; this is evident by the almost perfectly horizontal layering of the Tumblagooda sandstone. The alternating layers of red and white sediments whose origin is both wind and water borne over tidal flats, have formed the relatively soft plateau through which the Murchison River has cut the gorge. Many of the iron oxide coloured sands with their characteristically red hue are in stark contrast to the white sands that can comprise around fifty differing layers within the depth of one metre. It is interesting to note that many of the exposed rock slabs exhibit fine wave action on their horizontal surfaces, some of which contain fossilised tracks of ancient marine creatures.

Tumblagooda sandstone

The flora of this region is predominately arid heathland and Kalbarri National Park is centred in one of the best wildflower regions in Western Australia. The main species you will encounter on this walk include banksias, acacias, grevilleas, grass trees and spinifex. The river forms a corridor of life in this arid wilderness that supports vast numbers of nectar feeding birds and insects. Nocturnal mammals, notably bats, play their vital role in plant pollination. Rock-dwelling kangaroos and wallabies are also prevalent. You will most likely encounter water fowl such as cormorants, black swans and white herons, feeding on aquatic life in the deeper pools.

Eleven kilometres from Kalbarri, on the main Ajana–Kalbarri Road, turn left on to an unsealed road. Two wheel drive vehicles should only attempt this road in dry weather, which may be closed after heavy rain and particularly during the wet season. Beyond the park entrance (note that an entry fee applies) travel 19 km to a 'T' intersection. Here you turn left for 'the Loop'. Proceed a further 7 km to a carpark, toilets, picnic shelters and viewing platform with a view to the Gorge.

This marks the start of one of the most beautiful arid landscape walks in Australia

Murchison Gorge cliffs

via Natures Window and the Loop, where the river turns back on itself. It seems many visitors walk the short distance to Natures Window but few venture further into the equally stunning surrounds. In doing so you will most likely encounter wildlife, have the opportunity to swim the rock pools and laze on the beaches. You need sturdy footwear because of the presence of so much rock and the track to follow is best walked anticlockwise. The route is well defined with many white track markers (some of which have the Loop walk logo) along the way. On rare occasions high water levels of the river could make progress slower. Ensure you carry drinking water, wear a hat and sunscreen.

Take the traditional 500 m tourist walk route north from the carpark down to Natures Window. This feature is on the crest of the narrowest point of the river loop. Barely 300 m separates the river flow; to either side, the cliffs drop away some 100 m to the river below. The views improve significantly as you near the well photographed formation of Natures Window which is a wind-scoured hole in the spur crest.

Once across the narrow crest northwards, on much bare rock, turn to get a great view back towards Natures Window. Here you will find wind-scoured rock caverns with fine examples of sandstone layering. It is important to stay on the marked route and not venture too near potentially unstable cliffs. Note that the return track also joins at this point.

You next climb a little, following the well-marked track route to the highest point along the rim of the Gorge; here the river is 100 m below. Follow the rim track east, past many grass trees until you are

Murchison River

about 3 km from the walk start. Opposite, impressive ravines join the main gorge. Next, the track leaves the rim and descends steeply to the river at a spot where the flow turns abruptly north. There is a fine beach and pool where you meet the river. This could be a great place for a break. Fine, white-trunked red gums contrast with the red cliffs and myriad birds surround you.

From here, follow the track markers north on the west bank, mostly on stratified rock ledges, for about 1.5 km. When the river rises you need to climb on to higher ledges in a few spots. Note: at times of flood, debris is carried along the river and may block access to the route. Negotiating such obstacles may require you to deviate slightly. After this distance you see a rugged, narrow gorge entering the main gorge from the east. Vertical cliff-faces on the north-east side have remarkable 'hanging gardens'.

Gradually the river swings in an arc to flow west then south-west for another 3 km. Along this stretch, beaches and former river bed rock need to be crossed rather than rock ledges as previously traversed. Again, you need to be aware that after floods the track markers on the beaches may be indistinct. There seems to be a profusion of wildflowers on the sandy tracts due to large quantities of available underground water and stronger afternoon sunlight, unobscured by cliffs. You pass a prominent rock outcrop (which we have named Red Bluff) and a deep side canyon. Thereafter, the cliffs on your left give way to a gentle slope. Larger stands of red gums grow in this area. Eventually you reach broad, sandy river terraces immediately west of Natures Window and the near completion of the Loop.

Track markers show the way up to the terraces via a short rocky slope back to Natures Window. It is then a 500 m retrace south up to the carpark.

29 MOUNT BRUCE

Pilbara, Western Australia

Walk:	9.6 km retrace
Time required:	Including minimal breaks, 5 hours
Grade:	One day, medium
Environment:	Remote, exposed, rocky mountain ascent
Last review date:	September 2000 with update from park ranger October 2008
Map reference:	1:100 000 Mount Bruce and Map 29
Best time to visit:	May to September. Avoid November to March

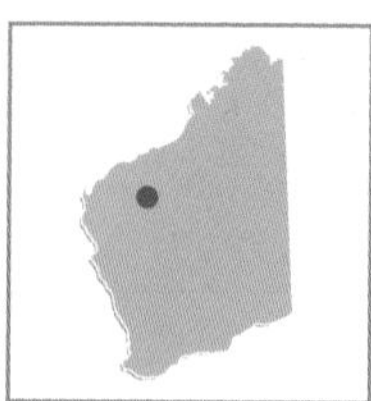

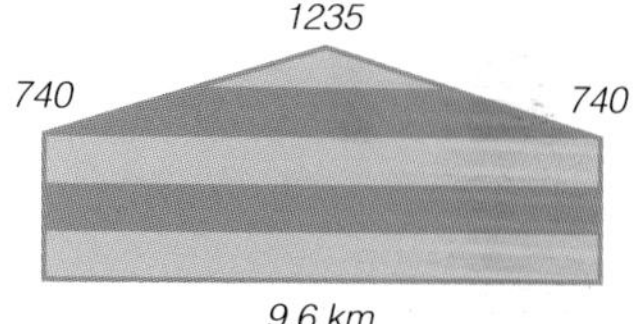

Long regarded as the highest mountain in Western Australia at 1235 m, Mount Bruce was in the 1980s found by iron ore prospecting teams to be a few metres lower than nearby 1250 m Mount Meharry. Early explorer F. T. Gregory traversed the surrounding Hamersley Ranges in the vast Pilbara region in 1861 and named them after his friend Hamersley. The traditional Aboriginal owners of the ranges call them Karijini. This resulted in the naming of the national park which covers the area. Mount Meharry is in an even more remote part of the Hamersley Ranges than Mount Bruce and is effectively inaccessible for walkers. The mining service town of Tom Price is the nearest settlement to Mount Bruce and is some 55 km south-west. Sealed mine access roads can be used to reach attractive Mount Bruce. Despite the remote location, only the last 3.5 km of road to the summit walking trackhead is unsealed.

This exposed peak rises 500 m higher than surrounding plains, consists of very ancient colourful reddish-brown rock with a high content of iron-oxide and silica which features in many of the high cliff-faces. Much of the rock is of square or oblong shape with large flat surfaces. The rock was laid down under an ancient sea and the pressure transformed banded sediments. Later, horizontal pressure caused the rock to buckle and form vertical cracks before lifting it to the surface as dry land. Following the retreat of the sea, erosion of the vertical cracks by streams (which today mostly only flow in the wet season) has created many attractive gorges in the surrounding region. Typically erosion has revealed the present landscape with its prominent banding as seen on Mount Bruce and many other mountains of the region.

Tom Price	J	F	M	A	M	J	J	A	S	O	N	D	Year
Rain av. mm	81	92	64	31	23	28	18	12	3	5	9	39	405
Temp av. max. °C	38	35	34	31	27	23	23	25	29	33	35	38	31
Temp av. min. °C	23	22	20	17	13	8	7	5	11	16	19	22	15

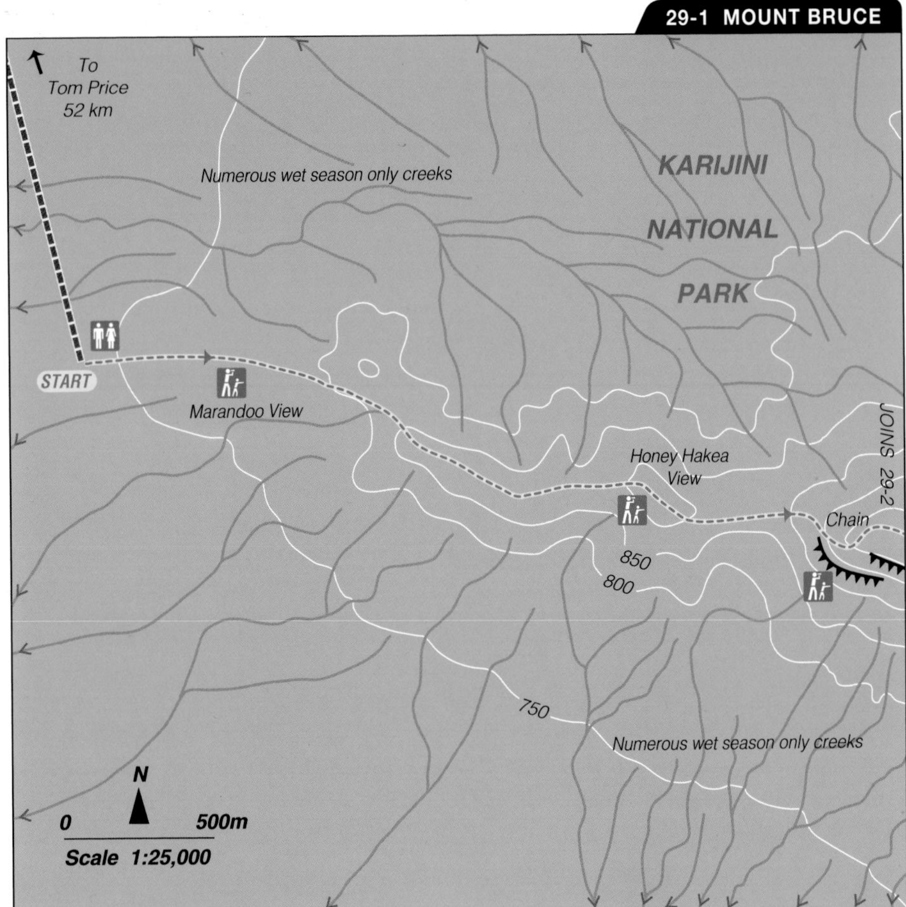

From the trackhead west of the peak there is a pronounced 3 kilometre-long spur to follow. This gives access through cliffs using a short stretch of hand chain. Vegetation, like that of most of the vast Pilbara, is quite sparse and low growing so that panoramic views occur throughout the walk. The outlook includes the huge Marandoo iron ore mine just 2–3 km south of Mount Bruce. You also see the 1 kilometre-long trains that transport the ore to the distant coast. The huge mine complex began operation in 1994 and employees mostly live in Tom Price.

Any ascent of Mount Bruce is best commenced before the heat of the day and you should always carry plenty of water and protect yourself from the strong sunlight. While winter nights can even experience frosts, by midday each day temperatures are usually in excess of 30 degrees and there is little or no shade. Frequently temperatures exceed 40 degrees and on those occasions you should abandon the ascent. Summer and its wet season need to be avoided as cyclones, thunder storms and road closures occur. The district is just north of the Tropic of Capricorn and is best described as a tropical, arid area. There is a quite dramatic seasonal variation and narrow window for walking in comfort and safety.

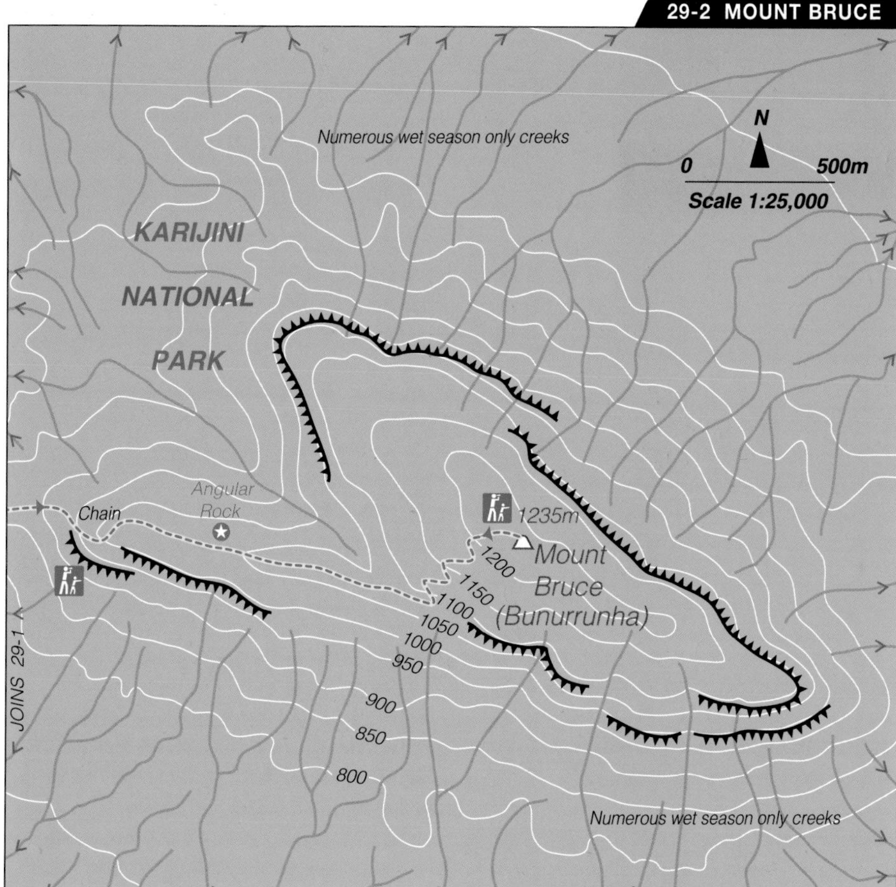

The predominant vegetation is the spiny tufts of the spinifex. There are a few scattered eucalyptus and wildflowers to be seen on the mountain with sparse mulga mainly on surrounding plains. The wildflowers mostly bloom promptly after rain and have an accelerated life cycle. Mulla mulla (of which there are some 35 species) especially the purple-pink varieties and yellow sennas (cassias) are quite attractive. Over the last 20 000 years firestick farming, an Aboriginal form of land management, has evidently been practised. This would no doubt favour the spinifex and other fire tolerant plant species such as hakea and eucalyptus.

Some scrambling at cliff-lines is needed but overall the foot track is very well defined and so is easy to follow. The presence of so many angular rocks along the way means good footwear is essential. At the trackhead carpark there is a toilet and small information shelter.

You begin to climb gradually right from the walk outset. The route is east and remains east for most of the way to the summit. Also the crest of the long access ridge is maintained for all but a short section within the first 1 km. Here you ascend the southern slopes of a small knob on the spur to bring you into a saddle 1.25 km from the walk start. There is a

Iron-oxide cliff

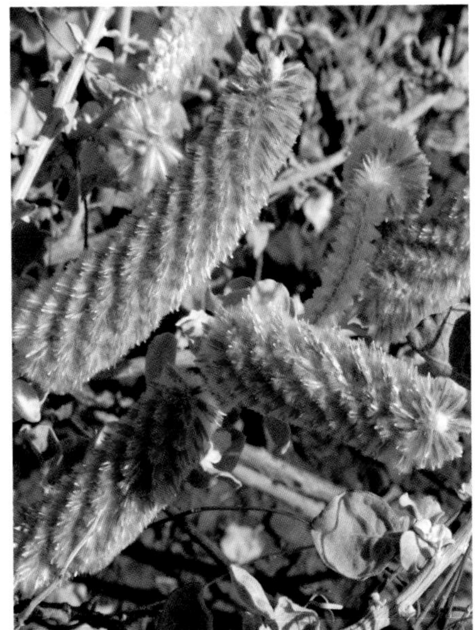
Mulla mulla

named lookout (Marandoo View) towards the Marandoo mine just 250 m up this first stage of the walk, but far better views occur later as you increase height.

Pilbara landscape

After 2.3 km and having gradually achieved 180 m rise in elevation, you reach Honey Hakea View then, soon afterwards, the steepest section. To this point there has even been some fairly level ridge crest walking. Suddenly there is a need to climb through dramatic cliffs and there are many zigzags up to a ledge where a chain is provided to help you. There is then a scramble up a short rock face that requires using your hands to grip the rocks and some extra care is needed. This brings you on to the ridge crest again for a high level fairly flat 1 km walk on remarkable expanses of angular rock. Off right over high cliffs is an almost aerial view of the vast iron ore mine complex and rail shipment system. In other directions there appears a never-ending sea of reddish-brown rocky mountains. The track leads into a saddle at the head of a north-west aligned rocky ravine. The locality seems to be one favoured by many geckos and other lizards.

Termite mounds and spinifex

From this lofty and windy saddle you start a steep zigzag climb for the final 750 m directly to the summit rock cairn at 1235 m. Here you get the feeling of being atop a very high mountain with massive cliffs all around, even though the summit in real height is not so remarkable. Mount Meharry lies south-east, in view about 60 km away.

After a summit break you need to retrace the same track taking particular care in rough, steep sections.

Bearded dragon

NORTHERN TERRITORY

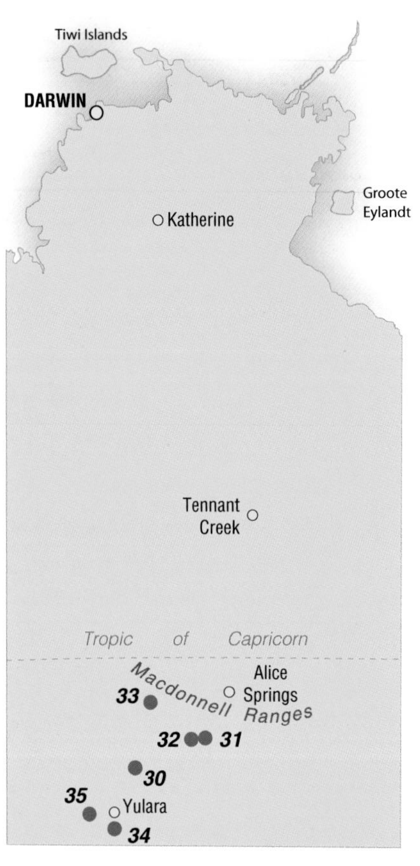

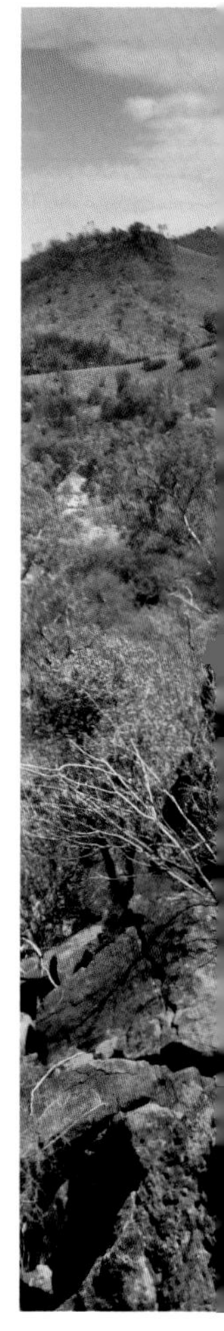

30	Kings Canyon	Watarrka National Park
31	Kalarranga-Mpaara	Finke Gorge National Park
32	Mpulungkinya	Finke Gorge National Park
33	Ormiston Gorge	West Macdonnell National Park
34	Uluṟu Circuit	Uluṟu–Kata Tjuṯa National Park
35	Kata Tjuṯa	Uluṟu–Kata Tjuṯa National Park

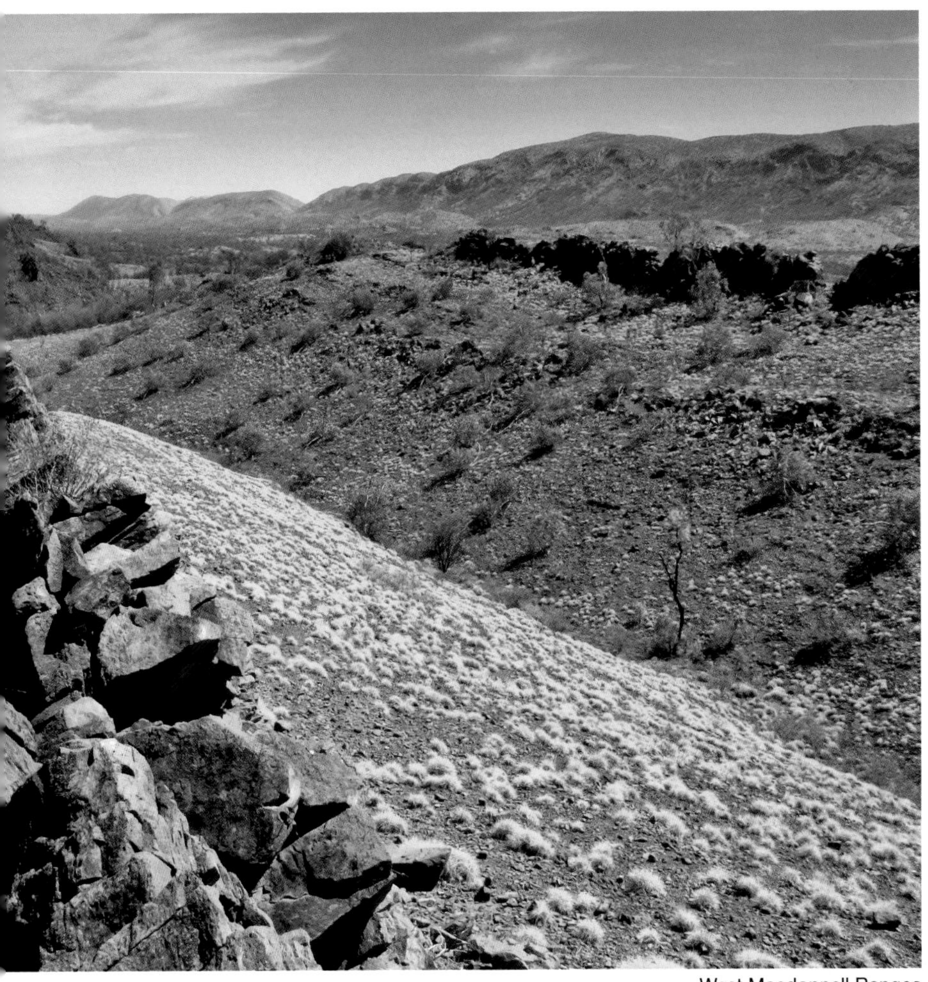

West Macdonnell Ranges

The 'Top End' of the Northern Territory, where the capital Darwin is situated, has terrain affected by heavy tropical monsoon rainfall. Nitmiluk (Katherine Gorge), 300 km south, is a great example of the relentless power of water from the monsoons. Another major attraction of the Top End is Kakadu National Park. The climate is often too hot for comfortable walking. By contrast the southern part of the territory or 'Red Centre' has a longer seasonal window for walking. There are truly great walks in remote Kings Canyon and Palm Valley. Around Alice Springs are the magnificent Macdonnell Ranges with the long-distance Larapinta Trail and Ormiston Gorge. Southwards at Kata Tjuṯa are massive domes through which a walk to the Valley of the Winds can be enjoyed. Nearby, Uluṟu lies almost at the geographic centre of the continent. The base walk around this huge rock is popular. The red centre is renowned for red sands, desert flora and dramatic sunsets.

KINGS CANYON

George Gill Range, Northern Territory

Walk:	10.5 km circuit
Time required:	Including minimal breaks, 4 hours 30 minutes
Grade:	One day, medium
Environment:	Remote sandstone canyon
Last review date:	September 2008
Map reference:	Map 30
Best time to visit:	May to September. Avoid hot days November to March

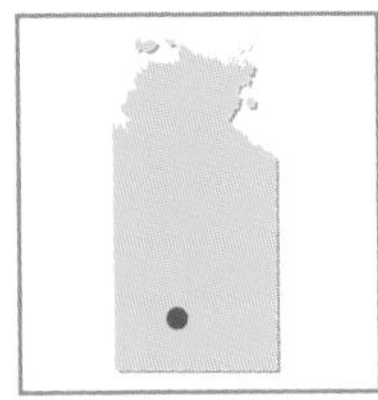

Watarrka National Park protects rugged gorges and waterholes in the very remote western end of the George Gill Range, some 450 km south-west of Alice Springs. The range abuts the enormous Western Desert plains. It is characteristically rugged with high cliffs allowing views across the vast plains of the Red Centre. Within the park, Kings Canyon is a scenic highlight with its red cliffs up to 100 m high. This loop walk, with several short side trips, leads through spectacular terrain including very special spots known as the Lost City and the Garden of Eden. You need to avoid hot days, start early in the day, wear a hat and sunscreen and carry plenty of water. (At least one litre per hour per person is recommended to avoid dehydration.) Emergency radio call devices (ECD) are located at several key spots along the way as a safety precaution.

Camping, other accommodation options, fuel and supplies are available at the nearby Kings Canyon resort. Although there is no camping facilities in the immediate canyon region, there are good picnic facilities and shelters at the main access carpark.

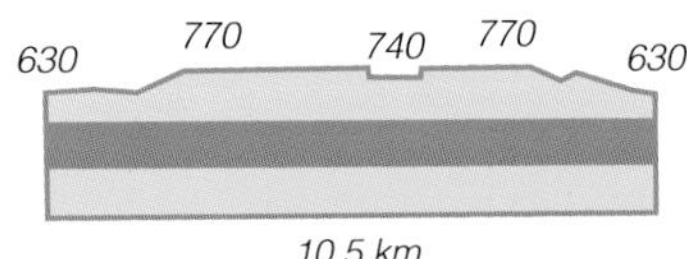

Kings Canyon gained worldwide fame as the movie *Priscilla Queen of the Desert* portrayed the three main characters climbing to the canyon rim. This walk suggestion explores the lower and upper reaches of the canyon including the rim.

Start the walk from the carpark and head along the excellent, easy grade Kings Creek Track as the creek meanders its way upstream for 1.25 km. You pass a cairn dedicated to John Cotterill after 500 m. He was a cattleman who played an integral part in opening the district to tourism. Onwards a few metres, you fork right at a track junction, which marks your later ongoing route. This first part of the walk takes you to a viewing deck and seats

Watarrka		J	F	M	A	M	J	J	A	S	O	N	D	Year
Rain	av. mm	32	47	28	15	23	20	15	5	7	25	44	36	293
Temp	av. max. °C	38	37	34	30	24	21	22	24	30	33	35	36	30
Temp	av. min. °C	24	23	20	17	11	7	6	8	13	17	20	22	16

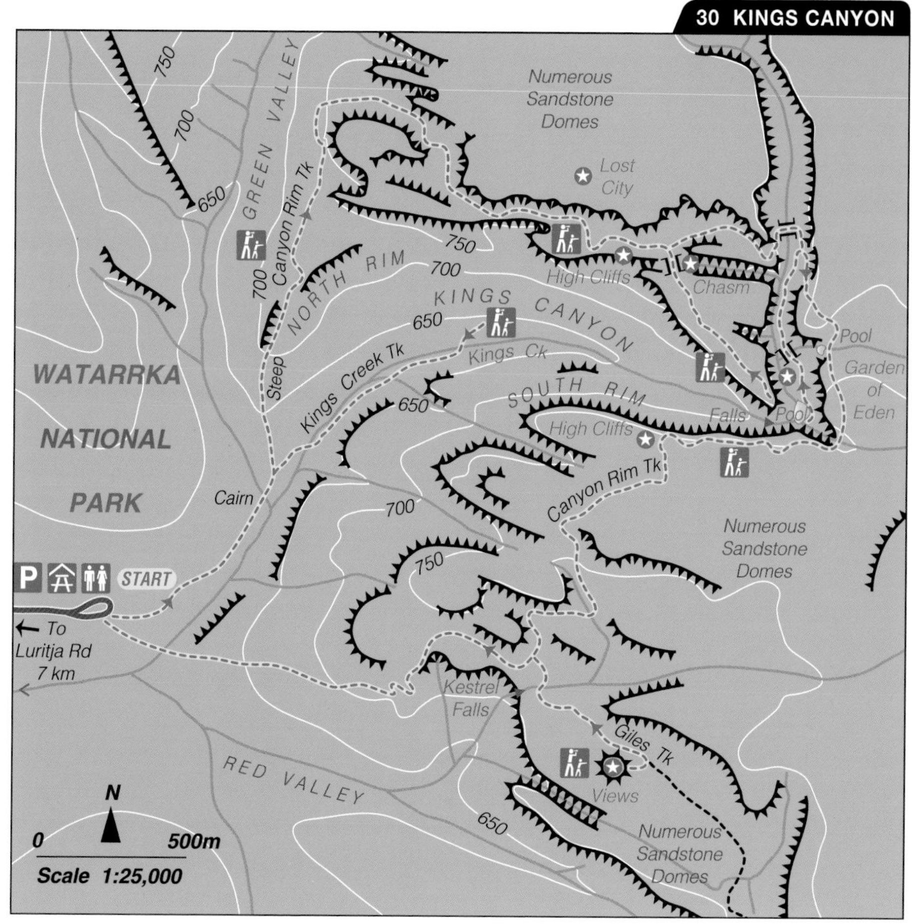

near the uppermost area of the canyon floor and creek valley. The deck affords fine views of the canyon walls towering some 100 m above you and to points where you will climb later. Red gums line the creek bed providing extensive shade. Many and varied plants grow under the canopy. The holly grevillea is a notable specimen here as is the very special Macdonnell Ranges cycad (*Macrozamia macdonnellii*). These cycads are reputedly up to 400 years old and the species has survived for some 50 million years since the time when rainforest covered inland Australia. It grows in cool, sheltered microclimates.

Beyond the viewing deck is a sacred place of the local Luritja Aboriginal people and you are asked to respect this culturally and environmentally sensitive area. Be content to view from the deck and not venture further upstream.

Two types of sandstone rock make up the canyon walls and the rubble-covered lower slopes. The lower reddish-brown rock is Carmichael sandstone some 440 million years old and the cliffs are of Mereenie sandstone some 400 million years old. The latter is hard and brittle with a high content of quartz grains cemented together with silica. It is said that coastal tidal flats

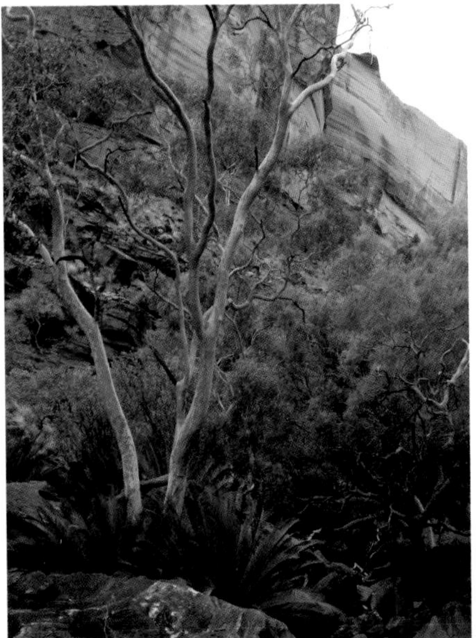

Kings Creek and cycads

followed by sand dunes once covered the region to form the sandstone. The land was geologically uplifted some 350 million years ago and has since been heavily eroded into fantastic forms.

Birds of the parrot family, minors, honeyeaters and fairy martins are the more common along the usually dry watercourse.

Retrace the 750 m back to the track junction and turn right to start climbing a steep spur crest to the tops and a fantastic plateau. This involves negotiating rocky steps as you climb Canyon Rim Track. The views to the canyon floor improve as you rise. Kings Creek valley is to your right and Green Valley is to your left. Cliffs begin to abut the track and in windy conditions you are advised to stay well clear of the edges. As you reach the tops you need to watch track markers closely so as not to lose your way. If necessary back-track to locate the appropriate next marker. In parts, the nearby cliff-rim becomes quite unstable and there are no protective measures, so keep well clear. The track too is quite rocky

Kings Canyon south rim

and uneven as it trends eastwards. It is, however, refreshing to not have many signs, fences and other man-made structures spoiling the natural wilderness atmosphere.

The plateau has a labyrinth of stratified domes somewhat akin to the beehive formations of the Bungle Bungles of Western Australia. Here they are known as the Lost City. There is a maze of domes intersected by cross-bedded ravines. Past earth movements squeezed and cracked the sandstone into joints that criss-cross the plateau at right angles forming blocks. Subsequently, weathering along the joints has created the dome shapes. Lilliput from Gullivers Travels is represented in a collection of pint-sized sandstone spires. Elsewhere, weathering of the stone has emulated chess pieces. At two points along the way you can look down to the canyon floor viewing deck where you were earlier.

After 4 km of walking you reach a track junction on the plateau and a 1 km return side trip off right is highly recommended. Near the outset, a footbridge spans a ravine at a remarkable example of cross-bedding of the rock. The way is south-east to Cotterills Lookout, an outlook above usually dry waterfalls at the head of the main canyon. On the way, you cross rock platforms amid very rugged terrain. At the track end the view is across the by now narrow main canyon from the northern rim to the southern rim. A large pool is below at the head of the waterfall. Also in view is the upper canyon in which the remarkable Garden of Eden lies, prolific with more cycads.

Retrace the 500 m back across the bridge and chasm and turn right. The way is due east down a series of steps and cliffs into the Garden of Eden within another 500 m. Here you are again surrounded by cycads and red gums. Cross the bridge which spans the creek and start to climb the eastern cliffs to some steps then turn

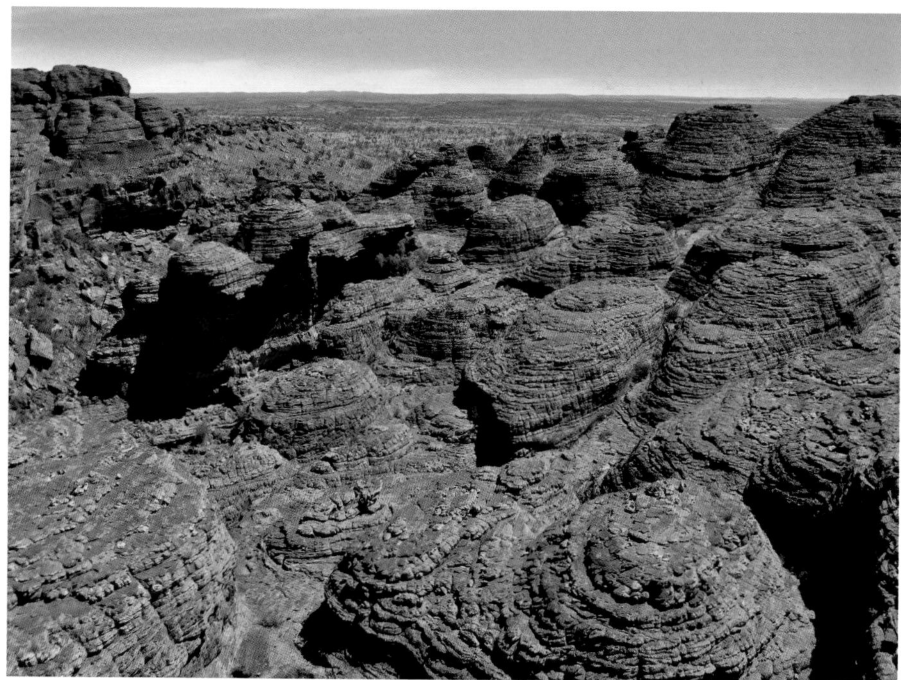

Sandstone rock domes

right (south) along the canyon in the Garden of Eden. This starts another 1 km return side trip southwards to the quiet seclusion and shady confines of the garden for a suggested idyllic lunch break. A pleasant beach under towering cliffs, by the large, deep and reliable pool at a bend in the gorge awaits you. The water tends to attract many birds because of an aquifer at the sandstone cliffs. The Garden of Eden cuts deep into the sandstone and taps an elevated (perched) water table at a layer of shale. This water supports lush ferns, cypress pines, cycads and red gums.

After lunch retrace the 500 m and climb the steps at the eastern side of the gorge on to the plateau. Next, head southwards then generally south-westwards. More cliff-rim views of the main canyon from its south rim are seen. You again pass through cross-bedded rock terrain with innumerable sandstone beehive-shaped domes. Like the rest of the plateau, vegetation is sparse. Gradually you descend through very rugged cliff-lines and reach a junction with the long-distance Giles Track. This is also near Kestrel Falls at the southern edge of the plateau and at Red Valley. Over time erosive forces of wind and water have created sandstone depressions, waterholes, chasms, cliffs and other formations. A number of species of birds of prey including kestrels can be found in the Kings Canyon region.

A final side trip of 1 km return on the Giles Track is a highlight of the entire walk. This takes you through an area of real wilderness to some of the best sandstone domes and broad views to the vast Western Desert plains. Track markers show the way and you should count them as you progress. Between markers 8 and 9 is a prominent rock stack which should be climbed to get an all-encompassing view of the domes. They almost resemble giant cow pats. You are less than 2 km from the walk end so relax and enjoy the views before retracing the 500 m to the main track circuit.

Turn left down via zigzags past usually dry Kestrel Falls where more great views of Red Valley and the vast plains exist. The track descends west from here directly into the carpark.

View from the Giles Track

31 KALARRANGA-MPAARA

Palm Valley, Northern Territory

Walk:	8 km circuit
Time required:	Including minimal breaks, 3 hours
Grade:	One day, medium
Environment:	Rocky sandstone cliffs, stacks and gullies
Last review date:	September 2008
Map reference:	Map 31
Best time to visit:	May to September. Avoid November to March

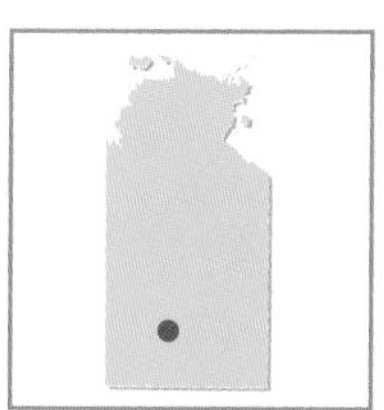

Some 125 km south-west of Alice Springs via sealed Larapinta Drive is the Aboriginal community of Hermannsburg and the usually dry Finke River. Access to this spectacular walk is from the west bank of the Finke River and south via designated four-wheel-drive track for a further 18 km. However, during dry weather, with care and a reasonably high ground clearance, most two-wheel-drive vehicles can travel the full distance. The river bed is crossed four times and for a few hundred metres of the way downstream, the river bed is used. A few short, sandy spots exist and where you enter the Finke Gorge National Park you must drive across an electrified cattle grid. The last section of four-wheel-drive track leads west up the broad Palm Creek subsidiary valley to a good campground with toilet block, solar-heated showers and information shelter. Any water available is untreated so you must carry plenty with you.

At camp especially, keep everything including shoes and clothing within the

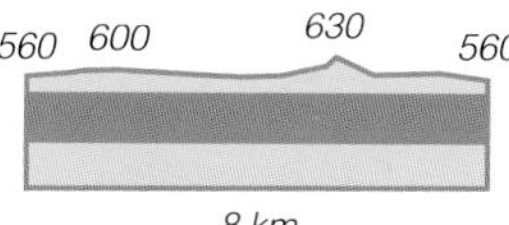

vehicle as dingoes will steal almost anything from the unwary. Around camp you are likely to see birds of the parrot family, such as corellas, cockatoos and the brilliant green Port Lincoln ringneck parrot.

South-east of the camp some 750 m distance is another information shelter and carpark at the access roadway. This marks the start of two adjoining walk circuits, which we suggest you combine to create a walk that will no doubt linger in your mind for life. These are the Kalarranga Walk 1.5 km long (45 minutes) and the Mpaara Walk 5 km long (1 hour 45 minutes), both of which we suggest you walk clockwise. Carry water and use sun protection. Alice Springs is the nearest place for accommodation and supplies.

From the camp take the good foot track south-east for the 750 m then start the Kalarranga Walk loop. Gradually

Alice Springs		J	F	M	A	M	J	J	A	S	O	N	D	Year
Rain	av. mm	37	42	31	17	19	14	14	9	8	22	27	37	279
Temp	av. max. °C	36	34	33	28	23	20	20	23	27	31	34	35	29
Temp	av. min. °C	21	21	18	13	8	5	4	6	10	15	18	20	13

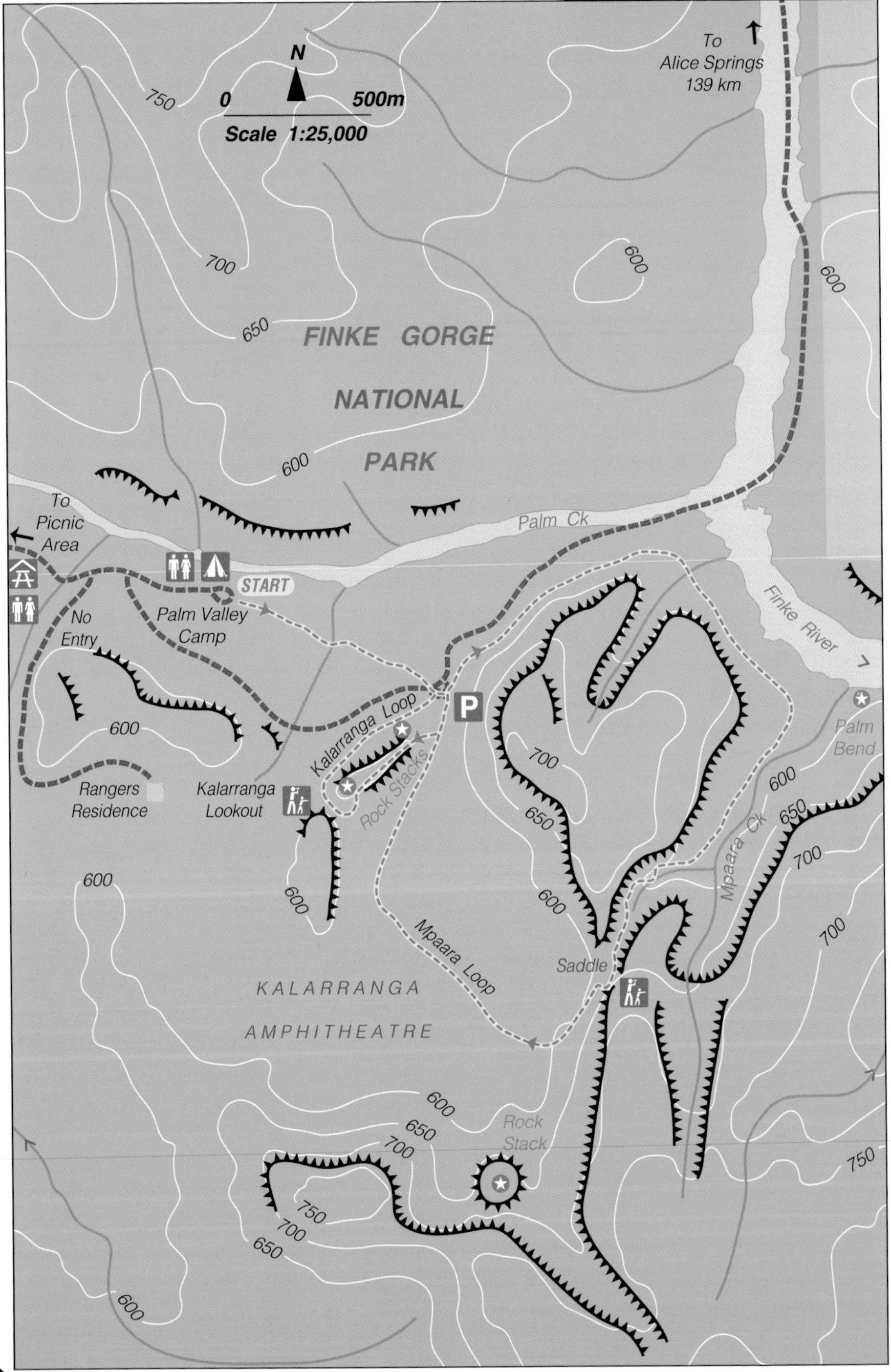

To Alice Springs 139 km

0 500m
Scale 1:25,000

FINKE GORGE NATIONAL PARK

750
700
650
600

To Picnic Area

Palm Ck

START

Palm Valley Camp

No Entry

Rangers Residence

Kalarranga Lookout

Kalarranga Loop

Rock Stacks

P

Finke River

Palm Bend

Mpaara Ck

Mpaara Loop

Saddle

KALARRANGA AMPHITHEATRE

Rock Stack

NT

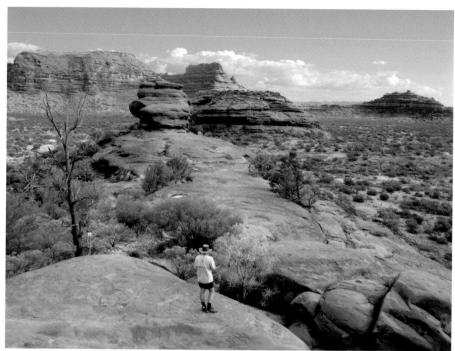

Kalarranga–Mparra rock stacks

climb south-west and turn right (west) at a junction to climb a little further on to a flattish bare rock ridge with two prominent rock stacks on it. Pause here for a 360 degree view from this ridge. It is especially good west upstream along Palm Creek and south to the huge Kalarranga rock amphitheatre surrounded by massive reddish-brown cliffs and rock stacks. At the second rock stack on the ridge the views are even better. From here you begin to descend and soon turn west then north-east to start the return to the carpark. This takes you near the base of the aforementioned ridge and directly back to the information shelter for a suggested short break.

The Mpaara Walk circuits what is essentially a very large rock stack or small plateau. Proceed north-east, downhill past rugged cliff-bases towards the confluence

Kalarranga Amphitheatre

Mpaara Rock

of Palm Creek and the Finke River. Once beside the broad, sandy Finke River turn right to walk near the banks towards some red cabbage palms at Palm Bend. Here the palms grow on average three times faster than the specimens in Palm Valley itself. This is due to the soil being deeper and more fertile with a permanent shallow water table. There are also large sandy beaches adjacent. The Finke is the largest river in central Australia.

Soon you reach the confluence of Mpaara Creek and the Finke River. Follow the well-marked track south-south-west up Mpaara Creek where you are amid huge cliffs, overhangs and caves. Towards the creek headwaters the track rises steeply to a saddle. Here you are suddenly confronted with the same huge amphitheatre and massive rock stacks seen before, but from a very different aspect. A rest and perhaps lunch is suggested near this saddle, A few shaded spots are available.

Next, descend to the floor of the amphitheatre via some short zigzags. Once down, the track swings north-west then north-east across fairly flat terrain. Plants that can withstand very tough environmental conditions, such as spinifex, senna, hakea, acacia and callitris, thrive. The track returns you directly to the carpark and access road. Finally, cross the road and retrace the 750 m on the foot track north-west down into camp.

MPULUNGKINYA

Palm Valley, Northern Territory

Walk:	13 km circuit
Time required:	Including minimal breaks, 5 hours 30 minutes
Grade:	One day, medium
Environment:	Arid rock landscapes and rare palm-filled gorge
Last review date:	September 2008
Map reference:	Map 32
Best time to visit:	May to September. Avoid November to March

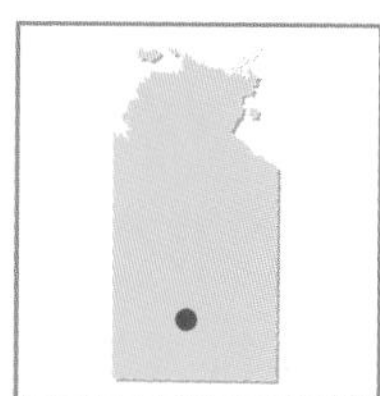

Palm Valley is famous for the endemic red cabbage palm (*Livingstonia australis*) that mainly grows along Palm Creek. There are reputedly only 1200 mature palms some of which are close to 300 years old and up to 26 m tall. Over the full 60 km square occurrence some 12 300 palms have been counted and protected within national park. The palm is a relic species from millions of years ago when rainforest existed in central Australia. They grow in a magnificent reddish-brown gorge and this walk to see the palms is most rewarding. Also seen are many cycads which date back to prehistoric rainforest conditions, however these cycads are far more widespread. Both types of palm only occur in sheltered and shaded places. Alice Springs has the nearest accommodation and supply options.

In remote country, 125 km south-west of Alice Springs via sealed Larapinta Drive, is the Aboriginal community of Hermannsburg and the usually dry Finke River. Access to this walk is from the west

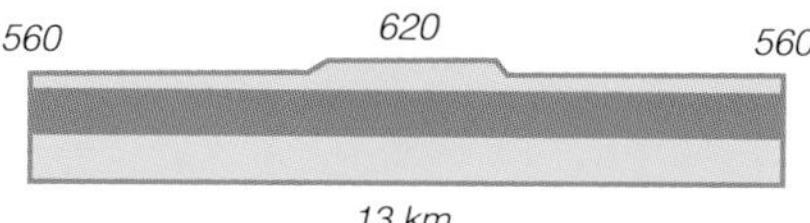

bank of the Finke River and south via a designated four-wheel-drive track for a further 18 km. However, during dry weather, with care and a reasonably high ground clearance, most two-wheel-drive vehicles can travel the full distance. The river bed is crossed four times and for a few hundred metres of the way downstream, the river bed is used. A few short, sandy spots exist and where you enter the Finke Gorge National Park you must drive across an electrified cattle grid. The last section of road leads west up the broad Palm Creek subsidiary valley to a good campground with toilet block, solar heated showers and information shelter. Any water available is untreated so you must carry plenty with you.

At camp especially, keep everything including shoes and clothing within the

Alice Springs	J	F	M	A	M	J	J	A	S	O	N	D	Year
Rain av. mm	37	42	31	17	19	14	14	9	8	22	27	37	279
Temp av. max. °C	36	34	33	28	23	20	20	23	27	31	34	35	29
Temp av. min. °C	21	21	18	13	8	5	4	6	10	15	18	20	13

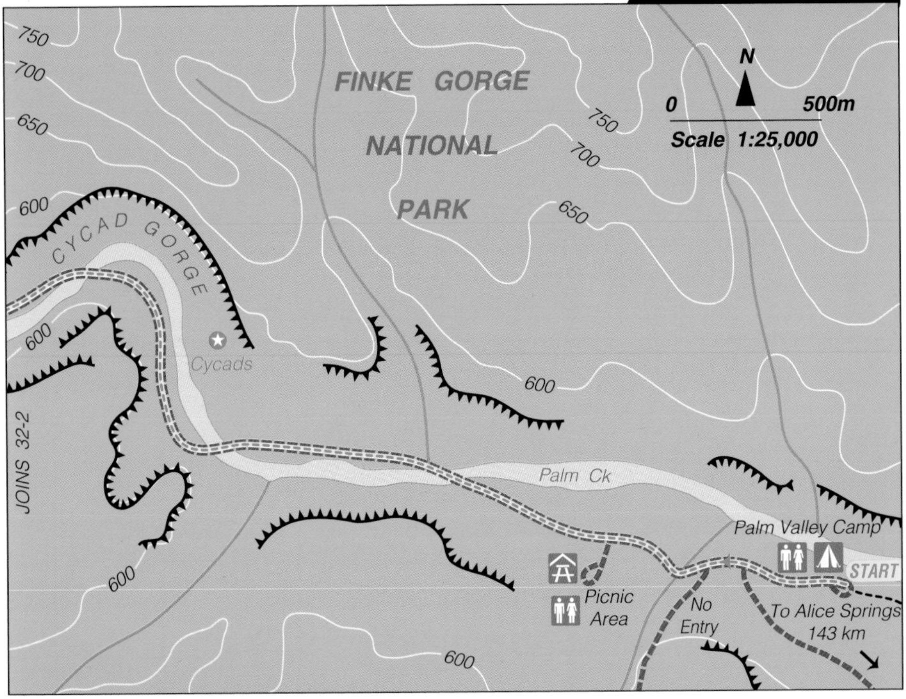

FINKE GORGE NATIONAL PARK
0 500m
Scale 1:25,000
N
750
700
650
600
CYCAD GORGE
Cycads
JOINS 32-2
Palm Ck
Palm Valley Camp
START
Picnic Area
No Entry
To Alice Springs 143 km

Red cabbage palms

750
700
650
600
GORGE
Palm Grove
Steps
Arankaia Loop
Shelter
PLATEAU
Mpulungkinya Loop
Palm Ck
JOINS 32-1
Rock Overhang
FINKE GORGE
NATIONAL
PARK
PALM
VALLEY
N
0 500m
Scale 1:25,000

Palm Valley gorge

vehicle as dingoes will steal almost anything from the unwary. Around camp you are likely to see zebra finches, crested pigeons, birds of prey and birds of the parrot family, such as corellas, cockatoos and the brilliant green Port Lincoln ringneck parrot.

Beyond camp a very rough four-wheel-drive road leads west past a picnic area 700 m away and up Palm Creek valley for a further 3.3 km to the road end and an information shelter. Here the Mpulungkinya 5 km walk loop begins, taking about 3 hours. This area is under the custodianship of the local Arrernte Aborigines. We strongly recommend not driving beyond the camp as damage to any vehicle is possible. Also, walking tends to be just as fast as four-wheel-drive travel. Intense reddish-brown sandstone cliffs with high iron-oxide content line both sides of Palm Creek with cycads in shaded areas of the south-facing cliffs so walking is most pleasant.

Walk the 4 km from camp west along the four-wheel-drive track. This includes four crossings of Palm Creek. You then start the Mpulungkinya walk clockwise following blue track markers to climb rock ledges and cliffs to a track junction within 400 m. There are good views, especially as you reach the cliff-rim and junction vicinity. The right fork is the short Arankaia Walk for tour groups and we suggest you keep left heading south-west. After a further short rise you cross a reasonably flat plateau through spinifex, ghost gums and acacias for 1.4 km. This brings you to an outlook at a cliff-rim with broad views upstream to part of the vast catchment of Palm Creek. In view are distant cliffs and rock stacks with stands of palms and cycads. Descend left (south-east) under rock overhangs to the creek bed, turn right and walk west about 200 m to a good lunch spot in shade on flat rocks near large pools. This is near the upper limit of the main gorge.

After lunch, follow the gorge downstream to see the best of the palms for 3 km and cross the stream bed through thick palm groves in two places. You will note that only the juvenile red cabbage palms have the red colouring. The age of the palms can be dated by the leaf rings on their trunks. You will also see tadpoles, frogs, dragon flies and evidence in the sand of snakes. About midway along the distance, you pass prominent steps up cliffs which mark the Arankaia Walk. Unless you want to climb the steps for a gorge view then retrace down them, you need simply continue down the creek bed eastwards back to the information shelter and retrace the 4 km back to camp. You could consider walking at least part of the dry creek bed instead of the four-wheel-drive track. The creek leads right past the camp.

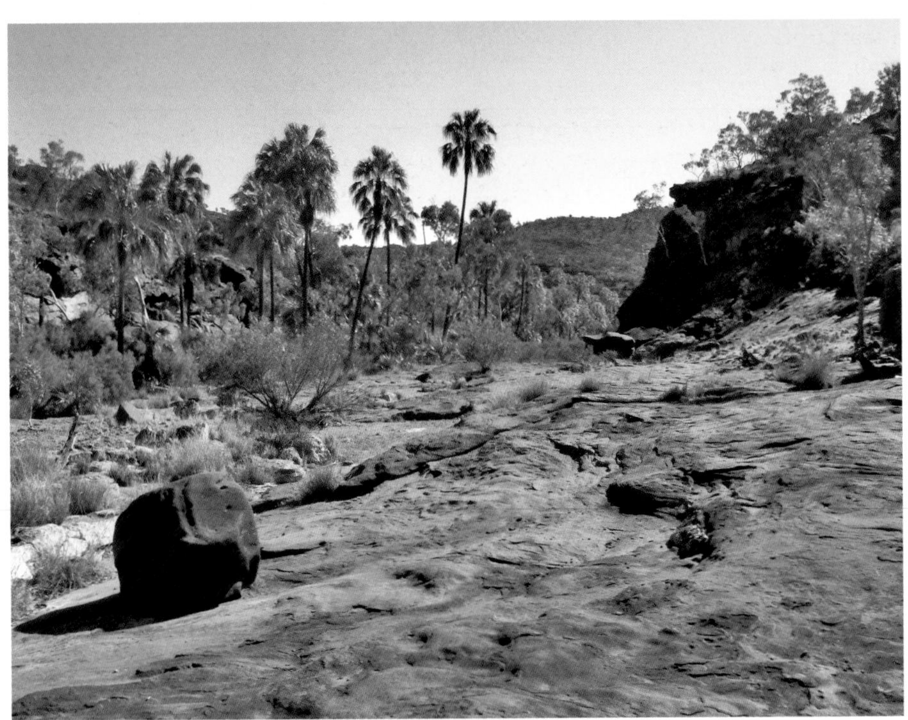

Palm Valley

33 ORMISTON GORGE

West Macdonnell Ranges, Northern Territory

Walk:	8.5 km circuit
Time required:	Including minimal breaks, 4 hours
Grade:	One day, medium
Environment:	Rugged, arid gorge, good views
Last review date:	September 2008
Map reference:	Map 33
Best time to visit:	May to September. Avoid November to March

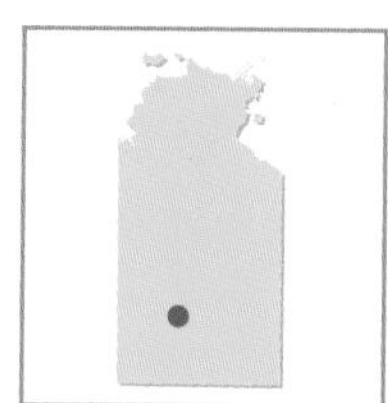

Ormiston Gorge is a significant central Australian attraction for both tourists and walkers alike. Ormiston Creek has carved a very rugged gorge through two pronounced tiers of red quartzite rock ridge to form huge walls and to drain large Ormiston Pound just upstream of the ridge. A loop walk leads through exceptionally beautiful red centre terrain and includes a near permanent waterhole up to 14 m deep. A ranger station, good picnic area

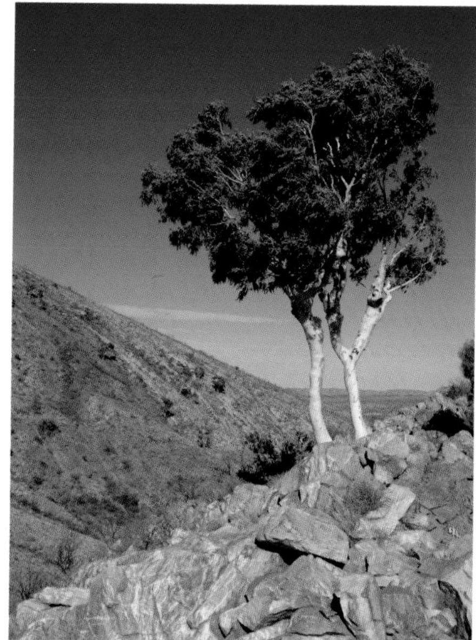

Ghost gums

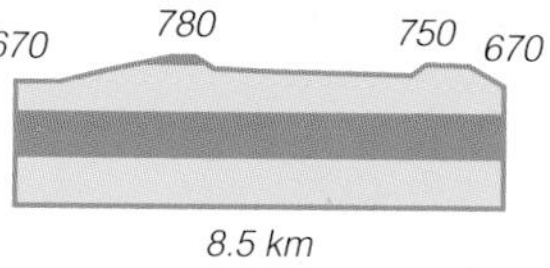

and campground are at the walk start. This is some 132 km west of Alice Springs via Larapinta Drive and Namatjira Drive. Ormiston Creek is a tributary of the Finke River, which is the biggest river in central Australia. The long-distance Larapinta Walking Trail also passes through the picnic and camp area. A short section of it is used for this suggested gorge circuit.

As with all walks in the outback, you should carry plenty of water. Start the walk early before the main heat of the day and avoid hot days. We recommend you walk the loop anticlockwise. Alice Springs is the nearest place with full accommodation and supplies.

Start from the visitor centre and follow the Larapinta Trail with its blue track markers south-east parallel to the access road and near the banks of Ormiston Creek. After 600 m, cross the creek to its east bank and 100 m later fork left as you leave the Larapinta Trail and creek flats to follow the gorge circuit. You climb a spur and walk generally eastwards through the head of gullies for 2 km to a saddle and the south rim of the massive Ormiston Pound.

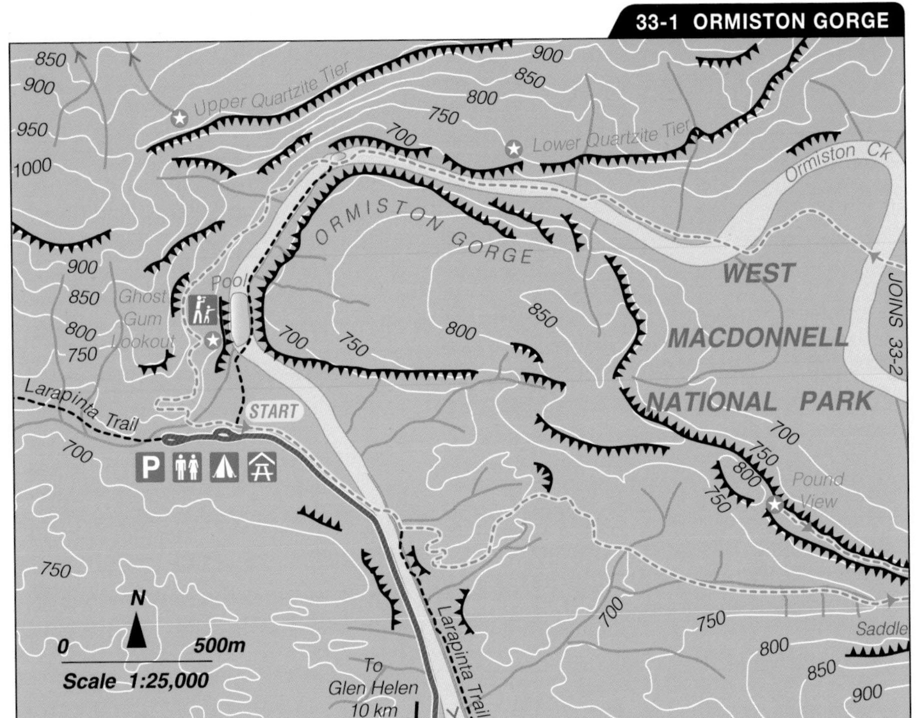

Spinifex covers the otherwise barren slopes except for a few acacias (mulga) and stunted ghost gums. The loose, rocky, infertile surface has little soil for vegetation to take hold. Shale and small rock rubble covers the track. Red and yellow tonings predominate everywhere and the freshness of morning light creates great contrasts. This landscape and indeed much of the Macdonnell Ranges has a beauty all of its own, well recognised by many artists and photographers, including the famous Aboriginal artist Albert Namatjira.

At the saddle, you turn left to the rim of the spectacular pound. This side trip 1 km return up the rock spine is your only elevated view of the whole of the pound formation and what a view it is. It encompasses the head of Ormiston Gorge, the lower and upper quartzite tiers of rock and distant pound perimeter cliffs as far away as Mount Giles to the east. Right on the rim crest are fine specimens of white-barked ghost gums (*Corymbia aparrerinja*). After rains, wildflowers are often seen along this rim. The desert rose, Sturt desert peas, native hops and daisies create a blaze of colour in this otherwise barren wilderness. These high tops can be windy and exposed, so we suggest you retrace the 500 m to the saddle then turn left (east) to descend across a small gully and on to a second gully within 500 m for a possible lunch break at a usually dry waterfall. There

Alice Springs	J	F	M	A	M	J	J	A	S	O	N	D	Year
Rain av. mm	37	42	31	17	19	14	14	9	8	22	27	37	279
Temp av. max. °C	36	34	33	28	23	20	20	23	27	31	34	35	29
Temp av. min. °C	21	21	18	13	8	5	4	6	10	15	18	20	13

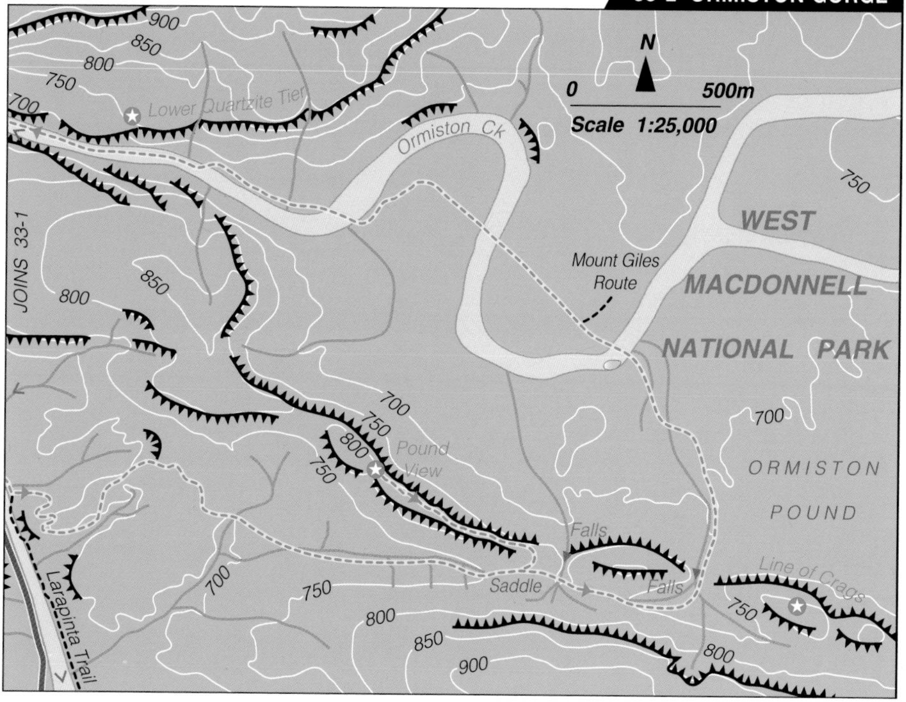

33-2 ORMISTON GORGE

Ormiston Pound

is a little shade at this spot. The area is remarkable for its line of folded, almost pleated strata, which are set on the slopes of a main range as if along a geological fault line.

Next, you head north down to the pound floor and within 1 km you meet and cross Ormiston Creek at a waterhole. Spinifex is the main vegetation except along the usually dry creek where ghost gums occur. Once across the creek, avoid the route off right to Mount Giles. It has orange track markers. Continue north-west across the pound floor and over the creek twice more within 1 km then head down the north bank towards the upper entrance of Ormiston Gorge. You are close to huge cliffs as you enter the gorge and are forced to walk the creek bed westwards.

Ormiston Pound floor

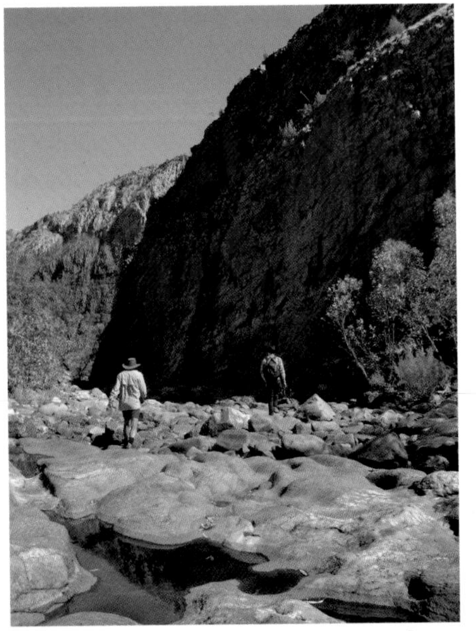

Ormiston Gorge

The creek bed is very rocky and includes some mudstone. After 1.2 km of walking between the spectacular cliffs, you reach a waterhole. Here you should look right and locate ascending track markers to Ghost Gum Lookout, 700 m further on via slopes high above the creek. Climb to the lookout for great views back up the gorge. Another large waterhole is seen directly below. Finally, descend via concrete steps for 400 m to the carpark and walk end, passing twisted layers of limestone, dolomite and mudstone formed about 800 million years ago. These are seen as rock ribs slanting across the hillside.

ULUṞU CIRCUIT

Red Centre, Northern Territory

Walk:	10.7 km circuit
Time required:	Including minimal breaks, 3 hours 30 minutes
Grade:	One day, medium
Environment:	Desert and monolith
Last review date:	September 2008
Map reference:	1:100 000 Uluṟu–Kata Tjuṯa National Park (limited use) and Map 34
Best time to visit:	May to September. Avoid November to March

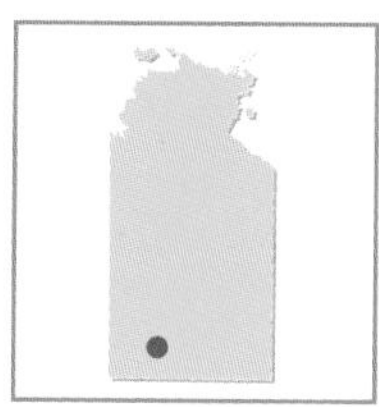

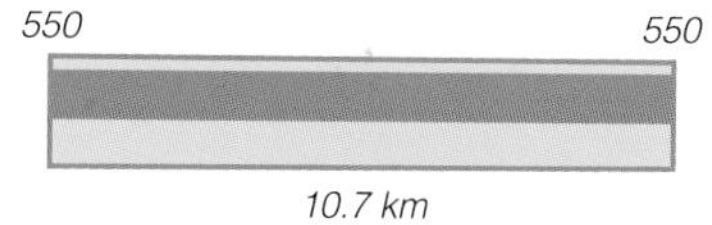

Uluṟu is second only to the Great Barrier Reef in importance as a unique Australian tourist attraction. It is a national icon and was previously known as Ayers Rock. It is 470 km by road south-west of Alice Springs. 'The Alice' is the most isolated sizeable town in Australia, so to say Uluṟu is isolated is quite an understatement.

The Uluṟu landscape consists of undulating dune country with vivid desert colours, lakes of dry salts and unusual plants and wildlife. Uluṟu itself is a vast rock mass protruding from under the desert sands with a circumference of 9.4 km and rising 343 m above the desert plains.

The A<u>n</u>angu have interesting stories of the creation of Uluṟu, which can best be appreciated at the cultural centre. The western scientific theory states that 550 million years ago, the early Petermann Ranges to the west were very much higher than today. Erosion produced layers of debris in fan-shaped horizontal flows which were subsequently covered by rising sea levels and further sediments. The enormous pressure gave rise to arkose, a sedimentary rock rich in feldspar and iron. Tectonic pressure buckled the layers into folds. Eventually the relentless forces of erosion exposed a near vertical, stratified section, which has been smoothed to the shape we see today. Uluṟu owes its red hue to the oxidation of ancient iron minerals laid down aeons ago.

Uluṟu is situated on A<u>n</u>angu Aboriginal land, leased to Parks Australia as the Uluṟu–Kata Tjuṯa National Park. It is managed with joint custodianship. Aboriginal law therefore must be respected in conjunction with national park regulations. An important belief is that the land and the people are as one in a living cultural landscape. Traditional Aboriginal law (Tjukurpa) treats these sites as sacred. There is separate law for Aboriginal men and women. As

Yulara		J	F	M	A	M	J	J	A	S	O	N	D	Year
Rain	av. mm	26	44	32	14	12	21	20	4	6	19	32	43	273
Temp	av. max. °C	38	37	34	30	24	20	20	23	29	32	35	36	30
Temp	av. min. °C	22	22	19	14	9	5	4	6	11	15	18	20	14

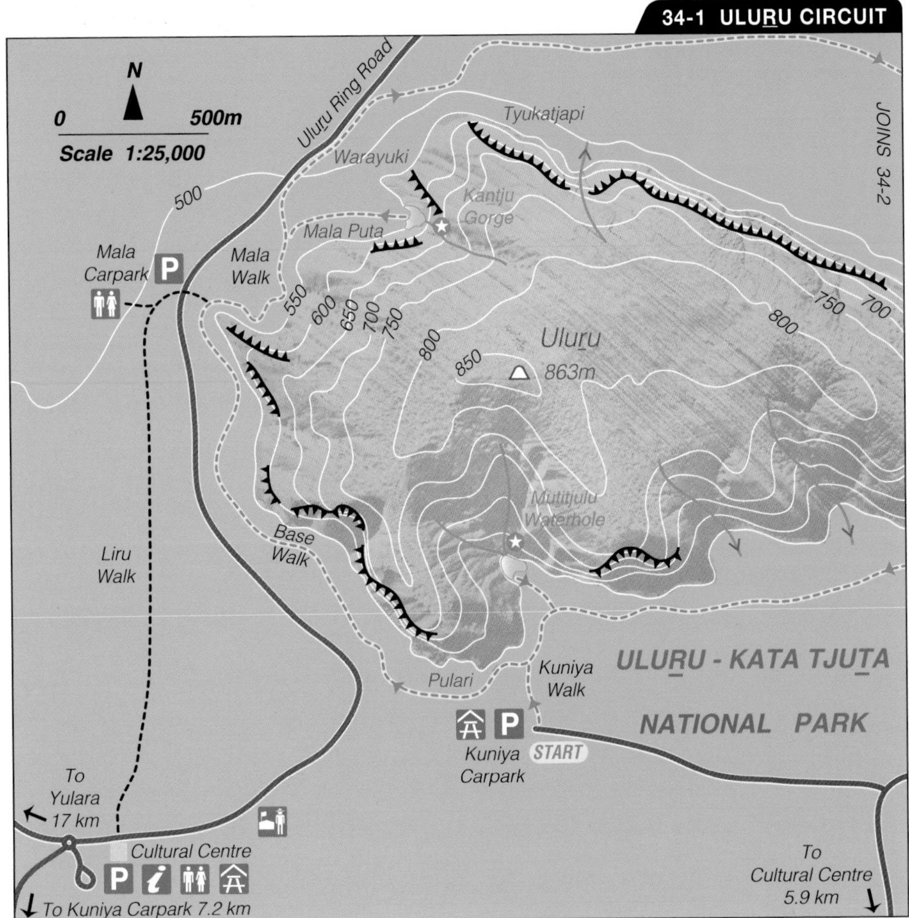

a result large areas are off limits to the general public so you need to stay on the marked tracks. There are significant curbs on photography, especially for commercial purposes. Signs are placed near areas that should not be photographed. To gain a better understanding of the Anangu beliefs it is best to visit the park cultural centre near Uluru before undertaking this suggested base walk from Kuniya carpark. Ideally visit the cultural centre on the day before your walk so you can make an early start and avoid the heat.

The Anangu consider Uluru sacred and would prefer visitors to refrain from making the ascent to the summit. This is traditionally reserved for those members of the Anangu who have attained a certain level of knowledge within their tribe. The national park authorities do not promote the climb, frequently close it when it is windy and recommend walking a circuit track around the circumference of the rock. These days only a few visitors arrive intent on climbing the icon and it is clearly only a matter of time before this irritating intrusion against the traditional owners' wishes will be stopped. The choice of whether or not to respect the Aboriginal preference that you not climb is yours, but we suggest you refrain.

The Aboriginal cultural centre is located some 1.5 km from the base of the

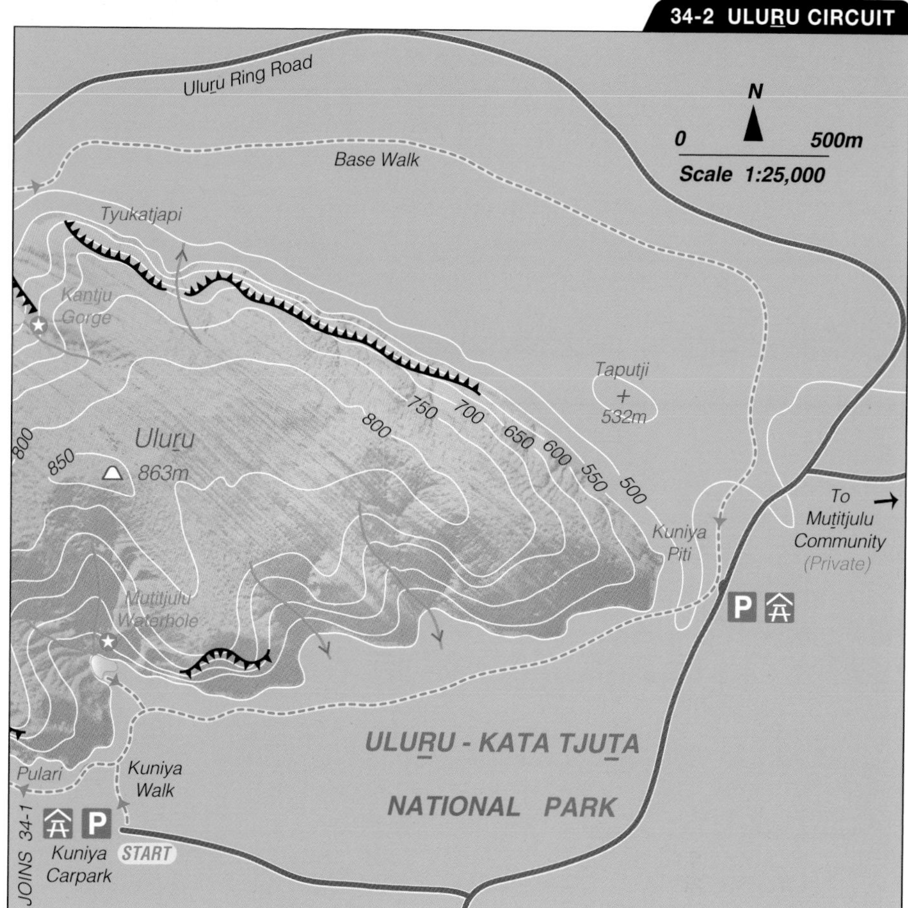

rock. A sealed road encircles the rock and has been re-aligned on the south side to take you some distance from culturally sensitive sites.

Yulara is set low between the sand dunes 20 km from Uluru and has the only camping, accommodation, supplies and fuel within the park. The next closest option is Curtin Springs, 84 km to the east.

The desert terrain of the Red Centre results in extreme temperatures and a lack of water so you need to carry plenty of drinking water, apply sunscreen and wear a long sleeved shirt and hat. Covering your skin with light clothing reduces exposure and helps to lessen dehydration. Rocky track conditions necessitate sturdy, rubber-soled boots or shoes. Start the walk early in the day to avoid heat and enjoy the early morning light, which creates different aspects of Uluru.

The walk suggestion starts from the Kuniya carpark. This avoids congestion at the other main carparks and ends the walk in relative shade on the south side of the monolith.

From the carpark, walk 200 m north then turn west to follow the rock base. The track runs roughly parallel with the road for 2 km to the Mala carpark. From here walk 400 m east then north to a track junction. On the way, pass two wind-scoured caves

Uluṟu southern side

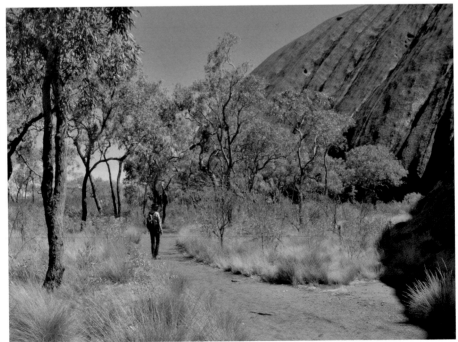

Uluṟu circuit track

containing rock art. Take an 800 m return side trip east to Kantju Gorge. Here you will find a cool, quiet ravine with large rock pool and sheer cliffs with overhangs. Retrace to the main track and turn right. The circuit then follows the roadside for 500 m before veering east into scrubby stands of mulga for 4 km. The track has been realigned away from the base. This is to avoid the most culturally sensitive sites on the entire north-east face. Many of these may only be viewed by either Aṉangu men or women respectively. Some of the most striking erosion formations can be viewed high up on the flanks.

Vegetation is fairly sparse but birds are likely to be seen, most often crested pigeons, mulga parrots, diamond doves, honeyeaters and eagles. With luck you may see an emu or kangaroo. Rain is rare with a low annual total which falls mostly in summer. When it does rain, water cascades in silvery threads down grooves and rock gullies to create waterholes for the wildlife.

The track leads to a shelter with a tank and emergency telephone. This is the eastern-most point of Uluṟu with some gently sloping rock expanses nearby, showing stratification in the sandstone.

The track turns west-south-west for the next 2 km, encountering some welcome shade. As you progress you will cross a number of dry gullies. Vegetation is denser on this cooler side of the rock. Mulga and other acacias, grevillea, eucalyptus and myrtle species all grow freely and budgerigars and honeyeaters inhabit the trees and shrubs.

After 2 km turn right at a track junction for the Miṯitjulu waterhole, 200 m away. Examples of rock art can be seen from viewing decks on overhanging cliffs near the track. This waterhole is said to be the most reliable throughout the year, attracting large numbers of wildlife. From here, retrace the 500 m south to the carpark and walk end.

Muṯitjulu Waterhole

KATA TJUṮA
Red Centre, Northern Territory

Walk:	7.4 km circuit
Time required:	Including minimal breaks, 3 hours
Grade:	One day, medium
Environment:	Desert and massive rock domes
Last review date:	July 2008
Map reference:	1:100 000 Uluṟu–Kata Tjuṯa National Park (limited use) and Map 35
Best time to visit:	May to September. Avoid November to March

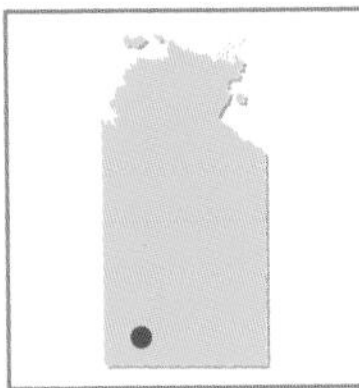

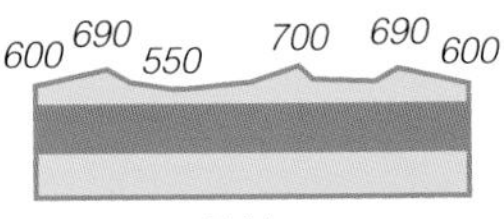

Kata Tjuṯa is comprised of 36 massive, red domes of conglomerate rock formed from granite, gneiss and basalt. Inundation by the sea cemented these together with sandstone some 600 million years ago. Later, with land uplifting and the sea retreating, the rock formations fractured along joints in a criss-cross fashion and weathering along the fractures created the remarkable domes visible before you today. The domes (geologically known as inselbergs) are spread over some 35 square kilometres and Mount Olga is the highest of the domes at 1066 m. It is about 450 m above the surrounding desert. Other domes are nearly as tall. Deep gorges exist between the domes and allow any rain water to be retained so assisting plant growth and attracting wildlife. Kata Tjuṯa is some 50 km west by road from Uluṟu and Yulara resort accommodation and village. Like Uluṟu, it is popular as a tourist destination and has World Heritage classification. The name Kata Tjuṯa means 'many heads' in the Aboriginal language.

Both Kata Tjuṯa and Uluṟu are situated on A̲nangu Aboriginal land leased to Parks Australia as the Uluṟu–Kata Tjuṯa National Park. It is managed with joint custodianship. Aboriginal law therefore must be respected in conjunction with the usual national park regulations. An important belief is that the land and the people are as one in a living cultural landscape. Traditional Aboriginal law (Tjukurpa) treats these sites as sacred and there are separate laws for both Aboriginal men and women. As a result large areas are off limits to the general public so you need to stay on the marked tracks. There are significant curbs on photography especially for commercial purposes. To gain a better understanding of the A̲nangu beliefs, you should visit the park cultural centre near Uluṟu before undertaking this suggested

Yulara	J	F	M	A	M	J	J	A	S	O	N	D	Year
Rain av. mm	26	44	32	14	12	21	20	4	6	19	32	43	273
Temp av. max. °C	38	37	34	30	24	20	20	23	29	32	35	36	30
Temp av. min. °C	22	22	19	14	9	5	4	6	11	15	18	20	14

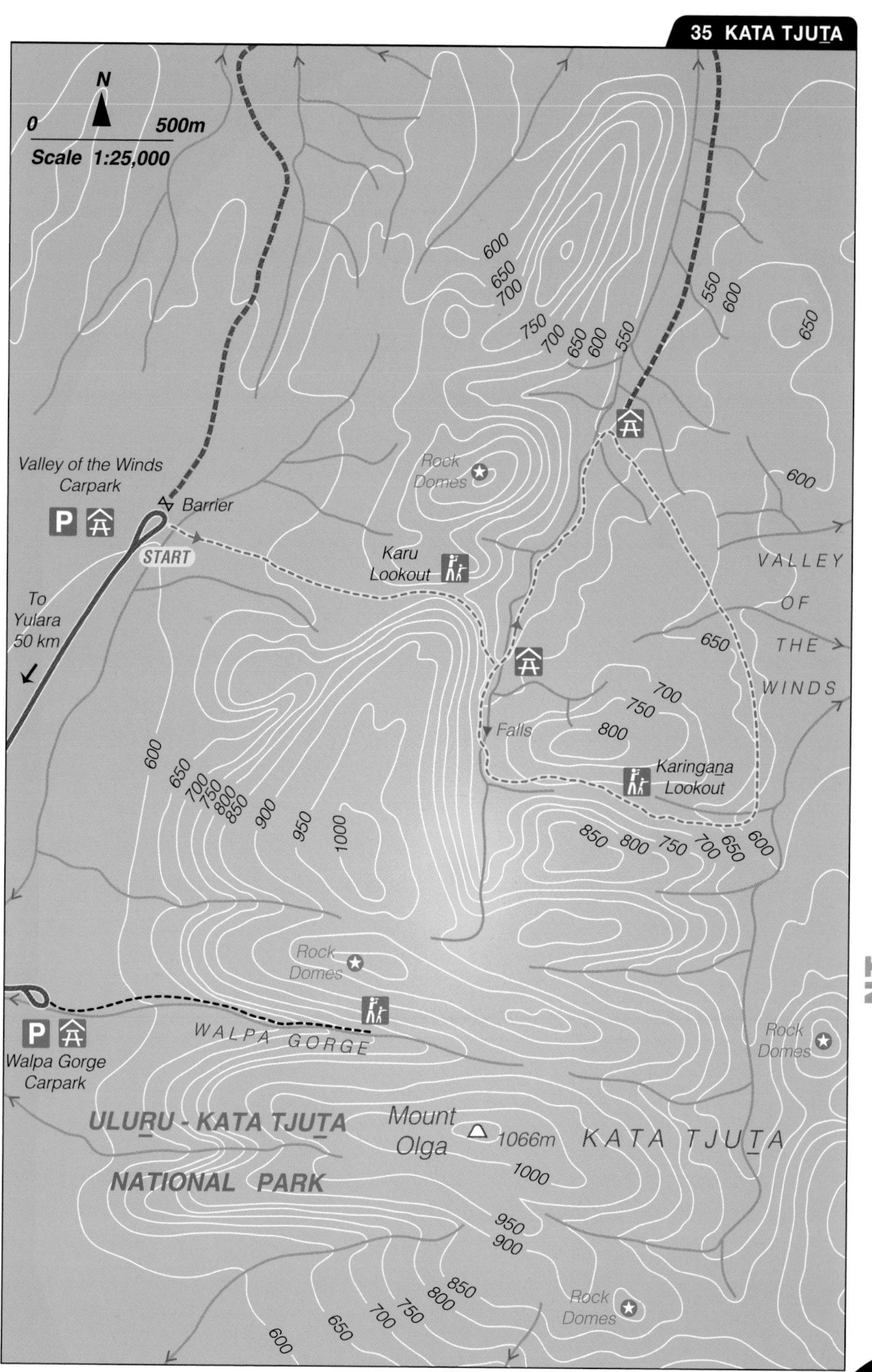
N
0
500m
Scale 1:25,000
Valley of the Winds
Carpark
Barrier
START
To
Yulara
50 km
Rock
Domes
Karu
Lookout
VALLEY
OF
THE
WINDS
Falls
Karingana
Lookout
Rock
Domes
WALPA GORGE
Walpa Gorge
Carpark
ULURU - KATA TJUṮA
NATIONAL PARK
Mount
Olga
1066m
KATA TJUṮA
Rock
Domes
Rock
Domes

Valley of the Winds walk. As such you need to visit the cultural centre the previous day, to enable an early start to the walk and so avoid the midday heat.

The desert terrain of the Red Centre results in extreme temperatures and a lack of water so you need to carry plenty of drinking water, apply sunscreen and wear a long sleeved shirt and hat. As the name implies, the Valley of the Winds is often windy so your hat needs to be secured with a strap. Covering your skin with light clothing reduces exposure and helps to lessen perspiration and dehydration. Rocky track conditions necessitate sturdy, rubber-soled boots or shoes. Start the walk early in the day to avoid heat and enjoy the early morning light on the domes.

From the Valley of Winds carpark and picnic area on the western side of Kata Tjuṯa you set off east on a well-formed path. You gradually climb for 1.1 km from the desert plains to Karu Lookout situated on a saddle between two domes. This is also known as First Lookout. During extremely hot or windy weather, the track ahead can be temporarily closed. The track can also be loose underfoot and steep in places as you descend for 600 m to a track junction. This is in a gully and marks the start of a 4 km loop walk which takes you in a clockwise direction.

Head down the gully north-north-east for 700 m to reach a shelter and tap. A four-wheel-drive track continues further, however, you should turn south-east for 400 m up to a ridge crest where you get a wide view including the desert beyond. Continue south-south-east descending gradually for 1.1 km to a creek bed with red gums. Especially to the west are the imposing domes through which the walk route climbs. Zebra finches and budgerigars are likely to be seen here.

Mount Olga and domes

Desert oaks

Follow the track west to enter one of the deepest chasms, you then climb quite steeply to Karingaṉa Lookout (Second Lookout) 800 m away. This rocky pass between imposingly high, sheer dome walls is perhaps the most spectacular part of the walk. It is often within shade so is a good place for a rest.

Next, descend the steep track for 300 m west and turn north through a deep ravine. The view back up the ravine is quite amazing. You then need to negotiate a smooth gentle slope at an intermittent waterfall, pass another shelter with tank and within 700 m complete the loop walk. Thereafter, turn left and retrace the 1.7 km back past Karu Lookout to the carpark.

To finish off the day, the traditional tourist sunset viewing of Uluṟu, from the dunes west of the monolith, is highly recommended.

Uluṟu at sunset

QUEENSLAND

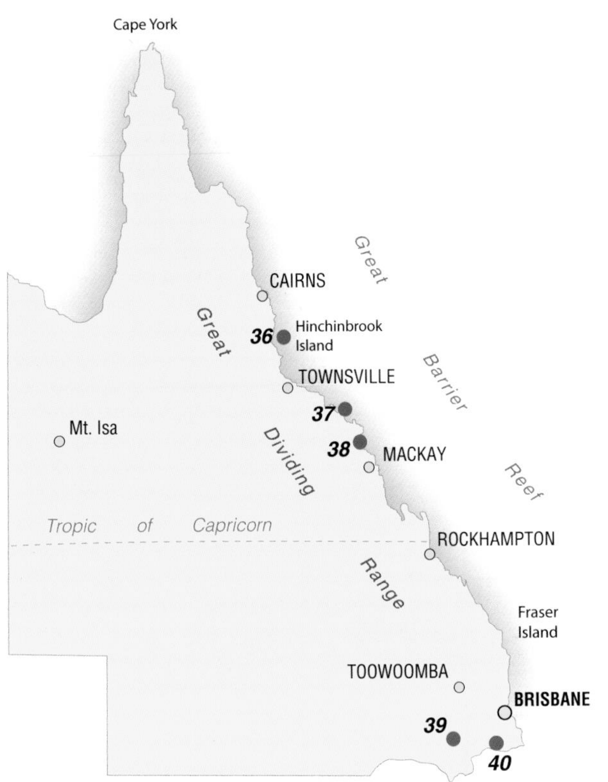

36	Macushla–Cape Richards	Hinchinbrook Island National Park
37	South Molle Island	Molle Islands National Park
38	Cape Hillsborough	Cape Hillsborough National Park
39	Mount Cordeaux	Main Range National Park
40	Green Mountains	Lamington National Park

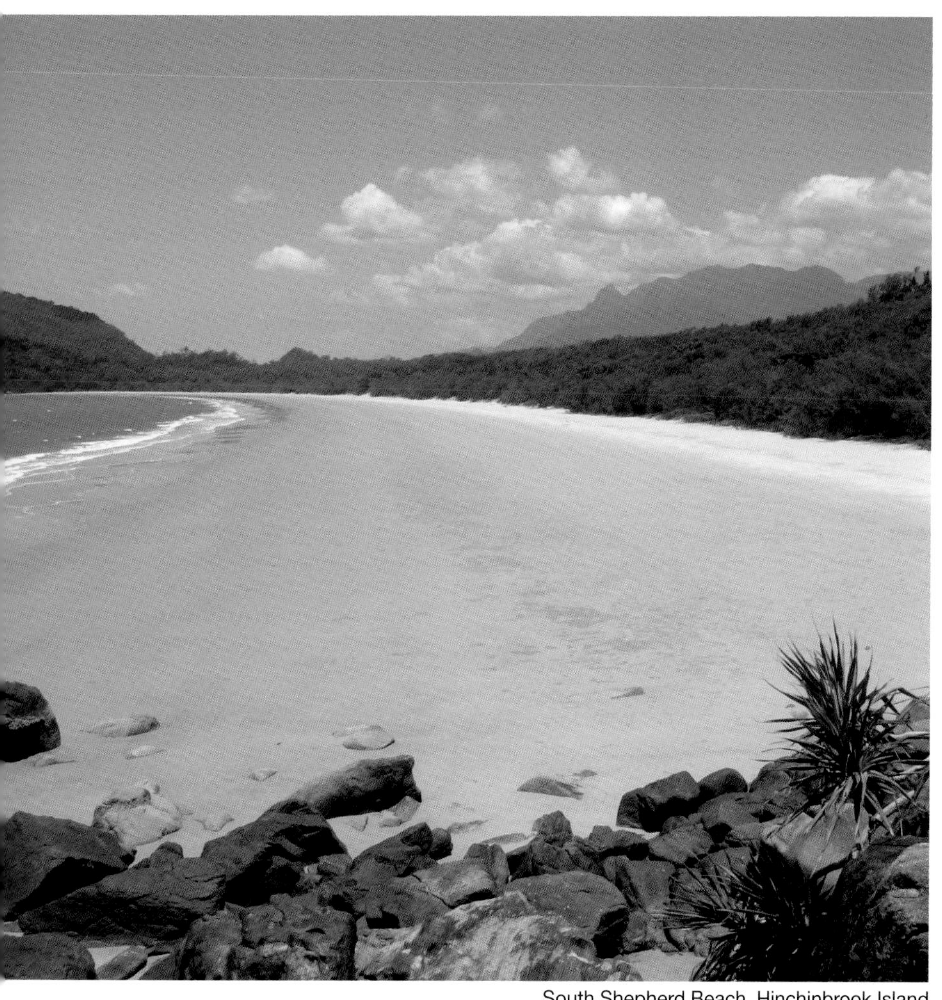

South Shepherd Beach, Hinchinbrook Island

Queensland has much of its mass in the tropics, although Brisbane, the capital is much further south. The Great Barrier Reef and adjacent rainforest on the coastal side of the Great Dividing Range are both captivating. The long-distance Thorsborne Trail on Hinchinbrook Island traverses tropical rainforest and coast. On the island at Macushla, one may camp or walk in splendid isolation. The Cape Richards walking track crosses the island into rich littoral coastal forest with giant buttressed trees, palms, vines and orchids. Towards the southern end of the Barrier Reef, in the Whitsunday Islands is South Molle Island and nearby Cape Hillsborough. Both coastal walks include stunning views from high points. In south-east Queensland, on the Great Dividing Range is an ascent amid rainforest to Mount Cordeaux and Bare Rock. Nearby, a splendid walk from O'Reillys at Lamington National Park, is through lush World Heritage rainforest with many waterfalls and orchids.

36 MACUSHLA–CAPE RICHARDS

Hinchinbrook Island, Queensland

Walk:	7 km one-way
Time required:	Including minimal breaks, 3 hours 30 minutes
Grade:	One day, easy
Environment:	Tropical coast, beach and rainforest
Last review date:	October 2008
Map reference:	1:50 000 Rockingham Bay and Map 36
Best time to visit:	May to October. Expect heavy rain January to April

Hinchinbrook Island has gained fame in recent years as an adventure wilderness walking area with Wet Tropics World Heritage classification. Many tourists from overseas and around Australia visit the large, pristine island. The traditional walking area is the east coast, long-distance Thorsborne Trail. Along this trail, it is wise to be prepared to encounter crocodiles, mosquitoes, march flies, sandflies, green tree ants, marine stingers, tidal range problems and flooding streams. Camping permits are scarce too, because of the popularity of the area. For many though, it is an icon walk with great rewards.

This walk option is mainly for those who want to spend time on magnificent Hinchinbrook, but consider the Thorsborne Trail too demanding. The boat access provides a great cruise passing a number of islands. Views south include spectacular Mount Bowen (1121 m) and a series of granitic crags that form the backbone of the island. You may see migrating Torres Strait pigeons, green turtles, dolphins and dugongs during the cruise and perhaps even a crocodile in the Missionary Bay tidal creeks of extensive mangrove forest.

Check in at Port Hinchinbrook marina just south of Cardwell, a small town on the Bruce Highway (No. 1) with good transport links, accommodation and supplies. You cruise across the broad Hinchinbrook Channel to the northern end of the 37 kilometre-long island for Cape Richards resort then on via channels through extensive mangroves to a Missionary Bay landing, which is the start of the Thorsborne Trail. Time is usually allotted here for a break at the adjacent Ramsay Bay beach fronting the Coral Sea. You then cruise further, landing at Macushla Point.

The walk from here explores the rainforest and beaches back to Cape Richards where, no doubt reluctantly, you

Innisfail	J	F	M	A	M	J	J	A	S	O	N	D	Year
Rain av. mm	530	600	700	480	300	190	130	120	90	80	150	270	3640
Temp av. max. °C	30	30	29	28	26	24	24	25	26	28	29	30	27
Temp av. min. °C	23	23	22	21	19	17	15	16	17	19	21	22	20

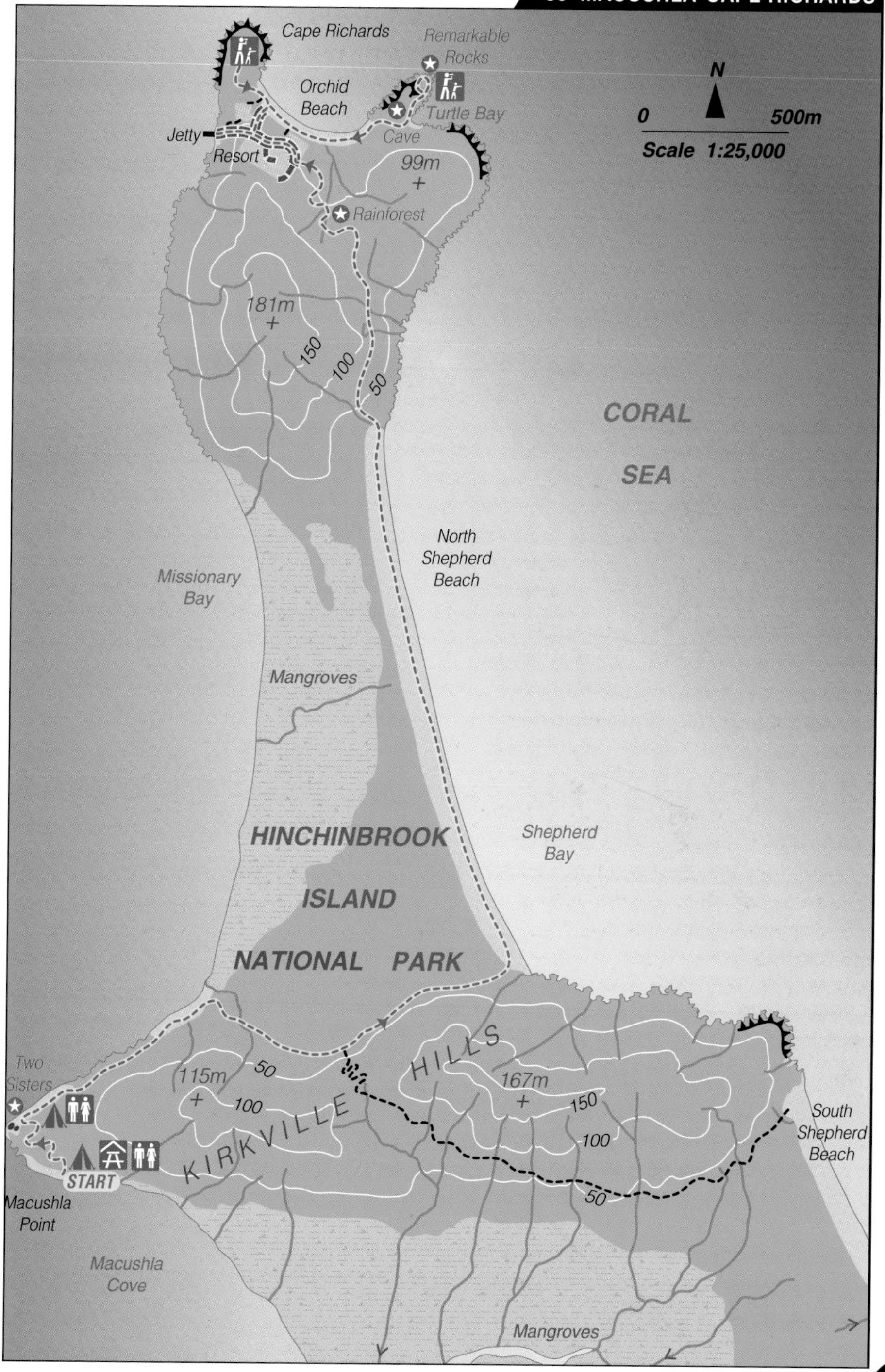

Cape Richards
Remarkable Rocks
Orchid Beach
Turtle Bay
Cave
Jetty
Resort
99m
Rainforest
N
0 500m
Scale 1:25,000
181m
150
100
50
CORAL SEA
North Shepherd Beach
Missionary Bay
Mangroves
HINCHINBROOK ISLAND NATIONAL PARK
Shepherd Bay
Two Sisters
115m
50
100
KIRKVILLE HILLS
167m
150
100
50
South Shepherd Beach
START
Macushla Point
Macushla Cove
Mangroves

QLD

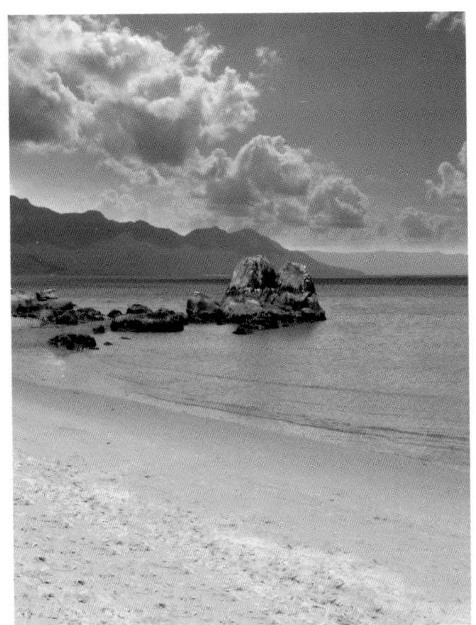

Two Sisters rocks, Macushla

need to leave. Boat times dictate that all but the very fittest of walkers should omit a possible side trip 5 km return over the Kirkville Hills to South Shepherd Beach. We strongly recommend you visit wonderful Turtle Bay instead.

The boat lands you right at the camp area on the south side of Macushla Point. You look south to massive peaks across Missionary Bay. The camp area has tables, shelter and seats plus a free gas barbecue. It is popular with fishermen. Be aware that crocodiles inhabit the area. Carry all drinking water and insect repellent.

You first need to use a very short pad over a rise to the north side of Macushla Point where prominent rocks called the Two Sisters rise out of the water. North-west across the water are Garden and Gould Islands. From near the east end of this beach, a track leads into forest and is the route to follow. It runs parallel to the rocky shore for a short distance then joins a third small beach. Again, go east until you reach a spot just before mangroves. A track then leads back into dense forest, which all but cuts out the light. Brush turkeys, which make giant mounds of leaf litter, may be seen scratching and your progress tends to disturb butterflies from the track. You cross an isthmus skirting the north side of the Kirkville Hills.

When 1.3 km from the boat landing point, you reach the South Shepherd Beach turnoff. Veer left for just 800 m within more forest on fairly level ground and you reach the southern end of North Shepherd Beach. Shade from overhanging casuarina and other trees, such as the pandani palm (*Pandanus pedunculatus*) with its interesting aerial prop roots, provide a good place for a lunch break on the edge of the sand. Cardwell cabbage (*Scaevola taccada*) with its lush green leaves and white flowers covers the ground at the back of the beach. This fine, 2 kilometre-long stretch of sand offers relatively safe swimming in the sea, unlike Macushla.

Cape Richards rainforest

Remarkable Rocks and Brook Islands

After lunch, walk the full length of the white sand beach, which fronts on to the Coral Sea, then return into forest for the 1.4 km walk to the resort fronting on to Orchid Beach at Cape Richards. After the beachcombing, you leave the coastal she oaks and cottonwoods and climb steadily through vine forest with lovely palm groves, strangler figs, curtain figs, and large-buttressed quandong trees. The blue quandong (*Elaeocarpus grandis*) fruit is commonly seen on the track. Strangely the fruit develops on the main trunk. You cross a ridge and descend amid fine stands of solitaire palm (*Ptychosperma elegans*) to reach the resort. There is a lookout platform as you enter the resort.

Once at the main building, bar and pool you should not miss the 1 km return side walk to Turtle Bay. You descend on to the lovely beach and go to its nearby east end. From here you climb over a low saddle within more rainforest to the rocky bay. There is a small beach littered with coral fragments, some pandani palms and a few mangroves, but the main attraction is up on to the rocks to your left. Follow small white-painted, turtle track markers and you pass a rock cave and climb to stunning views and vast expanses of rock. Explore this locality, perhaps making a loop so as to get the best vistas in each direction. You may see turtles feeding on sea grasses in the bay below you. Out to sea are the Brook and Family islands. One rock area looks just like the famous Remarkable Rocks at Kangaroo Island in South Australia.

Retrace to the north end of Orchid Beach in front of the resort and take a foot track for a 300 m return climb north to a great outlook on rocks at Cape Richards itself. Orchid Beach derived its name from the golden orchids (*Dendrobium discolor*) that spill over rocks in the vicinity. The jetty from which the boat leaves is some 200 m west of the main resort building. If time permits, afternoon tea at the resort might be in order to end a memorable day.

Orchid Beach

37 SOUTH MOLLE ISLAND

Whitsunday Islands, Queensland

Walk:	12.6 km circuit
Time required	Including minimal breaks, 5 hours
Grade:	One day, medium
Environment:	Great Barrier Reef mountainous island
Last review date:	October 2008
Map reference:	1:100 000 Proserpine (limited use) and Map 37
Best time to visit:	April to October. Expect heavy rain January and February

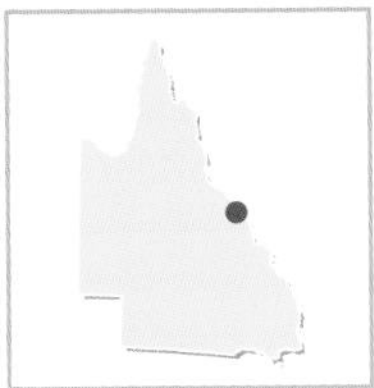

This island is in a somewhat central position amid the many Whitsunday Islands. It is the largest of the lesser Molle group of islands. Its main attraction is a low key resort on the north coast with a nine-hole golf course. For walkers, its greatest attraction is excellent tracks on open tops. These provide expansive vistas to the many other surrounding islands, islets and the mainland coast.

There is a very wide diversity of vegetation from tropical vine and rainforest, dry eucalyptus woodland, coconut groves, hoop pines, grass trees, mangroves and wind-swept coastal vegetation. Overgrazing by an early pastoralist before the present national park was created has resulted in the open tops. Wildlife is exceptionally good with colourful lorikeets, currawongs, curlews, brush turkeys, pigeons, kookaburras, butterflies, wallabies, fruit bats, goannas and other lizards. The lorikeets, curlews and wallabies are quite tame at the resort.

Access is by cruise boats from either Shute Harbour or Abel Point marina at the Whitsunday Islands tourist town of Airlie Beach. You should check timetables and use the service that gives you the most time on the island for the day. Some boat trips take you to other islands before your destination so you could end up getting quite a cruise. You really need at least six hours on the island. Other options are to camp at Paddle Bay bush camp 1.2 km west of the resort jetty or stay at the resort either before or after the walk. (A permit to camp would need to be arranged through the Parks and Wildlife Service website or district office.) The camp is right at the isthmus that links South Molle to Mid Molle at low tide. These and many other islands were once linked to the mainland and were created when ice melted from the last ice age some 10–12 000 years ago.

Proserpine	J	F	M	A	M	J	J	A	S	O	N	D	Year
Rain av. mm	280	321	149	135	78	36	19	30	21	39	79	169	1356
Temp av. max. °C	32	31	30	29	26	25	24	26	28	30	32	32	29
Temp av. min. °C	22	23	21	19	16	13	11	12	14	17	20	22	18

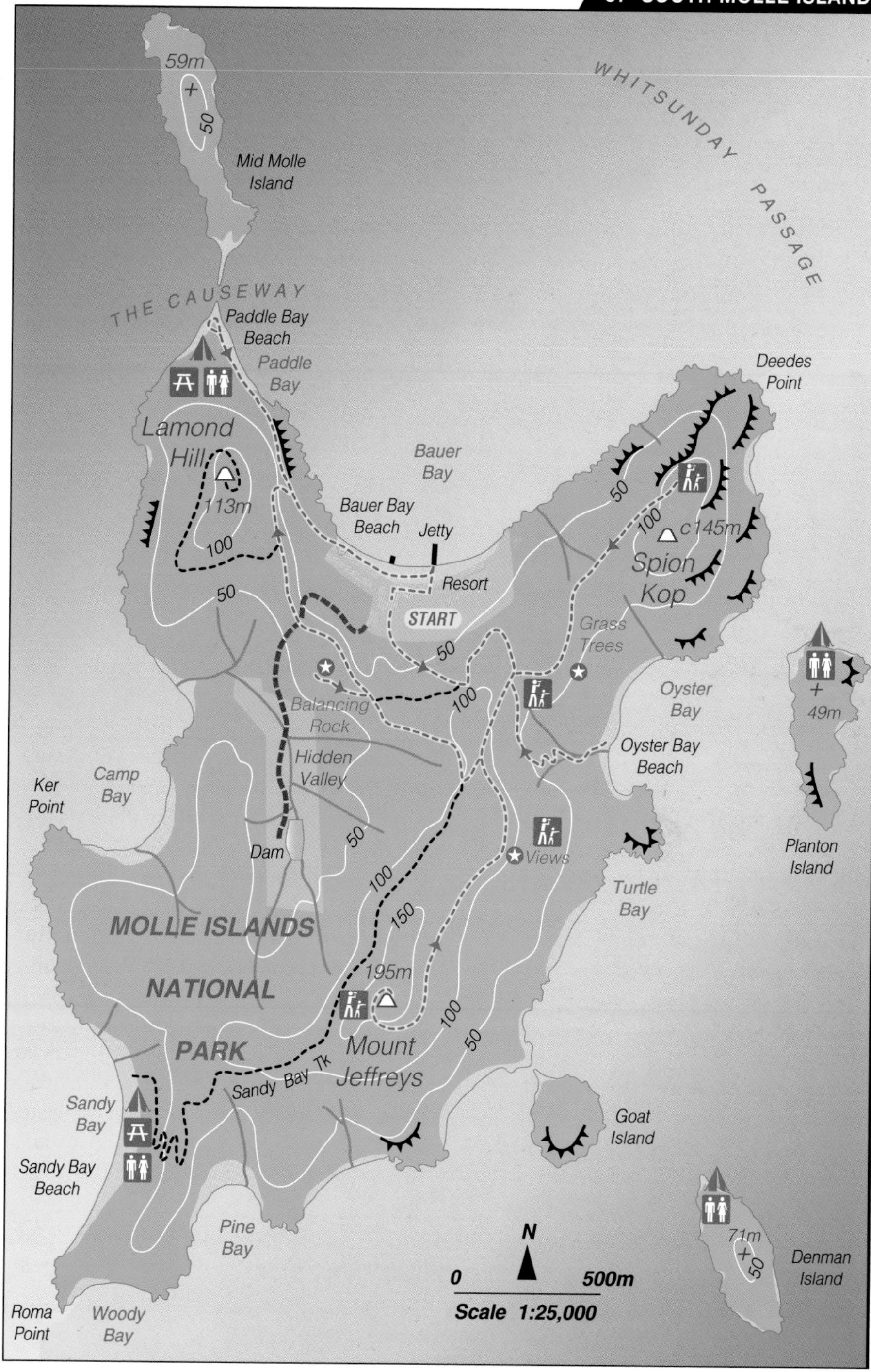

WHITSUNDAY PASSAGE
59m
50
Mid Molle Island
THE CAUSEWAY
Paddle Bay Beach
Paddle Bay
Lamond Hill
113m
100
50
Bauer Bay
Bauer Bay Beach
Jetty
Resort
START
Deedes Point
50
100
c145m
Spion Kop
Grass Trees
Oyster Bay
Oyster Bay Beach
49m
Planton Island
Balancing Rock
Hidden Valley
Dam
Camp Bay
Ker Point
Views
Turtle Bay
MOLLE ISLANDS NATIONAL PARK
195m
150
Mount Jeffreys
Sandy Bay Tk
Sandy Bay
Sandy Bay Beach
Goat Island
Pine Bay
71m
Denman Island
N
0
500m
Scale 1:25,000
Roma Point
Woody Bay

It is recommended that you climb to the open, eastern tops of the island at Spion Kop and Mount Jeffreys before the heat of the day and also to get the best light on crags, islands, the sea and the vegetation. Towards the afternoon you then tend to be more in shaded areas and amid forest. Carry plenty of water and wear protection from strong sunlight. Upon arrival at the jetty, you need to walk through the resort past a tennis court and south along the western perimeter of the small golf course in order to reach the walking track system and the edge of forest, some 400 m from the outer end of the jetty.

You begin to climb gradually within the forest and then pass a track off right after just 350 m. Another 500 m of gentle climbing sees you out of the forest and at a grassy saddle with broad views especially to the east. You see many islands including Planton Island in the foreground and distant Whitsunday Island. Grass trees are the main vegetation on these tops and are a sight to behold when their long flower spikes are in bloom. Also to the east is Oyster Bay with its rainforest gully and hoop pines (*Araucaria cunninghamii*). North-north-east 1.2 km away is craggy Spion Kop; your next objective. Another graded track leads upwards to it, partly through more forest on west-facing slopes, to a saddle and on to the track end at viewing platforms with great vistas to both east and west. This is in a very rocky spot amid a few hoop pines. To the west you see the resort below, Mid Molle Island, North Molle Island, West Molle (Daydream Island resort), Shute Harbour and the mainland.

Retrace the 1.2 km down to the saddle, go on just 20 m and take the side trip 1.7 km return down to lovely Oyster Bay on the east coast. The track is easy to follow. On the lower section you pass through rainforest. Under the shelter of the canopy there are many birds and butterflies darting about with brush turkeys scratching the leaf litter of the understorey. At the small beach and bay there are more hoop pines and a few mangroves. The bay

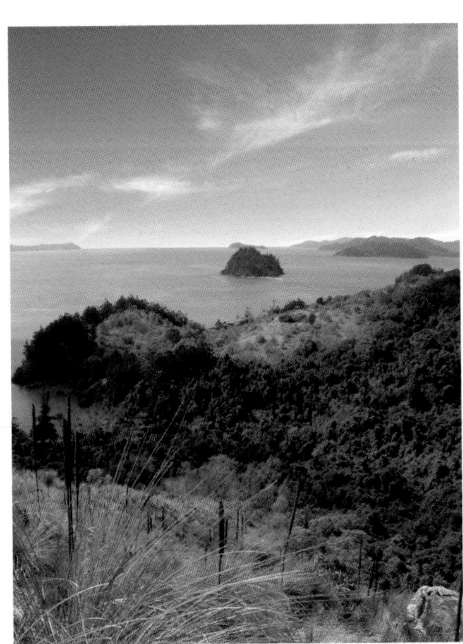

Oyster Bay and Denman Island

Oyster Bay and Planton Island

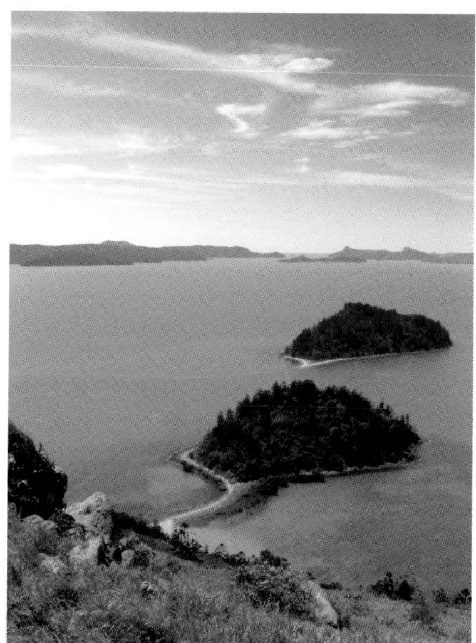

Goat and Denman Islands

tends to be a bit sheltered by neighbouring Planton Island. After a short break, climb back to the saddle on the crest.

The next goal is Mount Jeffreys, the highest point on the island. You walk south 400 m to another saddle then take the left-fork track for the 1.4 km gradual ascent generally south. Most of the way is open with tremendous views and more grass trees grow on the slopes. Small Denman and Goat islands, below, draw your attention with their tiny beaches and attractive hoop pines. At low tide, a sand bar joins Goat Island to South Molle Island. The track turns almost full circle at the Mount Jeffreys summit for the best possible vistas, during a lunch break.

Retrace 1.4 km, turn left for just 100 m down to meet the Sandy Bay Track in light forest then turn right. The route ahead is through dry eucalyptus forest westwards

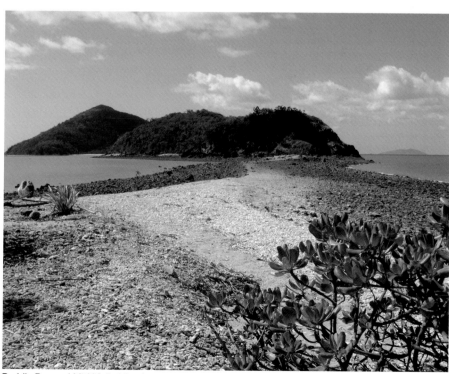

Paddle Bay and Mid Molle Island

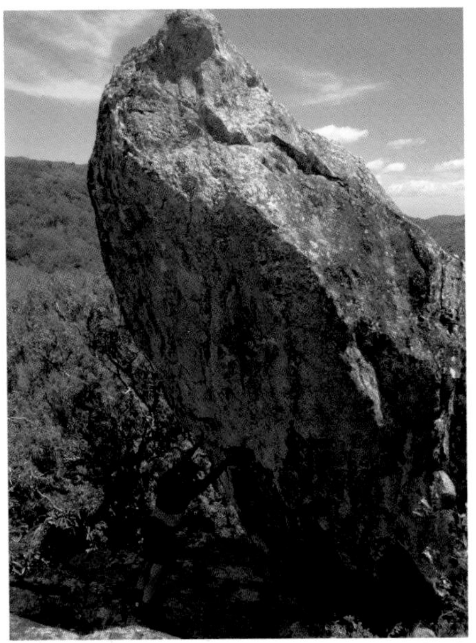
Balancing Rock

near a ridge crest for 700 m to another track junction on the crest at the back of the resort. Off right is a return track to the resort and off left is Balancing Rock just 150 m away. This huge granite boulder near a craggy summit is a real point of interest and you should take the side trip to it for more views especially towards the centre of the island with its resort water supply. After this, continue north-west, intersect a private road that links the resort and the water supply and within 400 m veer right to descend rather than go to Lamond Hill. An author called Lamond and his family were early settlers on the island. Head 250 m down through forest and meet the main resort to Paddle Bay walking track. Turn left and descend further for 250 m and you reach the Paddle Bay beach. Walk 250 m along the beach to the picnic and camp area at the point for another break. From the picnic facilities fine views are afforded of Mid Molle Island adjacent. West Molle Island (Daydream Island) with its resort is a little further away to the west.

To end the day you need to retrace the beach and access track for 500 m then veer left down the ongoing track to the end of the main beach and western extremity of the resort. It is then a short walk to the jetty along resort pathway or on the sand adjacent.

Spion Kop and jetty

38 CAPE HILLSBOROUGH

Mackay, Queensland

Walk:	9 km circuit
Time required:	Including minimal breaks, 4 hours
Grade:	One day, easy
Environment:	Tropical Coast
Last review date:	October 2008
Map reference:	1:100 000 Cumberland Islands (limited use) and Map 38
Best time to visit:	April to October. Expect heavy rain January to March

0 80 0 100 0

9 km

This beautiful cape, some 46 km north of the city of Mackay, is protected within Cape Hillsborough National Park and was named by Captain Cook. In past ages it was one of the many hilly islands of the Great Barrier Reef but is now linked to the mainland. Its walking tracks permit broad panoramas to a great many islands and along the coast. The tidal range in the area is up to 6.5 m so at low tide extra opportunities occur to explore the coast and to see soft coral and mangroves up close.

It is essential that tide times are checked before setting off to ensure you do not get stranded by fast rising tides. Sharp underwater rocks and the summertime presence of marine stingers make any wading most unwise. The low-key resort at the cape can advise when low tides occur and it is at low tide that you can better appreciate a number of points of interest. You should not attempt crossing to Orchid Rock but we recommend a low tide visit to Wedge Island.

Access is from the Bruce Highway north of Mackay, towards Seaforth then into the park. Once within the park you pass the popular 1.2 km Diversity Boardwalk circuit, which highlights mangroves and other environments. This walk and another at the nearby Hidden Valley Yuibera plant trail (also 1.2 km long) are highly recommended if you have the time. The park entry road leads to an isthmus with picnic area, camping and an adjacent small resort, complete with kiosk. There are walking tracks in both directions from the isthmus. These can be combined with beach walking for an excellent circuit. Carry water and protect yourself from the strong sunlight.

Geologically, the cape is very rugged, ancient, volcanic rhyolite rock exposed especially at headlands and where the hillsides plunge to the sea as cliffs. Wedge Island and Orchid Rock are adjacent to the main bay fronting the Coral Sea. Division Rocks extend out into the water midway

Mackay		J	F	M	A	M	J	J	A	S	O	N	D	Year
Rain	av. mm	335	318	308	152	94	68	41	26	40	46	74	164	1667
Temp	av. max. °C	30	30	29	27	25	23	22	23	25	28	29	30	27
Temp	av. min. °C	23	23	22	19	16	13	12	13	15	18	21	22	18

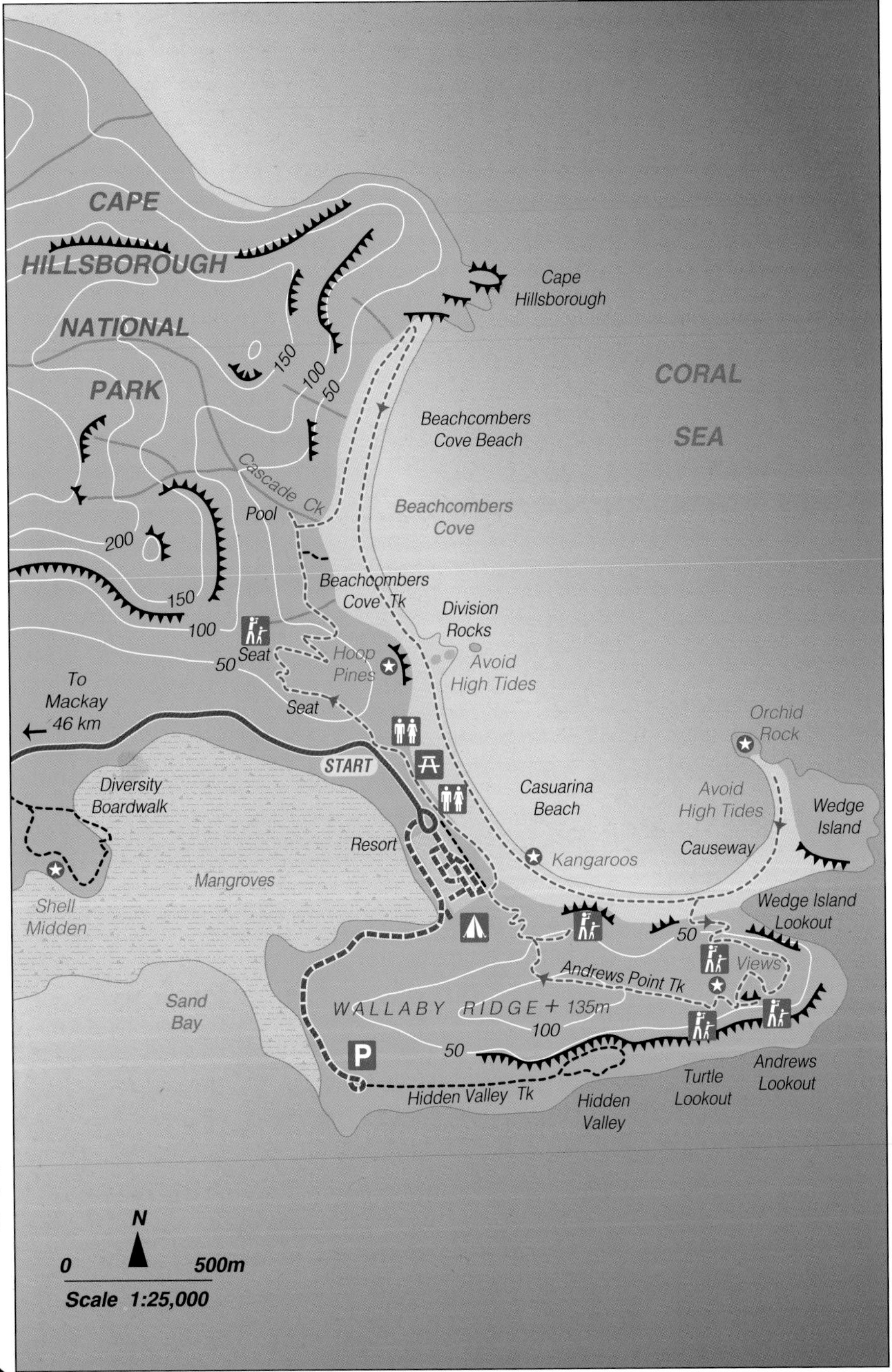

CAPE HILLSBOROUGH NATIONAL PARK
Cape Hillsborough
CORAL SEA
Beachcombers Cove Beach
Beachcombers Cove
Cascade Ck
Pool
200
150
100
50
Beachcombers Cove Tk
Division Rocks
Avoid High Tides
Seat
Hoop Pines
Seat
To Mackay 46 km
START
Orchid Rock
Diversity Boardwalk
Casuarina Beach
Avoid High Tides
Wedge Island
Resort
Kangaroos
Causeway
Shell Midden
Mangroves
Wedge Island Lookout
Views
Andrews Point Tk
Sand Bay
WALLABY RIDGE + 135m
Hidden Valley Tk
Hidden Valley
Turtle Lookout
Andrews Lookout
N
0 500m
Scale 1:25,000

QLD

Hoop Pines and Cumberland Islands

along the bay to separate Beachcombers Cove from Casuarina Beach.

Hand-reared kangaroos frequent the beach early each morning to be fed chaff. This is a preferred diet for these marsupials and you should not give them any other food. The cape appears to have more wildlife than other national parks. There are large numbers of brush turkeys, wallabies, kangaroos, kookaburras, fruit bats, possums, sand bubbler crabs, turtles, lizards, dolphins, 25 species of butterflies and 140 species of birds. If you are lucky you may see the brilliant blue Ulysses butterfly.

The vegetation is tropical with some dense rainforest including piccabeen palms, figs and birds nest ferns. Many large hoop pines (*Araucaria cunninghamii*) are on the higher ground. Coconut palms, broad-leaved tea tree and casuarinas line the beach in front of the resort and both pandani palms and mangroves border some of the coast.

Head off up the Beachcombers Cove track from the north-west end of the isthmus picnic area. The track rises a little to a saddle. As you climb, you reach a seat and can look out across mangroves. At the saddle and a second seat, you see volcanic cliffs off left and the Beachcombers Cove ahead. Go on down the pad via some zigzags and the beach is reached some 1.6 km from the walk start. The track divides just short of the beach near the mouth of a creek. Just upstream here via the left fork is an interesting, deep rock pool. From the beach, black volcanic sea cliffs dominate the north end of the bay at Cape Hillsborough itself. It is worth going to the rocks at the base of these cliffs to see the marine life when the tide is well out.

The next stage of the walk involves a 2.4 km section south-east along the full length of Beachcombers Cove and adjacent Casuarina Beach to a causeway at Wedge Island. Division Rocks are passed between the two bays and coconut palms mark the isthmus and resort as you pass them. Hoop

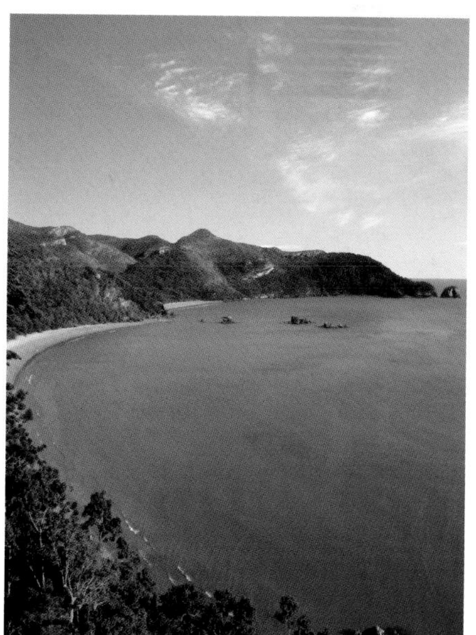

Cape Hillsborough and Division Rocks

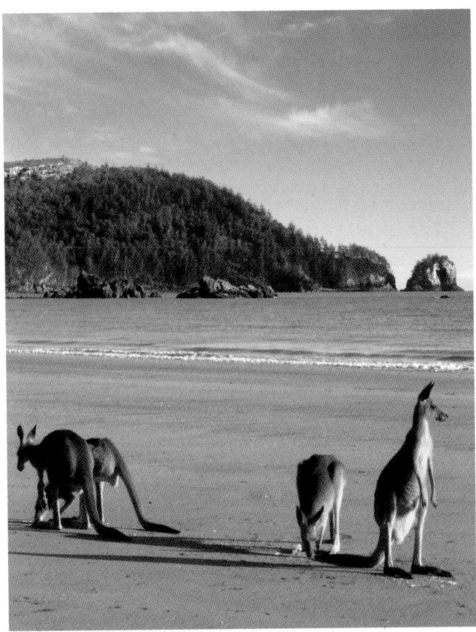

Kangaroos and Cape Hillsborough

pines grow on the bluffs near the beach and blue crabs scamper about when the tide is out. (When the tide is high it laps the cliff-base at several places to stop progress and blocks a causeway to Wedge Island.)

From the tidal causeway you should take a 1.2 km return side trip out to Wedge Island, along its western shore, so as to get a view to Orchid Rock and its golden orchids (*Dendrobium discolor*). The orchids flower on the rocks each September. Crabs and all manner of marine life are seen in the rocky areas at windswept Wedge Island. A few mangroves are at the causeway.

After the side trip, take a foot track off the beach at the southern end of the causeway so as to climb significantly into rainforest. Within 200 m you reach small Wedge Island lookout at a hairpin bend.

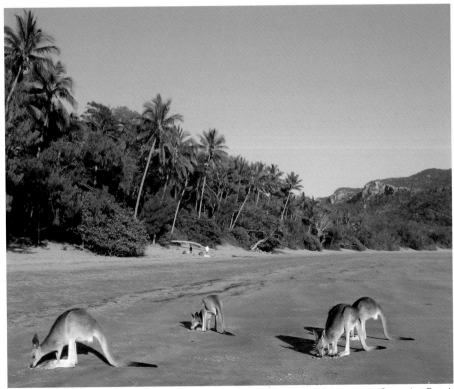

Kangaroos on Casuarina Beach

Then, 600 m later, after climbing in more dense forest around rocky volcanic bluffs, you reach the crest of Wallaby Ridge. Just 100 m east on a side track is Andrews Lookout, with limited views to some of the Barrier Reef islands. Double back and continue up the main track to reach Turtle Lookout within 200 m. From this viewing deck, turtles can sometimes be seen below feeding on sea grasses. There is a broad panorama.

Go further westwards and descend gradually off Wallaby Ridge. The area is fairly open, with some grass trees to be seen. After 700 m and within light forest, turn right and take a side trip (200 m return) to another viewing deck at Twin Beaches Lookout. This view will highlight the beautiful beaches, much of your earlier walk route and you can see the distant Cumberland Islands.

Thereafter, you head steeply down the main track via rocky bluffs within rainforest for 300 m. Steps assist with the descent via zigzags to reach Casuarina Beach at the east end of a camp area and the resort. A track leads through the palms in front of the resort, but it is best to head west (left) along the beach for 400 m, back to the picnic area and walk end.

View to Wedge Island

39 MOUNT CORDEAUX

Main Range, Queensland

Walk:	12.6 km retrace
Time required:	Including minimal breaks, 5 hours
Grade:	One day, medium
Environment:	Mountain ascent in sub-tropical area
Last review date:	August 2007
Map reference:	1:25 000 Cunninghams Gap and Map 39
Best time to visit:	Suited to any season but December to March can be hot and humid

This walk in the Main Range National Park is the best of several walk alternatives at Cunninghams Gap. The gap in the Great Dividing Range is 755 m high and through it passes the busy Cunningham Highway 115 km south-west of Brisbane. The pass was discovered by explorer Allan Cunningham in 1828 and he named the two abrupt peaks on either side the gap, Mount Mitchell (1168 m) and Mount Cordeaux (1144 m), after surveyor Major Mitchell and his assistant, Cordeaux. The Great Dividing Range in this vicinity is very rugged. The dramatic terrain ensured the gap was used only as a pass for a bridle track until 1927.

The range is mainly of heavily eroded basalt from a huge shield volcano some 23 million years old, but unlike nearby Mount Warning in New South Wales there is no known specific eruption point. Erosion of the volcanic material has been more pronounced on the eastern flanks leaving massive east-facing cliffs.

Rainforest covers the sheltered, moister parts of the range, while grass trees and low wind-pruned shrubs are predominant on the rocky tops. On exposed cliffs and steep slopes, the giant spear lily (*Doryanthes palmeri*) is a significant feature. It has huge flax-like leaves and a flower stalk, up to 4 m, with a brilliant red flower head. It blooms in late spring and early summer. Because the whole area has fertile volcanic soils, farms occupy all possible surrounding land, leaving only those places too steep to farm for the heavily forested park. This forest is part of the much larger World Heritage-classified Gondwana Rainforests of Australia.

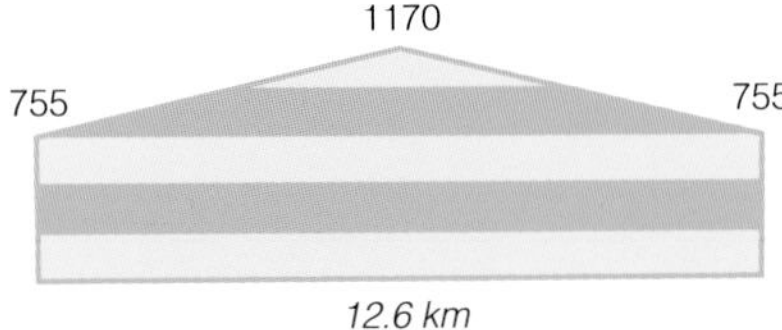

12.6 km

The suggested walk is north from Cunninghams Gap and includes what is known as the Rainforest Circuit. The track is very well graded via many zigzags, so the climb to the range crest is moderately easy.

Brisbane	J	F	M	A	M	J	J	A	S	O	N	D	Year
Rain av. mm	159	158	140	92	73	67	56	45	45	75	97	133	1149
Temp av. max. °C	29	29	28	26	23	20	20	21	24	26	27	29	25
Temp av. min. °C	20	20	19	16	13	10	9	10	12	15	18	19	1

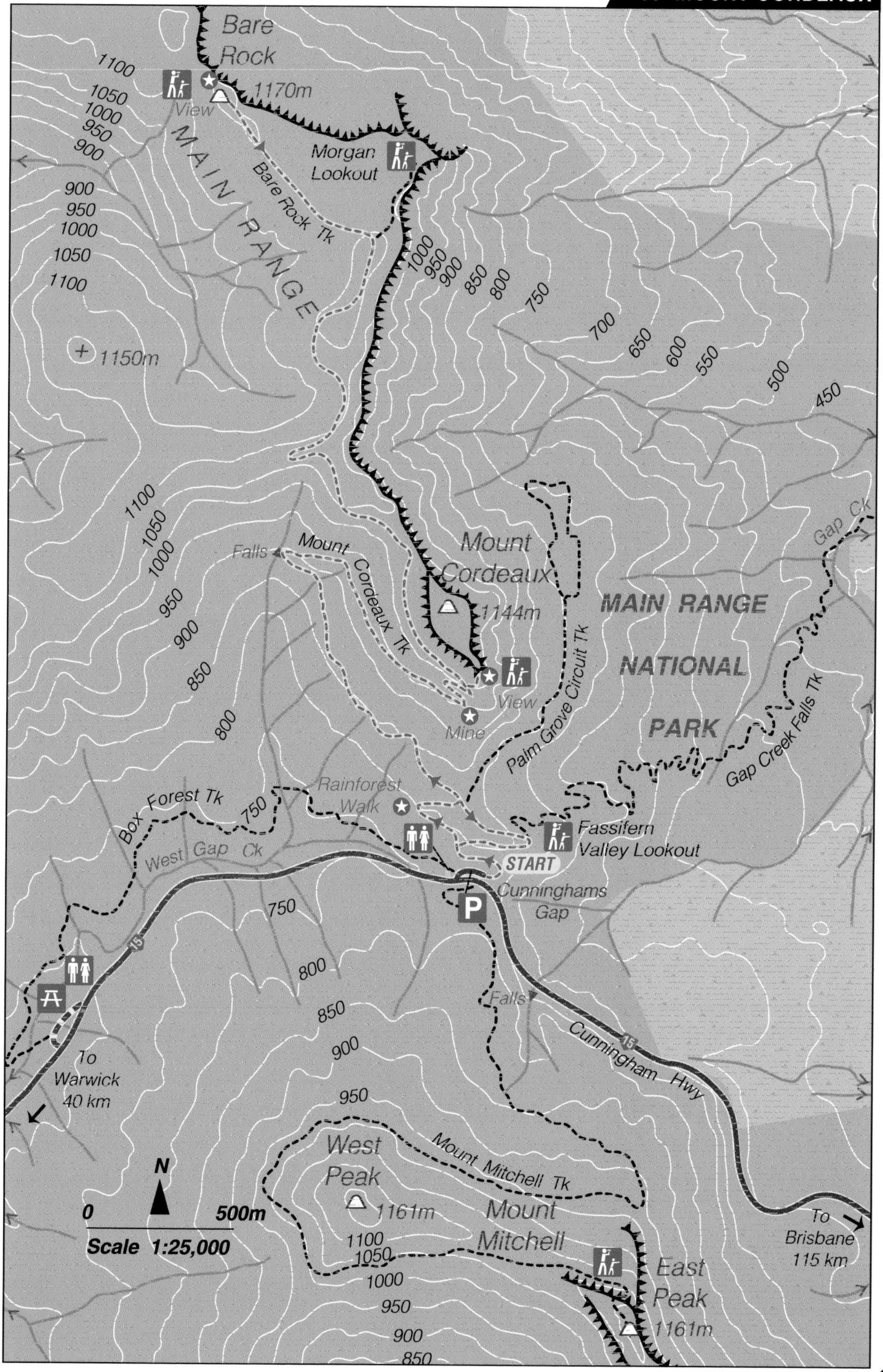

Bare Rock
1170m
View
Morgan Lookout
Bare Rock Tk
MAIN RANGE
1100
1050
1000
950
900
1150m
Mount Cordeaux
1144m
Falls
Mount Cordeaux Tk
View
Mine
Palm Grove Circuit Tk
MAIN RANGE NATIONAL PARK
Gap Ck
Gap Creek Falls Tk
700
650
600
550
500
450
850
800
750
Rainforest Walk
Box Forest Tk
West Gap Ck
Fassifern Valley Lookout
START
Cunninghams Gap
P
15
To Warwick 40 km
Falls
Cunningham Hwy
West Peak
1161m
Mount Mitchell Tk
Mount Mitchell
East Peak
1161m
To Brisbane 115 km
N
0 500m
Scale 1:25,000

Some 415 m elevation has to be gained to reach the objective at Bare Rock, but this rise is all but completed after the first 4 km. The rock has a commanding view of the massive cliffs along the escarpment and to the city skyline of Brisbane, approximately 115 km away. Mount Cordeaux Lookout is included in the walk, being only 65 m off the main track.

Private transport is best used for access to Cunninghams Gap and there is little accommodation in the immediate area. The small town of Aratula north-east of the gap has limited accommodation. The nearest large town facilities are at Boonah and Warwick, both some 40 km distant in opposing directions.

The track to follow leaves from the east end of the carpark at the gap. Do not leave valuables in vehicles at the gap as thieves evidently operate in the area. Also car parking spaces are quite limited, especially at weekends. You are therefore advised to arrive early. Carry water for lunch as the tops are usually dry. A toilet is available at the gap.

Shortly after departure, you pass a monument to Allan Cunningham. You soon reach a division of tracks which mark the two sides of the Rainforest Circuit. Go left so as to climb to a second track junction 700 m from the walk start. Some plants here are labelled. The tracks at the junction lead to Palm Grove, back down to the carpark and up to Mount Cordeaux. The last one is your route. It climbs gradually in and out of steep gullies, amid sheltered rainforest and soon you are away from the noise of trucks on the highway. Ensure you look up to view a complex plant community in the canopy. This includes birds nest ferns, orchids, epiphytes, vines and mosses.

After 1.4 km, near a grove of piccabeen palms (*Archontophoenix*

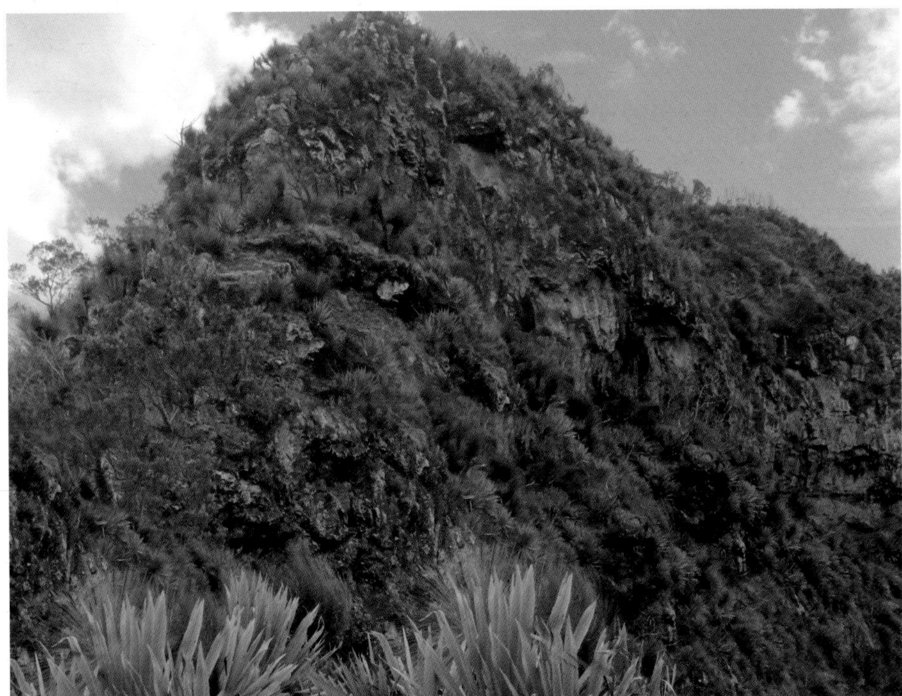

Mount Cordeaux and doryanthes

cunninghamiana), the track doubles back south-east at a small intermittent waterfall, but remains on the south-west slopes of Mount Cordeaux. These palms are known as bangalow palms in New South Wales. The track continues to rise gradually until it reaches the area of the main southern spur of Mount Cordeaux. At this point the track zigzags upwards several times and provides excellent views across Cunninghams Gap to Mount Mitchell as it rises above the rainforest canopy. There is an old open-cut gold mine at the zigzags. It has both a deep, horizontal cutting and a vertical shaft. Just after the turns, take the 65 metre-long side track to Mount Cordeaux Lookout. This rocky platform is adjacent to the sheer cliffs that ring the mountain summit. The actual top is dangerous to climb. The platform area is a great place to sit and enjoy the surrounding views.

Continue up the track along the south-west side of Mount Cordeaux. Soon a saddle is reached just north of the peak. Look back at the north-east side of the cliffs of the mountain to see the giant spear lilies and to better appreciate this rugged knob on the tops. Many orchids and grass trees (some with multi-trunks), up to 4 m tall, grow beside the track in this locality. Hoop pines (*Araucaria cunninghamii*) protrude above the canopy on the slopes westwards. This species existed at the time of Gondwana.

On again north-west along the range, the track re-enters rainforest with many tree ferns and climbs a little further. When some 2.1 km from Mount Cordeaux Lookout, the 350 metre-long and right-fork track to Morgan Lookout has a disappointing view so you could bypass it; although, it is a peaceful spot in the bush. We suggest you keep left and continue 680 m to reach Bare Rock. Its rocky summit is just above the rainforest, from which you can see one of the better views in south-east Queensland.

Bare Rock summit

Orchids

This makes it an ideal lunch spot. The variations in green of the forest below attract the eye, although the principal focus is along the Scenic Rim cliffs and north-eastwards. There is a 50 metre-long pad amid the scrub to rock on the south-west side of the summit where you get great views in that direction.

To return, retrace 5.5 km then complete the descent of 900 m via the alternative left-fork part of the Rainforest Circuit. It passes the Gap Falls Track and Fassifern Valley Lookout.

For those interested, an ascent of Mount Mitchell could be considered on another day. It leaves from the same carpark, is within our map coverage and also has stunning scenery.

Mount Mitchell East Peak

40 GREEN MOUNTAINS

South-East Rim, Queensland

Walk:	18.8 km circuit
Time required:	Including minimal breaks, 8 hours
Grade:	One day, hard
Environment:	Sub-tropical forest with many waterfalls
Last review date:	August 2007
Map reference:	1:25 000 Beechmont and Tyalgum and Map 40
Best time to visit:	Suited to any season but December to March can be hot and humid

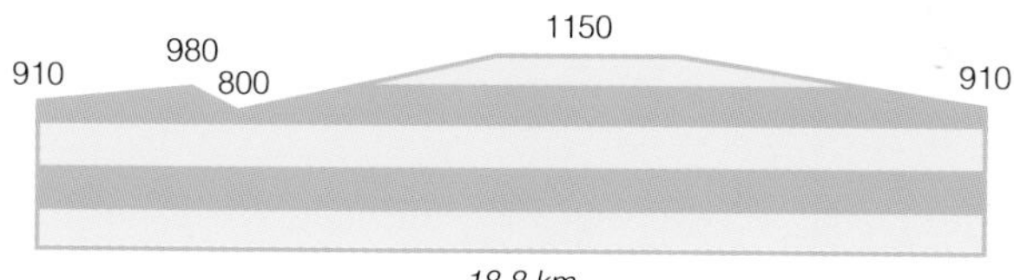

This longer walk in the Lamington National Park Green Mountains section includes numerous waterfalls along Canungra Creek West Branch and Toolona Creek. Rainforest covers most of the distance, including areas of an ancient crater rim on the Queensland–New South Wales state border. The walk is based from historic O'Reillys Guesthouse and the national park Green Mountains visitor centre across the road at 910 m elevation. The region is part of the large World Heritage classified Gondwana Rainforest of Australia and rainforest is in fact the prime attraction for this walk.

The outward route of this clockwise circuit has numerous stream crossings and waterfalls in the Toolona Gorge and beyond. Being a high rainfall belt, especially from December to March, these creek crossings could sometimes be awkward after prolonged rain. Slippery conditions occur at any time, especially at the creek crossings. You also need to carry a waterproof item upon which to sit during lunch and other breaks because of a lack of dry places to rest. It is essential, because of the length, to start this walk early in the day. You should regularly check yourself for possible ticks and leaches during and after the walk.

Private transport is needed for access from Canungra by very narrow, winding road. This town has numerous facilities and good accommodation. At O'Reilly

Tamborine Mtn	J	F	M	A	M	J	J	A	S	O	N	D	Year
Rain av. mm	228	221	199	118	110	101	90	55	58	95	119	152	1546
Temp av. max. °C	26	26	25	23	20	19	18	18	20	23	25	26	22
Temp av. min. °C	16	16	15	13	10	9	8	8	10	13	15	16	12

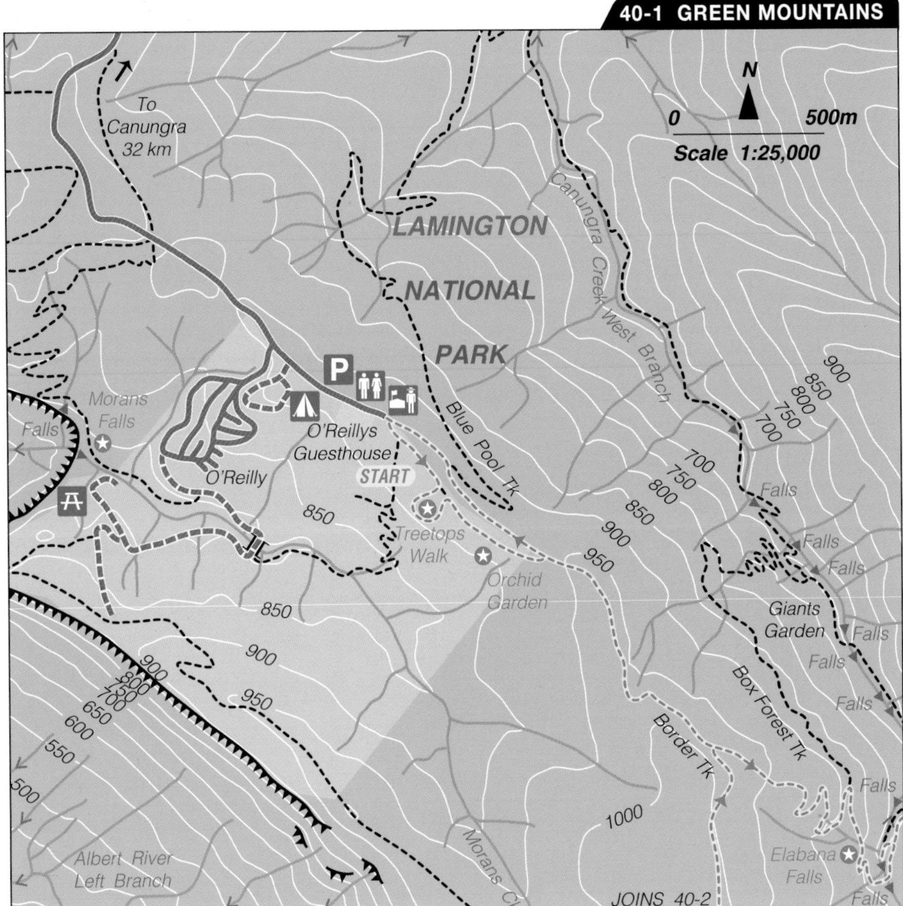

there is a park-operated basic, fuel stove only, camp area with levelled gravel sites to combat erosion and excess moisture. Accommodation is also available at the guesthouse. You should be aware that the former Pensioners Track shown on many maps has now been re-named as part of the Border Track and a parallel section of the Border Track has been downgraded to be an un-maintained route.

The guesthouse is heavily tourist orientated on a tract of private land surrounded by park. It contains a café, gift shop, its own network of walking tracks, garden for orchids and tropical plants and a treetops walk. It encourages bird feeding of colourful rosellas, lorikeets, brush turkeys, satin bower birds and regent bower birds for tourist viewing. This is in contrast to park signs across the road requesting that birds not be fed.

The state border escarpment rim is the eroded perimeter of the crater of the huge extinct Mount Warning shield volcano. It stands alone 15 km away in the centre of the crater as a volcanic plug of resistant igneous rock. The volcano is said to have been active about 23 million years ago. For this walk you climb to the rim of the caldera, follow the rim and then descend again. The basaltic rock has been heavily eroded by Toolona Creek and other

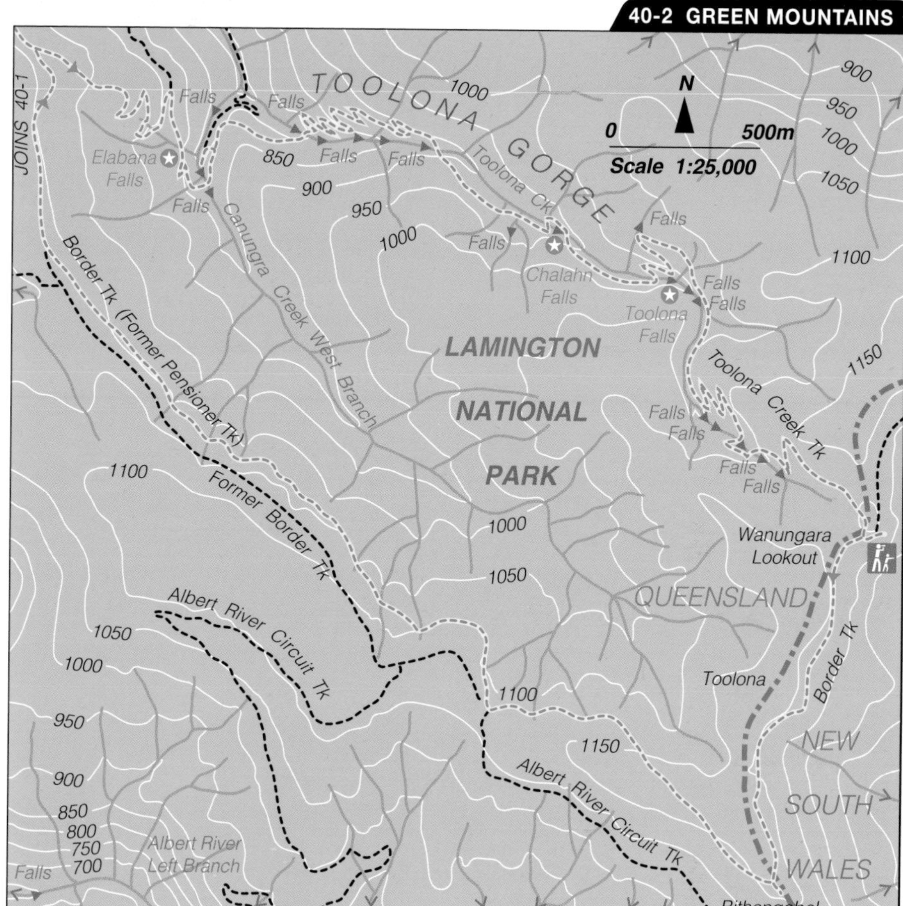

streams. However, the greatest erosion has been on the southern (New South Wales) side which is subject to prevailing weather.

Set off up past the guesthouse and respect the private land as you visit the treetops boardwalk, view the orchid garden briefly perhaps from across the fence. There is a long way to go so do not spend too much time in the garden. When 700 m from the walk start, you join the main Border Track. Some of the trees are labelled and are representative of those to be seen ahead in the nearby rainforest. They are sub tropical types often with large buttresses like the strangler fig trees (*Ficus watkinsiana*). Further into the forest there is a cool temperate type forest. Antarctic beech trees (*Nothofagus moorei*) are typically seen. Nothofagus support a fungus called beech orange, which is only found in Australia and South America. Both species existed at the time of Gondwana. As you continue, you will encounter colourful bracket fungi growing on rotting timber. It is one of many types of fungi seen in such damp places.

After another 1.1 km you veer left and start a descent into the rugged Canungra Creek West Branch valley. The way is down via zigzags into a cascading world of water and ferns. After 900 m you keep right to avoid the Box Forest Track and 600 m

Bowerbirds at O'Reilly

Elabana Falls

further down you reach Canungra Creek West Branch. Cross the creek above the first of some seventeen waterfalls to be seen ahead. Next, you should take a side trip to see beautiful two-tiered Elabana Falls. It is 400 m return. The other end of the Box Forest Track is near these falls and needs to be avoided.

After the detour, you go 400 m and reach Toolona Creek and from this creek crossing you climb the Toolona Creek Track for 5.7 km. There are many zigzags to negotiate and some falls drop more than 30 m. Chalahn Falls and Toolona Falls are particularly attractive. Multitudes of ferns are passed and there are aerial gardens of epiphytes, mosses, vines, ferns and other plants in the canopy. The track zigzags to visit many waterfalls as you ascend further and further into damp cloud forest. There are thousands of stream lilies growing in this mist-drenched area of gullies and cliffs. They flower in September and October and have a large flower stalk. The forest is most beautiful here at their flowering time. Eventually you arrive at the Mount Warning caldera rim and meet the Border Track junction.

Before you turn right, take the 70 metre-long side trip to Wanungara Lookout for its reasonably good view. At the time of review, some of the area was closed for revegetation. Next, follow the Border Track south close to the caldera rim in dense forest and within 1.3 km you reach Boolamoola where you leave the caldera rim. Antarctic beech trees (*Nothofagus moorei*), many mosses and ferns, plus lyrebirds are seen on this section. The beeches are up to 5000 years old and prefer the damp, mist-laden prevailing, south-easterly weather of the escarpment. The limbs are mostly draped with eerie mosses.

Turn back north-west and after a minor climb, you begin a descent. Within 1.1 km you reach the Albert River circuit track which links on the left. Just 50 m later the

Strangler fig

return junction of the circuit needs to be bypassed. The former Pensioner Track section of the Border Track (2.8 km long) takes you downhill gradually back into the sub tropical rainforest. Another 600 m on you rejoin your outward route. You retrace 1.1 km then keep right on to sealed path, which leads directly back to the park visitor centre. The Blue Pool Track from Canungra Creek West Branch links from the right just short of the walk end.

Time permitting you could explore the facilities at O'Reillys, enjoy afternoon tea and perhaps view the abundant birdlife. If you are not staying overnight at O'Reilly it is important that you make your way down the narrow winding road to Canungra before dark.

Waterfall on Toolona Creek

Safety and commonsense

Boardwalk, Cradle Valley, Tasmania

Bushwalking is a very enjoyable recreation and commonsense safety precautions will keep it that way. Be prepared for any problem that may arise. In the event of an emergency, free call 000 and ask for connection to fire, police, ambulance or search and rescue, or from a mobile phone call 112.

Planning

Plan your trip and leave details of your route, timing, vehicle registration, names and next of kin in writing with some responsible person reporting back to them on return.

Some parks provide intentions books for walkers but you should not rely upon park systems. It is unwise to divulge too much personal detail in trackhead intention books as unfortunately it could be used by thieves to their advantage.

Bushwalkers need to bear in mind that they practise a sport which entails a certain element of risk. You should be considerate and remember that the community is not impressed with having to meet expensive search costs because of incompetence. Pick the appropriate season and hopefully the right weather for your planned walk. Be sensible in regard to your safety and comfort and avoid very cold or hot days. Forget any walk on a day of proclaimed total fire ban or if a projected high risk of bushfire exists. On such fire risk days many national parks close. For your safety, do not stray from this advice.

Always carry maps, compass, mirror,

first-aid kit, pencil and paper, warm, brightly coloured, waterproof clothing, whistle, matches in a waterproof container, candle, small sharp knife, torch and emergency rations of food. It is of the utmost importance that you are able to confidently read maps and use a compass.

Accommodation and transport

The large size of the country results in great variations in accommodation availability and means of access to national parks and walking areas. Many parks have campgrounds and some have cabins or huts. A few mountain huts are free of charge but you should not rely upon their availability. Some are for emergency use only. As a general rule, motels are generally a quieter option to hotels, the latter having alcohol licences and public bars. Bed and breakfast should be considered and can be surprisingly affordable. Those on a budget may consider renting an on-site caravan at commercial campgrounds. There are many backpacker and youth hostels around the country, which can be very noisy. Free camping in remote areas, away from towns, is widely acceptable unless otherwise indicated. Tourist information offices in most towns of any real size can be helpful in locating suitable accommodation options.

There are usually no transport problems between cities and large towns using air, rail, or coach. Rental cars however, give the most flexibility, especially as travel beyond the large towns is often difficult without a vehicle. Some private operators provide transport to major parks, by coach or four-wheel-drive vehicle. Taxi cabs are in most towns, but can prove expensive if the walk area is distant.

Distance and timing

Never try to rush a trip. Think before you act, watch your route on a map and recognise your limitations, especially with distance. A good walker can cover three to five kilometres each hour on flat land, but in dense bush or hilly country, perhaps as little as five kilometres in a day. Always keep together when walking in a group. You are strongly advised to walk in a party of three or more in remote areas. (If one walker is injured, one can remain to assist while the other seeks help.)

Footwear

Sandshoes (sneakers or runners) with a good tread for grip are ideal for beach walks or for drier regions and on rock surfaces, but certainly not for snow conditions. Boots are needed for alpine country or very wet conditions. Some ankle support is always preferable. Never wear new boots for the first time on any long walk. Two pairs of cotton socks help prevent blisters and limit heat while woollen socks can cause too much heat.

Maps

When following suggested walk routes, ensure you obtain and use the latest maps so that the maximum amount of information is available to you. Where more than one map of an area is available, you are advised to use both. Maps frequently become obsolete and many government maps have not been updated for years. The detailed maps included in this book should be used in conjunction with other maps wherever possible. It would be easy to walk off the edge of our map coverage if you become disorientated. For your convenience and safety we have provided the additional map titles. Always carry a waterproof map case.

Information

Be aware that spelling of place names on maps, signposts and in books frequently does not correlate and while many names are official, others are not. Government maps are often outdated as to track and other man-made features. Some names in this book are widely recognised in the bushwalking fraternity but may not appear on official maps. No doubt, in the interest of safety, national park authorities and some other bodies appear to deliberately overstate distances and times in brochures and on signs. It is also policy in some parks to not show walking tracks that fail to meet their safety standards. This book attempts to state distances precisely to address these discrepancies. Much park literary and internet information is very superficial in its content especially hard copy hand out literature. Determining ever-changing government website names for reference, can be a major problem.

Conservation

Remember that care of the environment itself is very important. Many walk routes are in declared national parks and commonsense regulations must be respected. The landscape and the life within it are often in a delicate state of ecological balance and, of necessity, there must be no rubbish discarded or damage to wildlife and plants. For the sake of wildlife, pets are banned from all parks. Plants may not be taken from, or brought into national parks and fines often apply.

Campfires, fuel stoves and waste disposal

Green timber should not be cut or broken for fires and great care is required with any fire. Before leaving it make sure your camp fire is completely extinguished. Remember the adage, 'The bigger the fire, the bigger the fool'. On no account light a fire on a high fire-danger day. Most areas have fire risk indicator boards; again fines apply. Note that in some parks fires are totally banned at all times and you may need to carry a fuel stove for cooking.

The traditional bush campfire is still an expectation for many campers. However, the environmental footprint is bad and campfires should be actively discouraged. A fuel stove is always preferable to prevent escaping fire. All waste should be flattened and carried home for disposal. Burying of rubbish is not permitted. Human waste must be properly buried away from streams and drinking water.

Off-track walking

This book details walking tracks and with the exception of beaches, the tracks are well-defined, mostly park authority endorsed routes. Deviating from tracks and taking 'short cuts' can create erosion and may bring you into conflict with the park ranger. Official tracks are usually positioned to provide access to features of interest. The authors strongly advise against off-track walking for the ongoing protection of the environment.

Water

The purity of drinking water is of course important to walkers and as we all would realise, Australia is basically a very dry country with a shortage of water. Few pleasures can top a cool drink from a high-country lake or mountain stream on a hot day or after a big climb. Fortunately, in Australia we can still drink water from most mountain streams relatively safely. Use your map to ensure water quality from creeks has not been tainted from farmland, towns or industry upstream. At any location, still water is best avoided unless it is in an alpine tarn or large, remote lake. Inland lakes may be useless because of salt. If in doubt, boil water for about three to four minutes or use water purification tablets. Preferably you are advised to obtain water

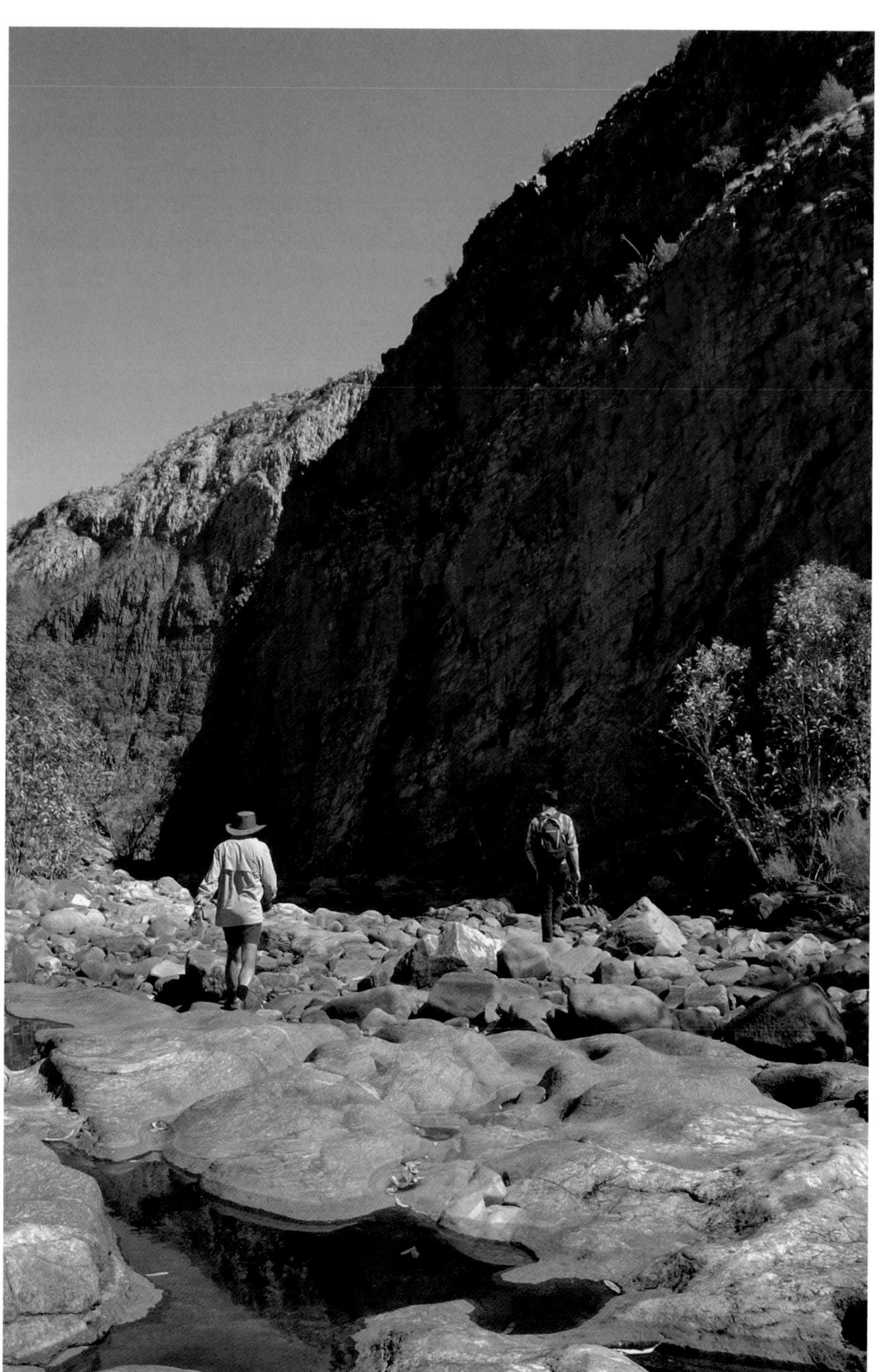
Walking in Ormiston Gorge, Northern Territory

from your usual source. This ensures that your body does not adversely react to changes in water quality. Always wash downstream from the camp site and collect drinking water upstream. Soap or detergent must not enter the watercourse.

Snow and exposure

Because of the variability of weather, violent changes and snow storms can occur even at the height of summer in the higher parts of southern Australia. In alpine areas of New South Wales, Victoria and Tasmania you should always carry protective and warm clothing. Make note of the position of huts or other shelter if needed. Good footwear is also very important. In winter, snow can fall as far north as the Queensland border.

If, in spite of planning, you do find yourself caught in snow when camping, stay in the tent. Do not try to walk out until the weather clears. Learn how to interpret cloud formations and winds in advance so that you do not get caught in exposed positions. You can then get off high, wild places well before foul weather sets in. Most situations where walkers have been holed up for days by snow or floods could have been avoided by reading the signs of the cloud formations and acting to avoid the problem. During electrical storms, lightning frequently strikes mountain tops. At such times keep off lookout towers and away from large or solitary trees, or metal objects.

Flooding

Flooded streams can cause delays and even prevent you from continuing along your intended route. Do not camp on sandy creek beds. A thunderstorm upstream can quickly turn a dry creek bed into a torrent. Some areas mentioned in these track notes are subject to flooding and you should use discretion. In this book, Murchison and Bunyeroo Gorges are two such examples where care should be exercised. Wet weather gear is essential in Tasmania virtually at all times.

Hot days

Over much of the country temperatures can rise to over 40 degrees Celsius. This applies to areas as far south as Melbourne. The northern one-third of the country is tropical and bushwalking is often uncomfortable. On hot days, especially if a northerly wind is predicted in southern Australia, start your walk early before the main heat of the day. Wet a small towel or similar item in a creek at the bottom of any big climb and cool off by mopping your brow. The towel should be left draped over your shoulders to dampen and cool you as you climb. Use sun screen, especially at high altitudes and wear a hat.

Lost?

If lost, STOP! Only move after you have sat down and logically and carefully thought things through. Generally it is best to stay in the spot until help arrives. Remember that any movement is normally best made on ridges and spurs, not in scrub-choked gullies. You should be absolutely sure of directions and should leave a prominent note indicating your intentions and time of leaving. Preferably wear brightly coloured and warm clothing and ration the food you have with you. Parties should not split up and the physically stronger should help others.

Once moving, check the compass frequently, remain on as straight a line as possible and leave notes along the route. If you become tired, stop and rest. Do not over-exert yourself. Remember that severe physical and mental strain, plus cold, can bring death by exposure. Over the years far too many people have died unnecessarily, or suffered serious injuries, mainly because

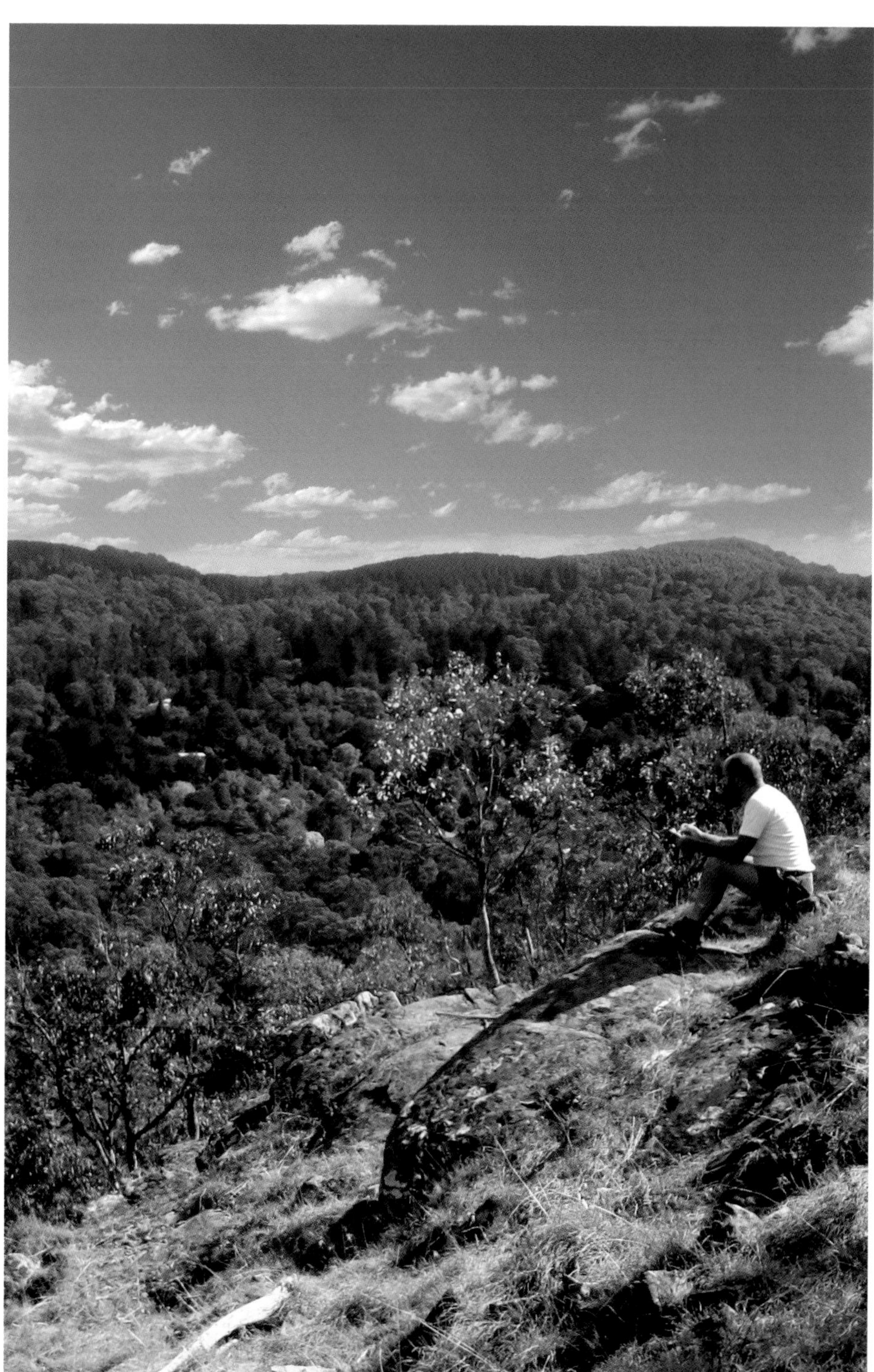

Mount Towrong outlook, Victoria

they have not understood the seriousness of being caught unprepared to cope with the situation. The accepted distress signal is three long whistles, coo-ees, mirror flashes, or any other signal repeated in threes every minute. Do not force yourself physically; rather, do things objectively and calmly, with plenty of rest. If you feel confused, make camp. If park or other regulations permit then consider lighting a small fire to create smoke where your location can be seen from the air.

Theft

Years ago, theft from a car left at a trackhead was rare. Now, equipment has become fancy, expensive and worth stealing. Wilderness trackheads are not a safe place to leave valuables, so take them on the walk with you or leave them at home.

Be wary of anyone waiting around when you arrive. A ploy used is for thieves to wear a rucksack on the back as if genuine walkers. After you leave, the thieves, having watched you hide your valuables, fill the rucksack with your belongings.

Families

Leaders attempting walking trips should at no time leave children unattended as becoming lost is a very unhappy experience for a child and parents alike. It must be emphasised that any walking along roads should usually be done facing oncoming traffic. (The Pinnacles Desert walk suggested in this book recommends walking against this advice, but extremely slow traffic is encountered there.) Children should be instructed not to wander away from the party and if they do become separated or lost, to wait where they are until help arrives. Children must be instructed not to drink from streams without supervision or eat tempting looking berries in the bush. Many leaves, fruit, berries and fungi, if not poisonous, can cause acute discomfort. It is unwise to take babies on walks that expose them to the hot sun, wind, undue jarring while walking or injuries from stumbling. Do not leave children (or pets) in vehicles while walking.

By using a little extra care and avoiding placing children in dangerous situations, great family times can be enjoyed. The environment is full of wonders and what better way is there to give children fresh air, exercise and first hand knowledge of nature?

Lichen

Equipment and food

The Razorback, Mount Feathertop, Victoria

Safety equipment

Carry: maps, compass, small mirror, paper, whistle, matches in a waterproof container, sharp knife, small candle, small torch, a waterproof marking pen, first aid kit, safety clothing (consisting of warm sweater or pullover, thick woollen socks, bright coloured shirt and bright coloured waterproof coat) and safety food rations (such as nourishing concentrated foods plus a little bulky food like dried fruit, chocolate, nuts, fruit and seed bars and brown rice).

Sunglasses and sunscreen are needed if snow is a possibility. A balaclava, mittens and wool trousers should be taken on all snow country walks. Waterproof over-trousers and gaiters provide comfort in wet and cold conditions. Remember that items that may leak such as toothpaste, sunscreen and shampoo, should be double wrapped in plastic bags to avoid a horrible mess in the bottom of your pack!

Other equipment

Overnight walks: tent, tent poles, tent pegs, tent guys, good quality sleeping bag, inner bag, ground sheet, toiletry items, a billy (saucepan), billy lifters, pot scourer and small fuel stove if you wish to cook. In wet weather plenty of plastic bags should be carried for waterproofing items in your pack. A pack liner also helps. Include a deck of cards or a book of crosswords for the days when you might be tent-bound.

All walks: shirt or blouse (woollen in winter), shorts, jeans, handkerchief, walking boots, runners or gym-boots with good tread and ankle support, mug, bowl, cutlery, small towel, lightweight bathers for summer, sunscreen, hat, waterbag (canvas type with zip top), water bottle (aluminium or plastic), can opener and backpack.

Food

In addition to the emergency rations (which are to be used only in an emergency), the following foods should be carried in quantities according to the number of days you will be walking: nuts, dried fruit, chocolate, fruit and seed bars, hard-boiled eggs, packet or cube soups, fruit drink powders, rice and packet rice preparations, pasta, fresh fruit, honey, pita bread, crispbread, savoury spreads, salami, fruit cake, coffee, tea or other hot drink, salted bacon, carrot, packet mashed potato or tuna and some muesli or porridge. Canned food should only be carried by people accustomed to heavy packs. Avoid the possibility of broken glass by decanting items (particularly sticky honey) into burst-proof polythene containers. Rubbish should be taken home for disposal. Thought should be given to the energy content of foods with respect to their weight.

Weight of backpack

The most important consideration when carrying an overnight pack is the combined weight of the contents. If you carry no more than stated in this list of equipment and food suggestions, you should not encounter trouble. Some extras, such as a camera, might be considered worthwhile. However, far too many people include that little extra item or two, or over estimate the quantity of food that they could possibly eat and so suffer the consequences when they climb a hill bearing 'a tonne of bricks'. They defeat the purpose of the walk by becoming too tired to enjoy the trip.

Frenchmans Cap from Donaghys Lookout, Tasmania

Mapping and navigation

Navigation procedures are best learned from experience in the field, using map and compass. This is sometimes difficult to arrange if one does not have a friend who can teach you in the field. Usually, there are excellent opportunities to learn navigation when walking with a bushwalking club.

Clubs help walkers with safety, advice, experience and companionship. Usually trips are organised and led by experienced leaders, often with transport arranged. Inquiries of a general nature and those concerning the various clubs can be made from the Federation of Walking Clubs in each state.

This book provides a map of the immediate area of every walk suggestion. To some extent the maps will assist with navigation, but to rely entirely on these maps would be unwise. (For example, you might travel off the map coverage while lost.) Our first walk map is at 1:12 500 scale and all others are at 1:25 000 scale. It is strongly recommended, therefore, that every endeavour be made to purchase the most updated government or other maps before setting out.

Apart from maps suggested in this book, additional maps are useful supplements. Such maps are available in the bigger cities at sales outlets of government departments, at larger book shops and especially shops catering for bushwalkers' needs. Map coverage is also available using the internet. The best government produced maps available for the walks in this book tend to be of the 1:25 000 scale sheets; there is broad coverage of walk areas in these series. The 1:50 000 and 1:100 000 scale sheets covering even greater areas are useful for planning and car touring. Remember that many government maps have been in circulation for a long time, often more than thirty years and so lack recent changes to roads, tracks and other man-made features. In Victoria 1:25 000 scale maps are being gradually replaced by 1:50 000 scale maps. These are less than ideal for bushwalkers so we recommend you use the older maps while stocks are available.

One important point with which all walkers should be familiar is that magnetic north is not constant and can vary by more that ten degrees from true north, depending on your location. Always consult your government map for this variation.

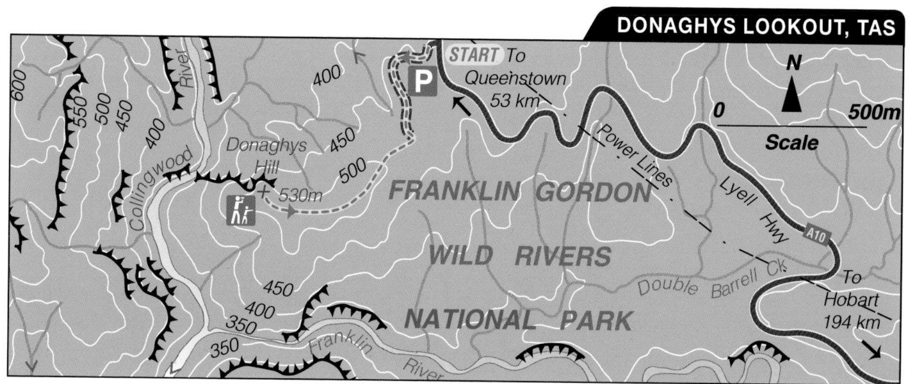

First aid at a glance

It is essential that any emergency can be dealt with promptly and smoothly. Free call 000 and ask for connection to ambulance or search and rescue services or call 112 from a mobile phone.

A first aid book and kit should be carried by at least one member of every walking party. First aid is not our field of expertise and we stress that reference to professional information is essential. Before you walk you need to prepare properly. Use the internet with links to first aid and printout information at

- www.stjohn.org.au
- www.redcross.org.au
- www.firstaidinternational.com.au
- www.bushwalkingaustralia.org.

As the name suggests, 'first aid' is an on-site basic treatment for patient comfort until you can seek professional medical attention.

The kit should include: bandages, safety pins, adhesive tape, small adhesive dressing strips, gauze pads, antiseptic cream, tweezers, small scissors, sunscreen, insect repellent, pain relief tablets, antifungal powder/cream, antacid tablets, antihistamine tablets, water purification tablets, dehydration treatment tablets and pen and paper to record details of any injury requiring further medical assistance.

The most likely troubles to be encountered are listed here for rapid reference. In virtually all serious situations the patient needs to be rested and reassured, often while another person obtains medical assistance. For this reason walk parties in any remote place should never be less than three in number. One walker should stay with the patient while the other goes for aid. Be aware in advance of any allergies or medical conditions present within your walk group and ensure their medications are carried.

COMPLAINT AND TREATMENT	
SERIOUS TRAUMA/ SPINAL/HEAD INJURIES	Immobilise completely with head slightly elevated, keep warm and seek urgent professional assistance.
BLISTERS	Apply a soft wound dressing; wear extra socks; if possible, do not break the blister as this increases the risk of infection. If blister breaks apply antiseptic cream.
HEAT EXHAUSTION	Replenish body fluids with plenty of water or fruit juice and take a little salt if badly dehydrated. Rest in a cool, shaded place and fan the patient. Remove excess clothing and sponge patient with cold water.
ABDOMINAL PAIN/ FEVERS	These conditions usually indicate that some deeper factor is involved and which needs to be investigated. Rest is essential. Give plenty of liquid to the patient.
BURNS	Immediately immerse burn area in cold water to chill for 10–20 minutes. Clean thoroughly, despite the pain, and apply a sterile dressing and bandage. Immobilise the burn area. Do not remove anything that is stuck to the skin.

COMPLAINT AND TREATMENT	
LACERATIONS	Control any external bleeding with pressure to the area using dressing and bandage where possible.
FRACTURES	Immobilise with compression bandaging and where practical, splinting. Use a support sling for arm or collarbone fracture.
EXPOSURE TO COLD	Do not rub the skin or apply direct heat or give alcohol. These cause blood to come to the skin surface which then returns to the heart, cooler. The body trunk and brain must be warmed. Insulate the entire body; give sugar in easily digested form (for example, sweetened condensed milk). Put the patient in a sleeping bag, preferably with a warm person. Cover the bag with insulation, provide a wind break and pitch a tent over the patient. If breathing stops, apply mouth-to-mouth resuscitation using the first aid book in your party for instruction on how to render this aid. Only move to a warmer place if in doing so the patient will in no way be physically exerted. Avoid standing the patient as fainting will follow. The recognisable signs of the onset of exposure are: pallor and shivering, listlessness, followed by slurred speech, poor vision, irrational and violent behaviour and eventual collapse. It is wet cold particularly that kills.
SPRAINS	Immobilise the area of the sprain and rest it. Promptly immerse in cold water (stream etc.) or apply cold pack or wet cloth.
INSECT AND SPIDER BITES/STINGS	Scrape sideways to remove any stinger barb that may be lodged. Apply cold treatment to reduce swelling and elevate any limb involved. For dangerous spider or scorpion bites treat the same as for snake bite.
SNAKE BITE	Most bites are of a minor nature but it is wise to treat all bites as if dangerous. Many people have a disproportionate fear of snake bite so need reassurance and rest. The majority of bites are to limbs rather than the body trunk, so first aid is easier. If bitten deeply by a full grown deadly snake on the neck many kilometres from anywhere then there is probably little that can be done and in these circumstances, prayer and writing your will seem like worthy options. However, the instances of such bites are extremely rare. For practically all bites, you need to restrict venom movement in the body. Therefore, a broad bandage should be applied to a limb bite area or pressure kept firmly on bites to the body trunk. The bite area should be kept immobilised, with pressure applied to bandage or pad until antivenene is received. Immobilisation can best be achieved by binding a splint to any limb bite area. The blood supply to the area must not be stopped for lengthy periods. Cutting the bite and washing venom off skin should not be attempted. Cutting upsets the patient, and can lead to complications. Venom retained on the skin can be tested later to identify the snake species. To maximise rest, transport should be brought to the patient. Apply mouth-to-mouth resuscitation and artificial respiration until medical aid is given. Refer to the first aid book in your party for the correct way of rendering artificial respiration procedures.

Glossary

adit an underground mine entrance
alluvial soil sand, silt and clay, resulting from deposition by streams, glaciers and lakes
amphitheatre semi-circular formation of cliffs resembling ancient man-made gallery for audience
anabranch former watercourse usually crescent shaped and often with billabong
anticlines deeply folded rock strata, the middle of which arches upwards
arable land normally used for growing grains for food
basalt hard, fine-grained, dark-coloured, extruded, volcanic rock
benched track a track that runs across a slope with a high-side embankment excavated to provide a flat walking surface
billabong a usually permanent waterhole found in the bed of a former stream or river, particularly anabranch
bushbash (also scrub-bash) to traverse trackless terrain amid bushland
bracket fungi the visible fruiting body resembling a round plate, often found on decaying trees especially in damp conditions
cairn usually small mound of rocks, erected to mark summits and track alignment, especially for un-maintained, minor tracks in rocky terrain
confluence the meeting of two streams
conglomerate pieces of various rock types naturally cemented together
continental drift movement of the tectonic plates that comprise the crust and surface of the Earth with respect to each other
endemic found only within a particular location
el niño (as opposed to **la niña**) weather system resulting from the combined effects of cold ocean currents and dry onshore winds causing reduced rainfall
epicormic cells specialised, dormant cells triggered into growth following damage such as fire, notably eucalyptus trees
escarpment rock formation often cliffs caused by sections of the crust being thrust to the surface during sideways compression along faults
fauna any form of animal life including insects
flora any form of plant life dependant on photosynthesis for growth
geo-synclines folded rock strata forming a central depression often with escarpments on the outer limits
GPS (Global Positioning System) a device used to define elevation and position by decoding satellite signals
granite course-grained, light-coloured, intrusive, volcanic rock formed deep underground and in places, later exposed by erosion
gulch a ravine or cleft, usually narrow, eroded by a stream or the sea
indigenous native to a particular region or country
isthmus narrow neck of land connecting promontory, point or cape to mainland
latitude divisions used to locate points on the surface of the Earth with respect to the equator and the poles, 0–90 degrees + north and 0–90 degrees – south where '0' is the equator

Anticline

Basalt

Bracket fungi

Granite

lava plug the solidified core of a volcanic vent following eruption, often exposed at the surface by erosion
longitude divisions in hours, minutes and seconds to locate points on the surface of the Earth parallel with the equator at any latitude, up to 24 hours from the Greenwich meridian near London
maar a volcanic crater that does not lie in a cone and was formed by a single volcanic event. Maars usually contain a lake
magma molten rock, often containing water and mineral elements. When ejected from a volcano forms lava and ash, when trapped underground forms granite
metamorphic rock chemically or structurally changed by intense heating and pressure
mineral deposits rocks and sediments containing ores including oil, coal and precious metals
monsoon usually torrential rainfall preceded by rising humidity particularly in the tropics, often with cyclones (hurricanes or typhoons)
monolith solid usually large rock formation devoid of variation in density or mineral composition
mudstone mud cemented by pressure and mineralisation
pad a minor, un-maintained walking track or defined animal track
pastoral land usually grazed by sheep and cattle for food or wool production
peakbag to reach the top of a significant peak for the first time
planeze low angle spur
pound common name for the depression within a geo-syncline, for example, Wilpena Pound in the Flinders Ranges, South Australia
rain shadow an area rendered dry because mountains regularly block prevailing weather and rainfall
saddle a low point along a ridge crest between two hills
sandstone sand cemented by pressure and mineralisation
sedimentary rock formed through the progressive deposition of particles on the bottom of lakes and seas, for example sandstone and mudstone
sidle to walk, following along a map contour or across the side of a hill
spur a sloping ridge that links lowlands with highlands
subduction zone a location where one continental plate slides under another plate
symbiosis a mutually beneficial association between two or more organisms, often differing species, for example a bacterium and a plant
synclines deeply folded rock strata, the middle of which arches downwards
tarn a small alpine lake
telegraph (line, station) early system of electronic communication utilising morse code to transmit the alphabet via overland wiring
tops the highest areas of high-country plateau, ridge crest or mountain
trackhead the starting point of a walking track, often at a road or carpark
treeline the upper limit at which trees will grow due to severe weather
trig point (trigonometric point) a marker on many significant mountain tops for survey mapping now largely superseded by satellite navigation
tropics the regions of the earth 23 degrees, 28 minutes north and south of the equator bounded by the Tropic of Capricorn in the south and the Tropic of Cancer in the north
volcano vent in the Earths crust through which magma escapes from the mantle, usually found close to the collision or separation of continental plates

Lava plug

Monolith

Sandstone

Tarn

Australian road atlas

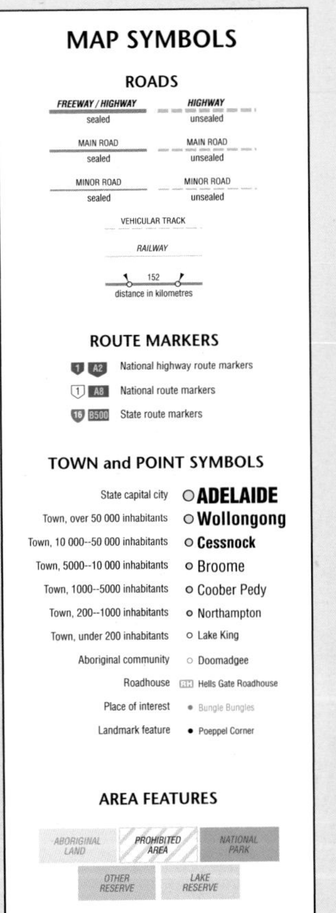
MAP SYMBOLS
ROADS
FREEWAY / HIGHWAY
sealed
HIGHWAY
unsealed
MAIN ROAD
sealed
MAIN ROAD
unsealed
MINOR ROAD
sealed
MINOR ROAD
unsealed
VEHICULAR TRACK
RAILWAY
152
distance in kilometres
ROUTE MARKERS
National highway route markers
National route markers
State route markers
TOWN and POINT SYMBOLS
State capital city ADELAIDE
Town, over 50 000 inhabitants Wollongong
Town, 10 000--50 000 inhabitants Cessnock
Town, 5000--10 000 inhabitants Broome
Town, 1000--5000 inhabitants Coober Pedy
Town, 200--1000 inhabitants Northampton
Town, under 200 inhabitants Lake King
Aboriginal community Doomadgee
Roadhouse Hells Gate Roadhouse
Place of interest Bungle Bungles
Landmark feature Poeppel Corner
AREA FEATURES
ABORIGINAL LAND
PROHIBITED AREA
NATIONAL PARK
OTHER RESERVE
LAKE RESERVE

247
Broome
Port Hedland
Nanutarra Roadhouse
Newman
Carnarvon
Mount Magnet
Geraldton
Southern Cross
PERTH
Margaret River
Manjimup
Albany
246

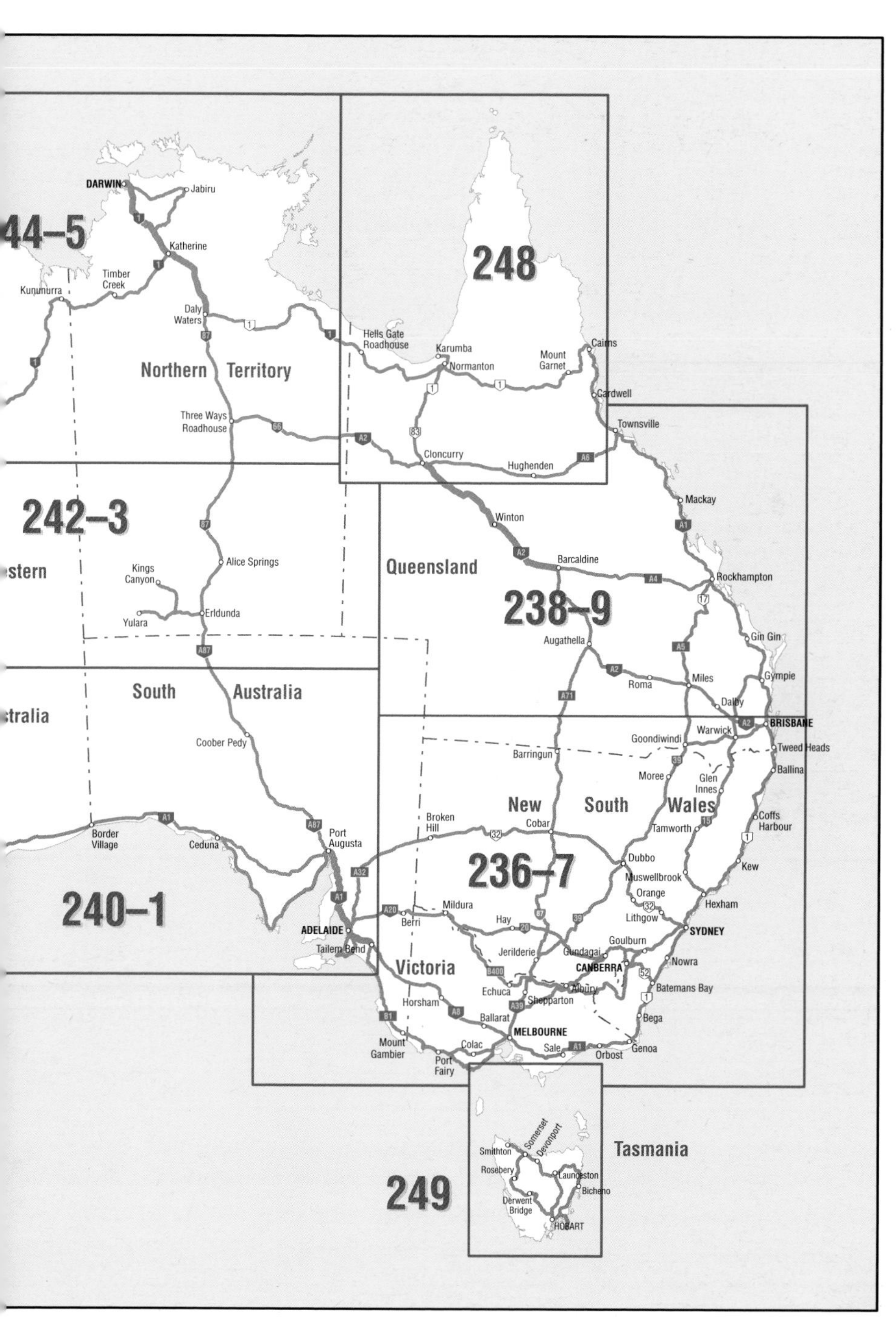

44–5
DARWIN
Jabiru
Katherine
Timber Creek
Kununurra
Daly Waters
Northern Territory
Hells Gate Roadhouse
Karumba
Normanton
Mount Garnet
Cairns
Cardwell
248
Three Ways Roadhouse
Townsville
Cloncurry
Hughenden
Mackay
Winton
242–3
Barcaldine
Queensland
Alice Springs
Kings Canyon
Rockhampton
238–9
Erldunda
Yulara
Augathella
Gin Gin
estern
South
Australia
Miles
Roma
Gympie
Dalby
stralia
Warwick
BRISBANE
Goondiwindi
Tweed Heads
Barringun
Coober Pedy
Moree
Ballina
Glen Innes
New
South
Wales
Broken Hill
Cobar
Coffs Harbour
Tamworth
Border Village
Ceduna
Port Augusta
236–7
Dubbo
Kew
Muswellbrook
Orange
240–1
Mildura
Hexham
Berri
Hay
Lithgow
ADELAIDE
SYDNEY
Jerilderie
Gundagai
Goulburn
Tailem Bend
Victoria
CANBERRA
Nowra
Echuca
Albury
Batemans Bay
Shepparton
Horsham
Ballarat
Bega
MELBOURNE
Mount Gambier
Colac
Sale
Orbost
Genoa
Port Fairy
Tasmania
Smithton
Somerset
Devonport
Rosebery
Launceston
249
Bicheno
Derwent Bridge
HOBART

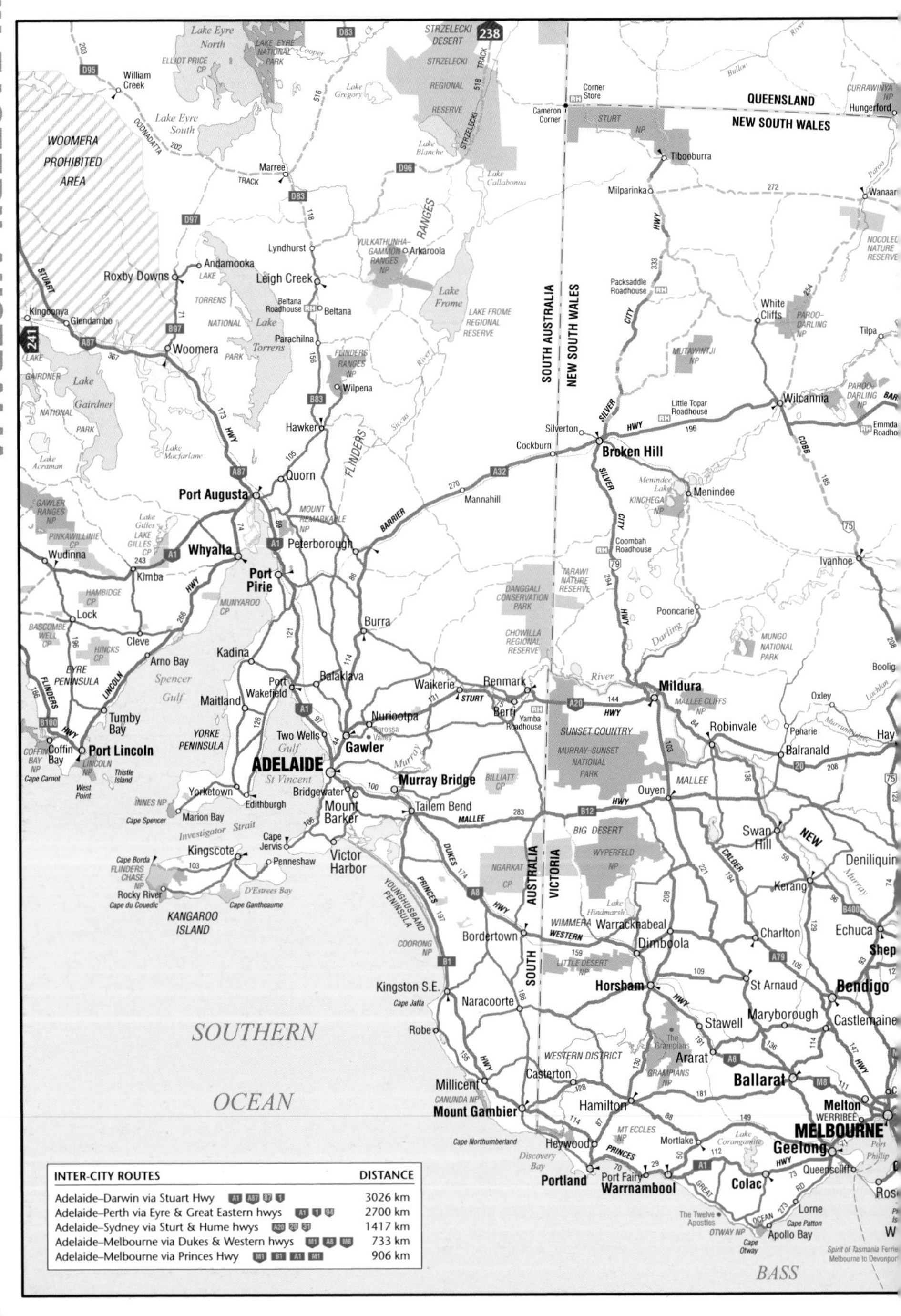

INTER-CITY ROUTES		DISTANCE
Adelaide–Darwin via Stuart Hwy	A1 A87 87 1	3026 km
Adelaide–Perth via Eyre & Great Eastern hwys	A1 1 94	2700 km
Adelaide–Sydney via Sturt & Hume hwys	A20 20 31	1417 km
Adelaide–Melbourne via Dukes & Western hwys	M1 A8 M8	733 km
Adelaide–Melbourne via Princes Hwy	M1 B1 A1 M1	906 km

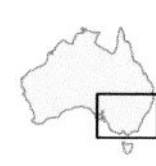

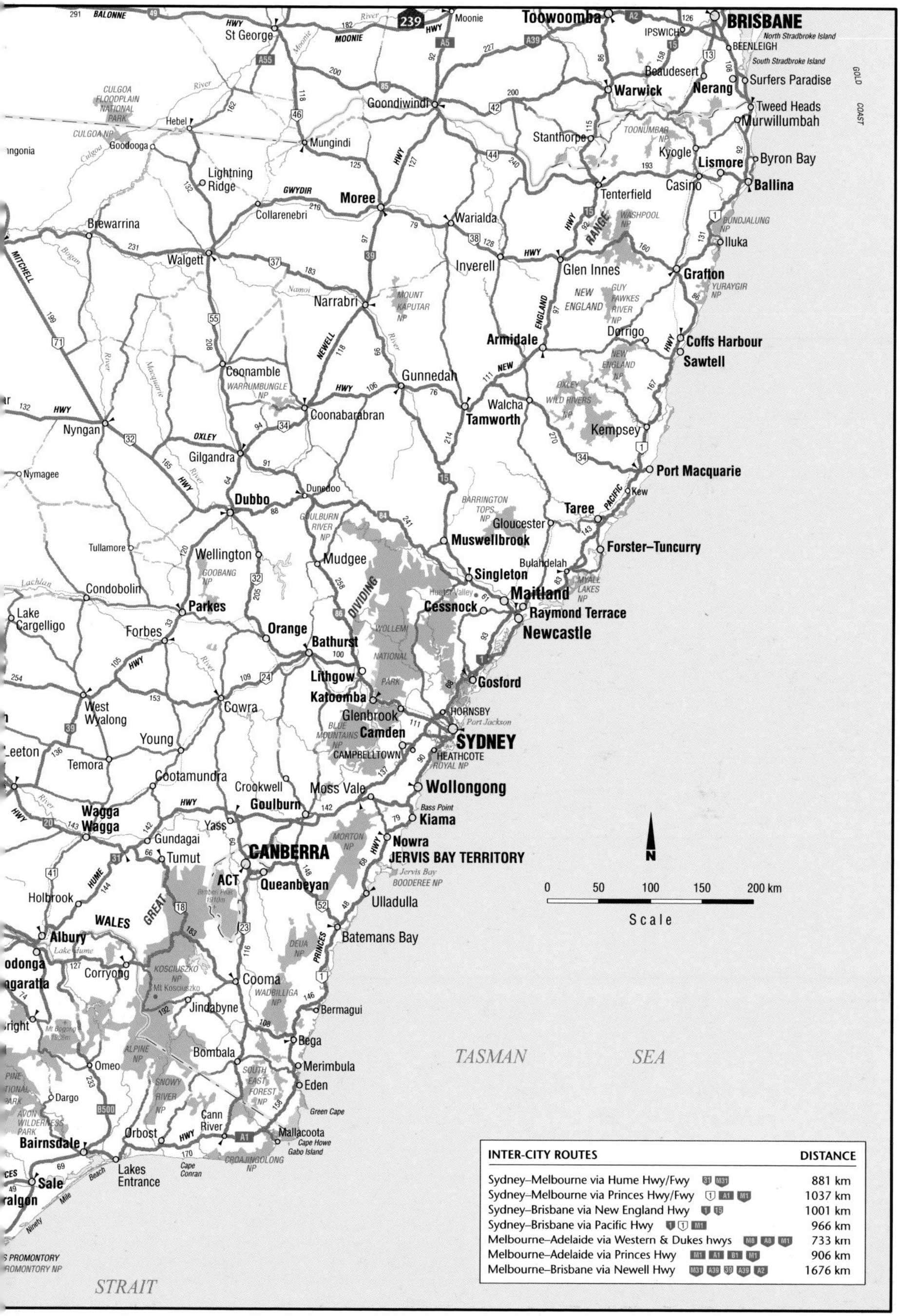

St George
Moonie
Toowoomba
BRISBANE
IPSWICH
North Stradbroke Island
BEENLEIGH
South Stradbroke Island
Beaudesert
Surfers Paradise
Nerang
Warwick
GOLD COAST
Goondiwindi
Tweed Heads
Murwillumbah
CULGOA FLOODPLAIN NATIONAL PARK
CULGOA NP
Hebel
Goodooga
Mungindi
Stanthorpe
TOONUMBAR NP
Kyogle
Lismore
Byron Bay
Lightning Ridge
Casino
Ballina
Tenterfield
Moree
Collarenebri
Brewarrina
Warialda
WASHPOOL NP
BUNDJALUNG NP
Iluka
Walgett
Inverell
Glen Innes
Grafton
YURAYGIR NP
NEW ENGLAND
GUY FAWKES RIVER NP
MOUNT KAPUTAR NP
Narrabri
Dorrigo
Armidale
Coffs Harbour
Sawtell
Coonamble
WARRUMBUNGLE NP
Gunnedah
NEW ENGLAND NP
OXLEY WILD RIVERS NP
Walcha
Tamworth
Nyngan
Coonabarabran
Kempsey
Gilgandra
Port Macquarie
Nymagee
Dunedoo
Kew
Dubbo
BARRINGTON TOPS NP
Taree
GOULBURN RIVER NP
Gloucester
Tullamore
Muswellbrook
Forster–Tuncurry
Wellington
GOOBANG NP
Mudgee
Bulahdelah
Singleton
MYALL LAKES NP
Condobolin
Hunter Valley
Maitland
Parkes
Cessnock
Raymond Terrace
Lake Cargelligo
Newcastle
Forbes
Orange
WOLLEMI NATIONAL PARK
Bathurst
Lithgow
Gosford
Katoomba
West Wyalong
Cowra
HORNSBY
Glenbrook
Port Jackson
BLUE MOUNTAINS NP
Camden
SYDNEY
Young
Leeton
CAMPBELLTOWN
HEATHCOTE ROYAL NP
Temora
Cootamundra
Crookwell
Moss Vale
Wollongong
Goulburn
Bass Point
Kiama
Wagga Wagga
Yass
MORTON NP
Gundagai
Nowra
Tumut
CANBERRA
JERVIS BAY TERRITORY
Jervis Bay
BOODEREE NP
ACT
Queanbeyan
Holbrook
Ulladulla
WALES
GREAT
DIVIDING
Albury
Lake Hume
Batemans Bay
Wodonga
Corryong
KOSCIUSZKO NP
Mt Kosciuszko
Cooma
Wangaratta
DEUA NP
WADBILLIGA NP
Jindabyne
Bermagui
Mt Bogong 1986m
Bega
Bombala
ALPINE NP
Omeo
Merimbula
SOUTH EAST FOREST NP
Eden
SNOWY RIVER NP
Dargo
Green Cape
AVON WILDERNESS PARK
Cann River
Orbost
Mallacoota
Cape Howe
Gabo Island
Bairnsdale
CROAJINGOLONG NP
Cape Conran
Lakes Entrance
Sale
Traralgon
Ninety Mile Beach
WILSONS PROMONTORY
PROMONTORY NP
STRAIT
TASMAN SEA

N

0 | 50 | 100 | 150 | 200 km

Scale

INTER-CITY ROUTES		DISTANCE
Sydney–Melbourne via Hume Hwy/Fwy	31 M31	881 km
Sydney–Melbourne via Princes Hwy/Fwy	1 A1 M1	1037 km
Sydney–Brisbane via New England Hwy	1 15	1001 km
Sydney–Brisbane via Pacific Hwy	1 1 M1	966 km
Melbourne–Adelaide via Western & Dukes hwys	M8 A8 M1	733 km
Melbourne–Adelaide via Princes Hwy	M1 A1 B1 M1	906 km
Melbourne–Brisbane via Newell Hwy	M31 A39 39 A39 A2	1676 km

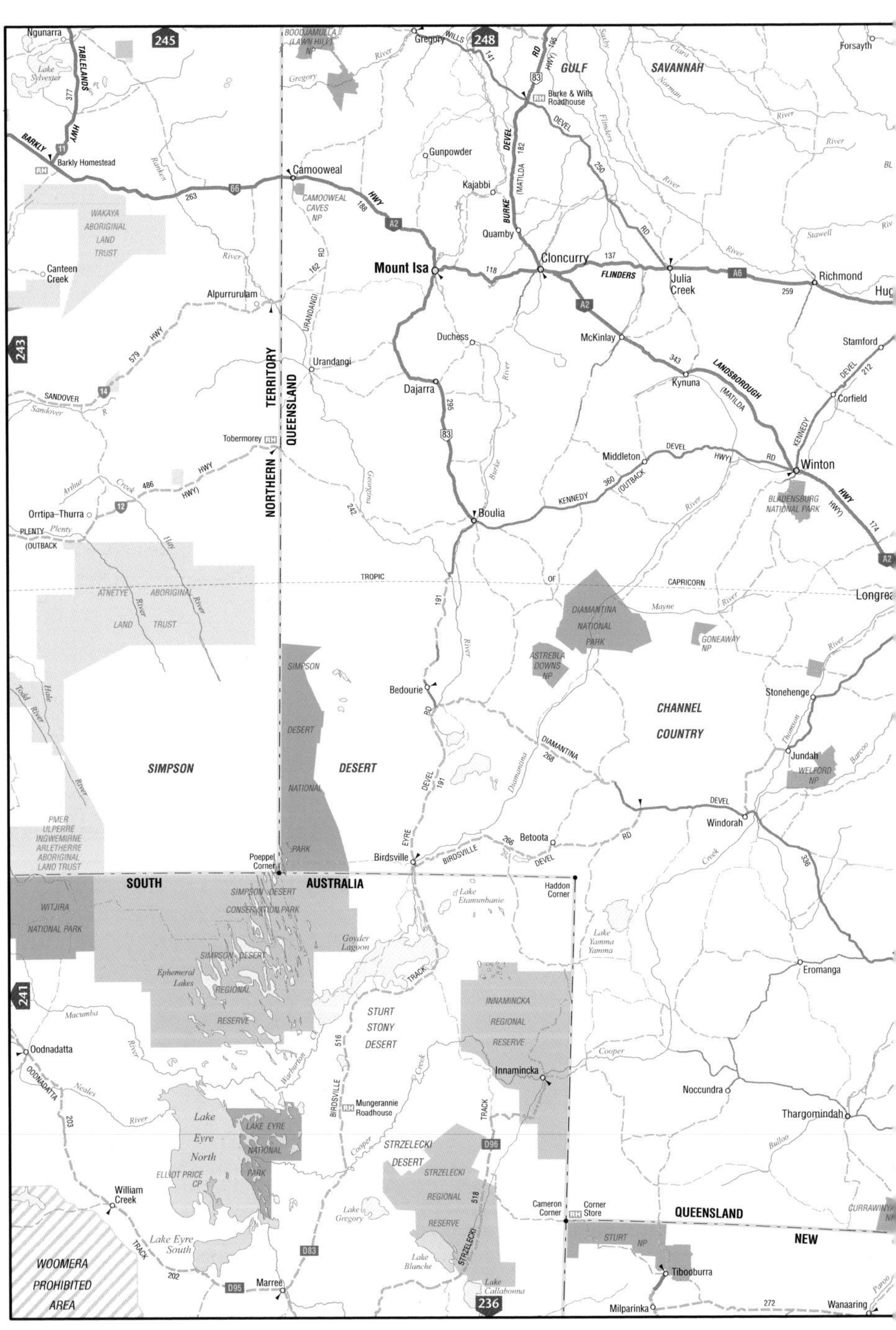
Ngunarra
245
248
BOODJAMULLA (LAWN HILL) NP
Gregory
Forsayth
GULF
SAVANNAH
Burke & Wills Roadhouse
Barkly Homestead
Camooweal
Gunpowder
Kajabbi
Quamby
WAKAYA ABORIGINAL LAND TRUST
CAMOOWEAL CAVES NP
Canteen Creek
Mount Isa
Cloncurry
Julia Creek
Richmond
Alpurrurulam
Duchess
McKinlay
Stamford
Urandangi
Dajarra
Kynuna
Corfield
243
NORTHERN TERRITORY
QUEENSLAND
Tobermorey
Middleton
Winton
Orrtipa–Thurra
Boulia
BLADENSBURG NATIONAL PARK
TROPIC
CAPRICORN
Longreach
ATNETYE ABORIGINAL LAND TRUST
DIAMANTINA NATIONAL PARK
GONEAWAY NP
ASTREBLA DOWNS NP
SIMPSON DESERT NATIONAL PARK
Bedourie
Stonehenge
CHANNEL COUNTRY
SIMPSON
DESERT
Jundah
WELFORD NP
Windorah
Betoota
PMER ULPERRE INGWEMIRNE ARLETHERRE ABORIGINAL LAND TRUST
Poeppel Corner
Birdsville
SOUTH
AUSTRALIA
Haddon Corner
WITJIRA NATIONAL PARK
SIMPSON DESERT CONSERVATION PARK
SIMPSON DESERT REGIONAL RESERVE
Lake Etamunbanie
Goyder Lagoon
Lake Yamma Yamma
Eromanga
241
STURT STONY DESERT
INNAMINCKA REGIONAL RESERVE
Oodnadatta
Innamincka
Noccundra
Mungerannie Roadhouse
Thargomindah
Lake Eyre North
LAKE EYRE NATIONAL PARK
ELLIOT PRICE CP
STRZELECKI DESERT
STRZELECKI REGIONAL RESERVE
William Creek
Cameron Corner
Corner Store
QUEENSLAND
NEW
Lake Gregory
STURT NP
Lake Eyre South
Lake Blanche
Tibooburra
WOOMERA PROHIBITED AREA
Marree
Lake Callabonna
236
Milparinka
Wanaaring

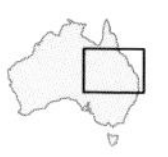

INTER-CITY ROUTES	DISTANCE
Brisbane–Sydney via New England Hwy 15 1	1001 km
Brisbane–Sydney via Pacific Hwy M1 1 1	966 km
Brisbane–Melbourne via Newell Hwy A2 A39 39 A39 M31	1676 km
Brisbane–Darwin via Warrego Hwy A2 66 87 1	3406 km
Brisbane–Cairns via Bruce Hwy M1 A1	1703 km

SOUTH PACIFIC OCEAN

0 50 100 150 200 km

Scale

LITTLE SANDY DESERT
GIBSON DESERT NATURE RESERVE
MUNGILLI ABORIGINAL LAND
NGAANYATJARRA ABORIGINAL LAND
Warakurna
Warakurna Roadhouse
Surveyor Generals Corner
Pipalyatjara
CENTRAL AUSTRALIA ABORIGINAL LAND TRUST
WESTERN AUSTRALIA
Warburton Roadhouse
Warburton
Carnegie Homestead
Lake Carnegie
Wiluna
Mount Keith
WANJARRI NATURE RESERVE
DE LA POER RANGE NATURE RESERVE
Tjukayirla Roadhouse
YEO LAKE NATURE RESERVE
Neale Junction
NEALE JUNCTION NATURE RESERVE
Cosmo Newbery
COSMO NEWBERY ABORIGINAL LAND
GREAT VICTORIA DESERT
GREAT VICTORIA DESERT NATURE RESERVE
Leinster
Laverton
Leonora
Kookynie
PLUMRIDGE LAKES NATURE RESERVE
NULLARBOR
Menzies
GOONGARRIE NP
MOUNT MANNING NATURE RESERVE
QUEEN VICTORIA SPRINGS NATURE RESERVE
Broad Arrow
Cundeelee
Kalgoorlie–Boulder
Coolgardie
Kambalda
Loongana
Rawlinna
Zanthus
Southern Cross
GOLDFIELDS WOODLAND NP
BURRA ROCK NR
BOORABBIN NP
Widgiemooltha
Mundrabilla Roadhouse
Madura
Cocklebiddy
Caiguna
Red Rocks Point
Marvel Loch
JILBADJI NATURE RESERVE
Norseman
Balladonia
DUNDAS NATURE RESERVE
Point Dover
NUYTSLAND NATURE RESERVE
Point Culver
Salmon Gums
Grass Patch
Varley
FRANK HANN NP
PEAK CHARLES NP
Lake King
CAPE ARID NP
Israelite Bay
Point Dempster
Ravensthorpe
Condingup
Esperance
Cape Pasley
CAPE LE GRAND NP
LAKE MAGENTA NR
Hopetoun
Jerramungup
FITZGERALD RIVER NP
Bremer Bay
Cheyne Bay
Ledge Point
0 50 100 150 200 km
Scale

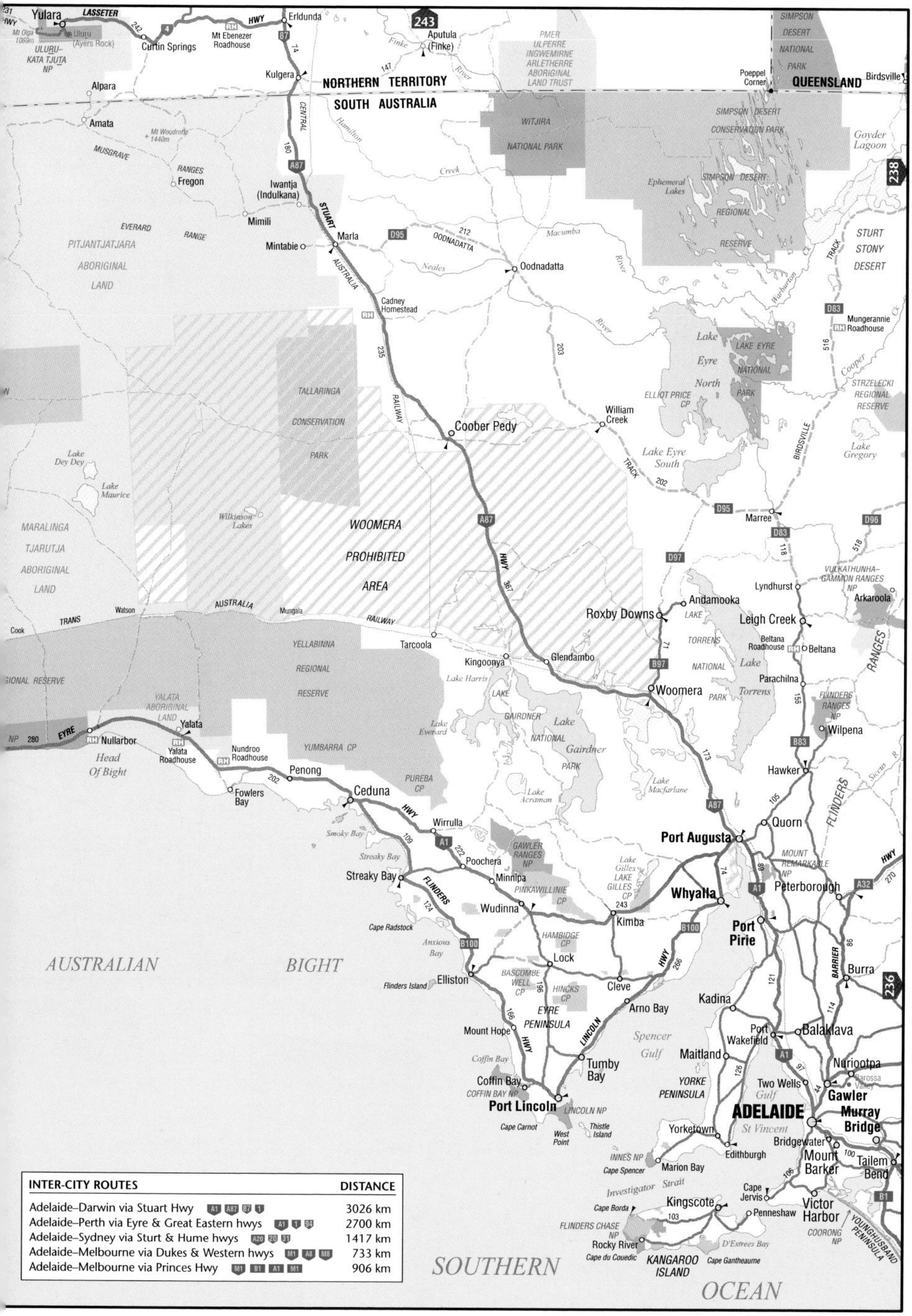

Yulara
LASSETER HWY
Uluru (Ayers Rock)
ULURU–KATA TJUTA NP
Curtin Springs
Mt Ebenezer Roadhouse
Erldunda
Aputula (Finke)
Kulgera
NORTHERN TERRITORY
SOUTH AUSTRALIA
QUEENSLAND
Poeppel Corner
Birdsville
SIMPSON DESERT NATIONAL PARK
PMER ULPERRE INGWEMIRNE ARLETHERRE ABORIGINAL LAND TRUST
WITJIRA NATIONAL PARK
SIMPSON DESERT CONSERVATION PARK
SIMPSON DESERT REGIONAL RESERVE
Goyder Lagoon
STURT STONY DESERT
Alpara
Amata
Mt Woodroffe 1440m
MUSGRAVE RANGES
Fregon
Iwantja (Indulkana)
Mimili
EVERARD RANGE
Marla
Mintabie
PITJANTJATJARA ABORIGINAL LAND
STUART HWY
Oodnadatta
ODNADATTA TRACK
Cadney Homestead
Mungerannie Roadhouse
Lake Eyre North
LAKE EYRE NATIONAL PARK
ELLIOT PRICE CP
STRZELECKI REGIONAL RESERVE
BIRDSVILLE TRACK
William Creek
Coober Pedy
TALLARINGA CONSERVATION PARK
Lake Dey Dey
Lake Maurice
Wilkinson Lakes
Lake Eyre South
Lake Gregory
Marree
MARALINGA TJARUTJA ABORIGINAL LAND
WOOMERA PROHIBITED AREA
Lyndhurst
VULKATHUNHA–GAMMON RANGES NP
Arkaroola
Andamooka
Roxby Downs
Leigh Creek
Beltana Roadhouse
Beltana
Parachilna
TRANS AUSTRALIA RAILWAY
Watson
Cook
Mungala
Tarcoola
Kingoonya
Glendambo
Woomera
LAKE TORRENS NATIONAL PARK
FLINDERS RANGES NP
Wilpena
YELLABINNA REGIONAL RESERVE
YALATA ABORIGINAL LAND
Yalata
Yalata Roadhouse
Nullarbor
Head Of Bight
EYRE HWY
Nundroo Roadhouse
YUMBARRA CP
Penong
Fowlers Bay
Ceduna
PUREBA CP
Lake Everard
LAKE GAIRDNER NATIONAL PARK
Lake Acraman
Lake Macfarlane
Hawker
Quorn
Port Augusta
Wirrulla
Smoky Bay
Streaky Bay
GAWLER RANGES NP
Poochera
Minnipa
PINKAWILLINIE CP
Lake Gilles
LAKE GILLES CP
Whyalla
MOUNT REMARKABLE NP
Peterborough
Wudinna
Kimba
Port Pirie
Cape Radstock
Anxious Bay
HAMBIDGE CP
Lock
Burra
AUSTRALIAN BIGHT
Flinders Island
Elliston
BASCOMBE WELL CP
HINCKS CP
Cleve
Arno Bay
Kadina
EYRE PENINSULA
Mount Hope
Spencer Gulf
Port Wakefield
Balaklava
Maitland
Nuriootpa
Barossa Valley
Tumby Bay
Coffin Bay
COFFIN BAY NP
Port Lincoln
LINCOLN NP
YORKE PENINSULA
Two Wells
Gawler
ADELAIDE
Murray Bridge
Gulf St Vincent
Cape Carnot
West Point
Thistle Island
Yorketown
Edithburgh
Bridgewater
Mount Barker
Tailem Bend
INNES NP
Cape Spencer
Marion Bay
Investigator Strait
Cape Jervis
Kingscote
Penneshaw
Victor Harbor
COORONG NP
YOUNGHUSBAND PENINSULA
Cape Borda
FLINDERS CHASE NP
Rocky River
Cape du Couedic
KANGAROO ISLAND
D'Estrees Bay
Cape Gantheaume
SOUTHERN OCEAN

INTER-CITY ROUTES	DISTANCE
Adelaide–Darwin via Stuart Hwy A1 A87 87 1	3026 km
Adelaide–Perth via Eyre & Great Eastern hwys A1 1 94	2700 km
Adelaide–Sydney via Sturt & Hume hwys A20 20 31	1417 km
Adelaide–Melbourne via Dukes & Western hwys M1 A8 M8	733 km
Adelaide–Melbourne via Princes Hwy M1 B1 A1 M1	906 km

243
238
236

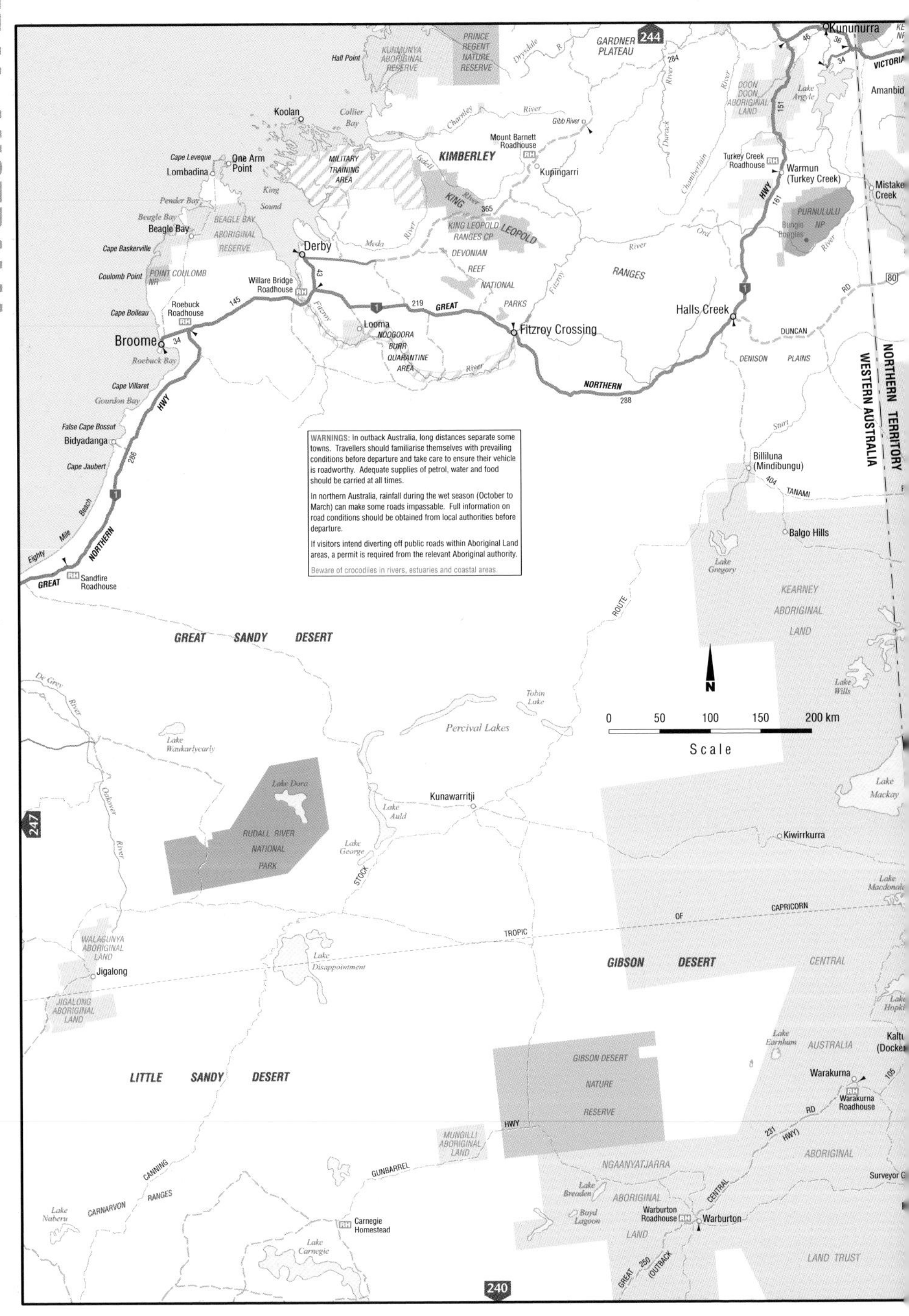

WARNINGS: In outback Australia, long distances separate some towns. Travellers should familiarise themselves with prevailing conditions before departure and take care to ensure their vehicle is roadworthy. Adequate supplies of petrol, water and food should be carried at all times.
In northern Australia, rainfall during the wet season (October to March) can make some roads impassable. Full information on road conditions should be obtained from local authorities before departure.
If visitors intend diverting off public roads within Aboriginal Land areas, a permit is required from the relevant Aboriginal authority.
Beware of crocodiles in rivers, estuaries and coastal areas.
0 50 100 150 200 km
Scale
N
Kununurra
244
247
240
GARDNER PLATEAU
PRINCE REGENT NATURE RESERVE
KUNMUNYA ABORIGINAL RESERVE
Hall Point
Koolan
Collier Bay
Cape Leveque
One Arm Point
Lombadina
MILITARY TRAINING AREA
King Sound
Pender Bay
Beagle Bay
BEAGLE BAY ABORIGINAL RESERVE
Cape Baskerville
Coulomb Point
POINT COULOMB NR
Derby
Willare Bridge Roadhouse
Cape Boileau
Roebuck Roadhouse
Broome
Roebuck Bay
Cape Villaret
Gourdon Bay
False Cape Bossut
Bidyadanga
Cape Jaubert
Eighty Mile Beach
GREAT NORTHERN HWY
Sandfire Roadhouse
Mount Barnett Roadhouse
KIMBERLEY
Kupingarri
Gibb River
KING LEOPOLD RANGES CP
DEVONIAN REEF NATIONAL PARKS
Looma
NOOGOORA BURR QUARANTINE AREA
Fitzroy Crossing
Fitzroy River
Meda River
Isdell River
Drysdale River
Durack River
Chamberlain River
Ord River
RANGES
Halls Creek
DOON DOON ABORIGINAL LAND
Lake Argyle
Turkey Creek Roadhouse
Warmun (Turkey Creek)
PURNULULU NP
Bungle Bungles
VICTORIA
Amanbid
Mistake Creek
DUNCAN RD
DENISON PLAINS
NORTHERN TERRITORY
WESTERN AUSTRALIA
Sturt
Billiluna (Mindibungu)
TANAMI ROUTE
Balgo Hills
Lake Gregory
KEARNEY ABORIGINAL LAND
Lake Wills
Lake Mackay
GREAT SANDY DESERT
De Grey River
Lake Waukarlycarly
Oakover River
Tobin Lake
Percival Lakes
Lake Dora
RUDALL RIVER NATIONAL PARK
Kunawarritji
Lake Auld
Lake George
STOCK
Kiwirrkurra
Lake Macdonald
TROPIC OF CAPRICORN
WALAGUNYA ABORIGINAL LAND
Jigalong
JIGALONG ABORIGINAL LAND
Lake Disappointment
GIBSON DESERT
CENTRAL AUSTRALIA ABORIGINAL LAND TRUST
Lake Hopkins
Lake Earnhum
Kaltu (Docker
LITTLE SANDY DESERT
GIBSON DESERT NATURE RESERVE
Warakurna
Warakurna Roadhouse
MUNGILLI ABORIGINAL LAND
GUNBARREL HWY
CANNING
CARNARVON RANGES
Lake Nabern
Carnegie Homestead
Lake Carnegie
NGAANYATJARRA ABORIGINAL LAND
Lake Breaden
Boyd Lagoon
Warburton Roadhouse
Warburton
CENTRAL RD
GREAT CENTRAL (OUTBACK) HWY
Surveyor G

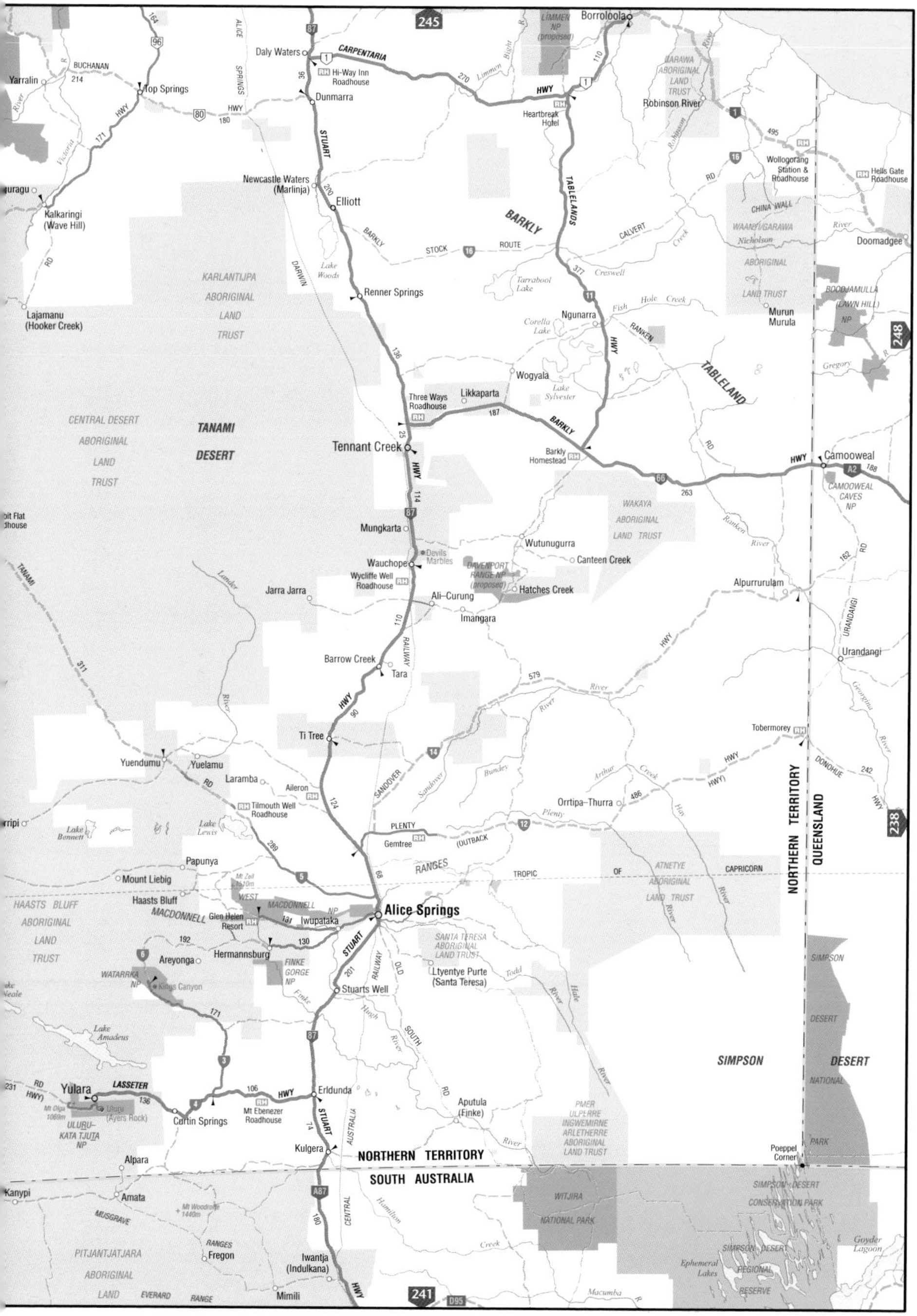

245
Borroloola
Daly Waters
CARPENTARIA HWY
Hi-Way Inn Roadhouse
Dunmarra
Top Springs
Yarralin
BUCHANAN
HWY
Heartbreak Hotel
Robinson River
Wollogorang Station & Roadhouse
Hells Gate Roadhouse
Newcastle Waters (Marlinja)
Elliott
Kalkaringi (Wave Hill)
BARKLY
TABLELANDS
STOCK ROUTE
CALVERT RD
CHINA WALL
WAANYI/GARAWA ABORIGINAL LAND TRUST
GARAWA ABORIGINAL LAND TRUST
Doomadgee
KARLANTIJPA ABORIGINAL LAND TRUST
Lake Woods
Renner Springs
Tarrabool Lake
Lajamanu (Hooker Creek)
Ngunarra
Corella Lake
Murun Murula
BOODJAMULLA (LAWN HILL) NP
248
Wogyala
Lake Sylvester
TABLELAND
Three Ways Roadhouse
Likkaparta
CENTRAL DESERT ABORIGINAL LAND TRUST
TANAMI DESERT
Tennant Creek
Barkly Homestead
BARKLY HWY
Camooweal
CAMOOWEAL CAVES NP
WAKAYA ABORIGINAL LAND TRUST
Mungkarta
Wutunugurra
Canteen Creek
Devils Marbles
Wauchope
Wycliffe Well Roadhouse
DAVENPORT RANGE NP (proposed)
Hatches Creek
Jarra Jarra
Ali-Curung
Imangara
Alpurrurulam
URANDANGI RD
Urandangi
Barrow Creek
Tara
RAILWAY
STUART HWY
Ti Tree
SANDOVER HWY
Tobermorey
DONOHUE HWY
Yuendumu
Yuelamu
Laramba
Aileron
Tilmouth Well Roadhouse
Orrtipa-Thurra
PLENTY HWY
Gemtree
(OUTBACK
RANGES
TROPIC OF CAPRICORN
Papunya
Mount Liebig
ATNETYE ABORIGINAL LAND TRUST
Haasts Bluff
HAASTS BLUFF ABORIGINAL LAND TRUST
WEST MACDONNELL NP
Glen Helen Resort
Iwupataka
Alice Springs
SANTA TERESA ABORIGINAL LAND TRUST
Hermannsburg
Areyonga
FINKE GORGE NP
WATARRKA NP
Kings Canyon
Ltyentye Purte (Santa Teresa)
Stuarts Well
NORTHERN TERRITORY
QUEENSLAND
238
SIMPSON DESERT NATIONAL PARK
Lake Amadeus
Yulara
LASSETER HWY
Uluru (Ayers Rock)
Mt Olga 1069m
ULURU-KATA TJUTA NP
Curtin Springs
Mt Ebenezer Roadhouse
Erldunda
Aputula (Finke)
PMER ULPERRE INGWEMIRNE ARLETHERRE ABORIGINAL LAND TRUST
SIMPSON DESERT
Kulgera
Poeppel Corner
NORTHERN TERRITORY
SOUTH AUSTRALIA
Alpara
Amata
Kanypi
Mt Woodroffe 1440m
MUSGRAVE RANGES
WITJIRA NATIONAL PARK
SIMPSON DESERT CONSERVATION PARK
SIMPSON DESERT REGIONAL RESERVE
Goyder Lagoon
Ephemeral Lakes
Fregon
PITJANTJATJARA ABORIGINAL LAND
EVERARD RANGE
Iwantja (Indulkana)
Mimili
241

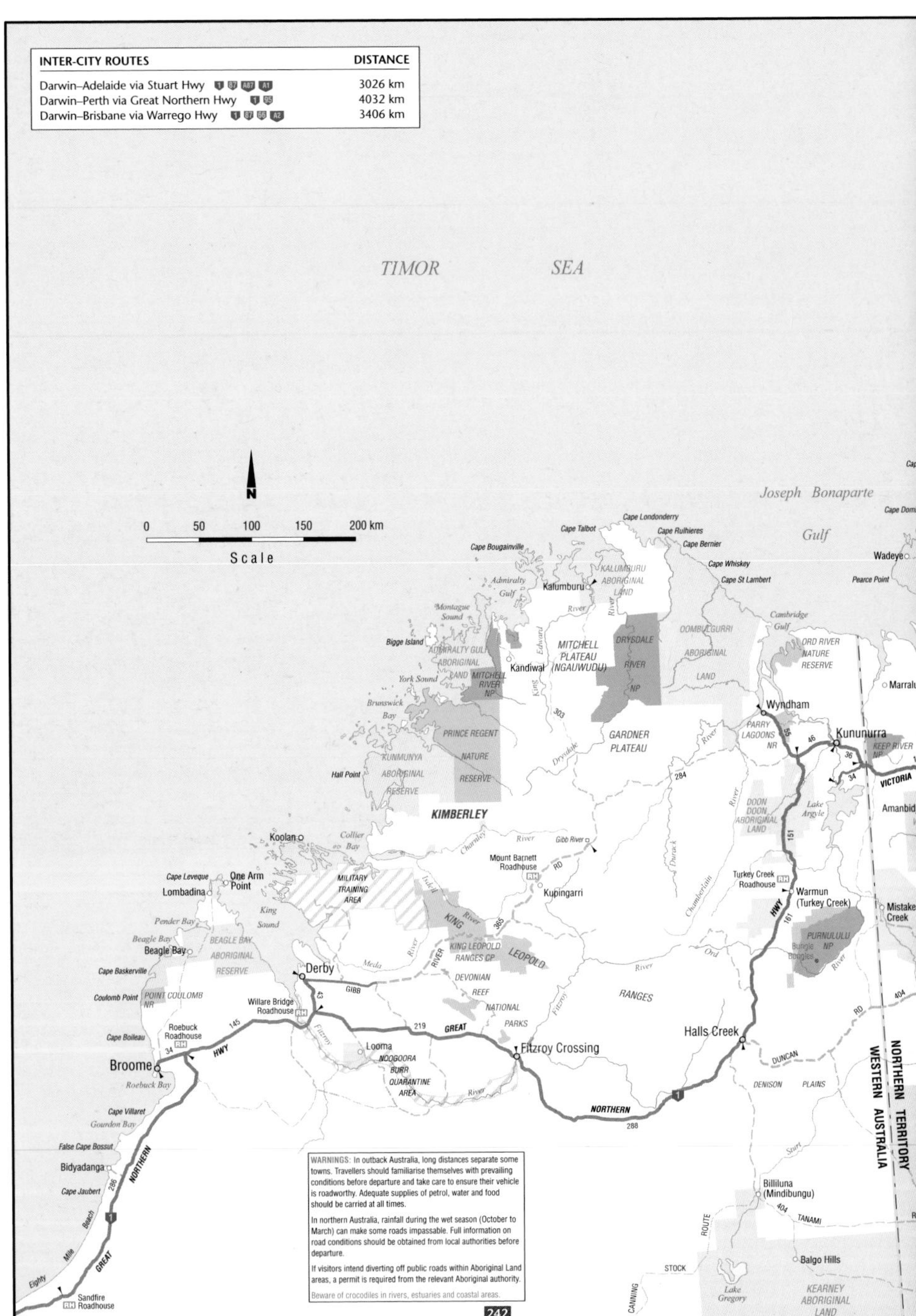
INTER-CITY ROUTES
DISTANCE
Darwin–Adelaide via Stuart Hwy 3026 km
Darwin–Perth via Great Northern Hwy 4032 km
Darwin–Brisbane via Warrego Hwy 3406 km
TIMOR SEA
N
0 50 100 150 200 km
Scale
Joseph Bonaparte Gulf
Cape Londonderry
Cape Talbot
Cape Rulhieres
Cape Bernier
Cape Bougainville
Cape Whiskey
Cape St Lambert
Wadeye
Pearce Point
Admiralty Gulf
Kalumburu
KALUMBURU ABORIGINAL LAND
Montague Sound
Cambridge Gulf
OOMBULGURRI ABORIGINAL LAND
Bigge Island
ADMIRALTY GULF ABORIGINAL LAND
MITCHELL PLATEAU (NGAUWUDU)
DRYSDALE RIVER NP
ORD RIVER NATURE RESERVE
Kandiwal
MITCHELL RIVER NP
York Sound
Marralu
Brunswick Bay
Wyndham
PRINCE REGENT NATURE RESERVE
GARDNER PLATEAU
PARRY LAGOONS NR
Kununurra
KEEP RIVER NP
KUNMUNYA ABORIGINAL RESERVE
VICTORIA
Hall Point
KIMBERLEY
DOON DOON ABORIGINAL LAND
Lake Argyle
Amanbidji
Koolan
Collier Bay
Gibb River
Mount Barnett Roadhouse
Cape Leveque
One Arm Point
MILITARY TRAINING AREA
Turkey Creek Roadhouse
Warmun (Turkey Creek)
Lombadina
Kupingarri
King Sound
Mistake Creek
Pender Bay
KING LEOPOLD RANGES CP
PURNULULU NP
Bungle Bungles
Beagle Bay
BEAGLE BAY ABORIGINAL RESERVE
Cape Baskerville
Derby
DEVONIAN REEF NATIONAL PARKS
Coulomb Point
POINT COULOMB NR
Willare Bridge Roadhouse
RANGES
Roebuck Roadhouse
GREAT
Halls Creek
Cape Boileau
Looma
Fitzroy Crossing
Broome
HWY
NOOGOORA BURR QUARANTINE AREA
DUNCAN
NORTHERN TERRITORY
WESTERN AUSTRALIA
Roebuck Bay
DENISON PLAINS
Cape Villaret
Gourdon Bay
NORTHERN
False Cape Bossut
Bidyadanga
Cape Jaubert
Billiluna (Mindibungu)
TANAMI
ROUTE
Eighty Mile Beach
Balgo Hills
STOCK
CANNING
Lake Gregory
KEARNEY ABORIGINAL LAND
Sandfire Roadhouse
WARNINGS: In outback Australia, long distances separate some towns. Travellers should familiarise themselves with prevailing conditions before departure and take care to ensure their vehicle is roadworthy. Adequate supplies of petrol, water and food should be carried at all times.
In northern Australia, rainfall during the wet season (October to March) can make some roads impassable. Full information on road conditions should be obtained from local authorities before departure.
If visitors intend diverting off public roads within Aboriginal Land areas, a permit is required from the relevant Aboriginal authority.
Beware of crocodiles in rivers, estuaries and coastal areas.
242

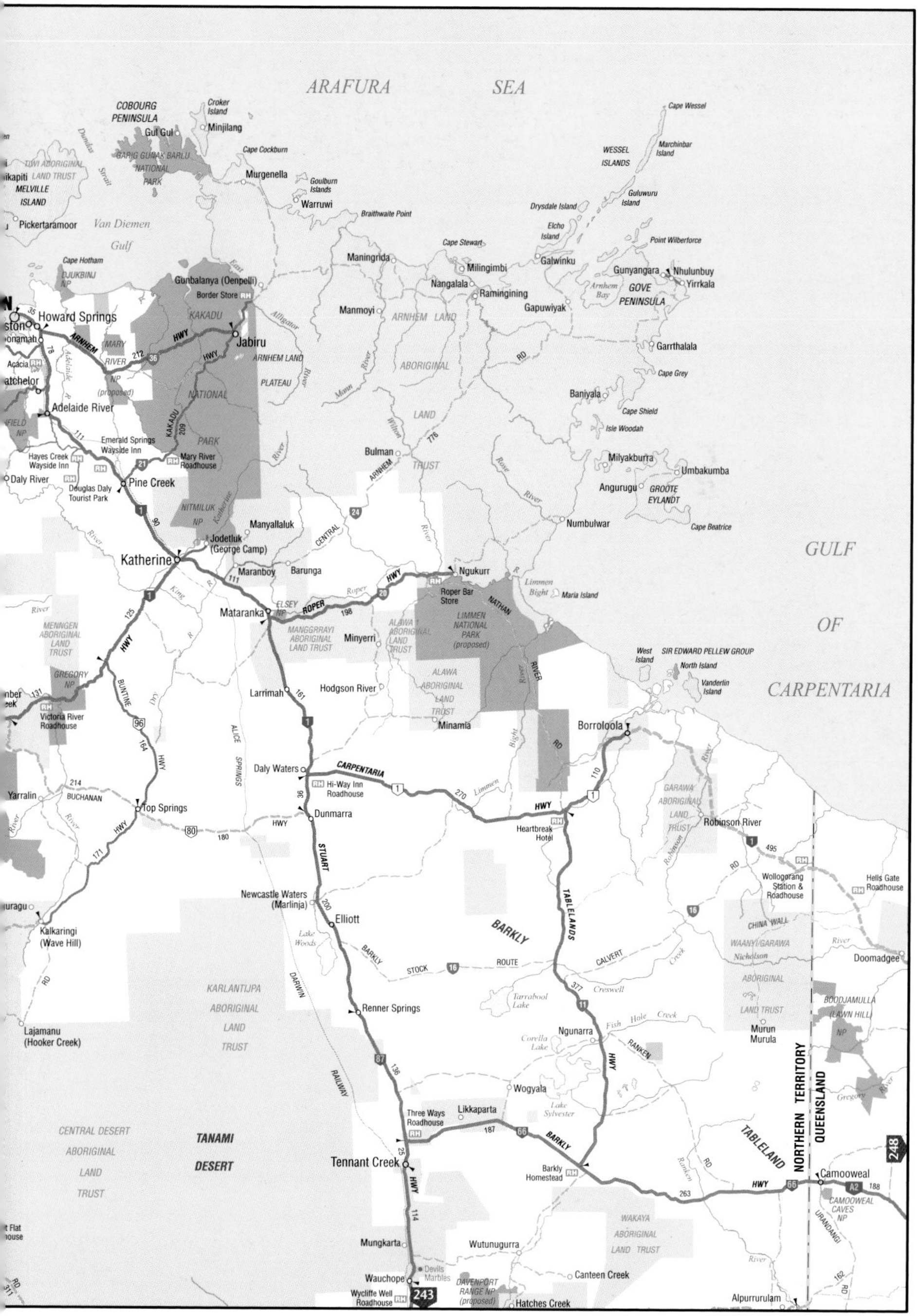

ARAFURA SEA
COBOURG PENINSULA
Croker Island
Minjilang
Gul Gul
Cape Wessel
Marchinbar Island
WESSEL ISLANDS
GARIG GUNAK BARLU NATIONAL PARK
Cape Cockburn
TIWI ABORIGINAL LAND TRUST
MELVILLE ISLAND
Dundas Strait
Murgenella
Goulburn Islands
Warruwi
Guluwuru Island
Braithwaite Point
Drysdale Island
Elcho Island
Pickertaramoor
Van Diemen Gulf
Cape Stewart
Point Wilberforce
Maningrida
Galwinku
Milingimbi
Cape Hotham
DJUKBINJ NP
Gunbalanya (Oenpelli)
East Alligator River
Border Store
Nangalala
Ramingining
Gunyangara
Nhulunbuy
Yirrkala
Arnhem Bay
GOVE PENINSULA
Gapuwiyak
Howard Springs
Manmoyi
ARNHEM LAND ABORIGINAL LAND TRUST
KAKADU NATIONAL PARK
MARY RIVER NP (proposed)
ARNHEM HWY
Jabiru
ARNHEM LAND PLATEAU
Garrthalala
Acacia
Batchelor
Adelaide River
Cape Grey
Mann River
Baniyala
Cape Shield
Isle Woodah
Emerald Springs Wayside Inn
Hayes Creek Wayside Inn
Mary River Roadhouse
KAKADU HWY
Bulman
Wilton River
Milyakburra
Umbakumba
Daly River
Douglas Daly Tourist Park
Pine Creek
ARNHEM
Rose River
Angurugu
GROOTE EYLANDT
NITMILUK NP
Katherine River
Manyallaluk
CENTRAL
Numbulwar
Cape Beatrice
Jodetluk (George Camp)
GULF OF CARPENTARIA
Katherine
Maranboy
Barunga
Ngukurr
King River
Roper River
ROPER HWY
Roper Bar Store
Limmen Bight
Maria Island
Mataranka
ELSEY NP
NATHAN RIVER
MENNGEN ABORIGINAL LAND TRUST
MANGGRRAYI ABORIGINAL LAND TRUST
ALAWA ABORIGINAL LAND TRUST
Minyerri
LIMMEN NATIONAL PARK (proposed)
West Island
SIR EDWARD PELLEW GROUP
North Island
Vanderlin Island
GREGORY NP
BUNTINE HWY
Larrimah
Hodgson River
ALAWA ABORIGINAL LAND TRUST
Victoria River Roadhouse
Minamia
Borroloola
ALICE SPRINGS
Daly Waters
CARPENTARIA HWY
Hi-Way Inn Roadhouse
Limmen Bight River
GARAWA ABORIGINAL LAND TRUST
Yarralin
BUCHANAN HWY
Top Springs
Dunmarra
Heartbreak Hotel
Robinson River
STUART HWY
Wollogorang Station & Roadhouse
Hells Gate Roadhouse
Newcastle Waters (Marlinja)
Elliott
TABLELANDS HWY
CHINA WALL
WAANYI/GARAWA ABORIGINAL LAND TRUST
Nicholson River
Kalkaringi (Wave Hill)
Lake Woods
BARKLY
BARKLY STOCK ROUTE
CALVERT
Doomadgee
Creswell
Tarrabool Lake
BOODJAMULLA (LAWN HILL) NP
KARLANTIJPA ABORIGINAL LAND TRUST
DARWIN
Renner Springs
Fish Hole Creek
Lajamanu (Hooker Creek)
Ngunarra
Corella Lake
RANKEN
Murun Murula
RAILWAY
Wogyala
Lake Sylvester
NORTHERN TERRITORY
QUEENSLAND
Gregory River
Three Ways Roadhouse
Likkaparta
CENTRAL DESERT ABORIGINAL LAND TRUST
TANAMI DESERT
BARKLY
TABLELAND
Tennant Creek
Barkly Homestead
BARKLY HWY
Camooweal
CAMOOWEAL CAVES NP
WAKAYA ABORIGINAL LAND TRUST
URANDANGI
Mungkarta
Wutunugurra
Devils Marbles
Wauchope
DAVENPORT RANGE NP (proposed)
Canteen Creek
Wycliffe Well Roadhouse
Hatches Creek
Alpurrurulam

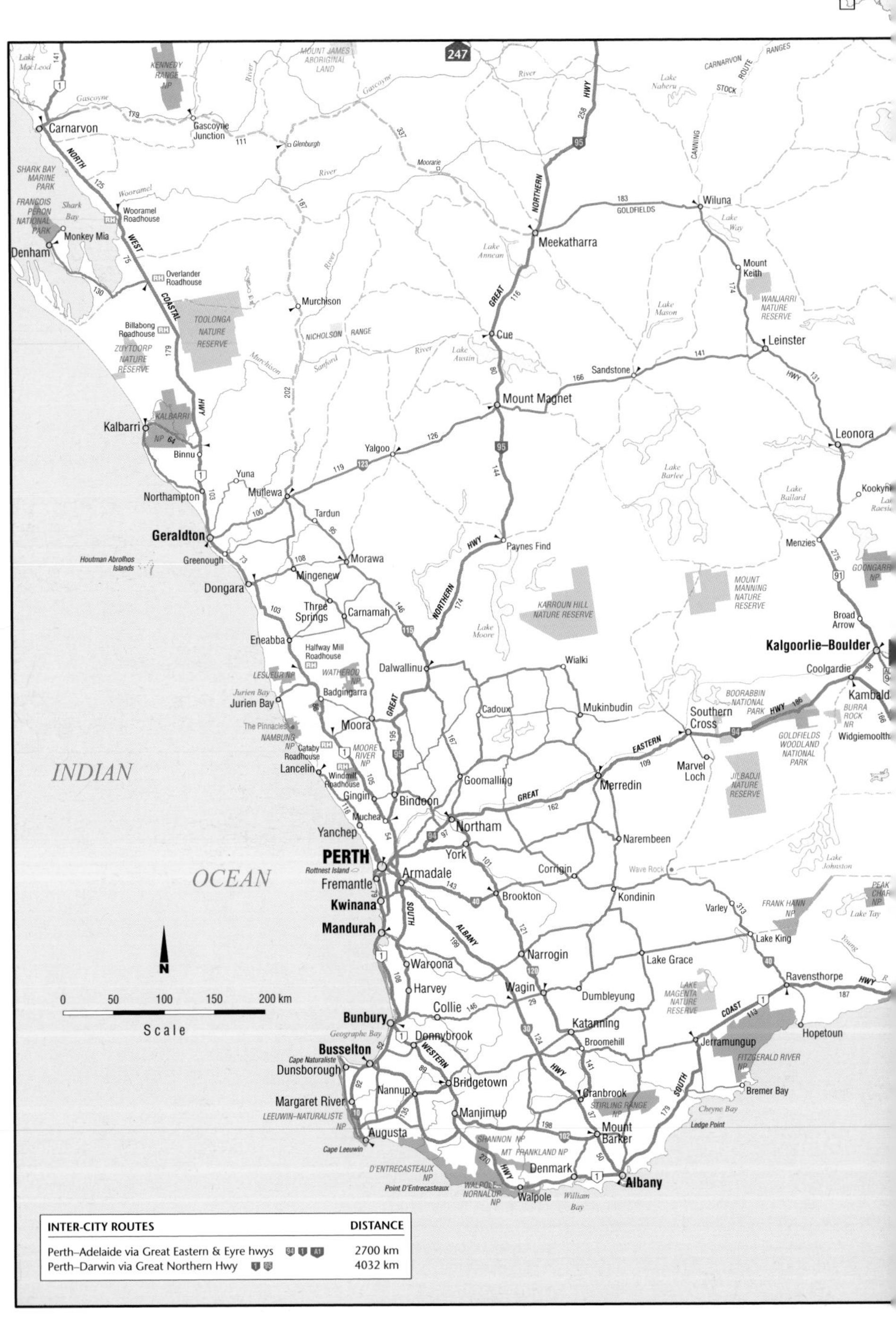

INTER-CITY ROUTES	DISTANCE
Perth–Adelaide via Great Eastern & Eyre hwys 94 1 A1	2700 km
Perth–Darwin via Great Northern Hwy 1 95	4032 km

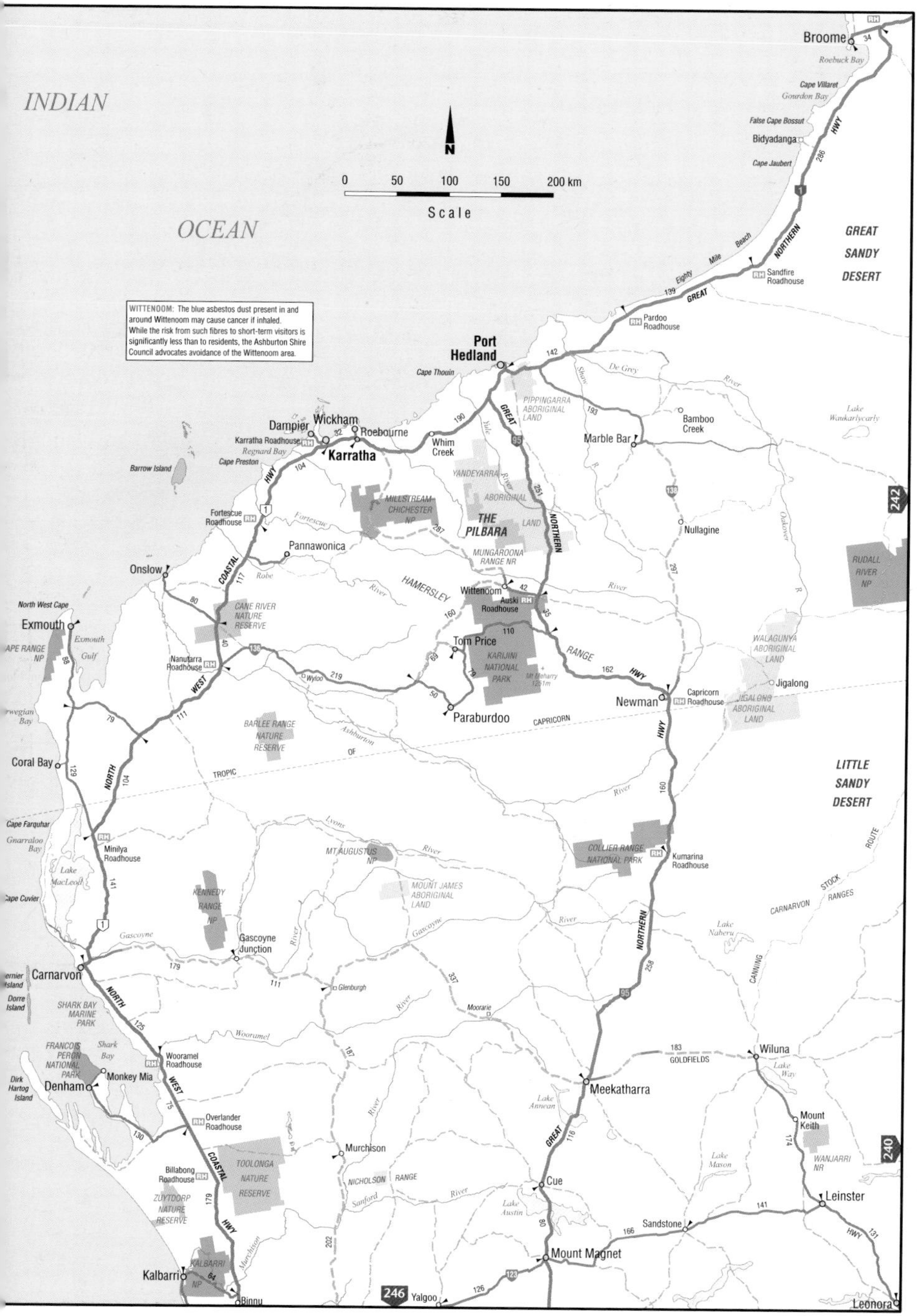

NORTH-WESTERN WESTERN AUSTRALIA

WITTENOOM: The blue asbestos dust present in and around Wittenoom may cause cancer if inhaled. While the risk from such fibres to short-term visitors is significantly less than to residents, the Ashburton Shire Council advocates avoidance of the Wittenoom area.

N

0 50 100 150 200 km

Scale

INDIAN OCEAN

Broome
Roebuck Bay
Cape Villaret
Gourdon Bay
False Cape Bossut
Bidyadanga
Cape Jaubert
Eighty Mile Beach
Sandfire Roadhouse
GREAT SANDY DESERT
Pardoo Roadhouse
GREAT NORTHERN HWY
Port Hedland
Cape Thouin
De Grey River
PIPPINGARRA ABORIGINAL LAND
Bamboo Creek
Lake Waukarlycarly
Marble Bar
Dampier
Wickham
Roebourne
Karratha Roadhouse
Karratha
Regnard Bay
Cape Preston
Whim Creek
Barrow Island
YANDEYARRA ABORIGINAL LAND
MILLSTREAM-CHICHESTER NP
THE PILBARA
Fortescue Roadhouse
Fortescue
Nullagine
MUNGAROONA RANGE NR
Pannawonica
Onslow
Robe
HAMERSLEY RANGE
Wittenoom
Auski Roadhouse
RUDALL RIVER NP
North West Cape
Exmouth
Exmouth Gulf
CAPE RANGE NP
CANE RIVER NATURE RESERVE
Tom Price
KARIJINI NATIONAL PARK
Mt Meharry 1251m
WALAGUNYA ABORIGINAL LAND
Nanutarra Roadhouse
NORTH WEST COASTAL HWY
Wyloo
Jigalong
Capricorn Roadhouse
Newman
JIGALONG ABORIGINAL LAND
Norwegian Bay
BARLEE RANGE NATURE RESERVE
Ashburton
Paraburdoo
TROPIC OF CAPRICORN
Coral Bay
LITTLE SANDY DESERT
Cape Farquhar
Gnarraloo Bay
Lyons
Minilya Roadhouse
MT AUGUSTUS NP
COLLIER RANGE NATIONAL PARK
Kumarina Roadhouse
Lake MacLeod
Cape Cuvier
KENNEDY RANGE NP
MOUNT JAMES ABORIGINAL LAND
CANNING STOCK ROUTE
CARNARVON RANGES
Lake Nabberu
Gascoyne
Gascoyne Junction
Carnarvon
Bernier Island
Dorre Island
Glenburgh
Moorarie
SHARK BAY MARINE PARK
Wooramel
Wooramel Roadhouse
GOLDFIELDS
Wiluna
Lake Way
FRANCOIS PERON NATIONAL PARK
Shark Bay
Monkey Mia
Dirk Hartog Island
Denham
Meekatharra
Lake Annean
Overlander Roadhouse
Mount Keith
Murchison
TOOLONGA NATURE RESERVE
Lake Mason
WANJARRI NR
Billabong Roadhouse
NICHOLSON RANGE
Cue
ZUYTDORP NATURE RESERVE
Sanford
Lake Austin
Leinster
Sandstone
Mount Magnet
KALBARRI NP
Kalbarri
Binnu
Yalgoo
Leonora

242
240
246

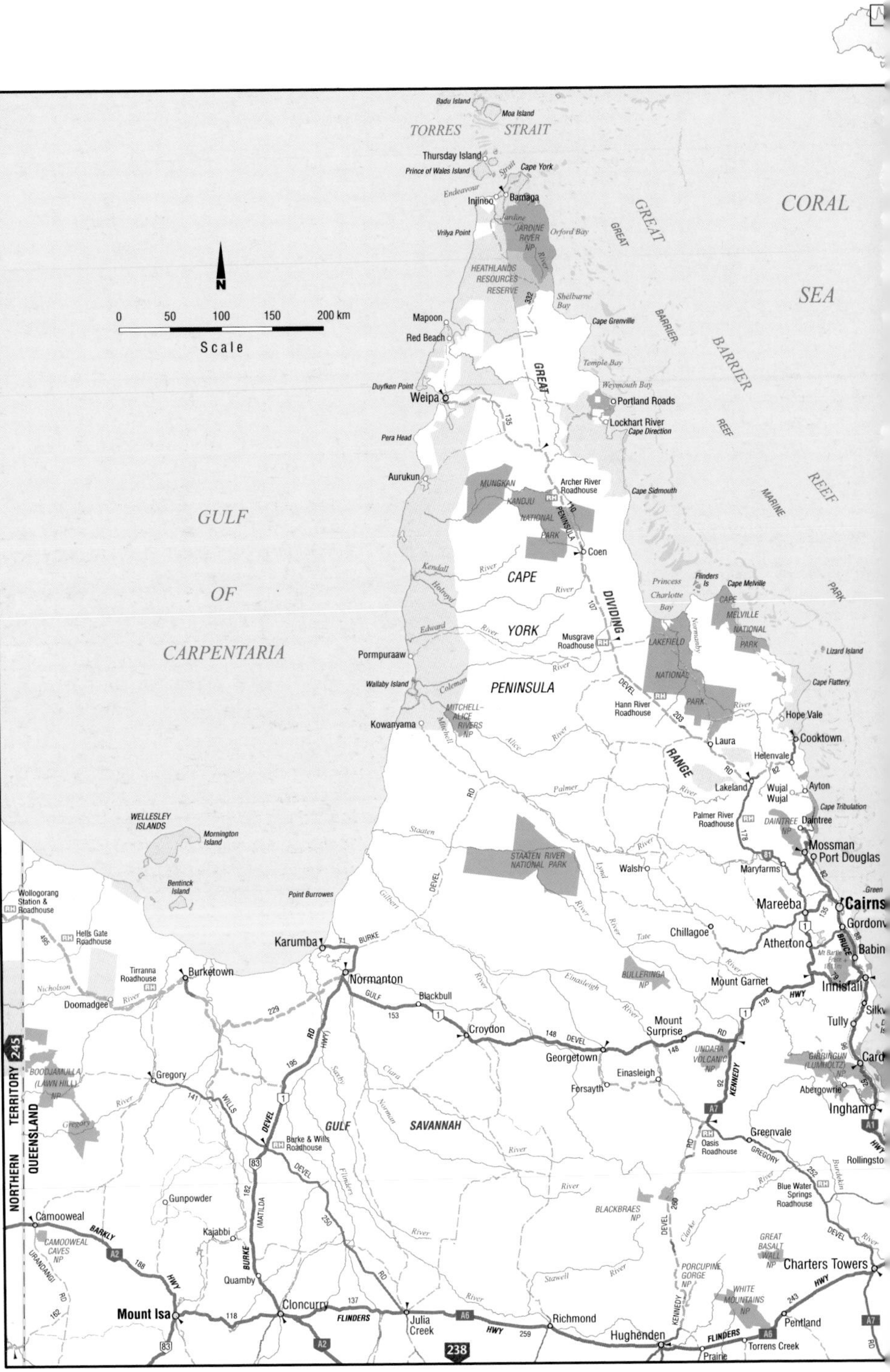

0 50 100 150 200 km

Scale

N

Badu Island
Moa Island
TORRES STRAIT
Thursday Island
Prince of Wales Island
Cape York
Endeavour Strait
Injinoo
Bamaga
Vrilya Point
JARDINE RIVER NP
Orford Bay
HEATHLANDS RESOURCES RESERVE
Shelburne Bay
CORAL SEA
GREAT BARRIER REEF MARINE PARK
Mapoon
Red Beach
Cape Grenville
Temple Bay
Duyfken Point
Weipa
Weymouth Bay
Portland Roads
Lockhart River
Cape Direction
Pera Head
Aurukun
MUNGKAN KANDJU NATIONAL PARK
Archer River Roadhouse
Cape Sidmouth
GULF OF CARPENTARIA
Coen
CAPE YORK PENINSULA
GREAT DIVIDING RANGE
Princess Charlotte Bay
Flinders Is
Cape Melville
CAPE MELVILLE NATIONAL PARK
Musgrave Roadhouse
LAKEFIELD NATIONAL PARK
Lizard Island
Pormpuraaw
Wallaby Island
Cape Flattery
Hann River Roadhouse
MITCHELL-ALICE RIVERS NP
Hope Vale
Kowanyama
Laura
Cooktown
Helenvale
Lakeland
Wujal Wujal
Ayton
Cape Tribulation
Palmer River Roadhouse
DAINTREE NP
Daintree
WELLESLEY ISLANDS
Mornington Island
STAATEN RIVER NATIONAL PARK
Mossman
Port Douglas
Walsh
Maryfarms
Bentinck Island
Wollogorang Station & Roadhouse
Point Burrowes
Mareeba
Cairns
Gordonvale
Chillagoe
Hells Gate Roadhouse
Karumba
Atherton
Babinda
Tirranna Roadhouse
Burketown
Normanton
BULLERINGA NP
Mount Garnet
Innisfail
Doomadgee
Blackbull
Croydon
Mount Surprise
Tully
Georgetown
UNDARA VOLCANIC NP
Cardwell
Einasleigh
Forsayth
GIRRINGUN (LUMHOLTZ) NP
Abergowrie
BOODJAMULLA (LAWN HILL) NP
Gregory
Ingham
GULF SAVANNAH
Burke & Wills Roadhouse
Greenvale
Oasis Roadhouse
Rollingstone
NORTHERN TERRITORY
QUEENSLAND
Gunpowder
Blue Water Springs Roadhouse
BLACKBRAES NP
Camooweal
CAMOOWEAL CAVES NP
Kajabbi
GREAT BASALT WALL NP
Charters Towers
PORCUPINE GORGE NP
Quamby
WHITE MOUNTAINS NP
Mount Isa
Cloncurry
Julia Creek
Richmond
Pentland
Hughenden
Prairie
Torrens Creek
BARKLY HWY
FLINDERS HWY
GULF DEVELOPMENTAL RD
BURKE DEVEL RD
KENNEDY DEVEL RD
GREGORY DEVEL RD
PENINSULA DEVEL RD
BRUCE HWY
WILLS DEVEL RD
BURKE (MATILDA) HWY
URANDANGI RD

245

238

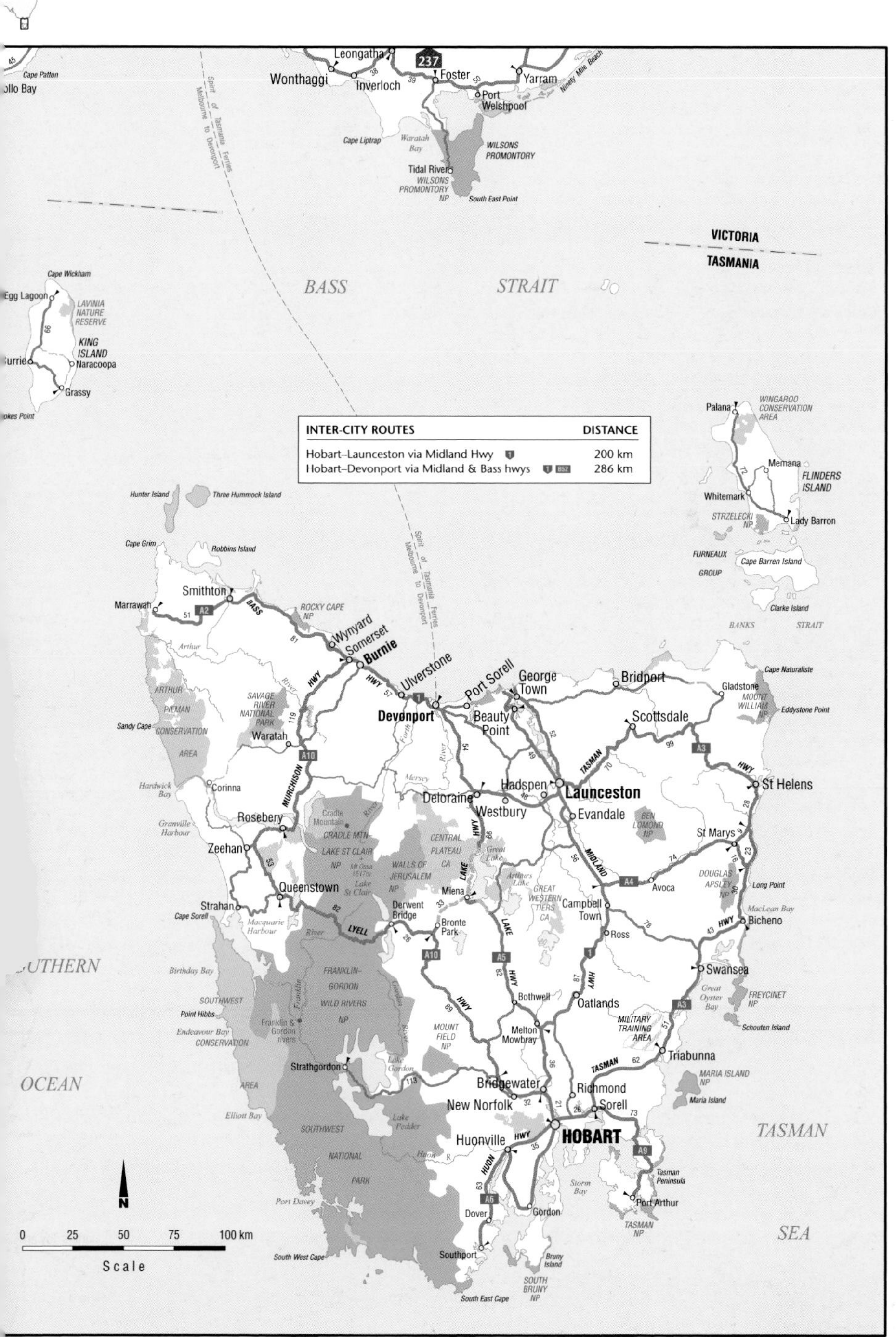

INTER-CITY ROUTES	DISTANCE
Hobart–Launceston via Midland Hwy	200 km
Hobart–Devonport via Midland & Bass hwys	286 km

Publisher's acknowledgements

Publications manager
Astrid Browne
Editor
Geraldine Corridon
Design
desertpony
Layout
Michael Kuszla
Photography credits
Front cover Kalarranga–Mpaara rock stacks, Palm Valley, Northern Territory by Andrew Close
Back cover Orchid Beach, Hinchinbrook Island, Queensland by Andrew Close
Images in this book are the work of Andrew Close, and are the copyright of Andrew Close, with the exception of the following:
Title page Ship Stern Bluff, Tunnel Bay, Tasmania by Tyrone Thomas
p. 4 Mount Connor and parakeelya, Northern Territory by Tyrone Thomas
p. 8 Hamersley Gorge, Western Australia by Greg Campbell
p. 11 Kangaroo paw by Greg Campbell
pp. 31–4 Photographs in Walk 3, New South Wales by Tyrone Thomas
p. 56 Mount Feathertop in winter, Victoria by Tyrone Thomas
p. 100 Lake Salome and scoparia, Tasmania by Doug Harris
p. 108 Barn Bluff, Tasmania by Sheryl Lockhart
pp. 162–3 Photographs in Walk 29, Western Australia by Greg Campbell
Graphic credits
pp. 6, 7, 9 Late Pangaea, The volcanic formation of the Great Dividing Range, The volcanic formation of Warrumbungles and Southern hemisphere climate by Roger Darby
State opener maps by Roger Darby
Our special thanks to Roger Darby who has been a valuable part of the survey team and has assisted greatly in the production of this book.
Thanks to Darren McGregor for his first aid advice.
Other publications by the authors
150 Walks in Victoria
Australia's Best Walks
100 Walks in Tasmania
Contact Tyrone Thomas and Andrew Close
PO Box 106
Mount Macedon, Victoria, 3441

Explore Australia Publishing Pty Ltd
85 High Street
Prahran, Victoria 3181, Australia
10 9 8 7 6 5 4 3 2 1

National Library of Australia Cataloguing-in-Publication entry

Author: Thomas, Tyrone T., 1938-
Title: 40 great walks in Australia / Tyrone Thomas, Andrew Close.
ISBN: 9781741172966 (pbk.)
Subjects: Trails—Australia—Guidebooks.
Walking—Australia—Guidebooks.
Australia—Guidebooks.
Other Authors/Contributors:
Close, Andrew.

Dewey Number: 919.404

Printed in China by C & C Offset Printing Company Limited
Publisher's Note: Every effort has been made to ensure that the information in this book is accurate at the time of going to press. The publisher welcomes information and suggestions for correction or improvement. Write to the Publications Manager, 85 High Street, Prahran, Victoria 3181, Australia or email: explore@hardiegrant.com.au
Disclaimers: The publisher cannot accept responsibility for any errors or omissions. The representation on the maps of any road or track is not necessarily evidence of public right of way. The publisher cannot be held responsible for any injury, loss or damage incurred during travel. Travellers should be aware that conditions in remote areas change; it is vital to research any proposed trip thoroughly and seek the advice of relevant state and travel organisations before you leave.